PENGUIN  CLASSICS

THE PORTABLE BENJAMIN FRANKLIN

BENJAMIN FRANKLIN (1706–1790) was the first American to achieve international celebrity. From the colonial period of his initial fame through to the twenty-first century, he has been regarded both at home and abroad as the one person who most clearly combines the many facets of the American character. He was the only person to sign all four major documents of the founding of the United States—the Declaration of Independence, the Constitution, the Treaty Alliance with France, and the Treaty of Peace with England—and his participation in these momentous events, his rise to wealth from humble beginnings, his practical inventions, such as bifocals, his scientific discoveries, most prominently in the field of electricity, his myriad contributions to both civic improvement and the betterment of everyday life, his philanthropic schemes, his sagacity, and his shrewd (and often earthy) wit all remain freshly available in the lucid prose of his many writings.

LARZER ZIFF has written books on many aspects of American literary and cultural history, including the period of Benjamin Franklin. Research professor at the Johns Hopkins University, he is a winner of the Christian Gauss Award and a member of the American Academy of Arts and Sciences.

The Portable
Benjamin Franklin

Edited with an Introduction and Notes by
LARZER ZIFF

PENGUIN BOOKS

PENGUIN BOOKS

Published by the Penguin Group
Penguin Group (USA) Inc., 375 Hudson Street, New York, New York 10014, U.S.A.
Penguin Group (Canada), 90 Eglinton Avenue East, Suite 700, Toronto, Ontario, Canada M4P 2Y3
(a division of Pearson Penguin Canada Inc.)
Penguin Books Ltd, 80 Strand, London WC2R 0RL, England
Penguin Ireland, 25 St Stephen's Green, Dublin 2, Ireland (a division of Penguin Books Ltd)
Penguin Group (Australia), 250 Camberwell Road, Camberwell, Victoria 3124, Australia
(a division of Pearson Australia Group Pty Ltd)
Penguin Books India Pvt Ltd, 11 Community Centre, Panchsheel Park, New Delhi – 110 017, India
Penguin Group (NZ), cnr Airborne and Rosedale Roads, Albany, Auckland 1310, New Zealand
(a division of Pearson New Zealand Ltd)
Penguin Books (South Africa) (Pty) Ltd, 24 Sturdee Avenue, Rosebank, Johannesburg 2196, South Africa

Penguin Books Ltd, Registered Offices:
80 Strand, London WC2R 0RL, England

First published in Penguin Books 2005

1 3 5 7 9 10 8 6 4 2

Grateful acknowledgment is made for permission to reprint excerpts from the following works:
Manuscript of *The Autobiography of Benjamin Franklin* as edited in *Benjamin Franklin's Memoirs:
Parallel Text Edition*, Max Farrand, editor (HM 9999). Used by permission of The Huntington Library,
San Marino, California.
The Papers of Thomas Jefferson, volume 18, November 1790–March 1791, edited by Julian P. Boyd.
Copyright © 1971 by Princeton University Press. Reprinted by permission of Princeton University Press.

LIBRARY OF CONGRESS CATALOGING IN PUBLICATION DATA
Franklin, Benjamin, 1706–1790.
The portable Benjamin Franklin / edited with an introduction and notes by Larzer Ziff.
p. cm.—(Penguin classics)
ISBN 0 14 30.3954 7
1. Franklin, Benjamin, 1706–1790. 2. Statesmen—United States—Biography. 3. Scientists—United
States—Biography. 4. Printers—United States—Biography. 5. United States—Politics and
government—To 1775. 6. United States—Politics and government—1775–1783. 7. United States—
Politics and government—1783–1789. I. Ziff, Larzer, 1927– II. Title. III. Series.
E302.F82 2006
973.3'092—dc22
[B] 2005053178

Printed in the United States of America
Set in Sabon

Contents

II. The Betterment of Life

IV. Religion: Belief and Critique

V. Bagatelles and Dalliances

VI. Virtuoso

Introduction

In 1756, John Adams, then an ambitious twenty-one-year-old schoolmaster in Worcester, Massachusetts, pondered the impossibility of his ever achieving fame, located as he was in a modest profession in a provincial colonial town thousands of miles from the political and cultural institutions that nurtured the famous. He attempted to rationalize the matter by telling his diary that those who love fame "descend to as mean tricks and artifices in pursuit of Honor as the Miser descends to in the pursuit of Gold." Yet fame, he knew, had already come to one—even if only one—American, "Mr. Franklin of Phyladelphia," who, he noted, possessed "a prodigious Genius cultivated with prodigious industry."

That same year the prodigious Franklin of Philadelphia, thirty years Adams's senior, was elected to the Royal Society of London, put a bill through the Pennsylvania Assembly that provided night watchmen and street lighting for Philadelphia, received an honorary master's degree from William and Mary College, toured the New York frontier to inspect military defenses against possible French attacks from Canada, and during a visit to Virginia on post office business met George Washington. It was a typical Franklin year, and yet so wide-ranging was his genius, and so conscientiously did he, as Adams surmised, "cultivate" it, that no year's activities could actually be termed typical. Each year brought new experiments, new offices, new ventures. In the following year, for instance, Franklin departed for London as his colony's agent in the commencement of what would prove to be a long and distinguished diplomatic career. Yet also and always a man of business and a writer of force, he improved the time afforded by the long sea voyage to write a preface to the newest edition of his *Poor Richard Improved*. In it Father Abraham, "a plain clean old Man with white Locks," advises his fellow villagers on the conduct of life by issuing a stream of proverbs to suit their daily activities. Later abstracted from the almanac and titled "The Way to Wealth," the proverbs attained a worldwide popularity that continues to this day.

In Adams's lifetime, fame did, of course, come to him, albeit in a condition different from that of Franklin's, affected as it was by the virulent abuses that partisan politics had invoked. As he looked back at his career from his retirement, Adams was alarmed by the abyss that had opened between the events he had gone through and their portrayal in the histories published by those too young to have participated in the nation's founding. The sad truth that age seemed to bring home to him was that the price one paid for making history was that history then made one over in its image regardless of the actuality one had lived. The only defense against such misrepresentation, as Benjamin Rush, another founding father, suggested to him, was to write "'a history of your own times' as far as you were an actor in them. Let them be published by your sons after your death. It will be more than a patent of nobility to your descendants to the end of time." And Adams likewise urged Rush to engage in the same task in order to defend his reputation against what he termed "the corruption of tradition and consequently . . . the corruption of history." Writing privately for the information of their children, both men produced such manuscripts.

Benjamin Franklin had been dead for some twenty years when Adams and Rush corresponded on the matter of protecting themselves from the corruption of history. Like them he, too, had written a memoir initially addressed to his son (the term "autobiography," not used in English before 1797, was to be applied to it by later editors). But there the resemblance ends in contrasts so striking as to overwhelm that slight similarity. Franklin was unconcerned with the corruption of history because his fame had never seriously been threatened. He did not aim at producing a patent of nobility for his descendants but at providing an account of his life that could assist them in conducting theirs.

Indeed, Franklin distrusted inherited honors. When in 1784 word reached him in Paris that disbanded officers of the Continental army had formed a hereditary Society of the Cincinnati—Washington and Hamilton were to be its first presidents—he was scornful of what he saw as a flagrant breach of republican principles and an affront to the good sense of the American people. He admired the Chinese custom of *ascending* honor, he wrote his daughter, Sarah Bache, according to which when one attained the rank of mandarin his parents were immediately entitled to the same honors on the supposition that it must have been owing to the education and example they provided that their son had attained his rank. This *ascending* honor, he said, "is therefore useful to the state" because it encourages parents to give their children a good and virtuous education. "But the *descending* honor to posterity who could have no share in obtaining it, is not only groundless and absurd, but often hurtful to that posterity, since it is apt to make them proud, disdaining to be employed in useful arts." He did not conceive of the history of his life as a patent of nobility for his descendants as his contemporaries saw theirs.

Franklin's son William, whom he addressed at the start of the *Autobiography,* was born out of wedlock to an unknown mother and taken into the family of Benjamin and Deborah Franklin after their marriage. Rather than appearing to defend the honor of an established family as did the other memorialists, in the *Autobiography* Franklin is, in effect, creating a new kind of family. The account of their immediate forebears that he gives William is essentially a story of discontinuities—ancestral removal within England, parental removal from England to America, and his own removal from Boston to Philadelphia—a story that underlies the work's demonstration that it is not a question of what or where you were at birth but what you make of life's opportunities regardless of place of birth. With such an underlying theme, the *Autobiography* effortlessly broadens from advice to a son to a manual for all young persons born into modest means.

From the very start of his recollections Franklin anticipated and disarmed the skeptics who were prepared to point out that his real aim was to celebrate himself, not instruct others. By putting his recollections into print so as to make them as durable as possible, Franklin says:

> I shall indulge the inclination so natural in old men to be talking of themselves and their own past actions; and I shall indulge it without being troublesome to others, who, through respect to age, might think themselves obliged to give me a hearing, since this may be read or not as one pleases. And lastly (I may as well confess it, since my denial of it will be believed by nobody), perhaps I shall a good deal gratify my own *vanity*. Indeed, I scarce ever heard or saw the introductory words, "Without vanity I may say," etc., but some vain thing immediately followed. Most people dislike vanity in others, whatever share they have of it in themselves; but I give it fair quarter wherever I meet with it, being persuaded that it is often productive of good to the possessor, and to others that are within his sphere of action; and therefore, in many cases, it would not be quite absurd if a man were to thank God for his vanity among the other comforts of life.

A brief paraphrase might run as follows: this indulgence is not really vanity, because if you don't like it you don't have to read it; well, I suppose it is vanity, but, then, we're all vain and, moreover, our wish to have others share our high estimation of ourselves may very well be the reason we do good things, not bad, so that we should perhaps thank God for our vanity rather than repent it. Each statement in Franklin's sequence anticipates and incorporates the statement that would counter it, the whole climaxed by the final suggestion that vanity is a gift of God. In the Christian doctrine of Franklin's parents, and, indeed, of most Americans of his day, pride was a cardinal sin, but Franklin who is aware of this does not mention it. In the *Autobiography,* as in many of his other writings, the arguments that he contests are not directly cited, but, rather, rendered obsolete by his development of an opposed viewpoint.

The writing of the *Autobiography* began in 1771, but Franklin's critical involvement in the large public affairs of the succeeding years forced him to put it aside. In 1784, while serving as American minister to France, however, he found time to continue the narrative, but by then William and he were estranged. During the Revolution, William had remained loyal to the Crown while his father in the same period had pursued a vehement course of opposition. As a consequence, after the 1784 resumption the tendency already present in the first part was amplified, and from its specific applicability to William, the narrative modulated into a text addressed to all young American men of plain beginnings. Over time, with the worldwide spread of capitalism and, much later, with the entry of women into the marketplace for talent, the *Autobiography* found an even wider applicability than the large one it had always enjoyed from its first publication.

That publication has had a tangled history. Franklin supervised the preparation of two fair copies of his manuscript, one of which he sent to Benjamin Vaughan in England and the other to Louis Guillaume le Veillard in France. Both copies disappeared and the *Autobiography*'s first publication (1791) was in French, a translation of part of the copy sent to le Veillard, while the first edition in English (1793) was a translation back from the imperfectly translated and incomplete French edition. Confusion was compounded in the next century as Franklin's grandson, William Temple Franklin, published a fuller edition based on a copy of one of the now-missing fair copies, but in it "improved" his grandfather's style so that it would meet the standards he thought to prevail, and John Bigelow in 1868 published an edition based on the copy sent to le Veillard, which he had discovered and purchased in Paris. Many other editions of the popular work, all in some degree faulty, were published into the following century. Finally, in 1949, modern bibliographical science addressed the problem in Max Farrand's "critical edition," which reconstructed the text by comparing the le Veillard copy recovered by Bigelow with those editions that could claim some connection with the lost Benjamin Vaughan copy. But the matter did not come to a complete rest even there. Further scholars have since been busy correcting minor faults.

Franklin's story of his life does not extend beyond 1766 when as a colonial agent in London he successfully worked for the repeal of the Stamp Act. Still to come were the great years of the Declaration of Independence, the Revolution, the Constitution, and the international recognition of the United States of America. But while Franklin's narrative of his intimate involvement in those events would certainly have made an unmatched contribution to the national history, his letters, satires, and polemical writings, a broad selection of which appears in this volume, provide a primary view of what he would have drawn upon. Moreover, the core fable of the *Autobiography* is, finally, independent of monumental public events. It is the success story of an individual—later to be trivialized in rags-to-riches folklore—with its assertion of the interdependence of private and civic improvement.

Franklin's account of himself was also, inevitably, an account of his country, not so much of the great national events in which he participated as of the reflexive relationship that existed between the advancement of his career and the well-being of his society; an account, that is, of how his civic environment shaped him and, consequently, of how he shaped it. Critics who have decried the self-help practices advocated in the *Autobiography* as petty and selfish have failed to take into account self-improvement's dependence upon civic improvement, a theme that runs throughout Franklin's narrative. In his account, he advanced because he worked toward shaping a world hospitable to individual well-being, and such a world served others as well as, if not far more than, himself.

The most influential critique of Franklin's outlook has been that of the German sociologist Max Weber in his powerfully argued *The Protestant Ethic and the "Spirit" of Capitalism* (1904–05). Examining the notorious chart of virtues in the *Autobiography,* Weber comments, "According to Franklin those virtues, like all others, are only in so far virtues as they are actually useful to the individual, and the surrogate of mere appearance is always sufficient when it accomplishes the end in view." This is so, and yet, as with his earlier argument about vanity, Franklin might well query whether the social value of the end in view is not the essential issue. A virtue such as temperance, for example, is indispensable for worldly success because intemperance leads to wasteful expenditure and inefficiency on the job. Mere appearance, therefore, will not suffice because even if others regard one as temperate, intemperance itself will have deleterious consequences. On the other hand, humility is beneficial because others are apt to trust and be persuaded by someone whom they regard as modest far more than they are to trust someone they perceive to be prideful. In this case, then, Franklin admitted, appearance will serve: "I cannot boast of much success in acquiring the *reality* of this virtue, but I had a good deal with regard to the *appearance* of it."

Needless to say, a host of theological, philosophical, or psychological objections have been raised against such a calculated detachment of behavior from character. By the standard of the Puritan patriarchs of Franklin's native Boston, for one example, any assertion that public behavior is a reliable source of information about an individual's true character—in their terms, of the state of his soul—is heretical. An individual's distinctive entity is not the product but the cause of his actions and that entity is determined by his relationship to God. He cannot truly do good, truly serve his fellow man, unless that service proceeds from a gracious soul. Franklin's letters to Josiah Franklin and Joseph Huey in this volume reflect his awareness of the uneasiness stirred among family and friends by his reversing these priorities and asserting that God's grace is, in effect, earned by moral behavior rather than the cause of it. Even the many who in Franklin's time had drifted from orthodoxy nevertheless held notions of individual identity as ultimately independent of social conduct. For them, America was a nation of yeoman farmers where the immanent self was formed by daily contact with nature and nature's god; the individual brought such an identity to society and there retained its irreducible core.

At the heart of Franklin's use of the terms *appearance* and *reality* is his concern with the relation of private to public life. Convinced that both personal success and the welfare of society depend upon the social conduct of individuals, he insisted upon the private development of virtues (or habits) that had a beneficial effect on public behavior, while he fully admitted that since other virtues—humility, for example—were in the keeping of the observer rather than the observed, no damage was done by the mere assumption of their appearance so long as the result was socially beneficial. Moreover, even those virtues one truly possessed were of limited value if one were not seen to possess them: "I took care not only to be in *reality* industrious and frugal, but to avoid all appearances to the contrary. . . . To show that I was not above my business I sometimes brought home the paper I purchased at the stores through the streets on a wheelbarrow."

To observe Franklin acting in this fashion is to recognize that to a degree unmatched by any other leader in the new nation, he was formed by the city, by the conditions of trade and the circumstances of daily intercourse with a range of his fellow citizens. Shaped by the city, he was also its shaper, founding the institutions of modern urban life such as hospitals, schools, fire companies, sanitation agencies, and streetlighting facilities. His boyhood apprenticeship to his brother, publisher of an intensely political newspaper, gave him daily glimpses into the crucial importance of acting in association with others rather than individually. At the age of sixteen he took the knowledge thus gained to Philadelphia, America's largest and the British empire's second-largest city, and his developing genius was further molded by urban conditions when he worked in London in his nineteenth and twentieth years.

Many of the foremost thinkers in Franklin's America, such as Jefferson, believed that the future happiness of the new nation depended upon its maintaining a rural character apart from the corruptions of the city, on one hand, and the savagery of the wilderness, on the other. While Franklin never differed from this ideal explicitly—he even briefly contemplated removing to Ohio—his philosophy clearly issued from urban circumstances. Inevitably, whether for better or worse, modern man lives in the city, and Franklin's *Autobiography* has endured because it speaks to the conditions of life in the city.

A half century after Franklin's death, what were seen as the pernicious consequences of his concentration on man as a social creature were challenged by the American transcendentalists. The one thing of value in the world, Emerson affirmed, is the active soul, and Thoreau dramatized this contention in *Walden*. His opening chapter with its penny-ha'penny accounting of expenditures mocks Franklin's bookkeeping habits while *Walden* as a whole may be read as a counter *Autobiography*. Subtitled "Life in the Woods," the book advocates the realization of self in solitude, the need to burrow beneath the alluvion of appearance to the immaterial rock of reality beneath it and there found one's character.

But although Franklin and Thoreau thus seem diametrically opposed—society vs. solitude, material advancement vs. spiritual growth—their differences may more aptly be seen as a dialogue within American culture. For most who pursue it, life in the woods, either literally, for example, by maintaining a house by a pond, or figuratively, for example, by making a retreat to an ashram, is a leisure activity underwritten by material success (to recognize which is not necessarily to impugn its sincerity). Thoreau saw the mass of men in his society leading lives of quiet desperation, but even as his America benefited from his pointing to other values, so he benefited from the civil liberties and modest everyday prosperity of the America Ben Franklin imagined and worked to create for him.

Franklin had arrived in both Philadelphia and London as a stranger and, accordingly, formed himself in terms of what the city required of young men. For want of other credentials, such as recognized family status or class affiliation, he had to give an account of himself in words and deeds, and the account he gave is what he became. To the moment of his death at the age of eighty-four, when he was known throughout the world, Franklin was still giving an account of himself. Dictating the final part of the *Autobiography* from his sickbed, he was fashioning a narrative that he thought should stand for—should be—Benjamin Franklin. Although from his day to ours, corrections and supplements to the details in that narrative have been undertaken on the basis of evidence external to it, still the Franklin of the *Autobiography* is the Franklin that persists because that Franklin incorporates his central perception of the public nature of private character.

Washington, Adams, and Jefferson, like almost all the other

founding fathers, were rooted in the regions of their birth; indeed, seemed to exemplify what it meant to be born and bred a Virginian or a Massachusetts Yankee. Public life may have removed them from their native regions, but when duty ceased to call they returned to them as the places where they could realize their best selves. But despite the close association that exists between Franklin and Philadelphia, so close that it is quite impossible to conceive of one without the other, Franklin was not a native son. The career that unfolds in the *Autobiography* provides the model of a pattern that would become typical of American life: the connection of upward social movement to outward geographic movement.

That pattern was not quite foreseen by Alexis de Tocqueville who visited the United States in 1831–32 in order to study "the shape of democracy." "The Union," he wrote:

> is a vast body and somewhat vague as the object of patriotism. But the state has precise shape and circumscribed boundaries, it represents a defined number of familiar things which are dear to those living there. It is identified with the soil, with the rights of property, the family memories of the past, activities of the present, dreams for the future. Patriotism, which is most often nothing but an extension of individual egoism, therefore remains attached to the state and has not yet been passed to the Union.

Yet by 1837 a British observer was writing that the American's "affections have more to do with the social and political system with which he is connected than with the soil which he inhabits. The man whose attachments converge upon a particular spot of earth, is miserable if removed from it; but give the American his institutions, and he cares little where you place him." The nation to which such an American was attached was not a physical space in which he lived the everyday life, nor a specific people with whom he felt a familial or ethnic identity, but a less visible community of shared ideals. D. H. Lawrence, historically the most eloquent of Franklin's critics—passionate to the point of melodrama—phrased the matter thus: "America has never been a blood home-land. Only an ideal home-land.

The home-land of the idea, of the *spirit*." The United States that claimed the loyalty of its citizens was not a family of those who shared a common soil and common traditions such as Tocqueville observed at the level of a single state. It was a nation of people united by their attachment to proclaimed ideals, an imagined community rather than an observable physical entity, one that depended for its existence upon the dissemination of shared ideals. As Wilbur Zelinsky phrased the matter in his study of nationhood, "The fact that members of . . . a nation are normally far too numerous for more than a limited face-to-face contact implies that nationalism can only flourish during an era when print and other advanced media of communication and tutelage are available." In eighteenth-century America, print was the only advanced medium of communication, and no one recognized its social and political potential more perceptively and deployed it more consequentially than "B. Franklin, Printer."

From the start the printed word served young Franklin as his entry into a superior social world. Books taught him how to write, how to dispute, and even how to plan his meals. And reading, of course, introduced him to the many fields his genius mastered. But, in addition, books were his passport to social and thence political advancement. He received an early indication of this when as a runaway of suspicious appearance he stopped at an inn in New Jersey and there began a lifelong friendship with its owner, Dr. Brown, when the older man discovered that the youth owned and read books. On a return journey to Boston, Franklin, still an unknown lad, was summoned to the house of Governor Burnet of New York because the governor had heard from the captain of the ship on which Franklin arrived that there was a young man aboard who owned a number of books. "The Governor treated me with great civility, showed me his library, which was a very large one, and we had a good deal of conversation about books and authors." When Franklin's employer, Keimer, received the commission to print New Jersey's currency, Franklin and he went to Burlington and in a three-month stay there executed the job under the close supervision of members of the colony's legislature. "My mind having been much more improved by reading than Keimer's," Franklin wrote, "I suppose it was for that reason my conversation seemed to be more valued. They had me to their houses, introduced me to their friends and showed me much civility. . . . These friends were afterwards of great use to me." When Franklin's rise in Philadelphia was substantially forwarded by his appointment as printer to the Pennsylvania Assembly, he learned that a new member of that body who promised to be influential was opposed to his continuing as printer and he therefore set out to win him over: "Having heard that he had in his library a certain very scarce and curious book, I wrote a note to him expressing my desire of perusing that book, and requesting he would do me the favor of lending it to me for a few days. He sent it immediately and I returned it in about a week, with another note expressing strongly my sense of the favor." Thus began another lifelong and politically profitable friendship.

Franklin's interest in books and his conversion of private reading into a body of knowledge superior to any university education available were, however, far from being a simple matter of calculated social climbing. Although he recognized that the mere fact of being familiar with books could gain him access to a higher social circle and did not hesitate to act upon it, he reached beyond this to establish the emerging class of ambitious, self-taught trades-and-crafts-men as a deciding political force in American society. In a world in which money to acquire and leisure to read books were the mark of the elite class he was displacing, Franklin had to avoid the appearance of leisure appropriate to that class: "A book, indeed, sometimes debauched me from my work; but this was seldom, snug and gave no scandal." But in his establishment of a library that would make books available to others like himself, he was also consciously undermining whatever superiority that class exercised simply because its members could afford financially to own books, and therefore, in a sense, to monopolize learning. The members of new associations, such as the Library Company and the Junto (later to become the American Philosophical Society), knew that knowledge not birth was the key to material success and civic power, and they proceeded accordingly.

Of even greater importance than Franklin's consumption of the printed word, however, was his production of it through his professional recognition not merely of the importance of print but of the print culture that was just coming into being. Although many writers were slow to grasp the fact, there was a difference between a written piece that was later printed and a piece written deliberately to be printed. Reflecting an oral culture, they proceeded from the assumptions that the writer—because of his rank, learning, or office—was in a position of authority relative to his readership, which was conceptualized as a determinate body of interested readers (very much as the writer of a sermon assumed a position of authority over the specific congregation he was to address). To the extent that such assumptions operated, literate culture was not yet print culture.

But Franklin did grasp the features that distinguished modern print culture. He saw that print's capacity to diffuse information, thought, and sentiments beyond the limits of place and moment meant that it need not address a specifically existing audience, such as members of a religious denomination, a particular occupation, or a certain social class, but that it could cross such boundaries in constructing its readership. Once a work was printed, the author had no control over who was to read it. The audience constituted by print was indeterminate, made up of individuals who neither knew nor lived in proximity to one another. Yet print could lead such a group to realize a potency greater than that of determinate, hence local, groups.

In the *Autobiography* Franklin describes the influence of Addison's *Spectator* essays upon the development of his style, a style that Dr. Johnson, speaking of Addison, characterized as "on grave subjects not formal, on light occasions not groveling." Of equal if not greater importance as a stylistic influence was his interest in the transactions of the Royal Society to which his electrical experiments gained him admission in 1756. One of the world's oldest scientific organizations, the Royal Society, founded in 1660, abandoned the empty theories of nature that had previously dominated scientific thinking to replace them with conclusions founded upon observation and experiment.

Additionally, its program called as vigorously for stylistic reform as it did for philosophical reform. In his *History of the Royal Society* (1667), Thomas Sprat said, "They have exacted from all their members, a close, naked, natural way of speaking; positive expressions; clear senses; a native easiness; bringing all things as near the Mathematical plainness, as they can: and preferring the language of Artizans, Countrymen, and Merchants, before that of Wits or Scholars."

Witty as he could be and scholarly as he was, Benjamin Franklin nevertheless rejoiced in his identity as an artisan—what he termed "a leather-apron man"—and consciously positioned his style in opposition to that of the professional men whose writings still remained within the assumptions of an oral culture. Writing about ministerial prose, for example, he rather gleefully proclaimed:

> Let them have the liberty of repeating the same sentence in other words; let them put an adjective to every substantive, and double every substantive with a synonyma, for this is more agreeable than hauking, spitting, taking snuff, or other means of concealing hesitation. Let them multiply definitions, comparisons, similitudes, and examples. Permit them to make a detail of causes and effects, enumerate all the consequences, and express one half by metaphor and circumlocution. Nay, allow the preacher to tell us whatever a thing is negatively, before he begins to tell what it is affirmatively; and permit him to divide and subdivide as far as *two and fiftiethly*.

But when a discourse is to be printed, "bound down upon paper," as Franklin puts it, then the brief, the perspicuous, and the direct are called for because the discourse must stand without the aid of the speaker's presence.

Similarly, Franklin lampooned the verbosity of legal writings in a day when print made them available to common readers: "You must abridge the performance to understand them; and when you find how little there is in a writing of vast bulk, you will be as much surpriz'd as a stranger at the opening of a pumpkin."

In short, Franklin knew that print meant a readership for sermons that was not to be treated as if it were passively sitting under the minister's gaze and a readership for legal matters that was larger than and distinct from those familiar with professional jargon. The principle could be extended into almost all areas of knowledge. His first published writings were designed for his brother's *New-England Courant,* and throughout his career he shaped his writing for an assumed audience of intelligent, busy people who had the ability to understand even technical subjects if they were presented in a clear and persuasive style. Influenced by American conditions, he accepted the indeterminate nature of his readership—neither ignorant nor learned; interested in gossip and interested in science; alert to personal profit and sympathetic to schemes of social benevolence—and he called forth the audience that from his day to this exists substantially yet amorphously under the title of the common reader.

To publish is to make publicly known, and Franklin, who published constantly, both as printer and author, had an extraordinary sense of the public ownership of all material written, spoken, or, even more radically, simply not maintained in silence. Famously, he declined to patent his widely copied stove, the "Pennsylvania Fireplace," because in publishing its pattern he believed he had relinquished ownership of it to all who wished to benefit from it (even though another man took his invention and did patent and profit from it). Similarly, he refused to surrender his allegiance to a preacher he supported when it was revealed that the man had preached the sermons of others which he had memorized: "I stuck by him," Franklin wrote in the *Autobiography,* "as I rather approved of his giving us good sermons composed by others, than bad ones of his own manufacture." Even more flagrantly, Franklin justified his making public confidential letters written by Governor Thomas Hutchinson that had fallen into his hands by saying, "It is in vain to say this would be betraying private correspondence, since if the truth only was written, no man need be ashamed or afraid of it being known; and if falsehoods have been maliciously covered under the cloak of confidence, 'tis perfectly just the incendiary writers should be exposed and punished." The corollary of such an extraordinary belief was that if you wished a thought to remain private, then you should remain silent, and for all his prolific writing Franklin famously, indeed notoriously, could keep his silence.

"Oratory in this age?" John Adams exclaimed in disgust at its decline, "Secrecy! Cunning! Silence! *Voila les grandes sciences des temps modernes.*" "Silence," he went on to say, "is most commonly design and intrigue," and it was most remarkable in Franklin who "was naturally a great talker." But the age of oratory had indeed passed, and if Adams was its chief mourner, Franklin was its mortician.

When one speaks, the words he utters are the thoughts of a personalized self. But writing is detached from personal presence. Writer and reader occupy separate places and separate moments in time, and the result is that both writer and reader are transformed from actual presences into the assumed presences that each believes the other to be. Even when the writer appears to invest his or her personality in the writing, that published self is essentially different from the personal self because the very process of reproduction and circulation in multiple copies converts the particular into the general.

Author, printer, publisher, Franklin recognized and collaborated with this inescapable process and enjoyed playing with readers who insisted on equating the published persona with a corporeal individual. In 1736, for example, Poor Richard reported that some wishing him ill have declared *"That there is no such a Man as I am."* He resents such uncivil treatment: "So long as I know my self to walk about, eat drink and sleep, I am satisfied that *there is really such a Man as I am*;" and he goes on to ask, "If there were no such Man as I am, how is it possible I should appear publickly to hundreds of People, as I have done for Several years past in print?" How, indeed? The last word of the question is also the answer.

To many during his lifetime and since, Franklin appeared to be evasive, to be hiding what they hypothesized to be a "real self" behind the personae of the written works. It is a fact, however, that all written discourse is uttered by a persona who is both different from the author yet expressive of him: the one, like Poor Richard, appears publicly; the other, like his creator, walks about, eats, drinks, sleeps, and, it should be added, dreams privately.

After the Battle of Marengo, Jean-Victor-Marie Moreau, one of Napoleon's generals, asked Napoleon why he had chosen the frozen St. Bernard route for his army when he could have followed a more direct and less dangerous road. "It was the scenery of the business," Napoleon answered. "I thought its boldness would have a good effect." No American of Franklin's day was as appreciative as he of the effect to be derived from "the scenery of the business." There are many portraits of him, as there are of the other great men of his day. But Franklin iconography places him against "the scenery of the business" far more than the iconography that celebrates the others. We do have Washington crossing the Delaware or, amusingly, with a child's body but the familiar adult head, standing by a felled cherry tree with his hatchet, but in almost all popular and classical portraiture he stands or sits in magisterial calm. In popular portraiture, however, Franklin acts against a specific background. He flies his kite into an electric storm (usually in his small clothes without protective outerwear) or is allegorized as grasping and taming the lightning even as he confronted and subdued tyranny. Benjamin West has him seated on airborne silk against the background of a stormy sky, his hair and kerchief windblown as he draws electricity from the sky while one group of cherubim above him to his left flies a kite into the menacing clouds and two other cherubim below to his right busy themselves with the laboratory apparatus that stores electricity.

Beyond his contemporaries Franklin invited anecdotal or narrative portraiture because he himself was adept at verbal pictures that suggested a meaning larger than the details of his particular appearance. The popular schoolbook picture of the youth strolling down Market Street eating a puffy roll and carrying another tucked under his arm while a young woman in a doorway, the future Deborah Franklin, smiles in amusement at the sight is drawn from a scene that Franklin not only paints in the *Autobiography* but then emblematizes: "I have been the more particular in this description . . . of my first entry into that city that you may in your mind compare such unlikely beginnings with the figure I have since made there." Another popular picture, that of the plainly dressed American symbolizing the egalitarian values of the new republic amid the silken opulence of the French court, was also painted verbally by Franklin. In a letter to a friend dated February 8, 1777, for example, he wrote: "Figure me in your mind as jolly as formerly, and as strong and hearty, only a few years older, very plainly dress'd, wearing my grey strait Hair, that peeps out from under my only Coiffure, a fine Fur Cap, which comes down to my Forehead almost to my Spectacles. Think how this must appear among the Powder'd Heads of Paris." (This is the image captured by his contemporary, August de Saint-Aubin and reproduced on the cover of this book.) From trundling the paper he had purchased through the streets of Philadelphia on a wheelbarrow to wearing his marten fur cap in the salons of Paris, he was a master at the art of visibly personifying the values he wished to communicate. As print diffused his person into the general, so his attention to physical display concentrated the general in his person.

It is small wonder that many of his contemporaries felt that there was more to Franklin than met their eyes and that he hid himself even when he was present in body. His cunning, they suspected, was not to be trusted. Yet with the range of his writings spread before them, today's readers do have the kind of access to him that those who met him did not possess, nor that many of his later critics who read only the *Autobiography* bothered to gain.

With an essay style modeled on Addison, a satiric technique informed by Swift, and a prose style that brought an uninsistent persuasiveness to social and political discussions, bringing them, as Thomas Sprat said of the reformed prose of the Royal Society, as near to mathematical plainness as possible, Franklin was very much an eighteenth-century English writer, albeit a colonial one. Yet compared with the prose of other notable Americans of his day, say Jonathan Edwards, on one hand, or Thomas Jefferson, on the other, Franklin's seems already to be anticipating a distinctively American articulation. As a writer he was first and foremost a journalist, and as a journalist he had a keen ear for the speech patterns of his readership. Poor Richard speaks as a countryman speaking to his fellow countrymen in the language they share. It is, to be sure, the English of the mother country, but in its loose informality and calculated moments of wink-and-nod vulgarity it also begins to pull away from it. Colloquialisms do not yet amount to a distinctly American vernacular style, but the seed is there, highlighted by Richard's delight in noting regional pronunciations. New Yorkers, he tells us, say "diss," for "this," those at Cape May say "keow" for "cow," while people in Connecticut and Maryland are unable to talk without saying "Sir" at the beginning or the end of their statements—and sometimes in both places.

The infant American novel of Franklin's day in its fascination with the theme of seduction and its consciously literary language was very much an English novel despite its American settings. Most such novels were epistolary, written by female characters within the novels and, with the exception of Charles Brockden Brown, the more outstanding novelists were women, which further heightened the tone of propriety connected with what was regarded as "literary" prose.

With Hannah Foster's *The Coquette* perhaps exempted, Poor Richard, Anthony Afterwit, Polly Baker, and other Franklin creations are far more palpably American than any of the characters in the novels of their day. Since they spoke the whole of the piece in which they appeared, colloquial speech was called upon to convey the entirety of whatever the reader was meant to infer, as opposed to speech framed within quotation marks by a more formal narrator who is, as it were, in charge of the feelings that are to be conveyed. It is some way from Franklin to Walt Whitman and Mark Twain (both also graduates of the print shop and journalism) and the establishment of American speech as a literary language, but Franklin is certainly their ancestor. In addition to his forays into the colloquial, Franklin shared with them an amused delight in the exuberance of American brag: "The very Tails of the American Sheep are so laden with Wooll, that each has a little Car or Waggon on four little Wheels, to support & keep it from trailing on the Ground," he wrote in a 1765 piece intended for an English newspaper. And inventor though he was, he delighted also in the frequently absurd tinkerings of his improvement-minded countrymen, which he pleasantly satirized in his instructions on the making of a striking sundial. To read such pieces is to sense one is in the company of a distinctly American writer.

Indeed, even Mark Twain's iconoclastic inversions of Poor Richard's maxims—"Fewer things are harder to put up with than a good example," says Pudd'nhead Wilson—can actually be seen to share the wry misgivings of human nature amply present in Poor Richard. It is Richard who says, "In the affairs of this world men are saved, not by faith, but by the want of it;" "Power to the bold and heaven to the virtuous." The humorous dimension of human fallibility which is so essential a part of what one marks as Twain's American tone can be heard in an earlier stage in a number of Franklin's pieces.

On June 36, 1755, Benjamin Franklin in Philadelphia wrote to Peter Collinson in London. He said that in an accompanying packet he was sending his paper on whirlwinds and waterspouts for publication if Collinson thought it would be welcome; sample sheets of asbestos; some superior grease-free candles and a few cakes of American soap, "best in the world for shaving and washing fine linens;" notations describing the North American woodchuck or groundhog; a paper on a worm found in a woman's liver; and "ten of my fireplace pieces" with a request that Collinson tell him of the reported improvements that one Harris had made of the fireplace. In the letter itself he reported on his activities in the Pennsylvania Assembly and on plans to establish settlements further west; discussed politics in America and England; outlined the present condition of the Library Company; described his mistaken efforts to mend a broken thermometer—"I only tell you this, that you and Mr. Bird may divert yourselves with laughing at me;" and requested that Collinson send him a copy of Johnson's dictionary and his wife sufficient satin for a gown, "somewhat darker than the enclosed pattern."

The range of interests and activities contained in the letter—from scientific observations, through inventions and notions that enhance the pleasures of living the everyday life, to a readiness to smile at his mistakes and offer them for the amusement of others—combines to provide a condensed tour of Benjamin Franklin's mind and temperament, and it is the intention of this volume to offer an expanded version of such a tour, deepening it by representing a range of Franklin's writings on the major areas of concern mentioned in the letter, and widening it by presenting writings in additional areas of ongoing concern to him such as religious belief and sexual conduct. Care has been taken, moreover, to provide access not just to Franklin's thoughts but to his temperament as manifested in his literary manner as well as his matter—the differing tones he sounds from the ferocity of political satires that are, nevertheless, comic, to the playful flirtations that are, nevertheless, imbued with a sense of loss.

Stated concisely, it is the intention of this volume to place the reader in Benjamin Franklin's presence.

Acknowledgments

Jason Hoppe assisted in the preparation and organization of this volume's contents. The treatment of Benjamin Franklin and print culture in the Introduction incorporates in revised form the discussion of the subject in Larzer Ziff, *Writing in the New Nation* (New Haven: Yale University Press, 1991), and appears here by permission of the publisher.

Note on the Texts

The text of the *Autobiography* is that established by Max Farrand in 1949.

Thomas Jefferson's anecdote appears in Julian P. Boyd, *The Papers of Thomas Jefferson,* vol. 18, November 1790–March 1791, © 1971 by Princeton University Press, and is here reprinted with the permission of the publisher. Some of the selections from the *Pennsylvania Gazette* are based on later reprintings, as are the "Dissertation on Liberty and Necessity, Pleasure and Pain" and "Advice to a Young Man." All other items, which is to say the overwhelming majority, are drawn from *The Writings of Benjamin Franklin* (New York: Macmillan Company, 1905–07), 10 volumes, edited by Albert Henry Smyth. Franklin wrote two of them, "The Elysian Fields" and "Conte," in French; they are here translated by Julia Kent.

The Portable
Benjamin Franklin

AUTOBIOGRAPHY

Twyford, at the Bishop of St Asaph's, 1771.

DEAR SON,

I have ever had a Pleasure in obtaining any little Anecdotes of my Ancestors. You may remember the Inquiries I made among the Remains of my Relations when you were with me in England; and the Journey I took for that purpose. Now imagining it may be equally agreeable to you to know the Circumstances of *my* Life, many of which you are yet unacquainted with; and expecting a Week's uninterrupted Leisure in my present Country Retirement, I sit down to write them for you. To which I have besides some other Inducements. Having emerg'd from the Poverty & Obscurity in which I was born & bred, to a State of Affluence & some Degree of Reputation in the World, and having gone so far thro' Life with a considerable Share of Felicity, the conducing Means I made use of, which, with the Blessing of God, so well succeeded, my Posterity may like to know, as they may find some of them suitable to their own Situations, & therefore fit to be imitated. That Felicity, when I reflected on it, has induc'd me sometimes to say, that were it offer'd to my Choice, I should have no Objection to a Repetition of the same Life from its Beginning, only asking the Advantages Authors have in a second Edition to correct some Faults of the first. So would I if I might, besides correcting the Faults, change some sinister Accidents & Events of it for others more favourable, but tho' this were deny'd, I should still accept the Offer. However, since such a Repetition is not to be expected, the next Thing most like living one's Life over again, seems to be a *Recollection* of that Life; and to make that Recollection as durable as possible, the putting it down in Writing. Hereby, too, I shall indulge the Inclination so natural in old Men, to be talking of themselves and their own past Actions, and I shall indulge it, without being troublesome to others who thro' respect to Age might think themselves oblig'd to give me a Hearing, since this may be read or not as any one pleases. And lastly, (I may as well confess it, since my Denial of it will be believ'd by nobody) perhaps I shall a good deal gratify my own *Vanity*. Indeed I scarce ever heard or saw the introductory Words, *Without Vanity I may say,* &c but some vain thing immediately follow'd. Most People dislike Vanity in others whatever Share they have of it themselves, but I give it fair Quarter wherever I meet with it, being persuaded that it is often productive of Good to the Possessor & to others that are within his Sphere of Action: And therefore in many Cases it would not be quite absurd if a Man were to thank God for his Vanity among the other Comforts of Life.

And now I speak of thanking God, I desire with all Humility to acknowledge, that I owe the mention'd Happiness of my past Life to his kind Providence, which led me to the Means I us'd & gave them Success. My Belief of this, induces me to *hope,* tho' I must not *presume,* that the same Goodness will still be exercis'd towards me in continuing that Happiness, or in enabling me to bear a fatal Reverse, which I may experience as others have done, the Complexion of my future Fortune being known to him only: and in whose Power it is to bless to us even our Afflictions.

The Notes one of my Uncles (who had the same kind of Curiosity in collecting Family Anecdotes) once put into my Hands, furnish'd me with several Particulars relating to our Ancestors. From these Notes I learned that the Family had liv'd in the same Village, Ecton in Northamptonshire, for 300 Years, & how much longer he knew not (perhaps from the Time when the Name *Franklin* that before was the Name of an Order of People, was assum'd by them for a Surname, when others took Surnames all over the Kingdom.—on a Freehold of about 30 Acres, aided by the Smith's Business which had continued in the Family till his Time, the eldest Son being always bred to that Business. A Custom which he & my Father both followed as to their eldest Sons. When I search'd the Register at Ecton, I found an Account of their Births, Marriages and Burials, from the Year 1555 only, there being no Register kept in that Parish at any time preceding. By that Register I perceiv'd that I was the youngest Son of the youngest Son for 5 Generations back. My Grandfather Thomas, who was born in 1598, lived at Ecton till he grew too old to follow Business longer, when he went to live with his Son John, a Dyer at Banbury in Oxfordshire, with whom my Father serv'd an Apprenticeship. There my Grandfather died and lies buried. We saw his Gravestone in 1758. His eldest Son Thomas liv'd in the House at Ecton, and left it with the Land to his only Child, a Daughter, who with her Husband, one Fisher of Wellingborough, sold it to Mr Isted, now Lord of the Manor there. My Grandfather had 4 Sons that grew up, viz. Thomas, John, Benjamin and Josiah. I will give you what Account I can of them at this distance from my Papers, and if they are not lost in my Absence, you will among them find many more Particulars. Thomas was bred a Smith under his Father, but being ingenious, and encourag'd in Learning (as all his Brothers like wise were) by an Esquire Palmer, then the principal Gentleman in that Parish, he qualify'd himself for the Business of Scrivener, became a considerable Man in the Country Affairs, was a chief Mover of all public Spirited Undertakings, for the Country, or Town of Northampton & his own Village, of which many Instances were told us at Ecton, and he was much taken Notice of and patroniz'd by the then Lord Halifax. He died in 1702, Jan. 6, old Style, just 4 Years to a Day before I was born. The Account we receiv'd of his Life & Character from some old People at Ecton, I remember struck you, as something extraordinary from its Similarity to what you knew of mine. Had he died on the same Day, you said one might have suppos'd a Transmigration. John was bred a Dyer, I believe of Woollens. Benjamin, was bred a Silk Dyer, serving an Apprenticeship at London. He was an ingenious Man, I remember him well, for when I was a Boy he came over to my Father in Boston, and lived in the House with us some Years. He lived to a great Age. His Grandson Samuel Franklin now lives in Boston. He left behind him two Quarto Volumes, M.S. of his own Poetry, consisting of little occasional Pieces address'd to his Friends and Relations, of which the following sent to me, is a Specimen. He had form'd a Shorthand of his own, which he taught me, but, never practising it I have now forgot it. I was nam'd after this Uncle, there being a particular Affection between him and my Father. He was very pious, a great Attender of Sermons of the best Preachers, which he took down in his Shorthand and had with him many Volumes of them. He was also much of a Politician, too much perhaps for his Station. There fell lately into my Hands in London a Collection he had made of all the principal Pamphlets relating to Public Affairs from 1641 to 1717. Many of the Volumes are wanting, as appears by the Numbering, but there still remains 8 Vols. Folio, and 24 in 4to & 8vo. A Dealer in old Books met with them, and knowing me by my sometimes buying of him, he brought them to me. It seems my Uncle must have left them here when he went to America, which was above 50 Years since. There are many of his Notes in the Margins.

This obscure Family of ours was early in the Reformation, and continu'd Protestants thro' the Reign of Queen Mary, when they were sometimes in Danger of Trouble on Account of their Zeal against Popery. They had got an English Bible, & to conceal & secure it, it was fastened open with Tapes under & within the Frame of a Joint Stool. When my Great Great Grandfather read in it to his Family, he turn'd up the Joint Stool upon his Knees, turning over the Leaves then under the Tapes. One of the Children stood at the Door to give Notice if he saw the Apparitor coming, who was an Officer of the Spiritual Court. In that Case the Stool was turn'd down again upon its feet, when the Bible remain'd conceal'd under it as before. This Anecdote I had from my Uncle Benjamin. The Family continu'd all of the Church of England till about the End of Charles the 2^{ds} Reign, when some of the Ministers that had been outed for Nonconformity, holding Conventicles in Northamptonshire, Benjamin & Josiah adher'd to them, and so continu'd all their Lives. The rest of the Family remain'd with the Episcopal Church.

Josiah, my Father, married young, and carried his Wife with three Children unto New England, about 1682. The Conventicles having been forbidden by Law, & frequently disturbed, induced some considerable Men of his Acquaintance to remove to that Country, and he was prevail'd with to accompany them thither, where they expected to enjoy their Mode of Religion with Freedom. By the same Wife he had 4 Children more born there, and by a second Wife ten more, in all 17, of which I remember 13 sitting at one time at his Table, who all grew up to be Men & Women, and married. I was the youngest Son, and the youngest Child but two, & was born in Boston, N. England. My Mother the 2ᵈ Wife was Abiah Folger, a Daughter of Peter Folger, one of the first Settlers of New England, of whom honorable mention is made by Cotton Mather; in his Church History of that Country, (entitled Magnalia Christi Americana) as a *godly learned Englishman,* if I remember the words rightly. I have heard that he wrote sundry small occasional Pieces, but only one of them was printed which I saw now many Years since. It was written in 1675, in the homespun Verse of that Time & People, and address'd to those then concern'd in the Government there. It was in favor of Liberty of Conscience, & in behalf of the Baptists, Quakers, & other Sectaries, that had been under Persecution; ascribing the Indian Wars & other Distresses, that had befallen the Country to that Persecution, as so many Judgments of God, to punish so heinous an Offense; and exhorting a Repeal of those uncharitable Laws. The whole appear'd to me as written with a good deal of Decent Plainness & manly Freedom. The six last concluding Lines I remember, tho' I have forgotten the two first of the Stanza, but the Purport of them was that his Censures proceeded from *Good Will,* & therefore he would be known as the Author,

> *because to be a Libeller, (says he)*
>   *I hate it with my Heart.*
> *From Sherburne Town where now I dwell,*
>   *My Name I do put here,*
> *Without Offense, your real Friend,*
>   *It is Peter Folgier.*

My elder Brothers were all put Apprentices to different Trades. I was put to the Grammar School at Eight Years of Age, my Father intending to devote me as the Tithe of his Sons to the Service of the Church. My early Readiness in learning to read (which must have been very early, as I do not remember when I could not read) and the Opinion of all his Friends that I should certainly make a good Scholar, encourag'd him in this Purpose of his. My Uncle Benjamin too approv'd of it, and propos'd to give me all his Shorthand Volumes of Sermons, I suppose as a Stock to set up with, if I would learn his Character. I continu'd however at the Grammar School not quite one Year, tho' in that time I had risen gradually from the Middle of the Class of that Year to be the Head of it, and farther was remov'd into the next Class above it, in order to go with that into the third at the End of the Year. But my Father in the mean time, from a View of the Expense of a College Education which, having so large a Family, he could not well afford, and the mean Living many so educated were afterwards able to obtain, Reasons that he gave to his Friends in my Hearing, altered his first Intention, took me from the Grammar School, and sent me to a School for Writing & Arithmetic kept by a then famous Man, Mr Geo. Brownell, very successful in his Profession generally, and that by mild encouraging Methods. Under him I acquired fair Writing pretty soon, but I fail'd in the Arithmetic, & made no Progress in it. At Ten Years old, I was taken home to assist my Father in his Business, which was that of a Tallow Chandler and Soap Boiler. A Business he was not bred to, but had assumed on his Arrival in New England & on finding his Dying Trade would not maintain his Family, being in little Request. Accordingly I was employed in cutting Wick for the Candles, filling the Dipping Mold, & the Molds for cast Candles, attending the Shop, going of Errands, &c. I dislik'd the Trade and had a strong Inclination for the Sea; but my Father declar'd against it; however, living near the Water, I was much in and about it, learned early to swim well, & to manage Boats, and when in a Boat or Canoe with other Boys I was commonly allow'd to govern, especially in any case of Difficulty; and upon other Occasions I was generally a Leader among the Boys, and sometimes led them into

Scrapes, of which I will mention one Instance, as it shows an early projecting public Spirit, tho' not then justly conducted. There was a Salt Marsh that bounded part of the Mill Pond, on the Edge of which at Highwater, we us'd to stand to fish for Minews. By much Trampling, we had made it a mere Quagmire. My Proposal was to build a Wharf there fit for us to stand upon, and I show'd my Comrades a large Heap of Stones which were intended for a new House near the Marsh, and which would very well suit our Purpose. Accordingly in the Evening when the Workmen were gone, I assembled a Number of my Playfellows, and working with them diligently like so many Emmets, sometimes two or three to a Stone, we brought them all away and built our little Wharf. The next Morning the Workmen were surpris'd at Missing the Stones; which were found in our Wharf; Inquiry was made after the Removers; we were discovered & complain'd of; several of us were corrected by our Fathers; and tho' I pleaded the Usefulness of the Work, mine convinc'd me that nothing was useful which was not honest.

I think you may like to know Something of his Person & Character. He had an excellent Constitution of body, was of middle Stature, but well set and very strong. He was ingenious, could draw prettily, was skill'd a little in Music and had a clear pleasing Voice; so that when he play'd Psalm Tunes on his Violin & sung withal as he sometimes did in an Evening after the Business of the Day was over, it was extremely agreeable to hear. He had a mechanical Genius too, and on occasion was very handy in the Use of other Tradesmen's Tools. But his great Excellence lay in a sound Understanding, and solid Judgment in prudential Matters, both in private & public Affairs. In the latter indeed he was never employed, the numerous Family he had to educate & the straitness of his Circumstances, keeping him close to his Trade, but I remember well his being frequently visited by leading People, who consulted him for his Opinion in Affairs of the Town or of the Church he belong'd to & show'd a good deal of Respect for his Judgment and Advice. He was also much consulted by private Persons about their Affairs when any Difficulty occur'd, & frequently chosen an Arbitrator between contending Parties. At his Table he lik'd to have as often as he could, some sensible Friend or Neighbor, to converse with, and always took care to start some ingenious or useful Topic for Discourse, which might tend to improve the Minds of his Children. By this means he turn'd our Attention to what was good, just, & prudent in the Conduct of Life; and little or no Notice was ever taken of what related to the Victuals on the Table, whether it was well or ill dressed, in or out of season, of good or bad flavor, preferable or inferior to this or that other thing of the kind; so that I was bro't up in such a perfect Inattention to those Matters as to be quite Indifferent what kind of Food was set before me; and so unobservant of it, that to this Day, if I am ask'd I can scarce tell, a few Hours after Dinner, what I din'd upon. This has been a Convenience to me in travelling, where my Companions have been sometimes very unhappy for want of a suitable Gratification of their more delicate because better instructed Tastes and Appetites.

My Mother had likewise an excellent Constitution. She suckled all her 10 Children. I never knew either my Father or Mother to have any Sickness but that of which they dy'd, he at 89 & she at 85 years of age. They lie buried together at Boston, where I some years since placed a Marble stone over their Grave with this Inscription

> Josiah Franklin
> And Abiah his Wife
> Lie here interred.
> They lived lovingly together in Wedlock
> Fifty-five Years.
> Without an Estate or any gainful Employment,
> By constant labor and Industry,
> With God's Blessing,
> They maintained a large Family
> Comfortably;
> And brought up thirteen Children,
> And seven Grand Children
> Reputably.
> From this Instance, Reader,
> Be encouraged to Diligence in thy Calling,

And distrust not Providence.
He was a pious & prudent Man,
She a discreet and virtuous Woman.
Their youngest Son,
In filial Regard to their Memory,
Places this Stone.
J.F. born 1655—Died 1744—Ætat 89
A.F. born 1667—died 1752———85

By my rambling Digressions I perceive myself to be grown old. I us'd to write more methodically. But one does not dress for private Company as for a public Ball. 'Tis perhaps only Negligence.

To return. I continu'd thus employ'd in my Father's Business for two Years, that is till I was 12 Years old; and my Brother John, who was bred to that Business, having left my Father, married and set up for himself at Rhode Island. There was all Appearance that I was destin'd to supply his Place and be a Tallow Chandler. But my Dislike to the Trade continuing, my Father was under Apprehensions that if he did not find one for me more agreeable, I should break away and get to Sea, as his Son Josiah had done to his great Vexation. He therefore sometimes took me to walk with him, and see Joiners, Bricklayers, Turners, Braziers, &c. at their Work, that he might observe my Inclination, & endeavor to fix it on some Trade or other on Land. It has ever since been a Pleasure to me to see good Workmen handle their Tools; and it has been useful to me, having learned so much by it, as to be able to do little Jobs myself in my House, when a Workman could not readily be got; & to construct little Machines for my Experiments while the Intention of making the Experiment was fresh & warm in my Mind. My Father at last fix'd upon the Cutler's Trade, and my Uncle Benjamin's Son Samuel, who was bred to that Business in London, being about that time establish'd in Boston, I was sent to be with him some time on liking. But his Expectations of a Fee with me displeasing my Father, I was taken home again.

From a Child I was fond of Reading, and all the little Money that came into my Hands was ever laid out in Books. Pleas'd with the Pilgrim's Progress, my first Collection was of John Bunyan's Works, in separate little Volumes. I afterwards sold them to enable me to buy R. Burton's Historical Collections; they were small Chapmen's Books and cheap, 40 or 50 in all. My Father's little Library consisted chiefly of Books in polemic Divinity, most of which I read, and have since often regretted, that at a time when I had such a Thirst for Knowledge, more proper Books had not fallen in my Way, since it was now re-solv'd I should not be a Clergyman. Plutarch's Lives there was, in which I read abundantly, and I still think that time spent to great Advantage. There was also a Book of Defoe's, called an Essay on Projects, and another of Dr. Mather's, call'd Essays to do Good which perhaps gave me a Turn of Thinking that had an Influence on some of the principal future Events of my Life.

This Bookish Inclination at length determin'd my Father to make me a Printer, tho' he had already one Son, (James) of that Profession. In 1717 my Brother James return'd from England with a Press & Letters to set up his Business in Boston. I lik'd it much better than that of my Father, but still had a Hankering for the Sea. To prevent the apprehended Effect of such an Incli-nation, my Father was impatient to have me bound to my Brother. I stood out some time, but at last was persuaded and signed the Indentures, when I was yet but 12 Years old. I was to serve as an Apprentice till I was 21 Years of Age, only I was to be allow'd Journeyman's Wages during the last Year. In a little time I made great Proficiency in the Business, and became a use-ful Hand to my Brother. I now had Access to better Books. An Acquaintance with the Apprentices of Booksellers, enabled me sometimes to borrow a small one, which I was careful to return soon & clean. Often I sat up in my Room reading the greatest Part of the Night, when the Book was borrow'd in the Evening & to be return'd early in the Morning lest it should be miss'd or wanted. And after some time an ingenious Tradesman Mr Matthew Adams who had a pretty Collection of Books, & who frequented our Printinghouse, took Notice of me, invited me to his Library, & very kindly lent me such Books as I chose to read. I now took a Fancy to Poetry, and made some little Pieces. My Brother, thinking it might turn to account encourag'd me,

& put me on composing two occasional Ballads. One was called the *Light House Tragedy,* & contain'd an Account of the drowning of Capt. Worthilake with his Two Daughters; the other was a Sailor Song on the Taking of *Teach* or Blackbeard the Pirate. They were wretched Stuff, in the Grubstreet Ballad Style, and when they were printed he sent me about the Town to sell them. The first sold wonderfully, the Event being recent, having made a great Noise. This flatter'd my Vanity. But my Father discourag'd me, by ridiculing my Performances, and telling me Verse-makers were always Beggars; so I escap'd being a Poet, most probably a very bad one. But as Prose Writing has been of great Use to me in the Course of my Life, and was a principal Means of my Advancement, I shall tell you how in such a Situation I acquir'd what little Ability I have in that Way.

There was another Bookish Lad in the Town, John Collins by Name, with whom I was intimately acquainted. We sometimes disputed, and very fond we were of Argument, & very desirous of confuting one another. Which disputatious Turn, by the way, is apt to become a very bad Habit, making People often extremely disagreeable in Company, by the Contradiction that is necessary to bring it into Practice, & thence, besides souring & spoiling the Conversation, is productive of Disgusts & perhaps Enmities where you may have occasion for Friendship. I had caught it by reading my Father's Books of Dispute about Religion. Persons of good Sense, I have since observ'd, seldom fall into it, except Lawyers, University Men, and Men of all Sorts that have been bred at Edinburgh. A Question was once somehow or other started between Collins & me, of the Propriety of educating the Female Sex in Learning, & their Abilities for Study. He was of Opinion that it was improper, & that they were naturally unequal to it. I took the contrary Side, perhaps a little for Dispute sake. He was naturally more eloquent, had a ready Plenty of Words, and sometimes as I thought bore me down more by his Fluency than by the Strength of his Reasons. As we parted without settling the Point, & were not to see one another again for some time, I sat down to put my Arguments in Writing, which I copied fair & sent to him. He answer'd & I reply'd. Three or four Letters of a Side had pass'd, when my

Father happen'd to find my Papers, and read them. Without entering into the Discussion, he took occasion to talk to me about the Manner of my Writing, observ'd that tho' I had the Advantage of my Antagonist in correct Spelling & pointing (which I ow'd to the Printinghouse) I fell far short in elegance of Expression, in Method and in Perspicuity, of which he convinc'd me by several Instances. I saw the Justice of his Remarks, & thence grew more attentive to the *Manner* in Writing, and determin'd to endeavor at Improvement.

About this time I met with an odd Volume of the Spectator. It was the third. I had never before seen any of them. I bought it, read it over and over, and was much delighted with it. I thought the Writing excellent, & wish'd if possible to imitate it. With that View, I took some of the Papers, & making short Hints of the Sentiment in each Sentence, laid them by a few Days, and then without looking at the Book, try'd to complete the Papers again, by expressing each hinted Sentiment at length & as fully as it had been express'd before, in any suitable Words, that should come to hand.

Then I compar'd my Spectator with the Original, discover'd some of my Faults & corrected them. But I found I wanted a Stock of Words or a Readiness in recollecting & using them, which I thought I should have acquir'd before that time, if I had gone on making Verses, since the continual Occasion for Words of the same Import but of different Length, to suit the Measure, or of different Sound for the Rhyme, would have laid me under a constant Necessity of searching for Variety, and also have tended to fix that Variety in my Mind, & make me Master of it. Therefore I took some of the Tales & turn'd them into Verse: And after a time, when I had pretty well forgotten the Prose, turn'd them back again. I also sometimes jumbled my Collections of Hints into Confusion, and after some Weeks, endeavor'd to reduce them into the best Order, before I began to form the full Sentences, & complete the Paper. This was to teach me Method in the Arrangement of Thoughts. By comparing my work afterwards with the original, I discover'd many faults and amended them; but I sometimes had the Pleasure of Fancying that in certain Particulars of small Import,

I had been lucky enough to improve the Method or the Language and this encourag'd me to think I might possibly in time come to be a tolerable English Writer, of which I was extremely ambitious.

My Time for these Exercises & for Reading, was at Night, after Work or before Work began in the Morning; or on Sundays, when I contrived to be in the Printinghouse alone, evading as much as I could the common Attendance on public Worship, which my Father used to exact of me when I was under his Care: And which indeed I still thought a Duty; tho' I could not, as it seemed to me, afford the Time to practise it.

When about 16 Years of Age, I happen'd to meet with a Book, written by one Tryon, recommending a Vegetable Diet. I determined to go into it. My Brother being yet unmarried, did not keep House, but boarded himself & his Apprentices in another Family. My refusing to eat Flesh occasioned an Inconveniency, and I was frequently chid for my singularity. I made myself acquainted with Tryon's Manner of preparing some of his Dishes, such as Boiling Potatoes or Rice, making Hasty Pudding, & a few others, and then propos'd to my Brother, that if he would give me Weekly half the Money he paid for my Board I would board myself. He instantly agreed to it, and I presently found that I could save half what he paid me. This was an additional Fund for buying Books: But I had another Advantage in it. My Brother and the rest going from the Printinghouse to their Meals, I remain'd there alone, and dispatching presently my light Repast, (which often was no more than a Biscuit or a Slice of Bread, a Handful of Raisins or a Tart from the Pastry Cook's, & a Glass of Water) had the rest of the Time till their Return, for Study, in which I made the greater Progress from that greater Clearness of Head & quicker Apprehension which usually attend Temperance in Eating & Drinking. And now it was that being on some Occasion made asham'd of my Ignorance in Figures, which I had twice failed in learning when at School, I took Cocker's Book of Arithmetic, & went thro' the whole by myself with great Ease. I also read Seller's & Sturmy's Books of Navigation, & became acquainted with the little Geometry they contain, but never proceeded far in that Science.

And I read about this Time Locke on Human Understanding, and the Art of Thinking by Messrs du Port Royal.

While I was intent on improving my Language, I met with an English Grammar (I think it was Greenwood's) at the End of which there were two little Sketches of the Arts of Rhetoric and Logic, the latter finishing with a Specimen of a Dispute in the Socratic Method. And soon after I procur'd Xenophon's Memorable Things of Socrates, wherein there are many Instances of the same Method. I was charm'd with it, adopted it, dropped my abrupt Contradiction, and positive Argumentation, and put on the humble Inquirer & Doubter. And being then, from reading Shaftsbury & Collins, become a real Doubter in many Points of our Religious Doctrine, I found this Method safest for myself & very embarrassing to those against whom I used it, therefore I took a Delight in it, practis'd it continually & grew very artful & expert in drawing People even of superior Knowledge into Concessions the Consequences of which they did not foresee, entangling them in Difficulties out of which they could not extricate themselves, and so obtaining Victories that neither myself nor my Cause always deserved. I continu'd this Method some few years, but gradually left it, retaining only the Habit of expressing myself in Terms of modest Diffidence, never using when I advance any thing that may possibly be disputed, the Words, *Certainly, undoubtedly,* or any others that give the Air of Positiveness to an Opinion; but rather say, *I conceive, or I apprehend* a Thing to be so or so, *It appears to me, or I should think it so or so for such & such Reasons,* or *I imagine* it to be so, or *it is so if I am not mistaken.* This Habit I believe has been of great Advantage to me, when I have had occasion to inculcate my Opinions & persuade Men into Measures that I have been from time to time engag'd in promoting. And as the chief Ends of Conversation are to *inform,* or to be *informed,* to *please* or to *persuade,* I wish well-meaning sensible Men would not lessen their Power of doing Good by a Positive assuming Manner that seldom fails to disgust, tends to create Opposition, and to defeat every one of those Purposes for which Speech was given us, to wit, giving or receiving Information, or Pleasure: For if you would *inform,* a positive dogmatical Manner in advancing your Sentiments, may provoke Contradiction & prevent a candid Attention. If you wish Information & Improvement from the Knowledge of others and yet at the same time express yourself as firmly fix'd in your present Opinions, modest sensible Men, who do not love Disputation, will probably leave you undisturb'd in the Possession of your Error; and by such a Manner you can seldom hope to recommend yourself in *pleasing* your Hearers, or to persuade those whose Concurrence you desire. Pope says, judiciously,

> *Men should be taught as if you taught them not,*
> *And things unknown propos'd as things forgot,*

farther recommending it to us,

> *To speak tho' sure, with seeming Diffidence.*

And he might have coupled with this Line that which he has coupled with another, I think less properly,

> *For Want of Modesty is Want of Sense.*

If you ask why, *less properly,* I must repeat the Lines;

> Immodest Words admit of *no* Defense;
> *For* Want of Modesty is Want of Sense.

Now is not *Want of Sense* (where a Man is so unfortunate as to want it) some Apology for his *Want of Modesty?* and would not the Lines stand more justly thus?

> Immodest Words admit *but this* Defense,
> That Want of Modesty is Want of Sense.

This however I should submit to better Judgments.

My Brother had in 1720 or 21, begun to print a Newspaper. It was the second that appear'd in America, & was called *The New England Courant.* The only one before it, was *The Boston*

News Letter. I remember his being dissuaded by some of his Friends from the Undertaking, as not likely to succeed, one Newspaper being in their Judgment enough for America. At this time 1771 there are not less than five & twenty. He went on however with the Undertaking, and after having work'd in composing the Types & printing off the Sheets I was employ'd to carry the Papers thro' the Streets to the Customers. He had some ingenious Men among his Friends who amus'd themselves by writing little Pieces for this Paper, which gain'd it Credit, & made it more in Demand; and these Gentlemen often visited us. Hearing their Conversations, and their Accounts of the Approbation their Papers were receiv'd with, I was excited to try my Hand among them. But being still a Boy, & suspecting that my Brother would object to printing any Thing of mine in his Paper if he knew it to be mine, I contriv'd to disguise my Hand, & writing an anonymous Paper I put it in at Night under the Door of the Printinghouse. It was found in the Morning & communicated to his Writing Friends when they call'd in as usual. They read it, commented on it in my Hearing, and I had the exquisite Pleasure, of finding it met with their Approbation, and that in their different Guesses at the Author none were named but Men of some Character among us for Learning & Ingenuity. I suppose now that I was rather lucky in my Judges. And that perhaps they were not really so very good ones as I then esteem'd them. Encourag'd however by this, I wrote and convey'd in the same Way to the Press several more Papers, which were equally approv'd, and I kept my Secret till my small Fund of Sense for such Performances was pretty well exhausted, & then I discovered it; when I began to be considered a little more by my Brother's Acquaintance, and in a manner that did not quite please him, as he thought, probably with reason, that it tended to make me too vain. And perhaps this might be one Occasion of the Differences that we frequently had about this Time. Tho' a Brother, he considered himself as my Master, & me as his Apprentice; and accordingly expected the same Services from me as he would from another; while I thought he demean'd me too much in some he requir'd of me, who from a Brother expected more Indulgence. Our Disputes were often brought before our

Father, and I fancy I was either generally in the right, or else a better Pleader, because the Judgment was generally in my favor: But my Brother was passionate & had often beaten me, which I took extremely amiss; and thinking my Apprenticeship very tedious, I was continually wishing for some Opportunity of shortening it, which at length offered in a manner unexpected.*

One of the Pieces in our Newspaper, on some political Point which I have now forgotten, gave Offense to the Assembly. He was taken up, censur'd and imprison'd for a Month by the Speaker's Warrant, I suppose because he would not discover his Author. I too was taken up & examin'd before the Council, but tho' I did not give them any Satisfaction, they contented themselves with admonishing me, and dismiss'd me, considering me perhaps as an Apprentice who was bound to keep his Master's Secrets. During my Brother's Confinement, which I resented a good deal, notwithstanding our private Differences, I had the Management of the Paper, and I made bold to give our Rulers some Rubs in it, which my Brother took very kindly, while others began to consider me in an unfavorable Light, as a young Genius that had a Turn for Libelling & Satire. My Brother's Discharge was accompany'd with an Order of the House, (a very odd one) *that James Franklin should no longer print the Paper called the New England Courant.* There was a Consultation held in our Printinghouse among his Friends what he should do in this Case. Some propos'd to evade the Order by changing the Name of the Paper; but my Brother seeing Inconveniences in that, it was finally concluded on as a better Way, to let it be printed for the future under the Name of *Benjamin Franklin.* And to avoid the Censure of the Assembly that might fall on him, as still printing it by his Apprentice, the Contrivance was, that my old Indenture should be return'd to me with a full Discharge on the Back of it, to be shown on Occasion; but to secure to him the Benefit of my Service I was to sign new Indentures for the Remainder of the Term, which were to

---

*Note. I fancy his harsh & tyrannical Treatment of me, might be a means of impressing me with that Aversion to arbitrary Power that has stuck to me thro' my whole Life.

be kept private. A very flimsy Scheme it was, but however it was immediately executed, and the Paper went on accordingly under my Name for several Months. At length a fresh Difference arising between my Brother and me, I took upon me to assert my Freedom, presuming that he would not venture to produce the new Indentures. It was not fair in me to take this Advantage, and this I therefore reckon one of the first Errata of my Life: But the Unfairness of it weigh'd little with me, when under the Impressions of Resentment, for the Blows his Passion too often urg'd him to bestow upon me. Tho' he was otherwise not an ill-natured Man: Perhaps I was too saucy & provoking.

When he found I would leave him, he took care to prevent my getting Employment in any other Printinghouse of the Town, by going round & speaking to every Master, who accordingly refus'd to give me Work. I then thought of going to New York as the nearest Place where there was a Printer: and I was the rather inclin'd to leave Boston, when I reflected that I had already made myself a little obnoxious to the governing Party; & from the arbitrary Proceedings of the Assembly in my Brother's Case it was likely I might if I stay'd soon bring myself into Scrapes; and farther that my indiscreet Disputations about Religion begun to make me pointed at with Horror by good People, as an Infidel or Atheist. I determin'd on the Point: but my Father now siding with my Brother, I was sensible that if I attempted to go openly, Means would be used to prevent me. My Friend Collins therefore undertook to manage a little for me. He agreed with the Captain of a New York Sloop for my Passage, under the Notion of my being a young Acquaintance of his that had got a naughty Girl with Child, whose Friends would compel me to marry her, and therefore I could not appear or come away publicly. So I sold some of my Books to raise a little Money, Was taken on board privately, and as we had a fair Wind in three Days I found myself in New York near 300 Miles from home, a Boy of but 17, without the least Recommendation to or Knowledge of any Person in the Place, and with very little Money in my Pocket.

My Inclinations for the Sea, were by this time worn out, or I might now have gratify'd them. But having a Trade, & supposing myself a pretty good Workman, I offer'd my Service to the Printer of the Place, old M^r W^m. Bradford, (who had been the first Printer in Pennsylvania, but remov'd from thence upon the Quarrel of Geo. Keith). He could give me no Employment, having little to do, and Help enough already: But, says he, my Son at Philadelphia has lately lost his principal Hand, Aquila Rose, by Death. If you go thither I believe he may employ you. Philadelphia was 100 Miles farther. I set out, however, in a Boat for Amboy, leaving my Chest and Things to follow me round by Sea. In crossing the Bay we met with a Squall that tore our rotten Sails to pieces, prevented our getting into the Kill, and drove us upon Long Island. In our Way a drunken Dutchman, who was a Passenger too, fell over board; when he was sinking I reach'd thro' the Water to his shock Pate & drew him up so that we got him in again. His Ducking sober'd him a little, & he went to sleep, taking first out of his Pocket a Book which he desir'd I would dry for him. It prov'd to be my old favorite Author Bunyan's Pilgrim's Progress in Dutch, finely printed on good Paper with copper Cuts, a Dress better than I had ever seen it wear in its own Language. I have since found that it has been translated into most of the Languages of Europe, and suppose it has been more generally read than any other Book except perhaps the Bible. Honest John was the first that I know of who mix'd Narration & Dialogue, a Method of Writing very engaging to the Reader, who in the most interesting Parts finds himself as it were brought into the Company, & present at the Discourse. Defoe in his Crusoe, his Moll Flanders, Religious Courtship, Family Instructor, & other Pieces, has imitated it with Success. And Richardson has done the same in his Pamela, &c.

When we drew near the Island we found it was at a Place where there could be no Landing, there being a great Surf on the stony Beach. So we dropped Anchor & swung round towards the Shore. Some People came down to the Water Edge & hallow'd to us, as we did to them. But the Wind was so high & the Surf so loud, that we could not hear so as to understand each other. There were Canoes on the Shore, & we made Signs & hallow'd that they should fetch us, but they either did not understand us, or thought it impracticable. So they went away, and Night coming on, we had no Remedy but to wait till the Wind should abate, and in the mean time the Boatman & I concluded to sleep if we could, and so crowded into the Scuttle with the Dutchman who was still wet, and the Spray beating over the Head of our Boat, leak'd thro' to us, so that we were soon almost as wet as he. In this Manner we lay all Night with very little Rest. But the Wind abating the next Day, we made a Shift to reach Amboy before Night, having been 30 Hours on the Water without Victuals, or any Drink but a Bottle of filthy Rum: The Water we sail'd on being salt.

In the Evening I found myself very feverish, & went in to Bed. But having read somewhere that cold Water drank plentifully was good for a Fever, I follow'd the Prescription, sweat plentifully most of the Night, my Fever left me, and in the Morning crossing the Ferry, I proceeded on my Journey, on foot, having 50 Miles to Burlington, where I was told I should find Boats that would carry me the rest of the Way to Philadelphia.

It rain'd very hard all the Day, I was thoroughly soak'd and by Noon a good deal tir'd, so I stopped at a poor Inn, where I stayed all Night, beginning now to wish I had never left home. I cut so miserable a Figure too, that I found by the Questions ask'd me I was suspected to be some runaway Servant, and in danger of being taken up on that Suspicion. However I proceeded the next Day, and got in the Evening to an Inn within 8 or 10 Miles of Burlington, kept by one Dr Brown.

He entered into Conversation with me while I took some Refreshment, and finding I had read a little, became very sociable and friendly. Our Acquaintance continu'd as long as he liv'd. He had been, I imagine, an itinerant Doctor, for there was no Town in England, or Country in Europe, of which he could not give a very particular Account. He had some Letters, & was ingenious, but much of an Unbeliever, & wickedly undertook some Years after to travesty the Bible in doggerel Verse as Cotton had done Virgil. By this means he set many of the Facts in a very ridiculous Light, & might have hurt weak minds if his Work had been publish'd, but it never was. At his House I lay that Night, and the next Morning reach'd Burlington.—But had the Mortification to find that the regular Boats were gone, a little before my coming, and no other expected to go till Tuesday, this being Saturday. Wherefore I return'd to an old Woman in the Town of whom I had bought Gingerbread to eat on the Water, & ask'd her Advice; she invited me to lodge at her House till a Passage by Water should offer: & being tired with my foot Travelling, I accepted the Invitation. She understanding I was a Printer, would have had me stay at that Town & follow my Business, being ignorant of the Stock necessary to begin with. She was very hospitable, gave me a Dinner of Ox Cheek with great Good Will, accepting only of a Pot of Ale in return. And I tho't myself fix'd till Tuesday should come. However walking in the Evening by the Side of the River a Boat came by, which I found was going towards Philadelphia, with several People in her. They took me in, and as there was no wind, we row'd all the Way; and about Midnight not having yet seen the City, some of the Company were confident we must have pass'd it, and would row no farther, the others knew not where we were, so we put towards the Shore, got into a Creek, landed near an old Fence with the Rails of which we made a Fire, the Night being cold, in October, and there we remain'd till Daylight. Then one of the Company knew the Place to be Cooper's Creek a little above Philadelphia, which we saw as soon as we got out of the Creek, and arriv'd there about 8 or 9 a Clock, on the Sunday morning, and landed at the Market street Wharf.

I have been the more particular in this Description of my Journey, & shall be so of my first Entry into that City, that you may in your Mind compare such unlikely Beginnings with the Figure I have since made there. I was in my Working Dress, my best Clothes being to come round by Sea. I was dirty from my Journey; my Pockets were stuff'd out with Shirts & Stockings; I knew no Soul, nor where to look for Lodging. I was fatigued with Travelling, Rowing & Want of Rest. I was very hungry, and my whole Stock of Cash consisted of a Dutch Dollar and about a Shilling in Copper. The latter I gave the People of the Boat for my Passage, who at first refus'd it on Account of my Rowing; but I insisted on their taking it, a Man being sometimes more generous when he has but a little Money than when he has plenty, perhaps thro' Fear of being thought to have but little. Then I walk'd up the Street, gazing about, till near the Market House I met a Boy with Bread. I had made many a Meal on Bread, & inquiring where he got it, I went immediately to the Baker's he directed me to in second Street; and ask'd for Biscuit, intending such as we had in Boston, but they it seems were not made in Philadelphia, then I ask'd for a three-penny Loaf, and was told they had none such: so not considering or knowing the Difference of Money & the greater Cheapness nor the Names of his Bread, I bad him give me three penny worth of any sort. He gave me accordingly three great Puffy Rolls. I was surpris'd at the Quantity, but took it, and having no room in my Pockets, walk'd off, with a Roll under each Arm, & eating the other. Thus I went up Market Street as far as fourth Street, passing by the Door of Mr Read, my future Wife's Father, when she standing at the Door saw me, & thought I made as I certainly did a most awkward ridiculous Appearance. Then I turn'd and went down Chestnut Street and part of Walnut Street, eating my Roll all the Way, and coming round found myself again at Market Street Wharf, near the Boat I came in, to which I went for a Draught of the River Water, and being fill'd with one of my Rolls, gave the other two to a Woman & her Child that came down the River in the Boat with us and were waiting to go farther. Thus refresh'd I walk'd again up the Street, which by this time had many clean dress'd People in it who were all walking the same Way; I join'd them, and thereby was led into the great Meeting House of the Quakers near the Market. I sat down among them, and after looking round a while & hearing nothing said, being very drowsy thro' Labor & want of Rest the preceding Night, I fell fast asleep, and continu'd so till the Meeting broke up, when one was kind enough to rouse me. This was therefore the first House I was in or slept in, in Philadelphia.

Walking again down towards the River, & looking in the Faces of People, I met a young Quaker Man whose Countenance I lik'd, and accosting him requested he would tell me where a Stranger could get Lodging. We were then near the Sign of the Three Mariners. Here, says he, is one Place that entertains

Strangers, but it is not a reputable House; if thee wilt walk with me, I'll show thee a better. He brought me to the Crooked Billet in Water-Street. Here I got a Dinner. And while I was eating it, several sly Questions were ask'd me, as it seem'd to be suspected from my youth & Appearance, that I might be some Runaway. After Dinner my Sleepiness return'd: and being shown to a Bed, I lay down without undressing, and slept till Six in the Evening; was call'd to Supper; went to Bed again very early and slept soundly till the next Morning. Then I made myself as tidy as I could, and went to Andrew Bradford the Printer's. I found in the Shop the old Man his Father, whom I had seen at New York, and who travelling on horseback had got to Philadelphia before me. He introduc'd me to his Son, who receiv'd me civilly, gave me a Breakfast, but told me he did not at present want a Hand, being lately supply'd with one. But there was another Printer in town lately set up, one Keimer, who perhaps might employ me; if not, I should be welcome to lodge at his House, & he would give me a little Work to do now & then till fuller Business should offer.

The old Gentleman said, he would go with me to the new Printer: And when we found him, Neighbor, says Bradford, I have brought to see you a young Man of your Business, perhaps you may want such a One. He ask'd me a few Questions, put a Composing Stick in my Hand to see how I work'd, and then said he would employ me soon, tho' he had just then nothing for me to do. And taking old Bradford whom he had never seen before, to be one of the Towns People that had a Good Will for him, enter'd into a Conversation on his present Undertaking & Prospects; while Bradford not discovering that he was the other Printer's Father, on Keimer's saying he expected soon to get the greatest Part of the Business into his own Hands, drew him on by artful Questions and starting little Doubts, to explain all his Views, what Interest he rely'd on, & in what manner he intended to proceed. I who stood by & heard all, saw immediately that one of them was a crafty old Sophister, and the other a mere Novice. Bradford left me with Keimer, who was greatly surpris'd when I told him who the old Man was.

Keimer's Printinghouse I found, consisted of an old shatter'd Press, and one small worn-out Fount of English, which he was then using himself, composing in it an Elegy on Aquila Rose before-mentioned, an ingenious young Man of excellent Character much respected in the Town, Clerk of the Assembly, & a pretty Poet. Keimer made Verses, too, but very indifferently. He could not be said to write them for his Manner was to compose them in the Types directly out of his Head; so there being no Copy, but one Pair of Cases, and the Elegy likely to require all the Letter, no one could help him. I endeavor'd to put his Press (which he had not yet us'd, & of which he understood nothing) into Order fit to be work'd with; & promising to come & print off his Elegy as soon as he should have got it ready, I return'd to Bradford's who gave me a little Job to do for the present, & there I lodged & dieted. A few Days after Keimer sent for me to print off the Elegy. And now he had got another Pair of Cases, and a Pamphlet to reprint, on which he set me to work.

These two Printers I found poorly Qualified for their Business. Bradford had not been bred to it, & was very illiterate; and Keimer tho' something of a Scholar, was a mere Compositor, knowing nothing of Presswork. He had been one of the French Prophets and could act their enthusiastic Agitations. At this time he did not profess any particular Religion, but something of all on occasion; was very ignorant of the World, & had, as I afterwards found, a good deal of the Knave in his Composition. He did not like my Lodging at Bradford's while I work'd with him. He had a House indeed, but without Furniture, so he could not lodge me: But he got me a Lodging at Mr Read's before-mentioned, who was the Owner of his House. And my Chest & Clothes being come by this time, I made rather a more respectable Appearance in the Eyes of Miss Read than I had done when she first happen'd to see me eating my Roll in the Street.

I began now to have some Acquaintance among the young People of the Town, that were Lovers of Reading with whom I spent my Evenings very pleasantly and gaining Money by my Industry & Frugality, I lived very agreeably, forgetting Boston as much as I could, and not desiring that any there should know where I resided, except my Friend Collins who was in my Secret, & kept it when I wrote to him. At length an Incident happened that sent me back again much sooner than I had intended.

I had a Brother-in-law, Robert Homes, Master of a Sloop, that traded between Boston and Delaware. He being at Newcastle 40 Miles below Philadelphia, heard there of me, and wrote me a letter, mentioning the Concern of my Friends in Boston at my abrupt Departure, assuring me of their Good Will to me, and that every thing would be accommodated to my Mind if I would return, to which he exhorted me very earnestly. I wrote an Answer to his Letter, thank'd him for his Advice, but stated my Reasons for quitting Boston fully, & in such a Light as to convince him I was not so wrong as he had apprehended. Sir William Keith, Governor of the Province, was then at New Castle, and Capt. Homes happening to be in Company with him when my Letter came to hand, spoke to him of me, and show'd him the Letter. The Governor read it, and seem'd surpris'd when he was told my Age. He said I appear'd a young Man of promising Parts, and therefore should be encouraged: The Printers at Philadelphia were wretched ones, and if I would set up there, he made no doubt I should succeed; for his Part, he would procure me the public Business, & do me every other Service in his Power. This my Brother-in-Law afterwards told me in Boston. But I knew as yet nothing of it; when one Day Keimer and I being at Work together near the Window, we saw the Governor and another Gentleman (which prov'd to be Col. French, of New Castle) finely dress'd, come directly across the Street to our House, & heard them at the Door. Keimer ran down immediately, thinking it a Visit to him. But the Governor inquir'd for me, came up, & with a Condescension & Politeness I had been quite unus'd to, made me many Compliments, desired to be acquainted with me, blam'd me kindly for not having made myself known to him when I first came to the Place, and would have me away with him to the Tavern where he was going with Col. French to taste as he said some excellent Madeira. I was not a little surpris'd, and Keimer star'd like a Pig poison'd. I went however with the Governor & Col. French, to a Tavern the Corner of Third Street, and over the Madeira he propos'd my Setting up my Business, laid before me the Probabilities of Success, & both he & Col. French assur'd me I should have their Interest & Influence in procuring the Public Business of both Governments. On my doubting whether my Father would assist me in it, Sir William said he would give me a Letter to him, in which he would state the Advantages, and he did not doubt of prevailing with him. So it was concluded I should return to Boston in the first Vessel with the Governor's Letter recommending me to my Father. In the mean time the Intention was to be kept secret, and I went on working with Keimer as usual, the Governor sending for me now & then to dine with him, a very great Honor I thought it, and conversing with me in the most affable, familiar, & friendly manner imaginable. About the End of April 1724, a little Vessel offer'd for Boston. I took Leave of Keimer as going to see my Friends. The Governor gave me an ample Letter, saying many flattering things of me to my Father, and strongly recommending the Project of my setting up at Philadelphia, as a Thing that must make my Fortune. We struck on a Shoal in going down the Bay & sprung a Leak, we had a blustering time at Sea, and were oblig'd to pump almost continually, at which I took my Turn. We arriv'd safe however at Boston in about a Fortnight. I had been absent Seven Months and my Friends had heard nothing of me; for my Br. Homes was not yet return'd; and had not written about me. My unexpected Appearance surpris'd the Family; all were however very glad to see me and made me Welcome, except my Brother. I went to see him at his Printinghouse: I was better dress'd than ever while in his Service, having a genteel new Suit from Head to foot, a Watch, and my Pockets lin'd with near Five Pounds Sterling in Silver. He receiv'd me not very frankly, look'd me all over, and turn'd to his Work again. The Journey-Men were inquisitive where I had been, what sort of a Country it was, and how I lik'd it? I prais'd it much, & the happy Life I led in it; expressing strongly my Intention of returning to it; and one of them asking what kind of Money we had there, I produc'd a handful of Silver and spread it before them, which was a kind of Raree-Show they had not been us'd to, Paper being the Money of Boston. Then I took an Opportunity of letting them see my Watch: and lastly, (my Brother still grum & sullen) I gave them a Piece of Eight to drink, & took my Leave. This Visit of mine offended him extremely. For when my Mother some time after spoke to him of a Reconciliation, & of her Wishes to see us on good Terms together, & that we might live for the future as Brothers, he said, I had insulted him in such a Manner before his People that he could never forget or forgive it. In this however he was mistaken.

My Father receiv'd the Governor's Letter with some apparent Surprise; but said little of it to me for some Days; when Capt. Homes returning, he show'd it to him, ask'd if he knew Keith, and what kind of a Man he was: Adding his Opinion that he must be of small Discretion, to think of setting a Boy up in Business who wanted yet 3 Years of being at Man's Estate. Homes said what he could in favor of the Project; but my Father was clear in the Impropriety of it; and at last gave a flat Denial to it. Then he wrote a civil Letter to Sir William thanking him for the Patronage he had so kindly offered me, but declining to assist me as yet in Setting up, I being in his Opinion too young to be trusted with the Management of a Business so important, & for which the Preparation must be so expensive.

My Friend & Companion Collins, who was a Clerk at the Post-Office, pleas'd with the Account I gave him of my new Country, determin'd to go thither also: And while I waited for my Father's Determination, he set out before me by Land to Rhode Island, leaving his Books which were a pretty Collection of Mathematics & Natural Philosophy, to come with mine & me to New York where he propos'd to wait for me. My Father, tho' he did not approve of Sir William's Proposition was yet pleas'd that I had been able to obtain so advantageous a Character from a Person of such Note where I had resided, and that I had been so industrious & careful as to equip myself so handsomely in so short a time: therefore seeing no Prospect of an Accommodation between my Brother & me, he gave his Consent to my Returning again to Philadelphia, advis'd me to behave respectfully to the People there, endeavor to obtain the general Esteem, & avoid lampooning & libelling to which he thought I had too much Inclination; telling me, that by steady Industry and a prudent Parsimony, I might save enough by the time I was One and Twenty to set me up, & that if I came near the Matter he would help me out with the rest. This was all I could obtain, except some small Gifts as Tokens of his & my Mother's Love, when I embark'd again for New York, now with their Approbation & their Blessing.

The Sloop putting in at Newport, Rhode Island, I visited my Brother John, who had been married & settled there some Years. He received me very affectionately, for he always lov'd me. A Friend of his, one Vernon, having some Money due to him in Pennsylvania, about 35 Pounds Currency, desired I would receive it for him, and keep it till I had his Directions what to remit it in. Accordingly he gave me an Order. This afterwards occasion'd me a good deal of Uneasiness. At Newport we took in a Number of Passengers for New York: Among which were two young Women Companions, and a grave, sensible Matron-like Quaker-Woman with her Attendants. I had shown an obliging readiness to do her some little Services which impress'd her I suppose with a degree of Good Will towards me. Therefore when she saw a daily growing Familiarity between me & the two Young Women, which they appear'd to encourage, she took me aside & said, Young Man, I am concern'd for thee, as thou has no Friend with thee, and seems not to know much of the World, or of the Snares Youth is expos'd to; depend upon it those are very bad Women, I can see it in all their Actions, and if thee art not upon thy Guard, they will draw thee into some Danger: they are Strangers to thee, and I advise thee in a friendly Concern for thy Welfare, to have no Acquaintance with them. As I seem'd at first not to think so ill of them as she did, she mention'd some Things she had observ'd & heard that had escap'd my Notice; but now convinc'd me she was right. I thank'd her for her kind Advice, and promis'd to follow it. When we arriv'd at New York, they told me where they liv'd, & invited me to come and see them: but I avoided it. And it was well I did: For the next Day, the Captain miss'd a Silver Spoon & some other Things that had been taken out of his Cabin, and knowing that these were a Couple of Strumpets,

he got a Warrant to search their Lodgings, found the stolen
Goods, and had the Thieves punish'd. So tho' we had escap'd a
sunken Rock which we scrap'd upon in the Passage, I thought
this Escape of rather more Importance to me. At New York
I found my Friend Collins, who had arriv'd there some Time
before me. We had been intimate from Children, and had read
the same Books together. But he had the Advantage of more
time for reading, & Studying and a wonderful Genius for
Mathematical Learning in which he far outstripped me. While I
liv'd in Boston most of my Hours of Leisure for Conversation
were spent with him, & he continu'd a sober as well as an industrious Lad; was much respected for his Learning by several
of the Clergy & other Gentlemen, & seem'd to promise making
a good Figure in Life: but during my Absence he had acquir'd a
Habit of Sotting with Brandy; and I found by his own Account
& what I heard from others, that he had been drunk every day
since his Arrival at New York, & behav'd very oddly. He had
gam'd too and lost his Money, so that I was oblig'd to discharge
his Lodgings, & defray his Expenses to and at Philadelphia:
Which prov'd extremely inconvenient to me. The then Governor of New York, Burnet, Son of Bishop Burnet hearing from
the Captain that a young Man, one of his Passengers, had a great
many Books, desired he would bring me to see him. I waited
upon him accordingly, and should have taken Collins with me
but that he was not sober. The Governor treated me with great
Civility, show'd me his Library, which was a very large one, &
we had a good deal of Conversation about Books & Authors.
This was the second Governor who had done me the Honor
to take Notice of me, which to a poor Boy like me was very
pleasing.

We proceeded to Philadelphia. I received on the Way Vernon's Money, without which we could hardly have finish'd our
Journey. Collins wish'd to be employ'd in some Counting
House; but whether they discover'd his Dramming by his Breath,
or by his Behavior, tho' he had some Recommendations, he met
with no Success in any Application, and continu'd Lodging &
Boarding at the same House with me & at my Expense. Knowing I had that Money of Vernon's he was continually borrowing

of me, still promising Repayment as soon as he should be in Business. At length he had got so much of it, that I was distress'd to think what I should do, in case of being call'd on to remit it. His Drinking continu'd, about which we sometimes quarrel'd, for when a little intoxicated he was very fractious. Once in a Boat on the Delaware with some other young Men, he refused to row in his Turn: I will be row'd home, says he. We will not row you, says I. You must, says he, or stay all Night on the Water, just as you please. The others said, Let us row; what signifies it? But my mind being soured with his other Conduct, I continu'd to refuse. So he swore he would make me row, or throw me overboard; and coming along stepping on the Thwarts towards me, when he came up & struck at me I clapped my Hand under his Crutch, and rising pitch'd him headforemost into the River. I knew he was a good Swimmer, and so was under little Concern about him; but before he could get round to lay hold of the Boat, we had with a few Strokes pull'd her out of his Reach. And ever when he drew near the Boat, we ask'd if he would row, striking a few Strokes to slide her away from him. He was ready to die with Vexation, & obstinately would not promise to row; however seeing him at last beginning to tire, we lifted him in; and brought him home dripping wet in the Evening. We hardly exchang'd a civil Word afterwards; and a West India Captain who had a Commission to procure a Tutor for the Sons of a Gentleman at Barbadoes, happening to meet with him, agreed to carry him thither. He left me then, promising to remit me the first Money he should receive in order to discharge the Debt. But I never heard of him after. The Breaking into this Money of Vernon's was one of the first great Errata of my Life. And this Affair show'd that my Father was not much out in his Judgment when he suppos'd me too Young to manage Business of Importance. But Sir William, on reading his Letter, said he was too prudent. There was great Difference in Persons, and Discretion did not always accompany Years, nor was Youth always without it. And since he will not set you up, says he, I will do it myself. Give me an Inventory of the Things necessary to be had from England, and I will send for them. You shall repay me when you are able; I am resolv'd to have a good Printer here, and I am sure you must succeed. This was spoken with such an Appearance of Cordiality that I had not the least doubt of his meaning what he said. I had hitherto kept the Proposition of my Setting up a Secret in Philadelphia, & I still kept it. Had it been known that I depended on the Governor, probably some Friend that knew him better would have advis'd me not to rely on him, as I afterwards heard it as his known Character to be liberal of Promises which he never meant to keep. Yet unsolicited as he was by me, how could I think his generous Offers insincere? I believ'd him one of the best Men in the World.

I presented him an Inventory of a little Printinghouse, amounting by my Computation to about 100£ Sterling. He lik'd it, but ask'd me if my being on the Spot in England to choose the Types & see that every thing was good of the kind, might not be of some Advantage. Then, says he, when there, you may make Acquaintances & establish Correspondencies in the Bookselling & Stationery Way. I agreed that this might be advantageous. Then says he, get yourself ready to go with Annis; which was the annual Ship, and the only one at that Time usually passing between London and Philadelphia. But it would be some Months before Annis sail'd, so I continu'd working with Keimer, fretting about the Money Collins had got from me; and in daily Apprehensions of being call'd upon by Vernon, which however did not happen for some Years after.

I believe I have omitted mentioning that in my first Voyage from Boston, being becalm'd off Block Island, our People set about catching Cod & haul'd up a great many. Hitherto I had stuck to my Resolution of not eating animal Food; and on this Occasion, I consider'd with my Master Tryon, the taking every Fish as a kind of unprovok'd Murder, since none of them had or ever could do us any Injury that might justify the Slaughter. All this seem'd very reasonable. But I had formerly been a great Lover of Fish, & when this came hot out of the Frying Pan, it smelled admirably well. I balanc'd some time between Principle & Inclination: till I recollected, that when the Fish were opened, I saw smaller Fish taken out of their Stomachs: Then thought I, if you eat one another, I don't see why we mayn't eat you. So I din'd upon Cod very heartily and continu'd to eat with other People, returning only now & then occasionally to a vegetable Diet. So convenient a thing it is to be a *reasonable Creature,* since it enables one to find or make a Reason for every thing one has a mind to do.

Keimer & I liv'd on a pretty good familiar Footing & agreed tolerably well: for he suspected nothing of my Setting up. He retain'd a great deal of his old Enthusiasms, and lov'd Argumentation. We therefore had many Disputations. I used to work him so with my Socratic Method, and had trapann'd him so often by Questions apparently so distant from any Point we had in hand, and yet by degrees led to the Point, and brought him into Difficulties & Contradictions that at last he grew ridiculously cautious, and would hardly answer me the most common Question, without asking first, *What do you intend to infer from that?* However it gave him so high an Opinion of my Abilities in the Confuting Way, that he seriously propos'd my being his Colleague in a Project he had of setting up a new Sect. He was to preach the Doctrines, and I was to confound all Opponents. When he came to explain with me upon the Doctrines, I found several Conundrums which I objected to, unless I might have my Way a little too, and introduce some of mine. Keimer wore his Beard at full Length, because somewhere in the Mosaic Law it is said, *thou shalt not mar the Corners of thy Beard.* He likewise kept the seventh day Sabbath; and these two Points were Essentials with him. I dislik'd both, but agreed to admit them upon Condition of his adopting the Doctrine of using no animal Food. I doubt, says he, my Constitution will not bear that. I assur'd him it would, & that he would be the better for it. He was usually a great Glutton, and I promis'd myself some Diversion in half-starving him. He agreed to try the Practice if I would keep him Company. I did so and we held it for three Months. We had our Victuals dress'd and brought to us regularly by a Woman in the Neighborhood, who had from me a List of 40 Dishes to be prepar'd for us at different times, in all which there was neither Fish Flesh nor Fowl, and the whim suited me the better at this time from the Cheapness of it, not costing us above 18^{d} Sterling each, per Week. I have since kept several Lents most strictly, Leaving the common Diet for that, and that for the common, abruptly, without the least Inconvenience: So that I think there is little in the Advice of making those Changes by easy Gradations. I went on pleasantly, but poor Keimer suffer'd grievously, tir'd of the Project, long'd for the Flesh Pots of Egypt, and order'd a roast Pig. He invited me & two Women Friends to dine with him, but it being brought too soon upon table, he could not resist the Temptation, and ate it all up before we came.

I had made some Courtship during this time to Miss Read. I had a great Respect & Affection for her, and had some Reason to believe she had the same for me: but as I was about to take a long Voyage, and we were both very young, only a little above 18, it was thought most prudent by her Mother to prevent our going too far at present, as a Marriage if it was to take place would be more convenient after my Return, when I should be as I expected set up in my Business. Perhaps too she thought my Expectations not so well founded as I imagined them to be.

My chief Acquaintances at this time were, Charles Osborne, Joseph Watson, & James Ralph; All Lovers of Reading. The two first were Clerks to an eminent Scrivener or Conveyancer in the Town, Charles Brockden; the other was Clerk to a Merchant. Watson was a pious sensible young Man, of great Integrity. The others rather more lax in their Principles of Religion, particularly Ralph, who as well as Collins had been unsettled by me, for which they both made me suffer. Osborne was sensible, candid, frank, sincere, and affectionate to his Friends; but in literary Matters too fond of Criticising. Ralph, was ingenious, genteel in his Manners, & extremely eloquent; I think I never knew a prettier Talker. Both of them great Admirers of Poetry, and began to try their Hands in little Pieces. Many pleasant Walks we four had together on Sundays into the Woods near Schuylkill, where we read to one another & conferr'd on what we read. Ralph was inclin'd to pursue the Study of Poetry, not doubting but he might become eminent in it and make his Fortune by it, alleging that the best Poets must when they first began to write, make as many Faults as he did. Osborne dissuaded him, assur'd him he had no Genius for Poetry,

& advis'd him to think of nothing beyond the Business he was bred to; that in the mercantile way tho' he had no Stock, he might by his Diligence & Punctuality recommend himself to Employment as a Factor, and in time acquire wherewith to trade on his own Account. I approv'd the amusing one's Self with Poetry now & then, so far as to improve one's Language, but no farther. On this it was propos'd that we should each of us at our next Meeting produce a Piece of our own Composing, in order to improve by our mutual Observations, Criticisms & Corrections. As Language & Expression was what we had in View, we excluded all Considerations of Invention, by agreeing that the Task should be a Version of the 18th Psalm, which describes the Descent of a Deity. When the Time of our Meeting drew nigh, Ralph call'd on me first, & let me know his Piece was ready, I told him I had been busy, & having little Inclination had done nothing. He then show'd me his Piece for my Opinion; and I much approv'd it, as it appear'd to me to have great Merit. Now, says he, Osborne never will allow the least Merit in any thing of mine, but makes 1000 Criticisms out of mere Envy. He is not so jealous of you. I wish therefore you would take this Piece, & produce it as yours. I will pretend not to have had time, & so produce nothing: We shall then see what he will say to it. It was agreed, and I immediately transcrib'd it that it might appear in my own hand. We met. Watson's Performance was read: there were some Beauties in it: but many Defects. Osborne's was read: It was much better. Ralph did it Justice, remark'd some Faults, but applauded the Beauties. He himself had nothing to produce. I was backward, seem'd desirous of being excus'd, had not had sufficient Time to correct; &c. but no Excuse could be admitted, produce I must. It was read and repeated; Watson and Osborne gave up the Contest; and join'd in applauding it immoderately. Ralph only made some Criticisms & propos'd some Amendments, but I defended my Text. Osborne was against Ralph, & told him he was no better a Critic than Poet; so he dropped the Argument. As they two went home together, Osborne express'd himself still more strongly in favor of what he thought my Production, having restrain'd himself before as he said, lest I should think it

Flattery. But who would have imagin'd, says he, that Franklin
had been capable of such a Performance; such Painting, such
Force! such Fire! he has even improv'd the Original! In his common Conversation, he seems to have no Choice of Words; he
hesitates and blunders; and yet, good God, how he writes!
When we next met, Ralph discover'd the Trick, we had played
him, and Osborne was a little laughed at. This Transaction fix'd
Ralph in his Resolution of becoming a Poet. I did all I could to
dissuade him from it, but He continued scribbling Verses, till
Pope cur'd him. He became however a pretty good Prose Writer.
More of him hereafter. But as I may not have occasion again to
mention the other two, I shall just remark here, that Watson died
in my Arms a few Years after, much lamented, being the best of
our Set. Osborne went to the West Indies, where he became an
eminent Lawyer & made Money, but died young. He and I had
made a serious Agreement, that the one who happen'd first to
die, should if possible make a friendly Visit to the other, and acquaint him how he found things in that Separate State. But he
never fulfill'd his Promise.

The Governor, seeming to like my Company, had me frequently to his House; & his Setting me up was always mention'd
as a fix'd thing. I was to take with me Letters recommendatory
to a Number of his Friends, besides the Letter of Credit to furnish me with the necessary Money for purchasing the Press &
Types, Paper, &c. For these Letters I was appointed to call at
different times, when they were to be ready, but a future time
was still named. Thus we went on till the Ship whose Departure
too had been several times postponed was on the Point of sailing. Then when I call'd to take my Leave & Receive the Letters,
his Secretary, Dr Bard, came out to me and said the Governor
was extremely busy, in writing, but would be down at Newcastle before the Ship, & there the Letters would be delivered
to me.

Ralph, tho' married & having one Child, had determined to
accompany me in this Voyage. It was thought he intended to establish a Correspondence, & obtain Goods to sell on Commission. But I found afterwards, that thro' some Discontent with
his Wife's Relations, he purposed to leave her on their Hands,

& never return again. Having taken leave of my Friends, & interchang'd some Promises with Miss Read, I left Philadelphia in the Ship, which anchor'd at Newcastle. The Governor was there. But when I went to his Lodging, the Secretary came to me from him with the civillest Message in the World, that he could not then see me being engag'd in Business of the utmost Importance; but should send the Letters to me on board, wish'd me heartily a good Voyage and a speedy Return, &c. I return'd on board, a little puzzled, but still not doubting.

Mr Andrew Hamilton, a famous Lawyer of Philadelphia, had taken Passage in the same Ship for himself and Son: and with Mr Denham a Quaker Merchant, & Messrs Onion & Russel Masters of an Iron Work in Maryland, had engag'd the Great Cabin; so that Ralph and I were forc'd to take up with a Berth in the Steerage: And none on board knowing us, were considered as ordinary Persons. But Mr Hamilton & his Son (it was James, since Governor) return'd from Newcastle to Philadelphia, the Father being recall'd by a great Fee to plead for a seized Ship. And just before we sail'd Col. French coming on board, & showing me great Respect, I was more taken Notice of, and with my Friend Ralph invited by the other Gentlemen to come into the Cabin, there being now Room. Accordingly we remov'd thither.

Understanding that Col. French had brought on board the Governor's Dispatches, I ask'd the Captain for those Letters that were to be under my Care. He said all were put into the Bag together; and he could not then come at them; but before we landed in England, I should have an Opportunity of picking them out. So I was satisfy'd for the present, and we proceeded on our Voyage. We had a sociable Company in the Cabin, and lived uncommonly well, having the Addition of all Mr Hamilton's Stores, who had laid in plentifully. In this Passage Mr Denham contracted a Friendship for me that continued during his Life. The Voyage was otherwise not a pleasant one, as we had a great deal of bad Weather.

When we came into the Channel, the Captain kept his word with me, & gave me an Opportunity of examining the Bag for the Governor's Letters. I found none upon which my Name was

put, as under my Care; I pick'd out 6 or 7 that by the Hand writing I thought might be the promis'd Letters, especially as one of
them was directed to Basket the King's Printer, and another to
some Stationer. We arriv'd in London the 24th of December,
1724. I waited upon the Stationer who came first in my Way,
delivering the Letter as from Gov. Keith. I don't know such a
Person, says he: but opening the Letter, O, this is from Riddlesden; I have lately found him to be a complete Rascal, and I will
have nothing to do with him, nor receive any Letters from him.
So putting the Letter into my Hand, he turn'd on his Heel & left
me to serve some Customer. I was surprised to find these were
not the Governor's Letters. And after recollecting and comparing Circumstances, I began to doubt his Sincerity. I found my
Friend Denham, and opened the whole Affair to him. He let
me into Keith's Character, told me there was not the least
Probability that he had written any Letters for me, that no one
who knew him had the smallest Dependence on him, and he
laughed at the Notion of the Governor's giving me a Letter of
Credit, having as he said no Credit to give. On my expressing
some Concern about what I should do: He advis'd me to endeavor getting some Employment in the Way of my Business.
Among the Printers here, says he, you will improve yourself;
and when you return to America, you will set up to greater
Advantage.

We both of us happen'd to know, as well as the Stationer,
that Riddlesden the Attorney, was a very Knave. He had half
ruin'd Miss Read's Father by drawing him in to be bound for
him. By his Letter it appear'd, there was a secret Scheme on
foot to the Prejudice of Hamilton, (Suppos'd to be then coming over with us,) and that Keith was concern'd in it with Riddlesden. Denham, who was a Friend of Hamilton's, thought he
ought to be acquainted with it. So when he arriv'd in England,
which was soon after, partly from Resentment & Ill-Will to
Keith & Riddlesden, & partly from Good Will to him: I waited
on him, and gave him the Letter. He thank'd me cordially, the
Information being of Importance to him. And from that time he
became my Friend, greatly to my Advantage afterwards on many
Occasions.

But what shall we think of a Governor's playing such pitiful Tricks, & imposing so grossly on a poor ignorant Boy! It was a Habit he had acquired. He wish'd to please every body; and, having little to give, he gave Expectations. He was otherwise an ingenious sensible Man, a pretty good Writer, & a good Governor for the People, tho' not for his Constituents the Proprietaries, whose Instructions he sometimes disregarded. Several of our best Laws were of his Planning, and pass'd during his Administration.

Ralph and I were inseparable Companions. We took Lodgings together in Little Britain at 3/6 per Week, as much as we could then afford. He found some Relations, but they were poor & unable to assist him. He now let me know his Intentions of remaining in London, and that he never meant to return to Philadelphia. He had brought no Money with him, the whole he could muster having been expended in paying his Passage. I had 15 Pistoles: So he borrowed occasionally of me, to subsist while he was looking out for Business. He first endeavored to get into the Playhouse, believing himself qualify'd for an Actor; but Wilkes, to whom he apply'd, advis'd him candidly not to think of that Employment, as it was impossible he should succeed in it. Then he propos'd to Roberts, a Publisher in Paternoster Row, to write for him a Weekly Paper like the Spectator, on certain Conditions, which Roberts did not approve. Then he endeavor'd to get Employment as a Hackney Writer to copy for the Stationers & Lawyers about the Temple but could find no Vacancy.

I immediately got into Work at Palmer's, then a famous Printinghouse in Bartholomew Close; and here I continu'd near a Year. I was pretty diligent; but spent with Ralph a good deal of my Earnings in going to Plays & other Places of Amusement. We had together consum'd all my Pistoles, and now just rubb'd on from hand to mouth. He seem'd quite to forget his Wife & Child, and I by degrees my Engagements with Miss Read, to whom I never wrote more than one Letter, & that was to let her know I was not likely soon to return. This was another of the great Errata of my Life, which I should wish to correct if I were to live it over again. In fact, by our Expenses, I was constantly kept unable to pay my Passage.

At Palmer's I was employ'd in composing for the second Edition of Woollaston's Religion of Nature. Some of his Reasonings not appearing to me well-founded, I wrote a little metaphysical Piece, in which I made Remarks on them. It was entitled, *A Dissertation on Liberty & Necessity, Pleasure and pain.* I inscrib'd it to my Friend Ralph. I printed a small Number. It occasion'd my being more consider'd by Mr Palmer, as a young Man of some Ingenuity, tho' he seriously expostulated with me upon the Principles of my Pamphlet which to him appear'd abominable. My printing this Pamphlet was another Erratum.

While I lodg'd in Little Britain I made an Acquaintance with one Wilcox a Bookseller, whose Shop was at the next Door. He had an immense Collection of second-hand Books. Circulating Libraries were not then in Use; but we agreed that on certain reasonable Terms which I have now forgotten, I might take, read & return any of his Books. This I esteem'd a great Advantage, & I made as much use of it as I could.

My Pamphlet by some means falling into the Hands of one Lyons, a Surgeon, Author of a Book entitled *The Infallibility of Human Judgment,* it occasioned an Acquaintance between us; he took great Notice of me, call'd on me often, to converse on those Subjects, carried me to the Horns, a pale Ale-House in [blank] Lane, Cheapside, and introduc'd me to Dr Mandeville, Author of the Fable of the Bees, who had a Club there, of which he was the Soul, being a most facetious entertaining Companion. Lyons too introduc'd me to Dr Pemberton, at Batson's Coffee House, who promis'd to give me an Opportunity some time or other of seeing Sir Isaac Newton, of which I was extremely desirous; but this never happened.

I had brought over a few Curiosities among which the principal was a Purse made of the Asbestos, which purifies by Fire. Sir Hans Sloane heard of it, came to see me, and invited me to his House in Bloomsbury Square; where he show'd me all his Curiosities, and persuaded me to let him add that to the Number, for which he paid me handsomely.

In our House there lodg'd a young Woman; a Milliner, who I think had a Shop in the Cloisters. She had been genteelly bred, was sensible & lively, and of most pleasing Conversation. Ralph read Plays to her in the Evenings, they grew intimate, she took another Lodging, and he follow'd her. They liv'd together some time, but he being still out of Business, & her Income not sufficient to maintain them with her Child, he took a Resolution of going from London, to try for a Country School, which he thought himself well qualify'd to undertake, as he wrote an excellent Hand, & was a Master of Arithmetic & Accounts. This however he deem'd a Business below him, & confident of future better Fortune when he should be unwilling to have it known that he once was so meanly employ'd, he chang'd his Name, & did me the Honor to assume mine. For I soon after had a Letter from him, acquainting me, that he was settled in a small Village in Berkshire, I think it was, where he taught reading & writing to 10 or a dozen Boys at 6 pence each per Week, recommending Mrs T. to my Care, and desiring me to write to him, directing for Mr Franklin Schoolmaster at such a Place. He continu'd to write frequently, sending me large Specimens of an Epic Poem, which he was then composing, and desiring my Remarks & Corrections. These I gave him from time to time, but endeavor'd rather to discourage his Proceeding. One of Young's Satires was then just publish'd. I copy'd & sent him a great Part of it, which set in a strong Light the Folly of pursuing the Muses with any Hope of Advancement by them. All was in vain. Sheets of the Poem continu'd to come by every Post. In the mean time Mrs T. having on his Account lost her Friends & Business, was often in Distresses, & us'd to send for me, and borrow what I could spare to help her out of them. I grew fond of her Company, and being at this time under no Religious Restraints, & presuming on my Importance to her, I attempted Familiarities, (another Erratum) which she repuls'd with a proper Resentment, and acquainted him with my Behavior. This made a Breach between us, & when he return'd again to London, he let me know he thought I had cancel'd all the Obligations he had been under to me. So I found I was never to expect his Repaying me what I lent to him or advanc'd for him.

This was however not then of much Consequence, as he was totally unable: And in the Loss of his Friendship I found myself reliev'd from a Burden. I now began to think of getting a little Money beforehand; and expecting better Work, I left Palmer's to work at Watts's near Lincoln's Inn Fields, a still greater Printinghouse. Here I continu'd all the rest of my Stay in London.

At my first Admission into this Printing House, I took to working at Press, imagining I felt a Want of the Bodily Exercise I had been us'd to in America, where Presswork is mix'd with Composing. I drank only Water; the other Workmen, near 50 in Number, were great Guzzlers of Beer. On occasion I carried up & down Stairs a large Form of Types in each hand, when others carried but one in both Hands. They wonder'd to see from this & several Instances that the water-American as they call'd me was *stronger* than themselves who drank *strong* Beer. We had an Alehouse Boy who attended always in the House to supply the Workmen. My Companion at the Press, drank every day a Pint before Breakfast, a Pint at Breakfast with his Bread and Cheese; a Pint between Breakfast and Dinner; a Pint at Dinner, a Pint in the Afternoon about Six o'Clock, and another when he had done his Day's-Work. I thought it a detestable Custom. But it was necessary, he suppos'd, to drink *strong* Beer that he might be *strong* to labor. I endeavor'd to convince him that the Bodily Strength afforded by Beer could only be in proportion to the Grain or Flour of the Barley dissolved in the Water of which it was made; that there was more Flour in a Penny-worth of Bread, and therefore if he would eat that with a Pint of Water, it would give him more Strength than a Quart of Beer. He drank on however, & had 4 or 5 Shillings to pay out of his Wages every Saturday Night for that muddling Liquor; an Expense I was free from. And thus these poor Devils keep themselves always under.

Watts after some Weeks desiring to have me in the Composing-Room, I left the Pressmen. A new *Bienvenu* or Sum for Drink, being 5/, was demanded of me by the Compositors. I thought it an Imposition, as I had paid below. The Master thought so too, and forbad my Paying it. I stood out two or three Weeks, was accordingly considered as an Excommunicate, and had so many little Pieces of private Mischief done me, by mixing my Sorts, transposing my Pages, breaking my Matter, &c, &c. if I were ever so little out of the Room, & all ascrib'd to the Chapel Ghost, which they said ever haunted those not regularly admitted, that notwithstanding the Master's Protection, I found myself oblig'd to comply and pay the Money; convinc'd of the Folly of being on ill Terms with those one is to live with continually. I was now on a fair Footing with them, and soon acquir'd considerable Influence. I propos'd some reasonable Alterations in their Chapel Laws, and carried them against all Opposition. From my Example a great Part of them left their muddling Breakfast of Beer & Bread & Cheese, finding they could with me be supply'd from a neighboring House with a large Porringer of hot Water-gruel, sprinkled with Pepper, crumb'd with Bread, & a Bit of Butter in it, for the Price of a Pint of Beer, viz, three half-pence. This was a more comfortable as well as cheaper Breakfast, & kept their Heads clearer. Those who continu'd sotting with Beer all day, were often, by not paying, out of Credit at the Alehouse, and us'd to make Interest with me to get Beer, *their Light,* as they phras'd it, *being out.* I watch'd the Pay table on Saturday Night, & collected what I stood engag'd for them, having to pay some times near Thirty Shillings a Week on their Accounts. This, and my being esteem'd a pretty good Riggite, that is a jocular verbal Satirist, supported my Consequence in the Society. My constant Attendance, (I never making a St. Monday), recommended me to the Master; and my uncommon Quickness at Composing, occasion'd my being put upon all Work of Dispatch which was generally better paid. So I went on now very agreeably.

My Lodging in Little Britain being too remote, I found another in Duke-street opposite to the Romish Chapel. It was two pair of Stairs backwards at an Italian Warehouse. A Widow Lady kept the House; she had a Daughter & a Maid Servant, and a Journeyman who attended the Warehouse, but lodg'd abroad. After sending to inquire my Character at the House where I last lodg'd, she agreed to take me in at the same Rate, 3/6 per Week, cheaper as she said from the Protection she expected in having a Man lodge in the House. She was a Widow, an elderly Woman, had been bred a Protestant, being a Clergyman's Daughter, but was converted to the Catholic Religion by her Husband, whose Memory she much revered; had lived much among People of Distinction, and knew a 1000 Anecdotes of them as far back as the Times of Charles the Second. She was lame in her Knees with the Gout, and therefore seldom stirr'd out of her Room, so sometimes wanted Company; and hers was so highly amusing to me; that I was sure to spend an Evening with her whenever she desired it. Our Supper was only half an Anchovy each, on a very little Strip of Bread & Butter, and half a Pint of Ale between us. But the Entertainment was in her Conversation. My always keeping good Hours, and giving little Trouble in the Family, made her unwilling to part with me; so that when I talk'd of a Lodging I had heard of, nearer my Business, for 2/ a Week, which, intent as I now was on saving Money, made some difference; she bid me not think of it, for she would abate me two Shillings a Week for the future, so I remain'd with her at 1/6 as long as I stayed in London.

In a Garret of her House there lived a Maiden Lady of 70 in the most retired Manner, of whom my Landlady gave me this Account, that she was a Roman Catholic, had been sent abroad when young & lodg'd in a Nunnery with an Intent of becoming a Nun: but the Country not agreeing with her, she return'd to England, where there being no Nunnery, she had vow'd to lead the Life of a Nun as near as might be done in those Circumstances: Accordingly she had given all her Estate to charitable Uses, reserving only Twelve Pounds a Year to live on, and out of this Sum she still gave a great deal in Charity, living herself on Water-gruel only, & using no Fire but to boil it. She had lived many Years in that Garret, being permitted to remain there gratis by successive Catholic Tenants of the House below, as they deem'd it a Blessing to have her there. A Priest visited her, to confess her every Day. I have ask'd her, says my Landlady, how she, as she liv'd, could possibly find so much Employment for a Confessor? O, says she, it is impossible to avoid *vain*

Thoughts. I was permitted once to visit her: She was cheerful & polite, & convers'd pleasantly. The Room was clean, but had no other Furniture than a Mattress, a Table with a Crucifix & Book, a Stool, which she gave me to sit on, and a Picture over the Chimney of St. *Veronica,* displaying her Handkerchief with the miraculous Figure of Christ's bleeding Face on it, which she explain'd to me with great Seriousness. She look'd pale, but was never sick, and I give it as another Instance on how small an Income Life & Health may be supported.

At Watts's Printinghouse I contracted an Acquaintance with an ingenious young Man, one Wygate, who having wealthy Relations, had been better educated than most Printers, was a tolerable Latinist, spoke French, & lov'd Reading. I taught him, & a Friend of his, to swim, at twice going into the River, & they soon became good Swimmers. They introduc'd me to some Gentlemen from the Country who went to Chelsea by Water to see the College and Don Saltero's Curiosities. In our Return, at the Request of the Company, whose Curiosity Wygate had excited, I stripped & leaped into the River, & swam from near Chelsea to Blackfriars, performing on the Way many Feats of Activity both upon & under Water, that surpris'd & pleas'd those to whom they were Novelties. I had from a Child been ever delighted with this Exercise, had studied & practis'd all Thevenot's Motions & Positions, added some of my own, aiming at the graceful & easy, as well as the Useful. All these I took this Occasion of exhibiting to the Company, & was much flatter'd by their Admiration. And Wygate, who was desirous of becoming a Master, grew more & more attach'd to me, on that account, as well as from the Similarity of our Studies. He at length propos'd to me travelling all over Europe together, supporting ourselves everywhere by working at our Business. I was once inclin'd to it. But mentioning it to my good Friend Mr Denham, with whom I often spent an Hour, when I had Leisure. He dissuaded me from it, advising me to think only of returning to Pennsylvania, which he was now about to do.

I must record one Trait of this good Man's Character. He had formerly been in Business at Bristol, but fail'd in Debt to a Number of People, compounded and went to America. There, by a close Application to Business as a Merchant, he acquir'd a plentiful Fortune in a few Years. Returning to England in the Ship with me, He invited his old Creditors to an Entertainment, at which he thank'd them for the easy Composition they had favor'd him with, & when they expected nothing but the Treat, every Man at the first Remove, found under his Plate an Order on a Banker for the full Amount of the unpaid Remainder with Interest.

He now told me he was about to return to Philadelphia, and should carry over a great Quantity of Goods in order to open a Store there: He propos'd to take me over as his Clerk, to keep his Books (in which he would instruct me) copy his Letters, and attend the Store. He added, that as soon as I should be acquainted with mercantile Business he would promote me by sending me with a Cargo of Flour & Bread &c. to the West Indies, and procure me Commissions from others; which would be profitable, & if I manag'd well, would establish me handsomely. The Thing pleas'd me, for I was grown tired of London, remember'd with Pleasure the happy Months I had spent in Pennsylvania, and wish'd again to see it. Therefore I immediately agreed, on the Terms of Fifty Pounds a Year, Pennsylvania Money; less indeed than my present Gettings as a Compositor, but affording a better Prospect.

I now took Leave of Printing, as I thought for ever, and was daily employ'd in my new Business; going about with Mr Denham among the Tradesmen, to purchase various Articles, & seeing them pack'd up, doing Errands, calling upon Workmen to dispatch, &c. and when all was on board, I had a few Days Leisure. On one of these Days I was to my Surprise sent for by a great Man I knew only by Name, a Sir William Wyndham and I waited upon him. He had heard by some means or other of my Swimming from Chelsea to Blackfriars, and of my teaching Wygate and another young Man to swim in a few Hours. He had two Sons about to set out on their Travels; he wish'd to have them first taught Swimming; and propos'd to gratify me handsomely if I would teach them. They were not yet come to Town and my Stay was uncertain, so I could not undertake it. But from this Incident I thought it likely, that if I were to remain in England and open a Swimming School, I might get a good deal of Money. And it struck me so strongly, that had the Overture been sooner made me, probably I should not so soon have returned to America. After many Years, you & I had something of more Importance to do with one of these Sons of Sir William Wyndham, become Earl of Egremont, which I shall mention in its Place.

Thus I spent about 18 Months in London. Most Part of the Time, I work'd hard at my Business, & spent but little upon myself except in seeing Plays & in Books. My Friend Ralph had kept me poor. He owed me about 27 Pounds; which I was now never likely to receive; a great Sum out of my small Earnings. I lov'd him notwithstanding, for he had many amiable Qualities. Tho' I had by no means improv'd my Fortune. But I had pick'd up some very ingenious Acquaintance whose Conversation was of great Advantage to me, and I had read considerably.

We sail'd from Gravesend on the 23^d of July 1726. For the Incidents of the Voyage, I refer you to my Journal, where you will find them all minutely related. Perhaps the most important Part of that Journal is the *Plan* to be found in it which I formed at Sea, for regulating my future Conduct in Life. It is the more remarkable, as being form'd when I was so young, and yet being pretty faithfully adhered to quite thro' to old Age. We landed in Philadelphia the 11th of October, where I found sundry Alterations. Keith was no longer Governor, being superseded by Major Gordon: I met him walking the Streets as a common Citizen. He seem'd a little asham'd at seeing me, but pass'd without saying any thing. I should have been as much asham'd at seeing Miss Read, had not her Friends, despairing with Reason of my Return, after the Receipt of my Letter, persuaded her to marry another, one Rogers, a Potter, which was done in my Absence. With him however she was never happy, and soon parted from him, refusing to cohabit with him, or bear his Name It being now said that he had another Wife. He was a worthless Fellow tho' an excellent Workman which was the Temptation to her Friends. He got into Debt, and ran away in 1727 or 28. Went to the West Indies, and died there. Keimer had got a better House, a Shop well supply'd with Stationery, plenty of new Types, a number of Hands tho' none good, and seem'd to have a great deal of Business.

Mr Denham took a Store in Water Street, where we open'd our Goods. I attended the Business diligently, studied Accounts, and grew in a little Time expert at selling. We lodg'd and boarded together, he counsell'd me as a Father, having a sincere Regard for me: I respected & lov'd him: and we might have gone on together very happily: But in the Beginning of Feby 1726/7 when I had just pass'd my 21st Year, we both were taken ill. My Distemper was a Pleurisy, which very nearly carried me off: I suffered a good deal, gave up the Point in my own mind, & was rather disappointed when I found myself recovering; regretting in some degree that I must now some time or other have all that disagreeable Work to do over again. I forget what his Distemper was. It held him a long time, and at length carried him off. He left me a small Legacy in a nuncupative Will, as a Token of his Kindness for me, and he left me once more to the wide World. For the Store was taken into the Care of his Executors, and my Employment under him ended: My Brother-in-law Homes, being now at Philadelphia, advis'd my Return to my Business. And Keimer tempted me with an Offer of large Wages by the Year to come & take the Management of his Printinghouse, that he might better attend his Stationer's Shop. I had heard a bad Character of him in London, from his Wife & her Friends, & was not fond of having any more to do with him. I try'd for farther Employment as a Merchant's Clerk; but not readily meeting with any, I clos'd again with Keimer.

I found in *his* House these Hands; Hugh Meredith a Welsh-Pennsylvanian, 30 Years of Age, bred to Country Work: honest, sensible, had a great deal of solid Observation, was something of a Reader, but given to drink: Stephen Potts, a young Country Man of full Age, bred to the Same: of uncommon natural Parts, & great Wit & Humor, but a little idle. These he had agreed with at extreme low Wages, per Week, to be rais'd a Shilling every 3 Months, as they would deserve by improving in their Business, & the Expectation of these high Wages to come on hereafter was what he had drawn them in with. Meredith was to work at Press, Potts at Bookbinding, which he by Agreement, was to teach them, tho' he knew neither one nor t'other. John ——— a wild Irishman brought up to no Business, whose Service for 4 Years Keimer had purchas'd from the Captain of a Ship. He too was to be made a Pressman. George Webb, an Oxford Scholar, whose Time for 4 Years he had likewise bought, intending him for a Compositor: of whom more presently. And David Harry, a Country Boy, whom he had taken Apprentice. I soon perceiv'd that the Intention of engaging me at Wages so much higher than he had been us'd to give, was to have these raw cheap Hands form'd thro' me, and as soon as I had instructed them, then, they being all articled to him, he should be able to do without me. I went on however, very cheerfully; put his Printinghouse in Order, which had been in great Confusion, and brought his Hands by degrees to mind their Business and to do it better.

It was an odd Thing to find an Oxford Scholar in the Situation of a bought Servant. He was not more than 18 Years of Age, & gave me this Account of himself; that he was born in Gloucester, educated at a Grammar School there, had been distinguish'd among the Scholars for some apparent Superiority in performing his Part when they exhibited Plays; belong'd to the Witty Club there, and had written some Pieces in Prose & Verse which were printed in the Gloucester Newspapers. Thence he was sent to Oxford; there he continu'd about a Year, but not well-satisfy'd, wishing of all things to see London & become a Player. At length receiving his Quarterly Allowance of 15 Guineas, instead of discharging his Debts, he walk'd out of Town, hid his Gown in a Furze Bush, and footed it to London, where having no Friend to advise him, he fell into bad Company, soon spent his Guineas, found no means of being introduc'd among the Players, grew necessitous, pawn'd his Clothes & wanted Bread. Walking the Street very hungry, & not knowing what to do with himself, a Crimp's Bill was put into his Hand, offering immediate Entertainment & Encouragement to such as would bind themselves to serve in America. He went directly, sign'd the Indentures, was put into the Ship & came over; never writing a Line to acquaint his Friends what was become of him. He was lively, witty, good-natur'd, and a pleasant Companion, but idle, thoughtless & imprudent to the last Degree.

John the Irishman soon ran away. With the rest I began to live very agreeably; for they all respected me, the more as they found Keimer incapable of instructing them, and that from me they learned something daily. We never work'd on a Saturday, that being Keimer's Sabbath. So I had two Days for Reading. My Acquaintance with Ingenious People in the Town, increased. Keimer himself treated me with great Civility, & apparent Regard; and nothing now made me uneasy but my Debt to Vernon, which I was yet unable to pay being hitherto but a poor Economist. He however kindly made no Demand of it.

Our Printinghouse often wanted Sorts, and there was no Letter Founder in America. I had seen Types cast at James's in London, but without much Attention to the Manner: However I now contriv'd a Mold, made use of the Letters we had, as Puncheons, struck the Matrices in Lead, and thus supply'd in a pretty tolerable way all Deficiencies. I also engrav'd several Things on occasion. I made the Ink, I was Warehouseman & every thing, in short quite a Factotum.

But however serviceable I might be, I found that my Services became every Day of less Importance, as the other Hands improv'd in the Business. And when Keimer paid my second Quarter's Wages, he let me know that he felt them too heavy, and thought I should make an Abatement. He grew by degrees less civil, put on more of the Master, frequently found Fault, was captious and seem'd ready for an Out-breaking. I went on nevertheless with a good deal of Patience, thinking that his incumber'd Circumstances were partly the Cause. At length a Trifle snapped our Connection. For a great Noise happening near the Courthouse, I put my Head out of the Window to see what was the Matter. Keimer being in the Street look'd up & saw me, call'd out to me in a loud voice and angry Tone to mind my Business, adding some reproachful Words that nettled me the more for their Publicity, all the Neighbors who were looking out on the same Occasion being Witnesses how I was treated. He came up immediately into the Printinghouse, continu'd the Quarrel, high Words pass'd on both Sides, he gave me the Quarter's Warning we had stipulated, expressing a Wish that he had not been oblig'd to so long a Warning. I told him his Wish was unnecessary for I would leave him that Instant; and so taking my Hat walk'd out of Doors; desiring Meredith whom I saw below to take care of some Things I left, & bring them to my Lodging.

Meredith came accordingly in the Evening, when we talk'd my Affair over. He had conceiv'd a great Regard for me, & was very unwilling that I should leave the House while he remain'd in it. He dissuaded me from returning to my native Country which I began to think of. He reminded me that Keimer was in debt for all he possess'd, that his Creditors began to be uneasy, that he kept his Shop miserably, sold often without Profit for ready Money, and often trusted without keeping Accounts. That he must therefore fail; which would make a Vacancy I might profit of. I objected my Want of Money. He then let me know, that his Father had a high Opinion of me, and from some Discourse that had pass'd between them, he was sure would advance Money to set us up, if I would enter into Partnership with him. My Time, says he, will be out with Keimer in the Spring. By that time we may have our Press & Types in from London: I am sensible I am no Workman. If you like it, Your Skill in the Business shall be set against the Stock I furnish; and we will share the Profits equally. The Proposal was agreeable, and I consented. His Father was in Town, and approv'd of it, the more as he saw I had great Influence with his Son, had prevail'd on him to abstain long from Dramdrinking, and he hop'd might break him of that wretched Habit entirely, when we came to be so closely connected. I gave an Inventory to the Father, who carry'd it to a Merchant; the Things were sent for; the Secret was to be kept till they should arrive, and in the mean time I was to get work if I could at the other Printinghouse. But I found no Vacancy there, and so remain'd idle a few Days, when Keimer, on a Prospect of being employ'd to print some Paper-money, in New Jersey, which would require Cuts & various Types that I only could supply, and apprehending Bradford might engage me & get the Job from him, sent me a very civil

Message, that old Friends should not part for a few Words, the Effect of sudden Passion, and wishing me to return. Meredith persuaded me to comply, as it would give more Opportunity for his Improvement under my daily Instructions. So I return'd, and we went on more smoothly than for some time before. The New Jersey Job was obtain'd. I contriv'd a Copper-Plate Press for it, the first that had been seen in the Country. I cut several Ornaments and Checks for the Bills. We went together to Burlington, where I executed the Whole to Satisfaction, & he received so large a Sum for the Work, as to be enabled thereby to keep his Head much longer above Water.

At Burlington I made an Acquaintance with many principal People of the Province. Several of them had been appointed by the Assembly a Committee to attend the Press, and take Care that no more Bills were printed than the Law directed. They were therefore by Turns constantly with us, and generally he who attended brought with him a Friend or two for Company. My Mind having been much more improv'd by Reading than Keimer's, I suppose it was for that Reason my Conversation seem'd to be more valu'd. They had me to their Houses, introduc'd me to their Friends and show'd me much Civility, while he, tho' the Master, was a little neglected. In truth he was an odd Fish, ignorant of common Life, fond of rudely opposing receiv'd Opinions, slovenly to extreme dirtiness, enthusiastic in some Points of Religion, and a little Knavish withal. We continu'd there near 3 Months, and by that time I could reckon among my acquired Friends, Judge Allen, Samuel Bustill, the Secretary of the Province, Isaac Pearson, Joseph Cooper & several of the Smiths, Members of Assembly, and Isaac Decow the Surveyor General. The latter was a shrewd sagacious old Man, who told me that he began for himself when young by wheeling Clay for the Brickmakers, learned to write after he was of Age, carry'd the Chain for Surveyors, who taught him Surveying, and he had now by his Industry acquir'd a good Estate; and says he, I foresee, that you will soon work this Man out of his Business & make a Fortune in it at Philadelphia. He had not then the least Intimation of my Intention to set up there or any where. These

Friends were afterwards of great Use to me, as I occasionally was to some of them. They all continued their Regard for me as long as they lived.

Before I enter upon my public Appearance in Business it may be well to let you know the then State of my Mind, with regard to my Principles and Morals, that you may see how far those influenc'd the future Events of my Life. My Parents had early given me religious Impressions, and brought me through my Childhood piously in the Dissenting Way. But I was scarce 15 when, after doubting by turns of several Points as I found them disputed in the different Books I read, I began to doubt of Revelation it self. Some Books against Deism fell into my Hands; they were said to be the Substance of Sermons preached at Boyle's Lectures. It happened that they wrought an Effect on me quite contrary to what was intended by them: For the Arguments of the Deists which were quoted to be refuted, appeared to me much Stronger than the Refutations. In short I soon became a thorough Deist. My Arguments perverted some others, particularly Collins & Ralph: but each of them having afterwards wrong'd me greatly without the least Compunction and recollecting Keith's Conduct toward me, (who was another Freethinker) and my own towards Vernon & Miss Read, which at Times gave me great Trouble, I began to suspect that this Doctrine tho' it might be true, was not very useful. My London Pamphlet, which had for its Motto those Lines of Dryden

> —Whatever is, is right.—
> Tho' purblind Man / Sees but a Part of
> the Chain, the nearest Link,
> His Eyes not carrying to the equal Beam,
> That poises all, above.

And from the Attributes of God, his infinite Wisdom, Goodness & Power concluded that nothing could possibly be wrong in the World, & that Vice & Virtue were empty Distinctions, no such Things existing: appear'd now not so clever a Performance as I once thought it; and I doubted whether some Error had not insinuated itself unperceiv'd, into my Argument, so as to infect all that follow'd, as is common in metaphysical Reasonings. I grew convinc'd that *Truth, Sincerity & Integrity* in Dealings between Man & Man, were of the utmost Importance to the Felicity of Life, and I form'd written Resolutions, (which still remain in my Journal Book) to practice them ever while I lived. Revelation had indeed no weight with me as such; but I entertain'd an Opinion, that tho' certain Actions might not be bad *because* they were forbidden by it, or good *because* it commanded them; yet probably those Actions might be forbidden *because* they were bad for us, or commanded *because* they were beneficial to us, in their own Natures, all the Circumstances of things considered. And this Persuasion, with the kind hand of Providence, or some guardian Angel, or accidental favorable Circumstances & Situations, or all together, preserved me (thro' this dangerous Time of Youth & the hazardous Situations I was sometimes in among Strangers, remote from the Eye & Advice of my Father) without any *wilful* gross Immorality or Injustice that might have been expected from my Want of Religion. I say *wilful,* because the Instances I have mentioned, had something of *Necessity* in them, from my Youth, Inexperience, & the Knavery of others. I had therefore a tolerable Character to begin the World with, I valued it properly, & determin'd to preserve it.

We had not been long return'd to Philadelphia, before the New Types arriv'd from London. We settled with Keimer, & left him by his Consent before he heard of it. We found a House to hire near the Market, and took it. To lessen the Rent, (which was then but 24£ a Year tho' I have since known it let for 70) We took in Thomas Godfrey, a Glazier, & his Family, who were to pay a considerable Part of it to us, and we to board with them. We had scarce opened our Letters & put our Press in Order, before George House, an Acquaintance of Mine, brought a Country-man to us; whom he had met in the Street inquiring for a Printer. All our Cash was now expended in the Variety of Particulars we had been obliged to procure & this Countryman's Five Shillings being our first Fruits, & coming so seasonably, gave me more Pleasure than any Crown I have since earn'd; and from the Gratitude I felt toward House, has made me often more ready, than perhaps I should otherwise have been to assist young Beginners.

There are Croakers in every Country always boding its Ruin. Such a one then lived in Philadelphia, a Person of Note, an elderly Man, with a wise Look, and very grave Manner of speaking. His Name was Samuel Mickle. This Gentleman, a Stranger to me, stopped one Day at my Door, and asked me if I was the young Man who had lately opened a new Printinghouse: Being answer'd in the Affirmative, he said he was sorry for me, because it was an expensive Undertaking & the Expense would be lost; for Philadelphia was a sinking Place, the People already half Bankrupts or near being so; all Appearances of the contrary, such as new Buildings & the Rise of Rents being to his certain Knowledge fallacious, for they were in fact among the Things that would soon ruin us. And he gave me such a Detail of Misfortunes, now existing or that were soon to exist, that he left me half-melancholy. Had I known him before I engag'd in this Business, probably I never should have done it. This Man continu'd to live in this decaying Place, and to declaim in the same Strain, refusing for many Years to buy a House there, because all was going to Destruction, and at last I had the Pleasure of seeing him give five times as much for one as he might have bought it for when he first began his Croaking.

I should have mention'd before, that in the Autumn of the preceding Year I had form'd most of my ingenious Acquaintances into a Club for mutual Improvement, which we called the Junto. We met on Friday Evening. The Rules I drew up requir'd that every Member in his Turn should produce one or more Queries on any Point of Morals, Politics or Natural Philosophy, to be discuss'd by the Company, and once in three Months produce & read an Essay of his own Writing on any Subject he pleased. Our Debates were to be under the Direction of a President, and to be conducted in the sincere Spirit of Inquiry after Truth, without Fondness for Dispute, or Desire of Victory; and to prevent Warmth all Expressions of Positiveness in Opinion or of direct Contradiction, were after some time made contraband & prohibited under small pecuniary Penalties. The first Members were Joseph Breintnal, a Copyer of Deeds for the Scriveners; a good-natur'd friendly middle-ag'd Man, a great Lover of Poetry, reading all he could meet with, & writing some that was tolerable; very ingenious in many little Nick-nackeries, & of sensible Conversation. Thomas Godfrey, a self-taught Mathematician, great in his Way, & afterwards Inventor of what is now call'd Hadley's Quadrant. But he knew little out of his way, and was not a pleasing Companion, as like most Great Mathematicians I have met with, he expected unusual Precision in every thing said, or was forever denying or distinguishing upon Trifles, to the Disturbance of all Conversation. He soon left us. Nicholas Scull, a Surveyor, afterwards Surveyor-General, Who lov'd Books, & sometimes made a few Verses. William Parsons, bred a Shoemaker, but loving Reading, had acquir'd a considerable Share of Mathematics, which he first studied with a View to Astrology that he afterwards laughed at. He also became Surveyor General. William Maugridge, a Joiner, a most exquisite Mechanic & a solid sensible Man. Hugh Meredith, Stephen Potts, & George Webb, I have Characteris'd before. Robert Grace, a young Gentleman of some Fortune, generous, lively & witty, a Lover of Punning and of his Friends. And William Coleman, then a Merchant's Clerk, about my Age, who had the coolest clearest Head, the best Heart, and the exactest Morals, of almost any Man I ever met with. He became afterwards a Merchant of great Note, and one of our Provincial Judges: Our Friendship continued without Interruption to his Death upwards of 40 Years. And the club continu'd almost as long and was the best School of Philosophy, Morals & Politics that then existed in the Province; for our Queries which were read the Week preceding their Discussion, put us on Reading with Attention upon the several Subjects, that we might speak more to the purpose: and here too we acquired better Habits of Conversation, every thing being studied in our Rules which might prevent our disgusting each other. From hence the long Continuance of the Club, which I shall have frequent Occasion to speak farther of hereafter; But my giving this Account of it here, is to show something of the Interest I had, every one of these exerting themselves in recommending Business to us. Breintnal particularly procur'd us from the Quakers, the Printing 40 Sheets of their History, the rest being to be done by Keimer: and upon this we work'd exceeding hard, for the Price was low. It was a Folio, Pro Patria Size, in Pica with Long Primer Notes. I compos'd of it a Sheet a Day, and Meredith work'd it off at Press. It was often 11 at Night and sometimes later, before I had finish'd my Distribution for the next days Work: For the little Jobs sent in by our other Friends now & then put us back. But so determin'd I was to continue doing a Sheet a Day of the Folio, that one Night when having impos'd my Forms, I thought my Day's Work over, one of them by accident was broken and two Pages reduc'd to Pie, I immediately distributed & compos'd it over again before I went to bed. And this Industry visible to our Neighbors began to give us Character and Credit; particularly I was told, that mention being made of the new Printing Office at the Merchants everynight-Club, the general Opinion was that it must fail, there being already two Printers in the Place, Keimer & Bradford; but Doctor Baird (whom you and I saw many Years after at his native Place, St. Andrews in Scotland) gave a contrary Opinion; for the Industry of that Franklin, says he, is superior to any thing I ever saw of the kind: I see him still at work when I go home from Club; and he is at Work again before his Neighbors are out of bed. This struck the rest, and we soon after had Offers from one of them to Supply us with Stationery. But as yet we did not choose to engage in Shop Business.

I mention this Industry the more particularly and the more freely, tho' it seems to be talking in my own Praise, that those of my Posterity who shall read it, may know the Use of that Virtue, when they see its Effects in my Favor throughout this Relation.

George Webb, who had found a Female Friend that lent him wherewith to purchase his Time of Keimer, now came to offer himself as a Journeyman to us. We could not then employ him, but I foolishly let him know, as a Secret, that I soon intended to begin a Newspaper, & might then have Work for him. My Hopes of Success as I told him were founded on this, that the then only Newspaper, printed by Bradford, was a paltry thing, wretchedly manag'd, & no way entertaining; and yet was profitable to him. I therefore thought a good Paper could scarcely fail of good Encouragement. I requested Webb not to mention it, but he told it to Keimer, who immediately, to be beforehand with me, published Proposals for Printing one himself, on which Webb was to be employ'd. I resented this, and to counteract them, as I could not yet begin our Paper, I wrote several Pieces of Entertainment for Bradford's Paper, under the Title of the Busy Body, which Breintnal continu'd some Months. By this means the Attention of the Public was fix'd on that Paper, & Keimer's Proposals which we burlesqu'd & ridicul'd, were disregarded. He began his Paper however, and after carrying it on three Quarters of a Year, with at most only 90 Subscribers, he offer'd it to me for a Trifle, & I having been ready some time to go on with it, took it in hand directly, and it prov'd in a few Years extremely profitable to me.

I perceive that I am apt to speak in the singular Number, though our Partnership still continu'd. The Reason may be, that in fact the whole Management of the Business lay upon me. Meredith was no Compositor, a poor Pressman, & seldom sober. My Friends lamented my Connection with him, but I was to make the best of it.

Our first Papers made a quite different Appearance from any before in the Province, a better Type & better printed: but some spirited Remarks of my Writing on the Dispute then going on between Governor Burnet and the Massachusetts Assembly, struck the principal People, occasion'd the Paper & the Manager of it to be much talk'd of, & in a few Weeks brought them all to be our Subscribers. Their Example was follow'd by many, and our Number went on growing continually. This was one of the first good Effects of my having learned a little to scribble. Another was, that the leading Men, seeing a Newspaper now in the hands of one who could also handle a Pen, thought it convenient to oblige & encourage me. Bradford still printed the Votes & Laws & other Public Business. He had printed an Address of the House to the Governor in a coarse blundering manner; We reprinted it elegantly & correctly, and sent one to every Member. They were sensible of the Difference, it strengthen'd the Hands of our Friends in the House, and they voted us their Printers for the Year ensuing.

Among my Friends in the House I must not forget Mr Hamilton before mentioned, who was now returned from England & had a Seat in it. He interested himself* for me strongly in that Instance, as he did in many others afterwards, continuing his Patronage till his Death. Mr Vernon about this time put me in mind of the Debt I ow'd him: but did not press me. I wrote him an ingenuous Letter of Acknowledgments, crav'd his Forbearance a little longer which he allow'd me, & as soon as I was able I paid the Principal with Interest & many Thanks. So that *Erratum* was in some degree corrected.

But now another Difficulty came upon me, which I had never the least Reason to expect. Mr Meredith's Father, who was to have paid for our Printinghouse according to the Expectations given me, was able to advance only one Hundred Pounds, Currency, which had been paid, & a Hundred more was due to the Merchant; who grew impatient & su'd us all. We gave Bail, but saw that if the Money could not be rais'd in time, the Suit must come to a Judgment & Execution, & our hopeful Prospects must with us be ruined, as the Press & Letters must be sold for Payment, perhaps at half Price. In this Distress two true Friends whose Kindness I have never forgotten nor ever shall forget while I can remember any thing, came to me separately unknown to each other, and without any Application from me, offering each of them to advance me all the Money that should be necessary to enable me to take the whole Business upon myself if that should be practicable, but they did not like my continuing the Partnership with Meredith, who as they said was often seen drunk in the Streets, & playing at low Games in Alehouses, much to our Discredit. These two Friends were *William Coleman* & *Robert Grace*. I told them I could not propose a Separation while any Prospect remain'd of the Merediths fulfilling their Part of our Agreement. Because I thought myself under great Obligations to them for what they had done & would do if they could. But if they finally fail'd in their Performance, & our Partnership must be disolv'd, I should then think myself at Liberty to accept the Assistance of my Friends. Thus the matter

*I got his Son once 500£.

rested for some time. When I said to my Partner, perhaps your Father is dissatisfied at the Part you have undertaken in this Affair of ours, and is unwilling to advance for you & me what he would for you alone: If that is the Case, tell me, and I will resign the whole to you & go about my Business. No says he, my Father has really been disappointed and is really unable; and I am unwilling to distress him farther. I see this is a Business I am not fit for. I was bred a Farmer, and it was a Folly in me to come to Town & put myself at 30 Years of Age an Apprentice to learn a new Trade. Many of our Welsh People are going to settle in North Carolina where Land is cheap: I am inclin'd to go with them, & follow my old Employment. You may find Friends to assist you. If you will take the Debts of the Company upon you, return to my Father the hundred Pound he has advanc'd, pay my little personal Debts, and give me Thirty Pounds & a new Saddle, I will relinquish the Partnership & leave the whole in your Hands. I agreed to this Proposal. It was drawn up in Writing, sign'd & seal'd immediately. I gave him what he demanded & he went soon after to Carolina; from whence he sent me next Year two long Letters, containing the best Account that had been given of that Country, the Climate, Soil, Husbandry, &c. for in those Matters he was very judicious. I printed them in the Papers, and they gave great Satisfaction to the Public.

As soon as he was gone, I recurr'd to my two Friends; and because I would not give an unkind Preference to either, I took half what each had offered & I wanted, of one, & half of the other; paid off the Company Debts, and went on with the Business in my own Name, advertising that the Partnership was dissolved. I think this was in or about the Year 1729.

About this Time there was a Cry among the People for more Paper Money, only 15,000£ being extant in the Province & that soon to be sunk. The wealthy Inhabitants oppos'd any Addition, being against all Paper Currency, from an Apprehension that it would depreciate as it had done in New England to the Prejudice of all Creditors. We had discuss'd this Point in our Junto, where I was on the Side of an Addition, being persuaded that the first small Sum struck in 1723 had done much good, by increasing the Trade, Employment, & Number of Inhabitants in the Province, since I now saw all the old Houses inhabited, & many new ones building, where as I remember'd well, that when I first walk'd about the Streets of Philadelphia, eating my Roll, I saw most of the Houses in Walnut Street between Second & Front Streets with Bills on their Doors, to be let; and many likewise in Chestnut Street, & other Streets; which made me then think the Inhabitants of the City were one after another deserting it. Our Debates possess'd me so fully of the Subject, that I wrote and printed an anonymous Pamphlet on it, entitled, *The Nature & Necessity of a Paper Currency*. It was well receiv'd by the common People in general; but the Rich Men dislik'd it; for it increas'd and strengthen'd the Clamor for more Money; and they happening to have no Writers among them that were able to answer it, their Opposition slacken'd, & the Point was carried by a Majority in the House. My Friends there, who conceiv'd I had been of some Service, thought fit to reward me, by employing me in printing the Money, a very profitable Job, and a great Help to me. This was another Advantage gain'd by my being able to write. The Utility of this Currency became by Time and Experience so evident, as never afterwards to be much disputed, so that it grew soon to 55,000£ and in 1739 to 80,000£ since which it arose during War to upwards of 350,000£. Trade, Building & Inhabitants all the while increasing. Tho' I now think there are Limits beyond which the Quantity may be hurtful.

I soon after obtain'd, thro' my Friend Hamilton, the Printing of the New Castle Paper Money, another profitable Job, as I then thought it; small Things appearing great to those in small Circumstances. And these to me were really great Advantages, as they were great Encouragements. He procured me also the Printing of the Laws and Votes of that Government which continu'd in my Hands as long as I follow'd the Business.

I now open'd a little Stationer's Shop. I had in it Blanks of all Sorts the correctest that ever appear'd among us, being assisted in that by my Friend Breintnal; I had also Paper, Parchment, Chapmen's Books, &c. One Whitemash a Compositor I had known in London, an excellent Workman, now came to me & work'd with me constantly & diligently, and I took an Apprentice the Son of Aquila Rose. I began now gradually to pay off the Debt I was under for the Printinghouse. In order to secure my Credit and Character as a Tradesman, I took care not only to be in *Reality* Industrious & frugal, but to avoid all *Appearances* of the Contrary. I dressed plainly; I was seen at no Places of idle Diversion; I never went out a-fishing or Shooting; a Book, indeed, sometimes debauch'd me from my Work; but that was seldom, snug, & gave no Scandal: and to show that I was not above my Business, I sometimes brought home the Paper I purchas'd at the Stores, thro' the Streets on a Wheelbarrow. Thus being esteem'd an industrious thriving young Man, and paying duly for what I bought, the Merchants who imported Stationery solicited my Custom, others propos'd supplying me with Books, & I went on swimmingly. In the mean time Keimer's Credit and Business declining daily, he was at last forc'd to sell his Printinghouse to satisfy his Creditors. He went to Barbadoes, & there lived some Years, in very poor Circumstances.

His Apprentice David Harry, whom I had instructed while I work'd with him, set up in his Place at Philadelphia, having bought his Materials. I was at first apprehensive of a powerful Rival in Harry, as his Friends were very able, & had a good deal of Interest. I therefore propos'd a Partnership to him; which he, fortunately for me, rejected with Scorn. He was very proud, dress'd like a Gentleman, liv'd expensively, took much Diversion & Pleasure abroad, ran in debt, & neglected his Business, upon which all Business left him; and finding nothing to do, he follow'd Keimer to Barbadoes; taking the Printinghouse with him. There this Apprentice employ'd his former Master as a Journeyman. They quarrel'd often, Harry went continually behindhand, and at length was forc'd to sell his Types, and return to his Country Work in Pennsylvania. The Person that bought them, employ'd Keimer to use them, but in a few years he died. There remain'd now no Competitor with me at Philadelphia, but the old one, Bradford, who was rich & easy, did a little Printing now & then by straggling Hands, but was not very anxious about the Business. However, as he kept the Post Office, it was imagined he had better Opportunities of obtaining News, his Paper was thought a better Distributer of Advertisements than mine, & therefore had many more, which was a profitable thing to him & a Disadvantage to me. For tho' I did indeed receive & send Papers by Post, yet the public Opinion was otherwise; for what I did send was by Bribing the Riders who took them privately: Bradford being unkind enough to forbid it: which occasion'd some Resentment on my Part; and I thought so meanly of him for it, that when I afterwards came into his Situation, I took care never to imitate it.

I had hitherto continu'd to board with Godfrey, who lived in Part of my House with his Wife & Children, & had one Side of the Shop for his Glazier's Business, tho' he work'd little, being always absorb'd in his Mathematics. Mrs Godfrey projected a Match for me with a Relation's Daughter, took Opportunities of bringing us often together, till a serious Courtship on my Part ensu'd, the Girl being in herself very deserving. The old Folks encourag'd me by continual Invitations to Supper, & by leaving us together, till at length it was time to explain. Mrs Godfrey manag'd our little Treaty. I let her know that I expected as much Money with their Daughter as would pay off my Remaining Debt for the Printinghouse, which I believe was not then above a Hundred Pounds. She brought me Word they had no such Sum to spare. I said they might mortgage their House in the Loan Office. The Answer to this after some Days was, that they did not approve the Match; that on Inquiry of Bradford they had been inform'd the Printing Business was not a profitable one, the Types would soon be worn out & more wanted, that S. Keimer & D. Harry had fail'd one after the other, and I should probably soon follow them; and therefore I was forbidden the House, & the Daughter shut up. Whether this was a real Change of Sentiment, or only Artifice, on a Supposition of our being too far engag'd in Affection to retract, & therefore that we should steal a Marriage, which would leave them at Liberty to give or withhold what they pleas'd, I know not: But I suspected the latter, resented it, and went no more. Mrs Godfrey brought me afterwards some more favorable Accounts of their Disposition, & would have drawn me on again: but I declared absolutely my Resolution to have nothing more to do with that Family. This was resented by the Godfreys, we differ'd, and they removed, leaving me the whole House, and I resolved to take no more Inmates. But this Affair having turn'd my Thoughts to Marriage, I look'd round me, and made Overtures of Acquaintance in other Places; but soon found that the Business of a Printer being generally thought a poor one, I was not to expect Money with a Wife unless with such a one, as I should not otherwise think agreeable. In the mean time, that hard-to-be-govern'd Passion of Youth, had hurried me frequently into Intrigues with low Women that fell in my Way, which were attended with some Expense & great Inconvenience, besides a continual Risk to my Health by a Distemper which of all Things I dreaded, tho' by great good Luck I escaped it.

A friendly Correspondence as Neighbors & old Acquaintances, had continued between me & Mrs Read's Family, who all had a Regard for me from the time of my first Lodging in their House. I was often invited there and consulted in their Affairs, wherein I sometimes was of service. I pity'd poor Miss Read's unfortunate Situation, who was generally dejected; seldom cheerful, and avoided Company. I consider'd my Giddiness & Inconstancy when in London as in a great degree the Cause of her Unhappiness; tho' the Mother was good enough to think the Fault more her own than mine, as she had prevented our Marrying before I went thither, and persuaded the other Match in my Absence. Our mutual Affection was revived, but there were now great Objections to our Union. That Match was indeed look'd upon as invalid, a preceding Wife being said to be living in England; but this could not easily be prov'd, because of the Distance. And tho' there was a Report of his Death, it was not certain. Then tho' it should be true, he had left many Debts which his Successor might be call'd on to pay. We ventured however, over all these Difficulties, and I took her to Wife Sept. 1. 1730. None of the Inconveniencies happened that we had apprehended, she prov'd a good & faithful Helpmate, assisted me much by attending the Shop, we throve together, and have ever mutually endeavor'd to make each other happy. Thus I corrected that great *Erratum* as well as I could.

About this Time our Club meeting, not at a Tavern, but in a little Room of Mr Grace's set apart for that Purpose; a Proposition was made by me that since our Books were often referr'd to in our Disquisitions upon the Queries, it might be convenient to us to have them all together where we met, that upon Occasion they might be consulted; and by thus clubbing our Books to a common Library, we should, while we lik'd to keep them together, have each of us the Advantage of using the Books of all the other Members, which would be nearly as beneficial as if each owned the whole. It was lik'd and agreed to, & we fill'd one End of the Room with such Books as we could best spare. The Number was not so great as we expected; and tho' they had been of great Use, yet some Inconveniencies occurring for want of due Care of them, the Collection after about a Year was separated, & each took his Books home again.

And now I set on foot my first Project of a public Nature, that for a Subscription Library. I drew up the Proposals, got them put into Form by our great Scrivener Brockden, and by the help of my Friends in the Junto, procur'd Fifty Subscribers of 40/ each to begin with & 10/ a Year for 50 years, the Term our Company was to continue. We afterwards obtain'd a Charter, the Company being increas'd to 100. This was the Mother of all the North American Subscription Libraries now so numerous. It is become a great thing itself, & continually increasing. These Libraries have improv'd the general Conversation of the Americans, made the common Tradesmen & Farmers as intelligent as most Gentlemen from other Countries, and perhaps have contributed in some degree to the Stand so generally made throughout the Colonies in Defense of their Privileges.

My Manner of acting to engage People in this & future Undertakings.

Mem°.

Thus far was written with the Intention express'd in the Beginning and therefore contains several little family Anecdotes of no Importance to others. What follows was written many Years after in compliance with the Advice contain'd in these Letters, and accordingly intended for the Public. The Affairs of the Revolution occasion'd the Interruption.

Letter from Mr Abel James with Notes of my Life, to be here inserted. Also

Letter from Mr Vaughan to the same purpose.

MY DEAR AND HONORED FRIEND,

I have often been desirous of writing to thee, but could not be reconciled to the thought that the letter might fall into the hands of the British, lest some printer or busy body should publish some part of the contents, and give our friend pain, and myself censure.

Some time since they fell into my hands, to my great joy, about twenty-three sheets in thy own handwriting, containing an account of the parentage and life of thyself, directed to thy son, ending in the year 1730, with which there were notes, likewise in thy writing; a copy of which I enclose, in hopes it may be a means, if thou continued it up to a later period, that the first and latter part may be put together; and if it is not yet continued, I hope thee will not delay it. Life is uncertain, as the preacher tells us; and what will the world say if kind, humane and benevolent Ben. Franklin, should leave his friends and the world deprived of so pleasing and profitable a work; a work which would be useful and entertaining not only to a few, but to millions. The influence writings under that class have on the minds of youth is very great, and has no where appeared to me so plain, as in our public friends' journals. It almost insensibly leads the youth into the resolution of endeavouring to become as good and eminent as the journalist. Should thine, for instance, when published, (and I think it could not fail of it,) lead the youth to equal the industry and temperance of thy early youth, what a blessing with that class would such a work be! I know of no character living, nor many of them put together, who has so much in his power as thyself to promote a greater spirit of industry and early attention to business, frugality, and temperance with the American youth. Not that I think the work would have no other merit and use in the world; far from it; but the first is of such vast importance, that I know nothing that can equal it.

I trust I need make no apology to my good friend for mentioning to him these matters, believing he continues a relish for every exertion of the sort, in confidence of which I rest with great truth and perfect esteem his

Very affectionate friend,
(Signed) Abel James

The foregoing letter and the minutes accompanying it being shown to a friend, I received from him the following:

Letter from Mr. Benjamin Vaughan.
Paris, January 31, 1783.

MY DEAREST SIR,

When I had read over your sheets of minutes of the principal incidents of your life, recovered for you by your Quaker acquaintance; I told you I would send you a letter expressing my reasons why I thought it would be useful to complete and publish it as he desired. Various concerns have for some time past prevented this letter being written, and I do not know whether it was worth any expectation: happening to be at leisure however at present, I shall by writing at least interest and instruct myself; but as the terms I am inclined to use may tend to offend a person of your manners, I shall only tell you how I would address any other person, who was as good and as great as yourself, but less diffident. I would say to him, Sir, I *solicit* the history of your life from the following motives.

Your history is so remarkable, that if you do not give it, somebody else will certainly give it; and perhaps so as nearly to do as much harm, as your own management of the thing might do good.

It will moreover present a table of the internal circumstances of your country, which will very much tend to invite to it settlers of virtuous and manly minds. And considering the eagerness with which such information is sought by them, and the extent of your reputation, I do not know of a more efficacious advertisement than your Biography would give.

All that has happened to you is also connected with the detail of the manners and situation of *a rising* people; and in this respect I do not think that the writings of Caesar and Tacitus can be more interesting to a true judge of human nature and society.

But these, Sir, are small reasons in my opinion, compared with the chance which your life will give for the forming of future great men; and in conjunction with your *Art of Virtue,* (which you design to publish) of improving the features of private character, and consequently of aiding all happiness both public and domestic.

The two works I allude to, Sir, will in particular give a noble rule and example of *self-education.* School and other education constantly proceed upon false principles, and show a clumsy apparatus pointed at a false mark; but your apparatus is simple, and the mark a true one; and while parents and young persons are left destitute of other just means of estimating and becoming prepared for a reasonable course in life, your discovery that the thing is in many a man's private power, will be invaluable!

Influence upon the private character late in life, is not only an influence late in life, but a weak influence. It is in *youth* that we plant our chief habits and prejudices; it is in youth that we take our party as to profession, pursuits, and matrimony. In youth therefore the turn is given; in youth the education even of the next generation is given; in youth the private and public character is determined; and the term of life extending but from youth to age, life ought to begin well from youth; and more especially *before* we take our party as to our principal objects.

But your Biography will not merely teach self-education, but the education of *a wise man;* and the wisest man will receive lights, and improve his progress, by seeing detailed the conduct of another wise man. And why are weaker men to be deprived of such helps, when we see our race has been blundering on in the dark, almost without a guide in this particular from the furthest trace of time? Show then, Sir, how much is to be done, *both to sons and fathers;* and invite all wise men to become like yourself; and other men to become wise.

When we see how cruel statesmen and warriors can be to the humble race, and how absurd distinguished men can be to their

acquaintance, it will be instructive to observe the instances
multiply of pacific acquiescing manners; and to find how com-
patible it is to be great and *domestic;* enviable and yet *good-
humored.*

The little private incidents which you will also have to relate,
will have considerable use, as we want above all things, *rules of
prudence in ordinary affairs;* and it will be curious to see how
you have acted in these. It will be so far a sort of key to life, and
explain many things that all men ought to have once explained
to them, to give them a chance of becoming wise by foresight.

The nearest thing to having experience of one's own, is to
have other people's affairs brought before us in a shape that is
interesting; this is sure to happen from your pen. Your affairs
and management will have an air of simplicity or importance
that will not fail to strike; and I am convinced you have conducted them with as much originality as if you had been conducting discussions in politics or philosophy; and what more
worthy of experiments and system, (its importance and its errors considered) than human life!

Some men have been virtuous blindly, others have speculated
fantastically, and others have been shrewd to bad purposes; but
you, Sir, I am sure, will give under your hand, nothing but what
is at the same moment wise, practical, and good.

Your account of yourself (for I suppose the parallel I am
drawing for Dr. Franklin, will hold not only in point of character but of private history), will show that you are ashamed of no
origin; a thing the more important, as you prove how little necessary all origin is to happiness, virtue, or greatness.

As no end likewise happens without a means, so we shall find,
Sir, that even you yourself framed a plan by which you became
considerable; but at the same time we may see that though the
event is flattering, the means are as simple as wisdom could make
them; that is, depending upon nature, virtue, thought, and habit.

Another thing demonstrated will be the propriety of every
man's waiting for his time for appearing upon the stage of the
world. Our sensations being very much fixed to the moment, we
are apt to forget that more moments are to follow the first, and
consequently that man should arrange his conduct so as to suit

the *whole* of a life. Your attribution appears to have been applied to your *life,* and the passing moments of it have been enlivened with content and enjoyment, instead of being tormented with foolish impatience or regrets. Such a conduct is easy for those who make virtue and themselves their standard, and who try to keep themselves in countenance by examples of other truly great men, of whom patience is so often the characteristic.

Your Quaker correspondent, Sir, (for here again I will suppose the subject of my letter resembling Dr. Franklin,) praised your frugality, diligence, and temperance, which he considered as a pattern for all youth: but it is singular that he should have forgotten your modesty, and your disinterestedness, without which you never could have waited for your advancement, or found your situation in the mean time comfortable; which is a strong lesson to show the poverty of glory, and the importance of regulating our minds.

If this correspondent had known the nature of your reputation as well as I do, he would have said; your former writings and measures would secure attention to your Biography and *Art of Virtue;* and your Biography and *Art of Virtue,* in return, would secure attention to them. This is an advantage attendant upon a various character, and which brings all that belongs to it into greater play; and it is the more useful, as perhaps more persons are at a loss for the *means* of improving their minds and characters, than they are for the time or the inclination to do it.

But there is one concluding reflection, Sir, that will show the use of your life as a mere piece of biography. This style of writing seems a little gone out of vogue, and yet it is a very useful one; and your specimen of it may be particularly serviceable, as it will make a subject of comparison with the lives of various public cutthroats and intriguers, and with absurd monastic self-tormentors, or vain literary triflers. If it encourages more writings of the same kind with your own, and induces more men to spend lives fit to be written; it will be worth all Plutarch's Lives put together.

But being tired of figuring to myself a character of which every feature suits only one man in the world, without giving him the praise of it; I shall end my letter, my dear Dr. Franklin, with a personal application to your proper self.

I am earnestly desirous then, my dear Sir, that you should let the world into the traits of your genuine character, as civil broils may otherwise tend to disguise or traduce it. Considering your great age, the caution of your character, and your peculiar style of thinking, it is not likely that any one besides yourself can be sufficiently master of the facts of your life, or the intentions of your mind.

Besides all this, the immense revolution of the present period, will necessarily turn our attention towards the author of it; and when virtuous principles have been pretended in it, it will be highly important to show that such have really influenced; and, as your own character will be the principal one to receive a scrutiny, it is proper (even for its effects upon your vast and rising country, as well as upon England and upon Europe), that it should stand respectable and eternal. For the furtherance of human happiness, I have always maintained that it is necessary to prove that man is not even at present a vicious and detestable animal; and still more to prove that good management may greatly amend him; and it is for much the same reason, that I am anxious to see the opinion established, that there are fair characters existing among the individuals of the race; for the moment that all men, without exception, shall be conceived abandoned, good people will cease efforts deemed to be hopeless, and perhaps think of taking their share in the scramble of life, or at least of making it comfortable principally for themselves.

Take then, my dear Sir, this work most speedily into hand: show yourself good as you are good, temperate as you are temperate; and above all things, prove yourself as one who from your infancy have loved justice, liberty, and concord, in a way that has made it natural and consistent for you to have acted, as we have seen you act in the last seventeen years of your life. Let Englishmen be made not only to respect, but even to love you. When they think well of individuals in your native country, they will go nearer to thinking well of your country; and when your countrymen see themselves well thought of by Englishmen, they will go nearer to thinking well of England. Extend your views even further; do not stop at those who speak the

English tongue, but after having settled so many points in nature and politics, think of bettering the whole race of men.

As I have not read any part of the life in question, but know only the character that lived it, I write somewhat at hazard. I am sure however, that the life, and the treatise I allude to (on the *Art of Virtue*), will necessarily fulfill the chief of my expectations; and still more so if you take up the measure of suiting these performances to the several views above stated. Should they even prove unsuccessful in all that a sanguine admirer of yours hopes from them, you will at least have framed pieces to interest the human mind; and whoever gives a feeling of pleasure that is innocent to man, has added so much to the fair side of a life otherwise too much darkened by anxiety, and too much injured by pain.

In the hope therefore that you will listen to the prayer addressed to you in this letter, I beg to subscribe myself, my dearest Sir, &c. &c.

Signed BENJ. VAUGHAN.

Continuation of the Account of my Life.
Begun at Passy 1784

It is some time since I receiv'd the above Letters, but I have been too busy till now to think of complying with the Request they contain. It might too be much better done if I were at home among my Papers, which would aid my Memory, & help to ascertain Dates. But my Return being uncertain, and having just now a little Leisure, I will endeavor to recollect & write what I can; If I live to get home, it may there be corrected and improv'd.

Not having any Copy here of what is already written, I know not whether an Account is given of the means I used to establish the Philadelphia public Library, which from a small Beginning is now become so considerable, though I remember to have come down to near the Time of that Transaction, 1730. I will therefore begin here, with an Account of it, which may be struck out if found to have been already given.

At the time I establish'd myself in Pennsylvania, there was not a good Bookseller's Shop in any of the Colonies to the Southward of Boston. In New York & Philadelphia the Printers were indeed Stationers, they sold only Paper, &c. Almanacks, Ballads, and a few common School Books. Those who lov'd Reading were oblig'd to send for their Books from England. The Members of the Junto had each a few. We had left the Alehouse where we first met, and hired a Room to hold our Club in. I propos'd that we should all of us bring our Books to that Room, where they would not only be ready to consult in our Conferences, but become a common Benefit, each of us being at Liberty to borrow such as he wish'd to read at home. This was accordingly done, and for some time contented us. Finding the Advantage of this little Collection, I propos'd to render the Benefit from Books more common by commencing a Public Subscription Library. I drew a Sketch of the Plan and Rules that would be necessary, and got a skilful Conveyancer, Mr Charles Brockden to put the whole in Form of Articles of Agreement to be subscribed; by which each Subscriber engag'd to pay a certain Sum down for the first Purchase of Books and an annual Contribution for increasing them. So few were the Readers at that time in Philadelphia, and the Majority of us so poor, that I was not able with great Industry to find more than Fifty Persons, mostly young Tradesmen, willing to pay down for this purpose Forty shillings each, & Ten Shillings per Annum. On this little Fund we began. The Books were imported. The Library was open one Day in the Week for lending them to the Subscribers, on their Promissory Notes to pay Double the Value if not duly returned. The Institution soon manifested its Utility, was imitated by other Towns and in other Provinces, the Libraries were augmented by Donations, Reading became fashionable, and our People having no public Amusements to divert their Attention from Study became better acquainted with Books, and in a few Years were observ'd by Strangers to be better instructed & more intelligent than People of the same Rank generally are in other Countries.

When we were about to sign the above-mentioned Articles, which were to be binding on us, our Heirs &c for fifty Years, Mr Brockden, the Scrivener, said to us, "You are young Men, but it is scarce probable that any of you will live to see the Expiration of the Term fix'd in this Instrument." A Number of us, however, are yet living: But the Instrument was after a few Years rendered null by a Charter that incorporated & gave Perpetuity to the Company.

The Objections, & Reluctances I met with in Soliciting the Subscriptions, made me soon feel the Impropriety of presenting one's self as the Proposer of any useful Project that might be suppos'd to raise one's Reputation in the smallest degree above that of one's Neighbors, when one has need of their Assistance to accomplish that Project. I therefore put myself as much as I could out of sight, and stated it as a Scheme of a *Number of Friends,* who had requested me to go about and propose it to such as they thought Lovers of Reading. In this way my Affair went on more smoothly, and I ever after practis'd it on such Occasions; and from my frequent Successes, can heartily recommend it. The present little Sacrifice of your Vanity will afterwards be amply repaid. If it remains a while uncertain to whom the Merit belongs, some one more vain than yourself will be encourag'd to claim it, and then even Envy will be dispos'd to do you Justice, by plucking those assum'd Feathers, & restoring them to their right Owner.

This Library afforded me the means of Improvement by constant Study, for which I set apart an Hour or two each Day; and thus repair'd in some Degree the Loss of the Learned Education my Father once intended for me. Reading was the only Amusement I allow'd myself. I spent no time in Taverns, Games, or Frolics of any kind. And my Industry in my Business continu'd as indefatigable as it was necessary. I was in debt for my Printinghouse, I had a young Family coming on to be educated, and I had to contend with for Business two Printers who were establish'd in the Place before me. My Circumstances however grew daily easier: my original Habits of Frugality continuing. And my Father having among his Instructions to me when a Boy, frequently repeated a Proverb of Solomon, *"Seest thou a Man diligent in his Calling, he shall stand before Kings, he shall not stand before mean Men."* I from thence consider'd Industry as a Means of obtaining Wealth and Distinction, which encourag'd me, tho' I did not think that I should ever literally stand before Kings, which however has since happened.—for I have stood before five, & even had the honor of sitting down with one, the King of Denmark, to Dinner.

We have an English Proverb that says,

> He that would thrive
> Must ask his Wife;

it was lucky for me that I had one as much dispos'd to Industry & Frugality as myself. She assisted me cheerfully in my Business, folding & stitching Pamphlets, tending Shop, purchasing old Linen Rags for the Paper-makers, &c. &c. We kept no idle Servants, our Table was plain & simple, our Furniture of the cheapest. For instance my Breakfast was a long time Bread & Milk, (no Tea) and I ate it out of a twopenny earthen Porringer with a Pewter Spoon. But mark how Luxury will enter Families, and make a Progress, in Spite of Principle. Being call'd one Morning to Breakfast, I found it in a China Bowl with a Spoon of Silver. They had been bought for me without my Knowledge by my Wife, and had cost her the enormous Sum of three and twenty Shillings, for which she had no other Excuse or Apology to make, but that she thought *her* Husband deserved a Silver Spoon & China Bowl as well as any of his Neighbors. This was the first Appearance of Plate & China in our House, which afterwards in a Course of Years as our Wealth increas'd augmented gradually to several Hundred Pounds in Value.

I had been religiously educated as a Presbyterian, and tho' some of the Dogmas of that Persuasion, such as the Eternal Decrees of God, Election, Reprobation, &c. appear'd to me unintelligible, others doubtful, & I early absented myself from the Public Assemblies of the Sect, Sunday being my Studying-Day, I never was without some religious Principles; I never doubted, for instance, the Existence of the Deity, that he made the World, & govern'd it by his Providence; that the most acceptable Service of God was the doing Good to Man; that our Souls are immortal; and that all Crime will be punished & Virtue rewarded either here or hereafter; these I esteem'd the Essentials of every

Religion, and being to be found in all the Religions we had in our Country I respected them all, tho' with different degrees of Respect as I found them more or less mix'd with other Articles which without any Tendency to inspire, promote or confirm Morality, serv'd principally to divide us & make us unfriendly to one another. This Respect to all, with an Opinion that the worst had some good Effects, induc'd me to avoid all Discourse that might tend to lessen the good Opinion another might have of his own Religion; and as our Province increas'd in People and new Places of worship were continually wanted, & generally erected by voluntary Contribution, my Mite for such purpose, whatever might be the Sect, was never refused.

Tho' I seldom attended any Public Worship, I had still an Opinion of its Propriety, and of its Utility when rightly conducted, and I regularly paid my annual Subscription for the Support of the only Presbyterian Minister or Meeting we had in Philadelphia. He us'd to visit me sometimes as a Friend, and admonish me to attend his Administrations, and I was now and then prevail'd on to do so, once for five Sundays successively. Had he been, *in my Opinion,* a good Preacher perhaps I might have continued, notwithstanding the occasion I had for the Sunday's Leisure in my Course of Study: But his Discourses were chiefly either polemic Arguments, or Explications of the peculiar Doctrines of our Sect, and were all to me very dry, uninteresting and unedifying, since not a single moral Principle was inculcated or enforc'd, their Aim seeming to be rather to make us Presbyterians than good Citizens. At length he took for his Text that Verse of the 4th Chapter of Philippians, *Finally, Brethren, Whatsoever Things are true, honest, just, pure, lovely, or of good report, if there be any virtue, or any praise, think on those Things;* & I imagin'd, in a Sermon on such a Text, we could not miss of having some Morality: But he confin'd himself to five Points only as meant by the Apostle, viz. 1. Keeping holy the Sabbath Day. 2. Being diligent in Reading the Holy Scriptures. 3. Attending duly the Public Worship. 4. Partaking of the Sacrament. 5. Paying a due Respect to

God's Ministers. These might be all good Things, but as they were not the kind of good Things that I expected from that Text, I despaired of ever meeting with them from any other, was disgusted, and attended his Preaching no more. I had some Years before compos'd a little Liturgy or Form of Prayer for my own Private Use, viz. in 1728, entitled, *Articles of Belief & Acts of Religion.* I return'd to the Use of this, and went no more to the public Assemblies. My Conduct might be blameable, but I leave it without attempting farther to excuse it, my present purpose being to relate Facts, and not to make Apologies for them.

It was about this time that I conceiv'd the bold and arduous Project of arriving at moral Perfection. I wish'd to live without committing any Fault at any time; I would conquer all that either Natural Inclination, Custom, or Company might lead me into. As I knew, or thought I knew, what was right and wrong, I did not see why I might not *always* do the one and avoid the other. But I soon found I had undertaken a Task of more Difficulty than I had imagined. While my *Attention was taken up* in guarding against one Fault, I was often surpris'd by another. Habit took the Advantage of Inattention. Inclination was sometimes too strong for Reason. I concluded at length, that the mere speculative Conviction that it was our Interest to be completely virtuous, was not sufficient to prevent our Slipping, and that the contrary Habits must be broken and good ones acquired and established, before we can have any Dependence on a steady uniform Rectitude of Conduct. For this purpose I therefore contriv'd the following Method.

In the various Enumerations of the moral Virtues I had met with in my Reading, I found the Catalogue more or less numerous, as different Writers included more or fewer Ideas under the same Name. Temperance, for Example, was by some confin'd to Eating & Drinking, while by others it was extended to mean the moderating every other Pleasure, Appetite, Inclination or Passion, bodily or mental, even to our Avarice & Ambition. I propos'd to myself, for the sake of Clearness, to use rather more Names with fewer Ideas annex'd to each, than a few Names with more Ideas; and I included under Thirteen Names

of Virtues all that at that time occurr'd to me as necessary or
desirable, and annex'd to each a short Precept, which fully express'd the Extent I gave to its Meaning.

These Names of Virtues with their Precepts were

1. Temperance.
Eat not to Dullness
Drink not to Elevation.

2. Silence.
Speak not but what may benefit others or yourself.
Avoid trifling Conversation.

3. Order.
Let all your Things have their Places.
Let each Part of your Business have its Time.

4. Resolution.
Resolve to perform what you ought.
Perform without fail what you resolve.

5. Frugality.
Make no Expense but to do good to others or yourself:
i.e. Waste nothing.

6. Industry.
Lose no Time. Be always employ'd in something
useful. Cut off all unnecessary Actions.

7. Sincerity.
Use no hurtful Deceit.
Think innocently and justly; and, if you speak, speak accordingly.

8. Justice.
Wrong none, by doing Injuries or omitting the
Benefits that are your Duty.

9. Moderation.
Avoid Extremes. Forbear resenting Injuries so much
as you think they deserve.

10. Cleanliness.
Tolerate no Uncleanness in Body, Clothes or Habitation.

11. Tranquillity.
Be not disturbed at Trifles, or at Accidents common
or unavoidable.

12. Chastity.
Rarely use Venery but for Health or Offspring; Never
to Dullness, Weakness, or the Injury of your own or
another's Peace or Reputation.

13. Humility.
Imitate Jesus and Socrates.

My Intention being to acquire the *Habitude* of all those
Virtues, I judg'd it would be well not to distract my Attention
by attempting the whole at once, but to fix it on one of them at
a time, and when I should be Master of that, then to proceed to
another, and so on till I should have gone thro' the thirteen. And
as the previous Acquisition of some might facilitate the Acquisition of certain others, I arrang'd them with that View as they
stand above. *Temperance* first, as it tends to procure that Cool-
ness & Clearness of Head, which is so necessary where constant Vigilance was to be kept up, and Guard maintained, against
the unremitting Attraction of ancient Habits, and the Force of
perpetual Temptations. This being acquir'd & establish'd, *Silence* would be more easy, and my Desire being to gain Knowledge at the same time that I improv'd in Virtue, and considering
that in Conversation it was obtain'd rather by the use of the Ears
than of the Tongue, & therefore wishing to break a Habit I was
getting into of Prattling, Punning & Joking, which only made me
acceptable to trifling Company, I gave *Silence* the second Place.
This, and the next, *Order,* I expected would allow me more Time
for attending to my Project and my Studies; RESOLUTION, once
become habitual, would keep me firm in my Endeavors to obtain
all the subsequent Virtues; *Frugality & Industry,* by freeing me
from my remaining Debt, & producing Affluence & Independence, would make more easy the Practice of *Sincerity* and *Justice,* &c. &c. Conceiving then that agreeable to the Advice of
Pythagoras in his Golden Verses daily Examination would be

necessary, I contriv'd the following Method for conducting that Examination.

I made a little Book in which I allotted a Page for each of the Virtues. I rul'd each Page with red Ink, so as to have seven Columns, one for each Day of the Week, marking each Column with a Letter for the Day. I cross'd these Columns with thirteen red Lines, marking the Beginning of each Line with the first Letter of one of the Virtues, on which Line & in its proper Column I might mark by a little black Spot every Fault I found upon Examination to have been committed respecting that Virtue upon that Day.

I determined to give a Week's strict Attention to each of the Virtues successively. Thus in the first Week my great Guard was to avoid every the least Offense against Temperance, leaving the other Virtues to their ordinary Chance, only marking every Evening the Faults of the Day. Thus if in the first Week I could keep my first Line marked T clear of Spots, I suppos'd the Habit of that Virtue so much strengthen'd and its opposite weaken'd, that I might venture extending my Attention to include the next, and for the following Week keep both Lines clear of Spots. Proceeding thus to the last, I could go thro' a Course complete in Thirteen Weeks, and four Courses in a Year. And like him who having a Garden to weed, does not attempt to eradicate all the bad Herbs at once, which would exceed his Reach and his Strength, but works on one of the Beds at a time, & having accomplish'd the first proceeds to a Second; so I should have, (I hoped) the encouraging Pleasure of seeing on my Pages the Progress I made in Virtue, by clearing successively my Lines of their Spots, till in the End by a Number of Courses, I should be happy in viewing a clean Book after a thirteen Weeks, daily Examination.

This my little Book had for its Motto these Lines from *Addison's Cato;*

Here will I hold: If there is a Pow'r above us,
(And that there is, all Nature cries aloud
Thro' all her Works) he must delight in Virtue,
And that which he delights in must be happy.

FORM OF THE PAGES

Temperance.							
Eat not to Dullness *Drink not to Elevation.*							
	S	**M**	**T**	**W**	**T**	**F**	**S**
T							
S	••	•		•		•	
O	•	•	•		•	•	•
R			•			•	
F		•			•		
I			•				
S							
J							
M							
Cl.							
T							
Ch.							
H							

Another from *Cicero*.

O Vitæ Philosophia Dux! O Virtutum indagatrix, expultrixque vitiorum! Unus dies bene, & ex preceptis tuis actus, peccanti immortalitati est anteponendus.

Another from the Proverbs of Solomon
speaking of Wisdom or Virtue;

Length of Days is in her right hand, and in her Left Hand Riches and Honors; Her Ways are Ways of Pleasantness, and all her Paths are Peace.

III, 16, 17.

And conceiving God to be the Fountain of Wisdom, I thought it right and necessary to solicit his Assistance for obtaining it; to this End I form'd the following little Prayer, which was prefix'd to my Tables of Examination; for daily Use.

O Powerful Goodness! bountiful Father! merciful Guide! Increase in me that Wisdom which discovers my truest Interests; Strengthen my Resolutions to perform what that Wisdom dictates. Accept my kind Offices to thy other Children, as the only Return in my Power for thy continual Favors to me.

I us'd also sometimes a little Prayer which I took from *Thomson's* Poems. viz

Father of Light and Life, thou Good supreme,
O teach me what is good, teach me thy self!
Save me from Folly, Vanity and Vice,
From every low Pursuit, and fill my Soul
With Knowledge, conscious Peace, & Virtue pure,
Sacred, substantial, neverfading Bliss!

The Precept of *Order* requiring that *every Part of my Business should have its allotted Time,* one Page in my little Book

The Morning Question, What Good shall I do this Day?	5 6 7	Rise, wash, and address *Powerful Goodness;* Contrive Day s Business and take the Resolution of the Day; prosecute the present Study: and breakfast?
	8 9 10 11	Work.
	12 1	Read, or overlook my Accounts, and dine.
	2 3 4 5	Work.
	6 7 8 9	Put Things in their Places, Supper, Music, or Diversion, or Conversation, Examination of the Day.
Evening Question, What Good have I done to day?	10 11 12 1 2 3 4	Sleep.

contain'd the following Scheme of Employment for the Twenty-four Hours of a natural Day,

I enter'd upon the Execution of this Plan for Self Examination, and continu'd it with occasional Intermissions for some time. I was surpris'd to find myself so much fuller of Faults than I had imagined, but I had the Satisfaction of seeing them diminish. To avoid the Trouble of renewing now & then my little Book, which by scraping out the Marks on the Paper of old Faults to make room for new Ones in a new Course, became full of Holes: I transferr'd my Tables & Precepts to the Ivory Leaves of a Memorandum Book, on which the Lines were drawn with red Ink that made a durable Stain, and on those Lines I mark'd my Faults with a black Lead Pencil, which Marks I could easily wipe out with a wet Sponge. After a while I went thro' one Course only in a Year, and afterwards only one in several Years, till at length I omitted them entirely, being employ'd in Voyages & Business abroad with a Multiplicity of Affairs, that interfered, but I always carried my little Book with me. My Scheme of ORDER, gave me the most Trouble, and I found, that tho' it might be practicable where a Man's Business was such as to leave him the Disposition of his Time, that of a Journey-man Printer for instance, it was not possible to be exactly observ'd by a Master, who must mix with the World, and often receive People of Business at their own Hours. *Order* too, with regard to Places for Things, Papers, &c. I found extremely difficult to acquire. I had not been early accustomed to *Method,* & having an exceeding good Memory, I was not so sensible of the Inconvenience attending Want of Method. This Article therefore cost me so much painful Attention & my Faults in it vex'd me so much, and I made so little Progress in Amendment, & had such frequent Relapses, that I was almost ready to give up the Attempt, and content myself with a faulty Character in that respect. Like the Man who in buying an Ax of a Smith my neighbor, desired to have the whole of its Surface as bright as the Edge; the Smith consented to grind it bright for him if he would turn the Wheel. He turn'd while the Smith press'd the broad Face of the Ax hard & heavily on the Stone, which made the Turning of it very fatiguing. The Man came every now & then from the Wheel to see how the Work went on; and at length would take his Ax as it was without farther Grinding. No, says the Smith, Turn on, turn on; we shall have it bright by and by; as yet 'tis only speckled. Yes, says the Man; but—*I think I like a speckled Ax best.* And I believe this may have been the Case with many who having for want of some such Means as I employ'd found the Difficulty of obtaining good, & breaking bad Habits, in other Points of Vice & Virtue, have given up the Struggle, & concluded that *a speckled Ax was best.* For something that pretended to be Reason was every now and then suggesting to me, that such extreme Nicety as I exacted of myself might be a kind of Foppery in Morals, which if it were known would make me ridiculous; that a perfect Character might be attended with the Inconvenience of being envied and hated; and that a benevolent Man should allow a few Faults in himself, to keep his Friends in Countenance. In Truth I found myself incorrigible with respect to *Order;* and now I am grown old, and my Memory bad, I feel very sensibly the want of it. But on the whole, tho' I never arrived at the Perfection I had been so ambitious of obtaining, but fell far short of it, yet I was by the Endeavor a better and a happier Man than I otherwise should have been, if I had not attempted it; As those who aim at perfect Writing by imitating the engraved Copies, tho' they never reach the wish'd for Excellence of those Copies, their Hand is mended by the Endeavor, and is tolerable while it continues fair & legible.

And it may be well my Posterity should be informed, that to this little Artifice, with the Blessing of God, their Ancestor ow'd the constant Felicity of his Life down to his 79th Year in which this is written. What Reverses may attend the Remainder is in the Hand of Providence: But if they arrive the Reflection on past Happiness enjoy'd ought to help his Bearing them with more Resignation. To *Temperance* he ascribes his long-continu'd Health, & what is still left to him of a good Constitution. To *Industry* and *Frugality* the early Easiness of his Circumstances, & Acquisition of his Fortune, with all that Knowledge which enabled him to be an useful Citizen, and obtain'd for him some Degree of Reputation among the Learned. To *Sincerity* & *Justice* the Confidence of his Country, and the honorable Employs it conferr'd upon him. And to the joint Influence of the whole Mass of the Virtues, even in the imperfect State he was able to acquire them, all that Evenness of Temper, & that Cheerfulness in Conversation which makes his Company still sought for, & agreeable even to his younger Acquaintance. I hope therefore that some of my Descendants may follow the Example & reap the Benefit.

It will be remark'd that, tho' my Scheme was not wholly without Religion there was in it no Mark of any of the distinguishing Tenets of any particular Sect. I had purposely avoided them; for being fully persuaded of the Utility and Excellency of my Method, and that it might be serviceable to People in all Religions, and intending some time or other to publish it, I would not have any thing in it that should prejudice any one of any Sect against it. I purposed writing a little Comment on each Virtue, in which I would have shown the Advantages of possessing it, & the Mischiefs attending its opposite Vice; and I should have called my Book the ART *of Virtue,* because it would have shown the *Means & Manner* of obtaining Virtue, which would have distinguish'd it from the mere Exhortation to be good, that does not instruct & indicate the Means; but is like the Apostle's Man of verbal Charity, who only, without showing to the Naked & the Hungry *how* or where they might get Clothes or Victuals, exhorted them to be fed & clothed. *James* II, 15, 16.

But it so happened that my Intention of writing & publishing this Comment was never fulfilled. I did indeed, from time to time put down short Hints of the Sentiments, Reasonings, &c. to be made use of in it; some of which I have still by me. But the necessary close Attention to private Business in the earlier part of Life, and public Business since, have occasioned my postponing it. For it being connected in my Mind with a *great and extensive Project* that required the whole Man to execute, and which an unforeseen Succession of Employs prevented my attending to, it has hitherto remain'd unfinish'd.

In this Piece it was my Design to explain and enforce this Doctrine, that vicious Actions are not hurtful because they are forbidden, but forbidden because they are hurtful, the Nature of Man alone consider'd: That it was therefore every one's

Interest to be virtuous, who wish'd to be happy even in this World; And I should from this Circumstance, there being always in the World a Number of rich Merchants, Nobility, States and Princes, who have need of honest Instruments for the Management of their Affairs, and such being so rare have endeavored to convince young Persons, that no Qualities were so likely to make a poor Man's Fortune as those of Probity & Integrity.

My List of Virtues contain'd at first but twelve: But a Quaker Friend having kindly inform'd me that I was generally thought proud; that my Pride show'd itself frequently in Conversation; that I was not content with being in the right when discussing any Point, but was overbearing & rather insolent; of which he convinc'd me by mentioning several Instances;—I determined endeavoring to cure myself if I could of this Vice or Folly among the rest, and I added *Humility* to my List, giving an extensive Meaning to the Word. I cannot boast of much Success in acquiring the *Reality* of this Virtue; but I had a good deal with regard to the *Appearance* of it. I made it a Rule to forbear all direct Contradiction to the Sentiments of others, and all positive Assertion of my own. I even forbid myself agreeable to the old Laws of our Junto, the Use of every Word or Expression in the Language that imported a fix'd Opinion; such as *certainly, undoubtedly,* &c. and I adopted instead of them, I *conceive,* I *apprehend,* or I *imagine* a thing to be so or so, or it so appears to me at present. When another asserted something, that I thought an Error, I deny'd myself the Pleasure of contradicting him abruptly, and of showing immediately some Absurdity in his Proposition; and in answering I began by observing that in certain Cases or Circumstances his Opinion would be right, but that in the present case there *appear'd* or *seem'd* to me some Difference, &c. I soon found the Advantage of this Change in my Manners. The Conversations I engag'd in went on more pleasantly. The modest way in which I propos'd my Opinions, procur'd them a readier Reception and less Contradiction; I had less Mortification when I was found to be in the wrong, and I more easily prevail'd with others to give up their Mistakes & join with me when I happen'd to be in the right. And this

Mode, which I at first put on, with some violence to natural Inclination, became at length so easy & so habitual to me, that perhaps for these Fifty Years past no one has ever heard a dogmatical Expression escape me. And to this Habit (after my Character of Integrity) I think it principally owing, that I had early so much Weight with my Fellow Citizens, when I proposed new Institutions, or Alterations in the old; and so much Influence in public Councils when I became a Member. For I was but a bad Speaker, never eloquent, subject to much Hesitation in my choice of Words, hardly correct in Language, and yet I generally carried my Points.

In reality there is perhaps no one of our natural Passions so hard to subdue as *Pride*. Disguise it, struggle with it, beat it down, stifle it, mortify it as much as one pleases, it is still alive, and will every now and then peep out and show itself. You will see it perhaps often in this History. For even if I could conceive that I had completely overcome it, I should probably be proud of my Humility.

Thus far written at Passy 1784

I am now about to write at home, Augt 1788.—but cannot have the help expected from my Papers, many of them being lost in the War: I have however found the following.

Having mentioned *a great & extensive Project* which I had conceiv'd, it seems proper that some Account should be here given of that Project and its Object. Its first Rise in my Mind appears in the following little Paper, accidentally preserv'd, viz.

OBSERVATIONS on my Reading History in Library, May 9, 1731.

"That the great Affairs of the World, the Wars, Revolutions, &c. are carried on and effected by Parties.

"That the View of these Parties is their present general Interest, or what they take to be such.

"That the different Views of these different Parties, occasion all Confusion.

"That while a Party is carrying on a general Design, each Man has his particular private Interest in View.

"That as soon as a Party has gain'd its general Point, each Member becomes Intent upon his particular Interest, which thwarting others, breaks that Party into Divisions, and occasions more Confusion.

"That few in Public Affairs act from a mere View of the Good of their Country, whatever they may pretend; and tho' their Actings bring real Good to their Country, yet Men primarily consider'd that their own and their Country's Interest was united, and did not act from a Principle of Benevolence.

"That fewer still in public Affairs act with a View to the Good of Mankind.

"There seems to me at present to be great Occasion for raising an united Party for Virtue, by forming the Virtuous and good Men of all Nations into a regular Body, to be govern'd by suitable good and wise Rules, which good and wise Men may probably be more unanimous in their Obedience to, than common People are to common Laws.

"I at present think, that whoever attempts this aright, and is well qualified, cannot fail of pleasing God & of meeting with Success. B.F."

Revolving this Project in my Mind, as to be undertaken hereafter when my Circumstances should afford me the necessary Leisure, I put down from time to time on Pieces of Paper such Thoughts as occurr'd to me respecting it. Most of these are lost; but I find one purporting to be the Substance of an intended Creed, containing as I thought the Essentials of every known Religion, and being free of every thing that might shock the Professors of any Religion. It is express'd in these Words. viz

"That there is one God who made all things.

"That he governs the World by his Providence.

"That he ought to be worshipped by Adoration, Prayer & Thanksgiving.

"But that the most acceptable Service of God is doing Good to Man.

"That the Soul is immortal.

"And that God will certainly reward Virtue and punish Vice either here or hereafter."

My Ideas at that time were, that the Sect should be begun & spread at first among young and single Men only; that each Person to be initiated should not only declare his Assent to such

Creed, but should have exercis'd himself with the Thirteen Weeks Examination and Practice of the Virtues as in the before mention'd Model; that the Existence of such a Society should be kept a Secret till it was become considerable to prevent Solicitations for the Admission of improper Persons; but that the Members should each of them search among his Acquaintance for ingenuous well-disposed Youths, to whom with prudent Caution the Scheme should be gradually communicated: That the Members should engage to afford their Advice Assistance and Support to each other in promoting one another's Interest, Business and Advancement in Life: That for Distinction, we should be call'd the Society of the *Free and Easy;* Free, as being by the general Practice and Habit of the Virtues, free from the Dominion of Vice, and particularly by the Practice of Industry & Frugality, free from Debt, which exposes a Man to Confinement and a Species of Slavery to his Creditors. This is as much as I can now recollect of the Project, except that I communicated it in part to two young Men, who adopted it with some Enthusiasm. But my then narrow Circumstances, and the Necessity I was under of sticking close to my Business, occasion'd my Postponing the farther Prosecution of it at that time, and my multifarious Occupations public & private induc'd me to continue postponing, so that it has been omitted till I have no longer Strength or Activity left sufficient for such an Enterprise: Tho' I am still of Opinion that it was a practicable Scheme, and might have been very useful, by forming a great Number of good Citizens: And I was not discourag'd by the seeming Magnitude of the Undertaking, as I have always thought that one Man of tolerable Abilities may work great Changes, & accomplish great Affairs among Mankind, if he first forms a good Plan, and, cutting off all Amusements or other Employments that would divert his Attention, makes the Execution of that same Plan his sole Study and Business.

In 1732 I first published my Almanack, under the Name of *Richard Saunders;* it was continu'd by me about 25 Years, commonly call'd *Poor Richard's* Almanack. I endeavor'd to make it both entertaining and useful, and it accordingly came to be in such Demand that I reap'd considerable Profit from it, vending annually near ten Thousand. And observing that it was generally read, scarce any Neighborhood in the Province being without it, I consider'd it as a proper Vehicle for conveying Instruction among the common People, who bought scarce any other Books. I therefore filled all the little Spaces that occurr'd between the Remarkable Days in the Calendar, with Proverbial Sentences, chiefly such as inculcated Industry and Frugality, as the Means of procuring Wealth and thereby securing Virtue, it being more difficult for a Man in Want to act always honestly, as (to use here one of those Proverbs) *it is hard for an empty Sack to stand upright.* These Proverbs, which contained the Wisdom of many Ages and Nations, I assembled and form'd into a connected Discourse prefix'd to the Almanack of 1757, as the Harangue of a wise old Man to the People attending an Auction. The bringing all these scatter'd Counsels thus into a Focus, enabled them to make greater Impression. The Piece being universally approved was copied in all the Newspapers of the Continent, reprinted in Britain on a Broadside to be stuck up in Houses, two Translations were made of it in French, and great Numbers bought by the Clergy & Gentry to distribute gratis among their poor Parishioners and Tenants. In Pennsylvania, as it discouraged useless Expense in foreign Superfluities, some thought, it had its share of Influence in producing that growing Plenty of Money which was observable for several Years after its Publication.

I consider'd my Newspaper also as another Means of Communicating Instruction, & in that View frequently reprinted in it Extracts from the Spectator and other moral Writers, and sometimes publish'd little Pieces of my own which had been first compos'd for Reading in our Junto. Of these are a Socratic Dialogue tending to prove, that, whatever might be his Parts and Abilities, a vicious Man could not properly be called a Man of Sense. And a Discourse on Self denial, showing that Virtue was not secure, till its Practice became a Habitude, & was free from the Opposition of contrary Inclinations. These may be found in the Papers about the beginning of 1735. In the Conduct of my Newspaper I carefully excluded all Libelling and Personal Abuse, which is of late Years become so disgraceful to our Country. Whenever I was solicited to insert any thing of that kind, and the Writers pleaded as they generally did, the Liberty of the Press, and that a Newspaper was like a Stage Coach in which any one who would pay had a Right to a Place, my Answer was, that I would print the Piece separately if desired, and the Author might have as many Copies as he pleased to distribute himself, but that I would not take upon me to spread his Detraction, and that having contracted with my Subscribers to furnish them with what might be either useful or entertaining, I could not fill their Papers with private Altercation in which they had no Concern without doing them manifest Injustice. Now many of our Printers make no scruple of gratifying the Malice of Individuals by false Accusations of the fairest Characters among ourselves, augmenting Animosity even to the producing of Duels, and are moreover so indiscreet as to print scurrilous Reflections on the Government of neighboring States, and even on the Conduct of our best national Allies, which may be attended with the most pernicious Consequences. These Things I mention as a Caution to young Printers, & that they may be encouraged not to pollute their Presses and disgrace their Profession by such infamous Practices, but refuse steadily; as they may see by my Example, that such a Course of conduct will not on the whole be injurious to their Interests.

In 1733, I sent one of my Journeymen to Charleston South Carolina where a Printer was wanting. I furnish'd him with a Press and Letters, on an Agreement of Partnership, by which I was to receive One Third of the Profits, of the Business, paying One Third of the Expense. He was a Man of Learning and honest, but ignorant in Matters of Account; and tho' he sometimes made me Remittances, I could get no Account from him, nor any satisfactory State of our Partnership while he lived. On his Decease, the Business was continued by his Widow, who being born & bred in Holland, where as I have been inform'd the Knowledge of Accompts makes a Part of Female Education, she not only sent me as clear a State as she could find of the Transactions past, but continu'd to account with the greatest Regularity & Exactitude every Quarter afterwards; and manag'd the Business with such Success that she not only brought up reputably a Family of Children, but at the Expiration of the Term was able to purchase of me the Printinghouse and establish her Son in it. I mention this Affair chiefly for the Sake of recommending that Branch of Education for our young Females, as likely to be of more Use to them & their children in Case of Widowhood than either Music or Dancing, by preserving them from Losses by Imposition of crafty Men, and enabling them to continue perhaps a profitable mercantile House with establish'd Correspondence till a Son is grown up fit to undertake and go on with it, to the lasting Advantage and enriching of the Family.

About the Year 1734, there arrived among us from Ireland, a young Presbyterian Preacher named Hemphill, who delivered with a good Voice, & apparently extempore, most excellent Discourses, which drew together considerable Numbers of different Persuasions, who join'd in admiring them. Among the rest I became one of his constant Hearers, his Sermons pleasing me as they had little of the dogmatical kind, but inculcated strongly the Practice of Virtue, or what in the religious Style are called Good Works. Those however, of our Congregation, who considered themselves as orthodox Presbyterians, disapprov'd his Doctrine, and were join'd by most of the old Clergy, who arraign'd him of Heterodoxy before the Synod, in order to have him silenc'd. I became his zealous Partisan, and contributed all I could to raise a Party in his Favor; and we combatted for him a while with some Hopes of Success. There was much Scribbling pro & con upon the Occasion; and finding that tho' an elegant Preacher he was but a poor Writer, I lent him my Pen and wrote for him two or three Pamphlets, and one Piece in the Gazette of April 1735. Those Pamphlets, as is generally the Case with controversial Writings, tho' eagerly read at the time, were soon out of Vogue, and I question whether a single Copy of them now exists. During the Contest an unlucky Occurrence hurt his Cause exceedingly. One of our Adversaries having heard him preach a Sermon that was much admired, thought he had somewhere read that Sermon before, or at least a part of it. On Search he found that Part quoted at length in one of the British Reviews, from a Discourse of Dr Forster's. This Detection gave many of our Party Disgust, who accordingly abandoned his Cause, and occasion'd our more speedy Discomfiture in the Synod. I stuck by him however, as I rather approv'd his giving us good Sermons compos'd by others, than bad ones of his own Manufacture; tho' the latter was the Practice of our common Teachers. He afterwards acknowledg'd to me that none of those he preach'd were his own; adding that his Memory was such as enabled him to retain and repeat any Sermon after one Reading only. On our Defeat he left us, in search elsewhere of better Fortune, and I quitted the Congregation, never joining it after, tho' I continu'd many Years my Subscription for the Support of its Ministers.

I had begun in 1733 to study Languages. I soon made myself so much a Master of the French as to be able to read the Books with Ease. I then undertook the Italian. An Acquaintance who was also learning it, us'd often to tempt me to play Chess with him. Finding this took up too much of the Time I had to spare for Study, I at length refus'd to play any more, unless on this Condition, that the Victor in every Game, should have a Right to impose a Task, either in Parts of the Grammar to be got by heart, or in Translation, &c. which Tasks the Vanquish'd was to perform upon Honor before our next Meeting. As we play'd pretty equally we thus beat one another into that Language. I afterwards with a little Pains-taking acquir'd as much of the Spanish as to read their Books also. I have already mention'd that I had only one Year's Instruction in a Latin School, and that when very young, after which I neglected that Language entirely. But when I had attained an Acquaintance with the French, Italian and Spanish, I was surpris'd to find on looking over a Latin Testament, that I understood so much more of that Language than I had imagined; which encouraged me to apply myself again to the Study of it, & I met with the more Success, as those preceding Languages had greatly smooth'd my Way. From these Circumstances I have thought that there is some Inconsistency in our common Mode of Teaching Languages. We are told that it is proper to begin first with the Latin, and having acquir'd that it will be more easy to attain those modern Languages which are deriv'd from it; and yet we do not begin with the Greek in order more easily to acquire the Latin. It is true, that if you can clamber & get to the Top of a Stair-Case without using the Steps, you will more easily gain them in descending: but certainly if you begin with the lowest you will with more Ease ascend to the Top. And I would therefore offer it to the Consideration of those who superintend the Educating of our Youth, whether, since many of those who begin with the Latin, quit the same after spending some Years, without having made any great Proficiency, and what they have learned becomes almost useless, so that their time has been lost, it would not have been better to have begun them with the French, proceeding to the Italian &c. for tho' after spending the same time they should quit the Study of Languages, & never arrive at the Latin, they would however have acquir'd another Tongue or two that being in modern Use might be serviceable to them in common Life.

After ten Years' Absence from Boston, and having become more easy in my Circumstances, I made a Journey thither to visit my Relations, which I could not sooner well afford. In returning I call'd at Newport, to see my Brother then settled there with his Printinghouse. Our former Differences were forgotten, and our Meeting was very cordial and affectionate. He was fast declining in his Health, and requested of me that in case of his Death, which he apprehended not far distant, I would take home his Son, then but 10 Years of Age, and bring him up to the Printing Business. This I accordingly perform'd, sending him a few Years to School before I took him into the Office. His Mother carry'd on the Business till he was grown up, when I assisted him with an Assortment of new Types, those of his Father being in a Manner worn out. Thus it was that I made my Brother ample Amends for the Service I had depriv'd him of by leaving him so early.

In 1736 I lost one of my Sons, a fine Boy of 4 Years old, by the Small Pox taken in the common way. I long regretted bitterly & still regret that I had not given it to him by Inoculation; This I mention for the Sake of Parents, who omit that Operation on the Supposition that they should never forgive themselves if a Child died under it; my Example showing that the

Regret may be the same either way, and that therefore the safer should be chosen.

Our Club, the Junto, was found so useful, & afforded such Satisfaction to the Members, that several were desirous of introducing their Friends, which could not well be done without exceeding what we had settled as a convenient Number, viz. Twelve. We had from the Beginning made it a Rule to keep our Institution a Secret, which was pretty well observ'd. The Intention was, to avoid Applications of improper Persons for Admittance, some of whom perhaps we might find it difficult to refuse. I was one of those who were against any Addition to our Number, but instead of it made in Writing a Proposal, that every Member separately should endeavor to form a subordinate Club, with the same Rules respecting Queries, &c. and without informing them of the Connection with the Junto. The Advantages propos'd were the Improvement of so many more young Citizens by the Use of our Institutions; Our better Acquaintance with the general Sentiments of the Inhabitants on any Occasion, as the Junto-Member might propose what Queries we should desire, and was to report to Junto what pass'd in his separate Club; the Promotion of our particular Interests in Business by more extensive Recommendations; and the Increase of our Influence in public Affairs & our Power of doing Good by spreading thro' the several Clubs the Sentiments of the Junto. The Project was approv'd, and every Member undertook to form his Club: but they did not all succeed. Five or six only were completed, which were call'd by different Names, as the Vine, the Union, the Band, &c. They were useful to themselves, & afforded us a good deal of Amusement, Information & Instruction, besides answering in some considerable Degree our Views of influencing the public Opinion on particular Occasions, of which I shall give some Instances in course of time as they happened.

My first Promotion was my being chosen in 1736 Clerk of the General Assembly. The Choice was made that Year without Opposition; but the Year following when I was again propos'd (the Choice, like that of the Members being annual) a new Member made a long Speech against me, in order to favor some other Candidate. I was however chosen; which was the more agreeable to me, as besides the Pay for immediate Service as Clerk, the Place gave me a better Opportunity of keeping up an Interest among the Members, which secur'd to me the Business of Printing the Votes, Laws, Paper Money, and other occasional Jobs for the Public, that on the whole were very profitable. I therefore did not like the Opposition of this new Member, who was a Gentleman of Fortune, & Education, with Talents that were likely to give him in time great Influence in the House, which indeed afterwards happened. I did not however aim at gaining his Favor by paying any servile Respect to him, but after some time took this other Method. Having heard that he had in his Library a certain very scarce & curious Book, I wrote a Note to him expressing my Desire of perusing that Book, and requesting he would do me the Favor of lending it to me for a few Days. He sent it immediately; and I return'd it in about a Week, with another Note expressing strongly my Sense of the Favor. When we next met in the House he spoke to me, (which he had never done before) and with great Civility. And he ever afterwards manifested a Readiness to serve me on all Occasions, so that we became great Friends, & our Friendship continu'd to his Death. This is another Instance of the Truth of an old Maxim I had learned, which says, *He that has once done you a Kindness will be more ready to do you another, than he whom you yourself have obliged.* And it shows how much more profitable it is prudently to remove, than to resent, return & continue inimical Proceedings.

In 1737, Col. Spotswood, late Governor of Virginia, & then Post-master, General, being dissatisfied with the Conduct of his Deputy at Philadelphia, respecting some Negligence in rendering, & Inexactitude of his Accounts, took from him the Commission & offered it to me. I accepted it readily, and found it of great Advantage; for tho' the Salary was small, it facilitated the Correspondence that improv'd my Newspaper, increas'd the Number demanded, as well as the Advertisements to be inserted, so that it came to afford me a very considerable Income. My old Competitor's Newspaper declin'd proportionably, and I was satisfy'd without retaliating his Refusal, while Postmaster, to permit my Papers being carried by the Riders. Thus he suffer'd greatly from his Neglect in due Accounting; and I mention it as a Lesson to those young Men who may be employ'd in managing Affairs for others that they should always render Accounts & make Remittances with Great Clearness and Punctuality. The Character of observing such a Conduct is the most powerful of all Recommendations to new Employments & Increase of Business.

I began now to turn my Thoughts a little to public Affairs, beginning however with small Matters. The City Watch was one of the first Things that I conceiv'd to want Regulation. It was managed by the Constables of the respective Wards in Turn. The Constable warn'd a Number of Housekeepers to attend him for the Night. Those who chose never to attend paid him Six Shillings a Year to be excus'd, which was suppos'd to be for hiring Substitutes; but was in reality much more than was necessary for that purpose, and made the Constableship a Place of Profit. And the Constable for a little Drink often got such Ragamuffins about him as a Watch, that reputable Housekeepers did not choose to mix with. Walking the rounds too was often neglected, and most of the Night spent in Tippling. I thereupon wrote a Paper to be read in Junto, representing these Irregularities, but insisting more particularly on the Inequality of this Six Shilling Tax of the Constables, respecting the Circumstances of those who paid it, since a poor Widow Housekeeper, all whose Property to be guarded by the Watch did not perhaps exceed the Value of Fifty Pounds, paid as much as the wealthiest Merchant who had Thousands of Pounds-worth of Goods in his Stores. On the whole I proposed as a more effectual Watch, the Hiring of proper Men to serve constantly in that Business; and as a more equitable Way of supporting the Charge, the levying a Tax that should be proportion'd to Property. This Idea being approv'd by the Junto, was communicated to the other Clubs, but as arising in each of them. And tho' the Plan was not immediately carried into Execution, yet by preparing the Minds of People for the Change, it paved the Way for the Law obtain'd a few Years after, when the Members of our Clubs were grown into more Influence.

About this time I wrote a Paper, (first to be read in Junto but it was afterwards publish'd) on the different Accidents and Carelessnesses by which Houses were set on fire, with Cautions against them, and Means proposed of avoiding them. This was much spoken of as a useful Piece, and gave rise to a Project, which soon followed it, of forming a Company for the more ready Extinguishing of Fires, and mutual Assistance in Removing & Securing of Goods when in Danger. Associates in this Scheme were presently found amounting to Thirty. Our Articles of Agreement oblig'd every Member to keep always in good Order and fit for Use, a certain Number of Leather Buckets, with strong Bags & Baskets (for packing & transporting of Goods) which were to be brought to every Fire; and we agreed to meet once a Month & spend a social Evening together, in discoursing and communicating such Ideas as occur'd to us upon the Subject of Fires as might be useful in our Conduct on such Occasions. The Utility of this Institution soon appear'd, and many more desiring to be admitted than we thought convenient for one Company, they were advised to form another, which was accordingly done. And this went on, one new Company being formed after another, till they became so numerous as to include most of the Inhabitants who were Men of Property; and now at the time of my Writing this, tho' upwards of Fifty Years since its Establishment, that which I first formed, called the Union Fire Company, still subsists and flourishes, tho' the first Members are all deceas'd but myself & one who is older by a Year than I am. The small Fines that have been paid by Members for Absence at the Monthly Meetings, have been apply'd to the Purchase of Fire-Engines, Ladders, Firehooks, and other useful Implements, for each Company, so that I question whether there is a City in the World better provided with the Means of putting a Stop to beginning Conflagrations; and in fact since those Institutions, the City has never lost by Fire more than one or two Houses at a time, and the Flames have often been extinguish'd before the House in which they began has been half consumed.

In 1739 arriv'd among us from England the Rev. Mr Whitefield, who had made himself remarkable there as an itinerant preacher. He was at first permitted to preach in some of our

Churches; but the Clergy taking a Dislike to him, soon refus'd him their Pulpits and he was oblig'd to preach in the Fields. The Multitudes of all Sects and Denominations that attended his Sermons were enormous, and it was matter of Speculation to me who was one of the Number, to observe the extraordinary Influence of his Oratory on his Hearers, and how much they admir'd & respected him; notwithstanding his common Abuse of them, by assuring them they were naturally *half Beasts and half Devils*. It was wonderful to see the Change soon made in the Manners of our Inhabitants; from being thoughtless or indifferent about Religion, it seem'd as if all the World were growing Religious; so that one could not walk thro' the Town in an Evening without Hearing Psalms sung in different Families of every Street. And it being found inconvenient to assemble in the open Air, subject to its Inclemencies, the Building of a House to meet in was no sooner propos'd and Persons appointed to receive Contributions, but sufficient Sums were soon receiv'd to procure the Ground and erect the Building which was 100 feet long & 70 broad, about the Size of Westminster-hall; and the Work was carried on with such Spirit as to be finished in a much shorter time than could have been expected. Both House and Ground were vested in Trustees, expressly for the Use of any Preacher of any religious Persuasion who might desire to say something to the People of Philadelphia, the Design in building not being to accommodate any particular Sect, but the Inhabitants in general, so that even if the Mufti of Constantinople were to send a Missionary to preach Mahometanism to us, he would find a Pulpit at his Service. (The Contributions being made by People of different Sects promiscuously, Care was taken in the Nomination of Trustees to avoid giving a Predominancy to any Sect, so that one of each was appointed, viz. one Church of England-man, one Presbyterian, one Baptist, one Moravian, &c.). Mr Whitefield, in leaving us, went preaching all the Way thro' the Colonies to Georgia. The Settlement of that Province had lately been begun; but instead of being made with hardy industrious Husbandmen accustomed to Labor, the only People fit for such an Enterprise, it was with Families of broken Shopkeepers and other insolvent Debtors,

many of idolent & idle habits, taken out of the Gaols, who being set down in the Woods, unqualified for clearing Land, &
unable to endure the Hardships of a new Settlement, perished in
Numbers, leaving many helpless Children unprovided for. The
Sight of their miserable Situation inspired the benevolent Heart
of Mr Whitefield with the Idea of building an Orphan House
there, in which they might be supported and educated. Returning northward he preach'd up this Charity, & made large Collections; for his Eloquence had a wonderful Power over the
Hearts and Purses of his Hearers, of which I myself was an Instance. I did not disapprove of the Design, but as Georgia was
then destitute of Materials & Workmen, and it was propos'd to
send them from Philadelphia at a great Expense, I thought it
would have been better to have built the House here & Brought
the Children to it. This I advis'd, but he was resolute in his
first Project, and rejected my Counsel, and I thereupon refus'd
to contribute. I happened soon after to attend one of his Sermons, in the Course of which I perceived he intended to finish
with a Collection, & I silently resolved he should get nothing
from me. I had in my Pocket a Handful of Copper Money, three
or four silver Dollars, and five Pistoles in Gold. As he proceeded
I began to soften, and concluded to give the Coppers. Another
Stroke of his Oratory made me asham'd of that, and determin'd
me to give the Silver; & he finish'd so admirably, that I empty'd
my Pocket wholly into the Collector's Dish, Gold and all. At
this Sermon there was also one of our Club, who being of my
Sentiments respecting the Building in Georgia, and suspecting a
Collection might be intended, had by Precaution emptied his
Pockets before he came from home; towards the Conclusion of
the Discourse however, he felt a strong Desire to give, and apply'd to a Neighbor who stood near him to borrow some
Money for the Purpose. The Application was unfortunately to
perhaps the only Man in the Company who had the firmness
not to be affected by the Preacher. His Answer was, *At any
other time, Friend Hopkinson, I would lend to thee freely; but
not now; for thee seems to be out of thy right Senses.*
    Some of Mr Whitefield's Enemies affected to suppose that he
would apply these Collections to his own private Emolument;

but I, who was intimately acquainted with him, (being employ'd in printing his Sermons and Journals, &c.) never had the least Suspicion of his Integrity, but am to this day decidedly of Opinion that he was in all his Conduct, a perfectly *honest Man.* And methinks my Testimony in his Favor ought to have the more Weight, as we had no religious Connection. He us'd indeed sometimes to pray for my Conversion, but never had the Satisfaction of believing that his Prayers were heard. Ours was a mere civil Friendship, sincere on both Sides, and lasted to his Death.

The following Instance will show something of the Terms on which we stood. Upon one of his Arrivals from England at Boston, he wrote to me that he should come soon to Philadelphia, but knew not where he could lodge when there, as he understood his old kind Host Mr Benezet was remov'd to Germantown. My Answer was; You know my House, if you can make shift with its scanty Accommodations you will be most heartily welcome. He reply'd, that if I made that kind Offer for Christ's sake, I should not miss of a Reward. And I return'd, *Don't let me be mistaken; it was not for Christ's sake, but for your sake.* One of our common Acquaintance jocosely remark'd, that knowing it to be the Custom of the Saints, when they receiv'd any favor, to shift the Burden of the Obligation from off their own Shoulders, and place it in Heaven, I had contriv'd to fix it on Earth.

The last time I saw Mr Whitefield was in London, when he consulted me about his Orphan House Concern, and his Purpose of appropriating it to the Establishment of a College.

He had a loud and clear Voice, and articulated his Words & Sentences so perfectly that he might be heard and understood at a great Distance, especially as his Auditories, however numerous, observ'd the most exact Silence. He preach'd one Evening from the Top of the Court House Steps, which are in the Middle of Market Street, and on the West Side of Second Street which crosses it at right angles. Both Streets were fill'd with his Hearers to a considerable Distance. Being among the hindmost in Market Street, I had the Curiosity to learn how far he could be heard, by retiring backwards down the Street towards the

River, and I found his Voice distinct till I came near Front-Street, when some Noise in that Street, obscur'd it. Imagining then a Semi-Circle, of which my Distance should be the Radius, and that it were fill'd with Auditors, to each of whom I allow'd two square feet, I computed that he might well be heard by more than Thirty-Thousand. This reconcil'd me to the Newspaper Accounts of his having preach'd to 25000 People in the Fields, and to the ancient Histories of Generals haranguing whole Armies, of which I had sometimes doubted.

By hearing him often I came to distinguish easily between Sermons newly compos'd, & those which he had often preach'd in the Course of his Travels. His Delivery of the latter was so improv'd by frequent Repetitions, that every Accent, every Emphasis, every Modulation of Voice, was so perfectly well turn'd and well plac'd, that without being interested in the Subject, one could not help being pleas'd with the Discourse, a Pleasure of much the same kind with that receiv'd from an excellent Piece of Music. This is an Advantage itinerant Preachers have over those who are stationary: as the latter cannot well improve their Delivery of a Sermon by so many Rehearsals.

His Writing and Printing from time to time gave great Advantage to his Enemies. Unguarded Expressions and even erroneous Opinions delivered in Preaching might have been afterwards explain'd, or qualify'd by supposing others that might have accompany'd them; or they might have been deny'd; But *litera scripta manet*. Critics attack'd his Writings violently, and with so much Appearance of Reason as to diminish the Number of his Votaries, and prevent their Increase. So that I am of Opinion, if he had never written any thing he would have left behind him a much more numerous and important Sect. And his Reputation might in that case have been still growing even after his Death; as there being nothing of his Writing on which to found a censure; and give him a lower Character, his Proselytes would be left at liberty to feign for him as great a Variety of Excellencies, as their enthusiastic Admiration might wish him to have possessed.

My Business was now continually augmenting, and my Circumstances growing daily easier, my Newspaper having become very profitable, as being for a time almost the only one in this and the neighboring Provinces. I experienc'd too the Truth of the Observation, that *after getting the first hundred Pound, it is more easy to get the second:* Money itself being of a prolific Nature.

The Partnership at Carolina having succeeded, I was encourag'd to engage in others, and to promote several of my Workmen who had behaved well, by establishing them with Printinghouses in different Colonies, on the same Terms with that in Carolina. Most of them did well, being enabled at the End of our Term, Six Years, to purchase the Types of me; and go on working for themselves, by which means several Families were raised. Partnerships often finish in Quarrels, but I was happy in this, that mine were all carry'd on and ended amicably; owing I think a good deal to the Precaution of having very explicitly settled in our Articles every thing to be done by or expected from each Partner, so that there was nothing to dispute, which Precaution I would therefore recommend to all who enter into Partnerships, for whatever Esteem Partners may have for & Confidence in each other at the time of the Contract, little Jealousies and Disgusts may arise, with Ideas of Inequality in the Care & Burden of the Business, &c. which are attended often with Breach of Friendship & of the Connection, perhaps with Lawsuits and other disagreeable Consequences.

I had on the whole abundant Reason to be satisfied with my being established in Pennsylvania. There were however two things that I regretted: There being no Provision for Defense, nor for a complete Education of Youth; No Militia nor any College. I therefore in 1743, drew up a Proposal for establishing an Academy; & at that time thinking the Revd Mr Peters, who was out of Employ, a fit Person to superintend such an Institution, I communicated the Project to him. But he having more profitable Views in the Service of the Proprietors, which succeeded, declin'd the Undertaking. And not knowing another at that time suitable for such a Trust, I let the Scheme lie a while dormant. I succeeded better the next Year, 1744, in proposing and establishing a Philosophical Society. The Paper I wrote for that purpose will be found among my Writings when collected.

With respect to Defense, Spain having been several Years at War against Britain, and being at length join'd by France, which brought us into greater Danger; and the labored & long-continued Endeavors of our Governor Thomas to prevail with our Quaker Assembly to pass a Militia Law, & make other Provisions for the Security of the Province having proved abortive, I determined to try what might be done by a voluntary Association of the People. To promote this I first wrote & published a Pamphlet, entitled, PLAIN TRUTH, in which I stated our defenseless Situation in strong Lights, with the Necessity of Union & Discipline for our Defense, and promis'd to propose in a few Days an Association to be generally signed for that purpose. The Pamphlet had a sudden & surprising Effect. I was call'd upon for the Instrument of Association: And having settled the Draft of it with a few Friends, I appointed a Meeting of the Citizens in the large Building before mentioned. The House was pretty full. I had prepared a Number of printed Copies, and provided Pens and Ink dispers'd all over the Room I harangu'd them a little on the Subject, read the Paper & explain'd it, and then distributed the Copies, which were eagerly signed, not the least Objection being made. When the Company separated, & the Papers were collected we found above Twelve hundred Hands; and other Copies being dispers'd in the Country the Subscribers amounted at length to upwards of Ten Thousand. These all furnish'd themselves as soon as they could with Arms; form'd themselves into Companies, and Regiments, chose their own Officers, & met every Week to be instructed in the manual Exercise, and other Parts of military Discipline. The Women, by Subscriptions among themselves, provided Silk Colors, which they presented to the Companies, painted with different Devices and Mottos which I supplied. The Officers of the Companies composing the Philadelphia Regiment, being met, chose me for their Colonel; but conceiving myself unfit, I declin'd that Station, & recommended Mr Lawrence, a fine Person and Man of Influence, who was accordingly appointed. I then propos'd a Lottery to defray the Expense of Building a Battery below the Town, and furnishing it with Cannon. It filled expeditiously and the Battery was soon erected, the Merlons being fram'd of

Logs & fill'd with Earth. We bought some old Cannon from Boston, but these not being sufficient, we wrote to England for more, soliciting at the same Time our Proprietaries for some Assistance, tho' without much Expectation of obtaining it. Mean while Colonel Lawrence, William Allen, Abram Taylor, Esquires, and myself were sent to New York by the Associators, commission'd to borrow some Cannon of Governor Clinton. He at first refus'd us peremptorily: but at a Dinner with his Council where there was great Drinking of Madeira Wine, as the Custom at that Place then was, he soften'd by degrees, and said he would lend us Six. After a few more Bumpers he advanc'd to Ten. And at length he very good-naturedly conceded Eighteen. They were fine Cannon, 18 pounders, with their Carriages, which we soon transported and mounted on our Battery, where the Associators kept a nightly Guard while the War lasted: And among the rest I regularly took my Turn of Duty there as a common Soldier.

My Activity in these Operations was agreeable to the Governor and Council; they took me into Confidence, & I was consulted by them in every Measure wherein their Concurrence was thought useful to the Association. Calling in the Aid of Religion, I propos'd to them the Proclaiming a Fast, to promote Reformation, & implore the Blessing of Heaven on our Undertaking. They embrac'd the Motion, but as it was the first Fast ever thought of in the Province, the Secretary had no Precedent from which to draw the Proclamation. My Education in New England, where a Fast is proclaim'd every Year, was here of some Advantage. I drew it in the accustomed Style, it was translated into German, printed in both Languages and divulg'd thro' the Province. This gave the Clergy of the different Sects an Opportunity of Influencing their Congregations to join in the Association; and it would probably have been general among all but Quakers if the Peace had not soon interven'd.

It was thought by some of my Friends that by my Activity in these Affairs, I should offend that Sect, and thereby lose my Interest in the Assembly where they were a great Majority. A young Gentleman who had likewise some Friends in the House, and wished to succeed me as their Clerk, acquainted me that it was decided to displace me at the next Election, and he therefore in Good Will advis'd me to resign, as more consistent with my Honor than being turn'd out. My Answer to him was, that I had read or heard of some Public Man, who made it a Rule never to ask for an Office, and never to refuse one when offer'd to him. I approve, says I, of his Rule, and will practise it with a small Addition; I shall never *ask*, never *refuse*, nor ever *resign* an Office. If they will have my Office of Clerk to dispose of to another, they shall take it from me. I will not by giving it up, lose my right of some time or other making Reprisals on my Adversaries. I heard however no more of this. I was chosen again, unanimously as usual, at the next Election. Possibly as they dislik'd my late Intimacy with the Members of Council, who had join'd the Governors in all the Disputes about military Preparations with which the House had long been harass'd, they might have been pleas'd if I would voluntarily have left them; but they did not care to displace me on Account merely of my Zeal for the Association; and they could not well give another Reason. Indeed I had some Cause to believe, that the Defense of the Country was not disagreeable to any of them, provided they were not requir'd to assist in it. And I found that a much greater Number of them than I could have imagined, tho' against offensive war, were clearly for the defensive. Many Pamphlets *pro* & *con* were publish'd on the Subject, and some by good Quakers in favor of Defense, which I believe convinc'd most of their younger People. A Transaction in our Fire Company gave me some Insight into their prevailing Sentiments. It had been propos'd that we should encourage the Scheme for building a Battery by laying out the present Stock, then about Sixty Pounds, in Tickets of the Lottery. By our Rules no Money could be dispos'd of but at the next Meeting after the Proposal. The Company consisted of Thirty Members, of which Twenty-two were Quakers, & Eight only of other Persuasions. We eight punctually attended the Meeting; but tho' we thought that some of the Quakers would join us, we were by no means sure of a Majority. Only one Quaker, Mr James Morris, appear'd to oppose the Measure. He express'd much Sorrow that it had ever been propos'd, as he said *Friends* were all against it, and it would create such Discord as might break up the Company. We told him, that we saw no reason for that; we were the Minority, and if *Friends* were against the Measure and outvoted us, we must and should, agreeable to the Usage of all Societies, submit. When the Hour for Business arriv'd, it was mov'd to put the Vote. He allow'd we might then do it by the Rules, but as he could assure us that a Number of Members intended to be present for the purpose of opposing it, it would be but candid to allow a little time for their appearing. While we were disputing this, a Waiter came to tell me two Gentlemen below desir'd to speak with me. I went down, and found they were two of our Quaker Members. They told me there were eight of them assembled at a Tavern just by; that they were determin'd to come and vote with us if there should be occasion, which they hop'd would not be the Case; and desir'd we would not call for their Assistance if we could do without it, as their Voting for such a Measure might embroil them with their Elders & Friends. Being thus secure of a Majority, I went up, and after a little seeming Hesitation, agreed to a Delay of another Hour. This Mr Morris allow'd to be extremely fair. Not one of his opposing Friends appear'd, at which he express'd great Surprise; and at the Expiration of the Hour, we carry'd the Resolution Eight to one; And as of the 22 Quakers, Eight were ready to vote with us and Thirteen by their Absence manifested that they were not inclin'd to oppose the Measure, I afterwards estimated the Proportion of Quakers sincerely against Defense as one to twenty one only. For these were all regular Members, of that Society, and in good Reputation among them, and had due Notice of what was propos'd at that Meeting.

The honorable & learned Mr Logan, who had always been of that Sect, was one who wrote an Address to them, declaring his Approbation of defensive War, and supporting his Opinion by many strong Arguments: He put into my Hands Sixty Pounds to be laid out in Lottery Tickets for the Battery, with Directions to apply what Prizes might be drawn wholly to that Service. He told me the following Anecdote of his old Master Wm Penn, respecting Defense. He came over from England, when a young Man, with that Proprietary, and as his Secretary. It was War

Time and their Ship was chas'd by an armed Vessel suppos'd to be an Enemy. Their Captain prepar'd for Defense, but told Wm Penn and his Company of Quakers, that he did not expect their Assistance, and they might retire into the Cabin; which they did, except James Logan, who chose to stay upon Deck, and was quarter'd to a Gun. The suppos'd Enemy prov'd a Friend; so there was no Fighting. But when the Secretary went down to communicate the Intelligence, Wm Penn rebuk'd him severely for staying upon Deck and undertaking to assist in defending the Vessel, contrary to the Principles of *Friends,* especially as it had not been required by the Captain. This Reproof being before all the Company, piqu'd the Secretary, who answer'd, *I being thy Servant, why did thee not order me to come down; but thee was willing enough that I should stay and help to fight the Ship when thee thought there was Danger.*

My being many Years in the Assembly, the Majority of which were constantly Quakers, gave me frequent Opportunities of seeing the Embarassment given them by their Principle against War, whenever Application was made to them by Order of the Crown to grant Aids for military Purposes. They were unwilling to offend Government on the one hand, by a direct Refusal, and their Friends the Body of Quakers on the other, by a Compliance contrary to their Principles. Hence a Variety of Evasions to avoid Complying, and Modes of disguising the Compliance when it became unavoidable. The common Mode at last was to grant Money under the Phrase of its being *for the King's Use,* and never to inquire how it was applied. But if the Demand was not directly from the Crown, that Phrase was found not so proper, and some other was to be invented. As when Powder was wanting, (I think it was for the Garrison at Louisburg,) and the Government of New England solicited a Grant of some from Pennsylvania, which was much urg'd on the House by Governor Thomas, they could not grant Money to buy Powder, because that was an Ingredient of War, but they voted an Aid to New England, of Three Thousand Pounds, to be put into the hands of the Governor, and appropriated it for the Purchasing of Bread, Flour, Wheat, *or other Grain.* Some of the Council desirous of giving the House still farther Embarrassment, advis'd the Governor not to accept Provision, as not being the Thing he had demanded. But he reply'd, "I shall take the Money, for I understand very well their Meaning; *Other Grain,* is Gunpowder;" which he accordingly bought; and they never objected to it. It was in Allusion to this Fact, that when in our Fire Company we feared the Success of our Proposal in favor of the Lottery, & I had said to my Friend Mr Syng, one of our Members, if we fail, let us move the Purchase of a Fire Engine with the Money; the Quakers can have no Objection to that: and then if you nominate me, and I you, as a Committee for that purpose, we will buy a great Gun, which is certainly a *Fire-Engine:* I see, says he, you have improv'd by being so long in the Assembly; your equivocal Project would be just a Match for their Wheat *or other Grain.*

These Embarassments that the Quakers suffer'd from having establish'd & published it as one of their Principles, that no kind of War was lawful, and which being once published, they could not afterwards, however they might change their minds, easily get rid of, reminds me of what I think a more prudent Conduct in another Sect among us; that of the Dunkers. I was acquainted with one of its Founders, Michael Welfare, soon after it appear'd. He complain'd to me that they were grievously calumniated by the Zealots of other Persuasions, and charg'd with abominable Principles and Practices to which they were utter Strangers. I told him this had always been the case with new Sects; and that to put a Stop to such Abuse, I imagin'd it might be well to publish the Articles of their Belief and the Rules of their Discipline. He said that it had been propos'd among them, but not agreed to, for this Reason; "When we were first drawn together as a Society, says he, it had pleased God to enlighten our Minds so far, as to see that some Doctrines which we once esteemed Truths were Errors, & that others which we had esteemed Errors were real Truths. From time to time he has been pleased to afford us farther Light, and our Principles have been improving, & our Errors diminishing. Now we are not sure that we are arriv'd at the End of this Progression, and at the Perfection of Spiritual or Theological Knowledge; and we fear that if we should once print our Confession of Faith, we should feel ourselves as if bound & confin'd by it, and perhaps be unwilling to receive farther Improvement; and our Successors still more so, as conceiving what we their Elders & Founders had done, to be something sacred, never to be departed from." This Modesty in a Sect is perhaps a singular Instance in the History of Mankind, every other Sect supposing itself in Possession of all Truth, and that those who differ are so far in the Wrong: Like a Man travelling in foggy Weather: Those at some Distance before him on the Road he sees wrapped up in the Fog, as well as those behind him, and also the People in the Fields on each side; but near him all appears clear. Tho' in truth he is as much in the Fog as any of them. To avoid this kind of Embarrassment the Quakers have of late Years been gradually declining the public Service in the Assembly & in the Magistracy. Choosing rather to quit their Power than their Principle.

In Order of Time I should have mentioned before, that having in 1742 invented an open Stove, for the better warming of Rooms and at the same time saving Fuel, as the fresh Air admitted was warmed in Entering, I made a Present of the Model to Mr Robert Grace, one of my early Friends, who having an Iron Furnace, I found the Casting of the Plates for these Stoves a profitable Thing, as they were growing in Demand. To promote that Demand I wrote and published a Pamphlet Entitled, *An Account of the New-Invented* PENNSYLVANIA FIRE PLACES: *Wherein their Construction & manner of Operation is particularly explained; their Advantages above every other Method of warming Rooms demonstrated; and all Objections that have been raised against the Use of them answered & obviated.* &c. This Pamphlet had a good Effect, Govr. Thomas was so pleas'd with the Construction of this Stove, as describ'd in it, that he offer'd to give me a Patent for the sole Vending of them for a Term of Years; but I declin'd it from a Principle which has ever weigh'd with me on such Occasions, viz. *That as we enjoy great Advantages from the Inventions of others, we should be glad of an Opportunity to serve others by any Invention of ours, and this we should do freely and generously.* An Ironmonger in London, however, after assuming a good deal of my Pamphlet,

& working it up into his own, and making some small Changes in the Machine, which rather hurt its Operation, got a Patent for it there, and made as I was told a little Fortune by it. And this is not the only Instance of Patents taken out for my Inventions by others, tho' not always with the same Success:—which I never contested, as having no Desire of profiting by Patents myself, and hating Disputes. The Use of these Fireplaces in very many Houses both of this and the neighboring Colonies, has been and is a great Saving of Wood to the Inhabitants.

Peace being concluded, and the Association Business therefore at an End, I turn'd my Thoughts again to the Affair of establishing an Academy. The first Step I took was to associate in the Design a Number of active Friends, of whom the Junto furnished a good Part: the next was to write and publish a Pamphlet entitled, *Proposals relating to the Education of Youth in Pennsylvania.* This I distributed among the principal Inhabitants gratis; and as soon as I could suppose their Minds a little prepared by the Perusal of it, I set on foot a Subscription for Opening and Supporting an Academy; it was to be paid in Quotas yearly for Five Years; by so dividing it I judg'd the Subscription might be larger, and I believe it was so, amounting to no less (if I remember right) than Five thousand Pounds. In the Introduction to these Proposals, I stated their Publication not as an Act of mine, but of some *public-spirited Gentlemen;* avoiding as much as I could, according to my usual Rule, the presenting myself to the Public as the Author of any Scheme for their Benefit.

The Subscribers, to carry the Project into immediate Execution chose out of their Number Twenty-four Trustees, and appointed Mr Francis, then Attorney General, and myself, to draw up Constitutions for the Government of the Academy, which being done and signed, a House was hired, Masters engag'd and the Schools opened I think in the same Year 1749. The Scholars Increasing fast, the House was soon found too small, and we were looking out for a Piece of Ground properly situated, with Intention to build, when Providence threw into our way a large House ready built, which with a few Alterations might well serve our purpose, this was the Building before mentioned erected by the Hearers of Mr Whitefield, and was obtain'd for us in the following Manner.

It is to be noted, that the Contributions to this Building being made by People of different Sects, Care was taken in the Nomination of Trustees, in whom the Building & Ground was to be vested, that a Predominancy should not be given to any Sect, lest in time that Predominancy might be a means of appropriating the whole to the Use of such Sect, contrary to the original Intention; it was therefore that one of each Sect was appointed, viz. one Church-of-England-man, one Presbyterian, one Baptist, one Moravian, &c. those in case of Vacancy by Death were to fill it by Election from among the Contributors. The Moravian happen'd not to please his Colleagues, and on his Death, they resolved to have no other of that Sect. The Difficulty then was, how to avoid having two of some other Sect, by means of the new Choice. Several Persons were named and for that reason not agreed to. At length one mention'd me, with the Observation that I was merely an honest Man, & of no Sect at all; which prevail'd with them to choose me. The Enthusiasm which existed when the House was built, had long since abated, and its Trustees had not been able to procure fresh Contributions for paying the Ground Rent, and discharging some other Debts the Building had occasion'd, which embarrass'd them greatly. Being now a Member of both Sets of Trustees, that for the Building & that for the Academy, I had good Opportunity of negotiating with both, & brought them finally to an Agreement, by which the Trustees for the Building were to cede it to those of the Academy, the latter undertaking to discharge the Debt, to keep forever open in the Building a large Hall for occasional Preachers according to the original Intention, and maintain a Free School for the Instruction of poor Children. Writings were accordingly drawn, and on paying the Debts the Trustees of the Academy were put in Possession of the Premises, and by dividing the great & lofty Hall into Stories, and different Rooms above & below for the several Schools, and purchasing some additional Ground, the whole was soon made fit for our purpose, and the Scholars remov'd into the Building. The

Care and Trouble of agreeing with the Workmen, purchasing Materials, and superintending the Work fell upon me, and I went thro' it the more cheerfully, as it did not then interfere with my private Business, having the Year before taken a very able, industrious & honest Partner, Mr David Hall, with whose Character I was well acquainted, as he had work'd for me four Years. He took off my Hands all Care of the Printing-Office, paying me punctually my Share of the Profits. This Partnership continued Eighteen Years, successfully for us both.

The Trustees of the Academy after a while were incorporated by a Charter from the Governor; their Funds were increas'd by Contributions in Britain, and Grants of Land from the Proprietaries, to which the Assembly has since made considerable Addition, and thus was established the present University of Philadelphia. I have been continued one of its Trustees from the Beginning, now near forty Years, and have had the very great Pleasure of seeing a Number of the Youth who have receiv'd their Education in it, distinguish'd by their improv'd Abilities, serviceable in public Stations, and Ornaments to their Country.

When I disengag'd myself as above mentioned from private Business, I flatter'd myself that by the sufficient tho' moderate Fortune I had acquir'd, I had secur'd Leisure during the rest of my Life, for Philosophical Studies and Amusements; I purchas'd all Dr Spence's Apparatus, who had come from England to lecture here; and I proceeded in my Electrical Experiments with great Alacrity, but the Public now considering me as a Man of Leisure, laid hold of me for their Purposes; every Part of our Civil Government, and almost at the same time, imposing some Duty upon me. The Governor put me into the Commission of the Peace; the Corporation of the City chose me of the Common Council, and soon after an Alderman; and the Citizens at large chose me a Burgess to represent them in Assembly. This latter Station was the more agreeable to me, as I was at length tired with sitting there to hear Debates in which as Clerk I could take no part, and which were often so unentertaining, that I was induc'd to amuse myself with making magic Squares, or Circles, or any thing to avoid Weariness. And I conceiv'd my becoming a Member would enlarge my Power of doing Good. I would not however insinuate that my Ambition was not flatter'd by all these promotions. It certainly was. For considering my low Beginning they were great Things to me. And they were still more pleasing, as being so many spontaneous Testimonies of the public's good Opinion, and by me entirely unsolicited.

The Office of Justice of the Peace I try'd a little, by attending a few Courts, and sitting on the Bench to hear Causes. But finding that more Knowledge of the Common Law than I possess'd, was necessary to act in that Station with Credit, I gradually withdrew from it, excusing myself by my being oblig'd to attend the higher Duties of a Legislator in the Assembly. My Election to this Trust was repeated every Year for Ten Years, without my ever asking any Elector for his Vote, or signifying either directly or indirectly any Desire of being chosen. On taking my Seat in the House, my Son was appointed their Clerk.

The Year following, a Treaty being to be held with the Indians at Carlisle, the Governor sent a Message to the House, proposing that they should nominate some of their Members to be join'd with some Members of Council as Commissioners for that purpose. The House nam'd the Speaker (Mr Norris) and myself; and being commission'd we went to Carlisle, and met the Indians accordingly. As those People are extremely apt to get drunk, and when so are very quarrelsome & disorderly, we strictly forbad the selling any Liquor to them; and when they complain'd of this Restriction, we told them that if they would continue sober during the Treaty, we would give them Plenty of Rum when Business was over. They promis'd this; and they kept their Promise—because they could get no Liquor—and the Treaty was conducted very orderly, and concluded to mutual Satisfaction. They then claim'd and receiv'd the Rum. This was in the Afternoon. They were near 100 Men, Women & Children, and were lodg'd in temporary Cabins built in the Form of a Square, just without the Town. In the Evening, hearing a great Noise among them, the Commissioners walk'd out to see what was the Matter. We found they had made a great Bonfire in the Middle of the Square. They were all drunk Men and Women, quarrelling and fighting. Their dark-color'd Bodies, half naked, seen only by the gloomy Light of the Bonfire, running after and beating one another with Firebrands, accompanied by their horrid Yellings, form'd a Scene the most resembling our Ideas of Hell that could well be imagin'd. There was no appeasing the Tumult, and we retired to our Lodging. At Midnight a Number of them came thundering at our Door, demanding more Rum; of which we took no Notice. The next Day, sensible they had misbehav'd in giving us that Disturbance, they sent three of their old Counsellors to make their Apology. The Orator acknowledg'd the Fault, but laid it upon the Rum; and then endeavor'd to excuse the Rum, by saying, *"The great Spirit who made all things made every thing for some Use, and whatever Use he design'd any thing for, that Use it should always be put to; Now, when he made Rum, he said,* LET THIS BE FOR INDI-ANS TO GET DRUNK WITH. *And it must be so."* And indeed if it be the Design of Providence to extirpate these Savages in order to make room for Cultivators of the Earth, it seems not improbable that Rum may be the appointed Means. It has already annihilated all the Tribes who formerly inhabited the Sea-coast.

In 1751, Dr Thomas Bond, a particular Friend of mine, conceiv'd the Idea of establishing a Hospital in Philadelphia, for the Reception and Cure of poor sick Persons, whether Inhabitants of the Province or Strangers. A very beneficent Design, which has been ascrib'd to me, but was originally his. He was zealous & active in endeavoring to procure subscriptions for it; but the Proposal being a Novelty in America, and at first not well understood, he met with small Success. At length he came to me, with the Compliment that he found there was no such thing as carrying a public Spirited Project through, without my being concern'd in it; "for," says he, "I am often ask'd by those to whom I propose Subscribing, Have you consulted Franklin upon this Business? and what does he think of it? And when I tell them that I have not, (supposing it rather out of your Line) they do not subscribe, but say they will consider of it." I inquir'd into the Nature, & probable Utility of his Scheme, and receiving from him a very satisfactory Explanation, I not only subscrib'd to it myself, but engag'd heartily in the Design of

Procuring Subscriptions from others. Previous however to the Solicitation, I endeavored to prepare the Minds of the People by writing on the Subject in the Newspapers, which was my usual Custom in such Cases, but which he had omitted. The Subscriptions afterwards were more free and generous, but beginning to flag, I saw they would be insufficient without some Assistance from the Assembly, and therefore propos'd to petition for it, which was done. The Country Members did not at first relish the Project. They objected that it could only be serviceable to the City, and therefore the Citizens should alone be at the Expense of it; and they doubted whether the Citizens themselves generally approv'd of it. My Allegation on the contrary, that it met with such Approbation as to leave no doubt of our being able to raise 2000£ by voluntary Donations, they considered as a most extravagant Supposition, and utterly impossible. On this I form'd my Plan; and asking Leave to bring in a Bill, for incorporating the Contributors according to the Prayer (of their) Petition, and granting them a blank Sum of Money, which Leave was obtain'd chiefly on the Consideration that the House could throw the Bill out if they did not like it, I drew it so as to make the important Clause a conditional One, viz. "And be it enacted by the Authority aforesaid That when the said Contributors shall have met and chosen their Managers and Treasurer, *and shall have raised by their Contributions a Capital Stock of 2000£ Value,* (the yearly Interest of which is to be applied to the Accommodating of the Sick Poor in the said Hospital, free of Charge for Diet, Attendance, Advice and Medicines) and *shall make the same appear to the Satisfaction of the Speaker of the Assembly* for the time being; that *then* it shall and may be lawful for the said Speaker, and he is hereby required to sign an Order on the Provincial Treasurer for the Payment of Two Thousand Pounds in two yearly Payments, to the Treasurer of the said Hospital, to be applied to the Founding, Building and Finishing of the same." This Condition carried the Bill through; for the Members who had oppos'd the Grant, and now conceiv'd they might have the Credit of being charitable without the Expense, agreed to its Passage; And then in soliciting Subscriptions among the People we urg'd the conditional Promise of the Law as an additional Motive to give, since every Man's Donation would be doubled. Thus the Clause work'd both ways. The Subscriptions accordingly soon exceeded the requisite sum, and we claim'd and receiv'd the Public Gift, which enabled us to carry the Design into Execution. A convenient and handsome Building was soon erected, the Institution has by constant Experience been found useful, and flourishes to this Day. And I do not remember any of my political Maneuvers, the Success of which gave me at the time more Pleasure. Or that in after-thinking of it, I more easily excus'd myself for having made some Use of Cunning.

It was about this time that another Projector, the Revd Gilbert Tennent, came to me, with a Request that I would assist him in procuring a Subscription for erecting a new Meeting-house. It was to be for the Use of a Congregation he had gathered among the Presbyterians who were originally Disciples of Mr Whitefield. Unwilling to make myself disagreeable to my fellow Citizens, by too frequently soliciting their Contributions, I absolutely refus'd. He then desir'd I would furnish him with a List of the Names of Persons I knew by Experience to be generous and public-spirited. I thought it would be unbecoming in me, after their kind Compliance with my Solicitations, to mark them out to be worried by other Beggars, and therefore refus'd also to give such a List. He then desir'd I would at least give him my Advice. That I will readily do, said I; and, in the first Place, I advise you to apply to all those whom you know will give something; next to those whom you are uncertain whether they will give any-thing or not; and show them the List of those who have given: and lastly, do not neglect those who you are sure will give nothing; for in some of them you may be mistaken. He laugh'd, thank'd me, and said he would take my Advice. He did so, for he ask'd of *every body;* and he obtain'd a much larger Sum than he expected, with which he erected the capacious and very elegant Meeting-house that stands in Arch Street.

Our City, tho' laid out with a beautiful Regularity, the Streets large, straight, and crossing each other at right Angles, had the Disgrace of suffering those Streets to remain long unpav'd, and in wet Weather the Wheels of heavy Carriages plough'd them into a Quagmire, so that it was difficult to cross them. And in dry Weather the Dust was offensive. I had liv'd near what was called the Jersey Market, and saw with Pain the Inhabitants wading in Mud while purchasing their Provisions. A Strip of Ground down the middle of that Market was at length pav'd with Brick, so that being once in the Market they had firm Footing, but were often over Shoes in Dirt to get there. By talking and writing on the Subject, I was at length instrumental in getting the Street pav'd with Stone between the Market and the brick'd Foot Pavement that was on each Side next the Houses. This for some time gave an easy Access to the Market, dryshod. But the rest of the Street not being pav'd, whenever a Carriage came out of the Mud upon this Pavement, it shook off and left its Dirt on it, and it was soon cover'd with Mire, which was not remov'd, the City as yet having no Scavengers. After some Inquiry I found a poor industrious Man, who was willing to undertake keeping the Pavement clean, by sweeping it twice a week & carrying off the Dirt from before all the Neighbors' Doors, for the Sum of Sixpence per Month, to be paid by each House. I then wrote and printed a Paper, setting forth the Advantages to the Neighborhood that might be obtain'd by this small Expense; the greater Ease in keeping our Houses clean, so much Dirt not being brought in by People's Feet; the Benefit to the Shops by more Custom, as Buyers could more easily get at them, and by not having in windy Weather the Dust blown in upon their Goods, &c. &c. I sent one of these Papers to each House, and in a Day or two went round to see who would subscribe an Agreement to pay these Sixpences. It was unanimously sign'd, and for a time well executed. All the Inhabitants of the City were delighted with the Cleanliness of the Pavement that surrounded the Market, it being a Convenience to all; and this rais'd a general Desire to have all the Streets paved; & made the People more willing to submit to a Tax for that purpose. After some time I drew a Bill for Paving the City, and brought it into the Assembly. It was just before I went to England in 1757, and did not pass till I was gone, and then with an Alteration in the Mode of Assessment, which I thought not for the better, but with an additional Provision for lighting as well as Paving the Streets; which was a great Improvement. It was by a private Person, the late Mr John Clifton, his giving a Sample of the Utility of Lamps by placing one at his Door, that the People were first impress'd with the Idea of enlightening all the City. The Honor of this public Benefit has also been ascrib'd to me, but it belongs truly to that Gentleman. I did but follow his Example; and have only some Merit to claim respecting the Form of our Lamps as differing from the Globe Lamps we at first were supply'd with from London. Those we found inconvenient in these respects; they admitted no Air below, the Smoke therefore did not readily go out above, but circulated in the Globe, lodg'd on its Inside, and soon obstructed the Light they were intended to afford; giving, besides, the daily Trouble of wiping them clean; and an accidental Stroke on one of them would demolish it, & render it totally useless. I therefore suggested the composing them of four flat Panes, with a long Funnel above to draw up the Smoke, and Crevices admitting Air below, to facilitate the Ascent of the Smoke. By this means they were kept clean, and did not grow dark in a few Hours as the London Lamps do, but continu'd bright till Morning; and an accidental Stroke would generally break but a single Pane, easily repair'd. I have sometimes wonder'd that the Londoners did not from the Effect Holes in the Bottom of the Globe Lamps us'd at Vauxhall, have in keeping them clean, learn to have such Holes in their Street Lamps. But those Holes being made for another purpose, viz. to communicate Flame more suddenly to the Wick, by a little Flax hanging down thro' them, the other Use of letting in Air seems not to have been thought of. And therefore, after the Lamps have been lit a few Hours, the Streets of London are very poorly illuminated.

The Mention of these Improvements puts me in mind of one I propos'd when in London, to Dr Fothergill, who was among the best Men I have known, and a great Promoter of useful Projects. I had observ'd that the Streets when dry were never swept and the light Dust carried away, but it was suffer'd to accumulate till wet Weather reduced it to Mud and then after lying some Days so deep on the Pavement that there was no Crossing but in Paths kept clean by poor People with Brooms, it was with great Labor rak'd together & thrown up into Carts open above, the Sides of which suffer'd some of the Slush at every jolt on the Pavement to shake out and fall, some times to the Annoyance of Foot-Passengers. The Reason given for not sweeping the dusty Streets was, that the Dust would fly into the Windows of Shops and Houses. An accidental Occurrence had instructed me how much Sweeping might be done in a little Time. I found at my Door in Craven Street one Morning a poor Woman sweeping my Pavement with a birch Broom. She appeared very pale & feeble as just come out of a Fit of Sickness. I ask'd who employ'd her to sweep there. She said, "Nobody; but I am very poor and in Distress, and I sweeps before Gentlefolkeses Doors, and hopes they will give me something." I bid her sweep the whole Street clean and I would give her a Shilling. This was at 9 a Clock. At 12 she came for the Shilling. From the slowness I saw at first in her Working, I could scarce believe that the Work was done so soon, and sent my Servant to examine it, who reported that the whole Street was swept perfectly clean, and all the Dust plac'd in the Gutter which was in the Middle. And the next Rain wash'd it quite away, so that the Pavement & even the Kennel was perfectly clean. I then judg'd that if that feeble Woman could sweep such a Street in 3 Hours, a strong active Man might have done it in half the time. And here let me remark the Convenience of having but one Gutter in such a narrow Street, running down its Middle instead of two, one on each Side near the Footway. For where all the Rain that falls on a Street runs from the Sides and meets in the middle, it forms there a Current strong enough to wash away all the Mud it meets with: But when divided into two Channels, it is often too weak to cleanse either, and only makes the Mud it finds more fluid, so that the Wheels of Carriages and Feet of Horses throw and dash it up on the Foot Pavement which is thereby rendered foul and slippery, and sometimes splash it upon those who are walking. My Proposal communicated to the good Doctor, was as follows:

"For the more effectual cleaning and keeping clean the Streets of London and Westminster, it is proposed,

"That the several Watchmen be contracted with to have the Dust swept up in dry Seasons, and the Mud rak'd up at other Times, each in the several Streets & Lanes of his Round.

"That they be furnish'd with Brooms and other proper Instruments for these purposes, to be kept at their respective Stands, ready to furnish the poor People they may employ in the Service.

"That in the dry Summer Months the Dust be all swept up into Heaps at proper Distances, before the Shops and Windows of Houses are usually opened: when the Scavengers with close-covered Carts shall also carry it all away.

"That the Mud when rak'd up be not left in Heaps to be spread abroad again by the Wheels of Carriages & Trampling of Horses; but that the Scavengers be provided with Bodies of Carts, not plac'd high upon Wheels, but low upon Sliders; with Lattice Bottoms, which being cover'd with Straw, will retain the Mud thrown into them, and permit the Water to drain from it, whereby it will become much lighter, Water making the greatest Part of its Weight. These Bodies of Carts to be plac'd at convenient Distances, and the Mud brought to them in Wheelbarrows, they remaining where plac'd till the Mud is drain'd, and then Horses brought to draw them away."

I have since had Doubts of the Practicability of the latter Part of this Proposal, on Account of the Narrowness of some Streets, and the Difficulty of placing the Draining Sleds so as not to encumber too much the Passage: But I am still of Opinion that the former, requiring the Dust, to be swept up & carry'd away before the Shops are open, is very practicable in the Summer, when the Days are long: For in Walking thro' the Strand and Fleetstreet one Morning at 7 a Clock I observ'd there was not one shop open tho' it had been Daylight & the Sun up above three Hours. The Inhabitants of London choosing voluntarily to live much by Candle Light, and sleep by Sunshine; and yet often complain a little absurdly, of the Duty on Candles and the high Price of Tallow.

Some may think these trifling Matters not worth minding or relating. But when they consider, that tho' Dust blown into the Eyes of a single Person, or into a single Shop on a windy Day, is but of small Importance, yet the great Number of the Instances in a populous City, and its frequent Repetitions give it Weight & Consequence; perhaps they will not censure very severely those who bestow some of Attention to Affairs of this seemingly low Nature. Human Felicity is produc'd not so much by great Pieces of good Fortune that seldom happen, as by little Advantages that occur every Day. Thus if you teach a poor young Man to shave himself and keep his Razor in order, you may contribute more to the Happiness of his Life than in giving him a 1000 Guineas. The Money may be soon spent, the Regret only remaining of having foolishly consum'd it. But in the other Case he escapes the frequent Vexation of waiting for Barbers, & of their some times, dirty Fingers, offensive Breaths and dull Razors. He shaves when most convenient to him, and enjoys daily the Pleasure of its being done with a good Instrument. With these Sentiments I have hazarded the few preceding Pages, hoping they may afford Hints which some time or other may be useful to a City I love, having lived many Years in it very happily; and perhaps to some of our Towns in America.

Having been for some time employed by the Postmaster General of America, as his Comptroller in regulating the several Offices, and bringing the Officers to account, I was upon his Death in 1753 appointed jointly with Mr William Hunter to succeed him, by a Commission from the Postmaster General in England. The American Office had never hitherto paid any thing to that of Britain. We were to have 600£ a Year between us if we could make that Sum out of the Profits of the Office. To do this, a Variety of Improvements were necessary; some of these were inevitably at first expensive; so that in the first four Years the Office became above 900£ in debt to us. But it soon after began to repay us, and before I was displac'd, by a Freak of the Minister's, of which I shall speak hereafter, we had brought it to yield *three times* as much clear Revenue to the Crown as the Post-Office of Ireland. Since that imprudent Transaction, they have receiv'd from it—Not one Farthing.

The Business of the Post-Office occasion'd my taking a Journey this Year to New England, where the College of Cambridge of their own Motion, presented me with the Degree of Master

of Arts. Yale College in Connecticut, had before made me a
similar Compliment. Thus without studying in any College I
came to partake of their Honors. They were confer'd in Consideration of my Improvements & Discoveries in the electric
Branch of Natural Philosophy.

In 1754, War with France being again apprehended, a Con-
gress of Commissioners from the different Colonies, was by an
Order of the Lords of Trade, to be assembled at Albany, there
to confer with the Chiefs of the Six Nations, concerning the
Means of defending both their Country and ours. Governor
Hamilton, having receiv'd this Order, acquainted the House
with it, requesting they would furnish proper Presents for the
Indians to be given on this Occasion; and naming the Speaker
(Mr Norris) and myself, to join Mr Thomas Penn & Mr Secretary Peters, as Commissioners to act for Pennsylvania. The
House approv'd the Nomination, and provided the Goods for
the Present, tho' they did not much like treating out of the
Province, and we met the other Commissioners and met at Albany about the Middle of June. In our Way thither, I projected
and drew up a Plan for the Union of all the Colonies, under one
Government so far as might be necessary for Defense, and other
important general Purposes. As we pass'd thro' New York, I
had there shown my Project to Mr James Alexander & M^r
Kennedy, two Gentlemen of great Knowledge in public Affairs,
and being fortified by their Approbation I ventur'd to lay it before the Congress. It then appear'd that several of the Commissioners had form'd Plans of the same kind. A previous Question
was first taken whether a Union should be established, which
pass'd in the Affirmative unanimously. A Committee was then
appointed one Member from each Colony, to consider the several Plans and report. Mine happen'd to be prefer'd, and with a
few Amendments was accordingly reported. By this Plan, the
general Government was to be administered by a President
General appointed and supported by the Crown, and a Grand
Council to be chosen by the Representatives of the People of the
several Colonies met in their respective Assemblies. The Debates upon it in Congress went on daily hand in hand with the
Indian Business. Many Objections and Difficulties were started,

but at length they were all overcome, and the Plan was unanimously agreed to, and Copies ordered to be transmitted to the Board of Trade and to the Assemblies of the several Provinces. Its Fate was singular. The Assemblies did not adopt it as they all thought there was too much *prerogative* in it; and in England it was judg'd to have too much of the *Democratic:* The Board of Trade therefore did not approve it; nor recommend it for the Approbation of his Majesty; but another Scheme was form'd (suppos'd better to answer the same Purpose) whereby the Governors of the Provinces with some Members of their respective Councils were to meet and order the raising of Troops, building of Forts, &c. &c. to draw on the Treasury of Great Britain for the Expense, which was afterwards to be refunded by an Act of Parliament laying a Tax on America. My Plan, with my Reasons in support of it, is to be found among my political Papers that are printed.

Being the Winter following in Boston, I had much Conversation with Govr Shirley upon both the Plans. Part of what pass'd between us on the Occasion may also be seen among those Papers. The different & contrary Reasons of dislike to my Plan, makes me suspect that it was really the true Medium; & I am still of Opinion it would have been happy for both Sides the Water if it had been adopted. The Colonies so united would have been sufficiently strong to have defended themselves; there would then have been no need of Troops from England; of course the subsequent Pretense for Taxing America, and the bloody Contest it occasioned, would have been avoided. But such Mistakes are not new; History is full of the Errors of States & Princes.

> "Look round the habitable World, how few
> Know their own Good, or knowing it pursue."

Those who govern, having much Business on their hands, do not generally like to take the Trouble of considering and carrying into Execution new Projects. The best public Measures are therefore seldom *adopted from previous Wisdom,* but *forc'd by the Occasion.*

The Governor of Pennsylvania in sending it down to the

Assembly, express'd his Approbation of the Plan "as appearing to him to be drawn up with great Clearness & Strength of Judgment, and therefore recommended it as well worthy their closest & most serious Attention." The House however, by the Management of a certain Member, took it up when I happen'd to be absent, which I thought not very fair, and reprobated it without paying any Attention to it at all, to my no small Mortification.

In my Journey to Boston this Year I met at New York with our new Governor, Mr Morris, just arriv'd there from England; with whom I had been before intimately acquainted. He brought a Commission to supersede Mr Hamilton, who, tir'd with the Disputes his Proprietary Instructions subjected him to, had resigned. Mr Morris ask'd me, if I thought he must expect as uncomfortable an Administration. I said, No; you may on the contrary have a very comfortable one, if you will only take care not to enter into any Dispute with the Assembly. "My dear Friend," says he, pleasantly, "how can you advise my avoiding Disputes. You know I love Disputing; it is one of my greatest Pleasures: However, to show the Regard I have for your Counsel, I promise you I will if possible avoid them." He had some Reason for loving to dispute, being eloquent, an acute Sophister, and therefore generally successful in argumentative Conversation. He had been brought up to it from a Boy, his Father (as I have heard) accustoming his Children to dispute with one another for his Diversion while sitting at Table after Dinner. But I think the Practice was not wise, for in the Course of my Observation, these disputing, contradicting & confuting People are generally unfortunate in their Affairs. They get Victory sometimes, but they never get Good Will, which would be of more use to them. We parted, he going to Philadelphia, and I to Boston. In returning, I met at New York with the Votes of the Assembly, by which it appear'd that notwithstanding his Promise to me, he and the House were already in high Contention, and it was a continual Battle between them, as long as he retain'd the Government. I had my Share of it; for as soon as I got back to my Seat in the Assembly, I was put on every Committee for answering his Speeches and Messages, and by the Committees always desired to make the Drafts. Our Answers as well as his Messages were often tart, and sometimes indecently abusive. And as he knew I wrote for the Assembly, one might have imagined that when we met we could hardly avoid cutting Throats. But he was so good-natur'd a Man, that no personal Difference between him and me was occasion'd by the Contest, and we often din'd together. One Afternoon in the height of this public Quarrel, we met in the Street. "Franklin," says he, "you must go home with me and spend the Evening. I am to have some Company that you will like"; and taking me by the Arm he led me to his House. In gay Conversation over our Wine after Supper he told us Jokingly that he much admir'd the Idea of Sancho Panza, who when it was propos'd to give him a Government, requested it might be a Government of *Blacks*, as then, if he could not agree with his People he might sell them. One of his Friends who sat next me, says, "Franklin, why do you continue to side with these damn'd Quakers? had not you better sell them? the Proprietor would give you a good Price." The Governor, says I, has not yet *black'd* them enough. He had indeed labor'd hard to blacken the Assembly in all his Messages, but they wip'd off his Coloring as fast as he laid it on, and plac'd it in return thick upon his own Face; so that finding he was likely to be negrify'd himself, he as well as Mr Hamilton, grew tir'd of the Contest, and quitted the Government.

These public Quarrels were all at bottom owing to the Proprietaries, our hereditary Governors; who when any Expense was to be incurr'd for the Defense of their Province, with incredible Meanness instructed their Deputies to pass no Act for levying the necessary Taxes, unless their vast Estates were in the same Act expressly excused; and they had even taken Bonds of these Deputies to observe such Instructions. The Assemblies for three Years held out against this Injustice, tho' constrain'd to bend at last. At length Capt. Denny, who was Governor Morris's Successor, ventur'd to disobey those instructions; how that was brought about I shall show hereafter.

But I am got forward too fast with my Story; there are still some Transactions to be mentioned that happened during the Administration of Governor Morris.

War being, in a manner, commenced with France, the Government of Massachusetts Bay projected an Attack upon

Crown Point, and sent Mr Quincy to Pennsylvania, and Mr Pownall, afterwards Govr Pownall, to N. York to solicit Assistance. As I was in the Assembly, knew its Temper, & was Mr Quincy's Countryman, he apply'd to me for my Influence & Assistance. I dictated his Address to them which was well receiv'd. They voted an Aid of ten Thousand Pounds; to be laid out in Provisions. But the Governor refusing his Assent to their Bill, (which included this with other Sums granted for the Use of the Crown) unless a Clause were inserted exempting the Proprietary Estate from bearing any Part of the Tax that would be necessary, the Assembly, tho' very desirous of making their Grant to New England effectual, were at a Loss how to accomplish it. Mr Quincy labored hard with the Governor to obtain his Assent, but he was obstinate. I then suggested a Method of doing the Business without the Governor, by Orders on the Trustees of the Loan-Office, which by Law the Assembly had the Right of Drawing. There was indeed little or no Money at that time in the Office, and therefore I propos'd that the Orders should be payable in a Year and to bear an Interest of Five per C^t. With these Orders I suppos'd the Provisions might easily be purchas'd. The Assembly with very little Hesitation adopted the Proposal. The Orders were immediately printed, and I was one of the Committee directed to sign and dispose of them. The Fund for Paying them was the Interest of all the Paper Currency then extant in the Province upon Loan, together with the Revenue arising from the Excise which being known to be more than sufficient, they obtain'd instant Credit, and were not only receiv'd in Payment for the Provisions, but many money'd People who had Cash lying by them, vested it in those Orders, which they found advantageous, as they bore Interest while upon hand, and might on any Occasion be used as Money: So that they were eagerly all bought up, and in a few Weeks none of them were to be seen. Thus this important Affair was by my means completed, Mr Quincy return'd Thanks to the Assembly in a handsome Memorial, went home highly pleas'd with the Success of his Embassy, and ever after bore for me the most cordial and affectionate Friendship.

The British Government not choosing to permit the Union of the Colonies, as propos'd at Albany, and to trust that Union with their Defense, lest they should thereby grow too military, and feel their own Strength, Suspicions & Jealousies at this time being entertain'd of them; sent over General Braddock with two Regiments of Regular English Troops for that purpose. He landed at Alexandria in Virginia, and thence march'd to Frederic Town in Maryland, where he halted for Carriages. Our Assembly apprehending, from some Information, that he had conceived violent Prejudices against them, as averse to the Service, wish'd me to wait upon him, not as from them, but as Postmaster General, under the guise of proposing to settle with him the Mode of conducting with most Celerity and Certainty the Dispatches between him and the Governors of the several Provinces, with whom he must necessarily have continual Correspondence, and of which they propos'd to pay the Expense. My Son accompanied me on this Journey. We found the General at Frederic Town, waiting impatiently for the Return of those he had sent thro' the back Parts of Maryland & Virginia to collect Wagons. I stayed with him several Days, Din'd with him daily, and had full Opportunity of removing all his Prejudices, by the Information of what the Assembly had before his Arrival actually done and were still willing to do to facilitate his Operations. When I was about to depart, the Returns of Wagons to be obtain'd were brought in, by which it appear'd that they amounted only to twenty-five, and not all of those were in serviceable Condition. The General and all the Officers were surpris'd, declar'd the Expedition was then at an End, being impossible, and exclaim'd against the Ministers for ignorantly landing them in a Country destitute of the Means of conveying their Stores, Baggage, &c. not less than 150 Wagons being necessary. I happen'd to say, I thought it was pity they had not been landed rather in Pennsylvania, as in that Country almost every Farmer had his Wagon. The General eagerly laid hold of my Words, and said, "Then you, Sir, who are a Man of Interest there, can probably procure them for us; and I beg you will undertake it." I ask'd what Terms were to be offer'd the Owners of the Wagons; and I was desir'd to put on Paper the Terms that appear'd to me necessary. This I did, and they were agreed to, and a Commission and Instructions accordingly prepar'd immediately.

What those Terms were will appear in the Advertisement I publish'd as soon as I arriv'd at Lancaster; which being, from the
great and sudden Effect it produc'd, a Piece of some Curiosity,
I shall insert at length, as follows.

"ADVERTISEMENT."
"*Lancaster, April 26, 1753.*"

"Whereas, 150 wagons, with 4 horses to each wagon, and
1500 saddle or pack horses, are wanted for the service of his
Majesty's forces, now about to rendezvous at Wills's Creek;
and his Excellency General Braddock having been pleased to
empower me to contract for the hire of the same; I hereby give
notice, that I shall attend for that purpose at Lancaster from this
day to next Wednesday evening; and at York from next Thursday
morning, till Friday evening; where I shall be ready to agree for
wagons and teams; or single horses, on the following terms:
viz. 1. That there shall be paid for each wagon with four good
horses and a driver, fifteen shillings per diem. And for each able
horse with a pack-saddle, or other saddle and furniture, two
shillings per diem. And for each able horse without a saddle,
eighteen pence per diem. 2. That the pay commence from the
time of their joining the forces at Wills's Creek (which must
be on or before the 20th May ensuing) and that a reasonable
allowance be paid over and above for the time necessary for
their travelling to Wills's Creek and home again after their discharge. 3. Each wagon and team, and every saddle or pack-horse,
is to be valued by indifferent persons chosen between me and
the owner; and in case of the loss of any wagon, team or other
horse in the service, the price according to such valuation is to be
allowed and paid. 4. Seven days' pay is to be advanced and paid
in hand by me to the owner of each wagon and team, or horse, at
the time of contracting, if required; and the remainder to be
paid by General Braddock, or by the paymaster of the army, at
the time of their discharge; or from time to time as it shall be
demanded. 5. No drivers of wagons, or persons taking care of
the hired horses, are on any account to be called upon to do the
duty of soldiers, or be otherwise employed than in conducting or

taking care of their carriages or horses. 6. All oats, indian corn, or other forage, that wagons or horses bring to the camp, more than is necessary for the subsistence of the horses, is to be taken for the use of the army, and a reasonable price paid for the same."

"Note—My son, William Franklin, is empowered to enter into like contracts, with any person in Cumberland County.

"B. FRANKLIN."

"To the Inhabitants of the Counties
of Lancaster, York, and Cumberland.

"FRIENDS AND COUNTRYMEN,

"Being occasionally at the camp at Frederic, a few days since, I found the general and officers extremely exasperated on account of their not being supplied with horses and carriages, which had been expected from this province, as most able to furnish them; but through the dissensions between our Governor and Assembly, money had not been provided, nor any steps taken for that purpose.

"It was proposed to send an armed force immediately into these counties, to seize as many of the best carriages and horses as should be wanted, and compel as many persons into the service, as would be necessary to drive and take care of them.

"I apprehended that the progress of British soldiers through these counties on such an occasion, (especially considering the temper they are in, and their resentment against us,) would be attended with many and great inconveniences to the inhabitants, and therefore more willingly took the trouble of trying first what might be done by fair and equitable means. The people of these back counties have lately complained to the Assembly that a sufficient currency was wanting; you have an opportunity of receiving and dividing among you a very considerable sum; for if the service of this expedition should continue (as it is more than probable it will) for 120 days, the hire of these wagons and horses will amount to upwards of thirty thousand pounds; which will be paid you in silver and gold of the King's money.

"The service will be light and easy, for the army will scarce march above twelve miles per day, and the wagons and baggage horses, as they carry those things that are absolutely necessary to the welfare of the army, must march with the army, and no faster; and are for the army's sake, always placed where they can be most secure, whether in a march or in a camp.

"If you are really, as I believe you are, good and loyal subjects to His Majesty, you may now do a most acceptable service, and make it easy to yourselves; for three or four of such as cannot separately spare from the business of their plantations, a wagon and four horses and a driver, may do it together; one furnishing the wagon, another one or two horses, and another the driver, and divide the pay proportionably between you: but if you do not this service to your King and country voluntarily, when such good pay and reasonable terms are offered to you, your loyalty will be strongly suspected: the King's business must be done: so many brave troops, come so far for your defense, must not stand idle through your backwardness to do what may be reasonably expected from you: wagons and horses must be had, violent measures will probably be used; and you will be to seek for a recompence where you can find it, and your case perhaps be little pitied or regarded.

"I have no particular interest in this affair, as (except the satisfaction of endeavoring to do good) I shall have only my labor for my pains. If this method of obtaining the wagons and horses is not likely to succeed, I am obliged to send word to the General in fourteen days; and I suppose, Sir John St. Clair, the hussar, with a body of soldiers, will immediately enter the province for the purpose; which I shall be sorry to hear, because I am very sincerely and truly

> "Your friend and well-wisher,
> "B. FRANKLIN."

I receiv'd of the General about 800£ to be disburs'd in Advance-money to the Wagon-Owners &c: but that Sum being insufficient, I advanc'd upwards of 200£ more, and in two Weeks, the 150 Wagons with 259 carrying Horses were on their March for the Camp. The Advertisement promised Payment according to the Valuation, in case any Wagon or Horse should be lost. The Owners however, alleging they did not know General Braddock, or what dependance might be had on his Promise, insisted on my Bond for the Performance, which I accordingly gave them.

While I was at the Camp, supping one Evening with the Officers of Col. Dunbar's Regiment, he represented to me his concern for the Subalterns, who he said were generally not in Affluence, and could ill afford in this dear Country to lay in the Stores that might be necessary in so long a March thro' a Wilderness where nothing was to be purchas'd. I commiserated their case, and resolved to endeavor procuring them some relief. I said nothing, however, to him of my Intention, but wrote the next Morning to the Committee of Assembly, who had the Disposition of some public Money, warmly recommending the Case of these Officers to their Consideration, and proposing that a Present should be sent them of Necessaries & Refreshments. My Son, who had had some Experience of a Camp Life, and of its Wants, drew up a List for me, which I inclos'd in my Letter. The Committee approv'd, and used such Diligence, that conducted by my Son, the Stores arrived at the Camp as soon as the Wagons. They consisted of 20 Parcels, each containing

> 6 lb Loaf Sugar
> 6 lb good Muscovado D°
> 1 lb good Green Tea
> 1 lb good Bohea D°
> 6 lb good ground Coffee
> 6 lb Chocolate
> ½ Cʷᵗ. best white Biscuit
> ½ lb Pepper
> 1 Quart best white Wine Vinegar
> 1 Gloucester Cheese
> 1 Kegg containing 20 lb good Butter
> 2 Doz. old Madeira Wine
> 2 Gallons Jamaica Spirits
> 1 Bottle Flour of Mustard
> 2 well-cur'd Hams
> ½ Doz. dry'd Tongues
> 6 lb Rice
> 6 lb Raisins.

These 20 Parcels well pack'd were plac'd on as many Horses, each Parcel with the Horse, being intended as a Present for one Officer. They were very thankfully receiv'd, and the Kindness acknowledg'd by Letters to me from the Colonels of both Regiments in the most grateful Terms. The General too was highly satisfied with my Conduct in procuring him the Wagons, &c. and readily paid my Account of Disbursements; thanking me repeatedly and requesting my farther Assistance in sending Provisions after him. I undertook this also, and was busily employ'd in it till we heard of his Defeat, advancing, for the Service, of my own Money, upwards of 1000£ Sterling, of which I sent him an Account. It came to his Hands luckily for me a few Days before the Battle, and he return'd me immediately an Order on the Paymaster for the round Sum of 1000£ leaving the Remainder to the next Account. I consider this Payment as good Luck; having never been able to obtain that Remainder, of which more hereafter.

This General was I think a brave Man, and might probably have made a Figure as a good Officer in some European War. But he had too much self-confidence, too high an Opinion of the Validity of Regular Troops, and too mean a One of both Americans and Indians. George Croghan, our Indian Interpreter, join'd him on his March with 100 of those People, who might have been of great Use to his Army as Guides, Scouts, &c. if he had treated them kindly; but he slighted & neglected them, and they gradually left him. In Conversation with him one day, he was giving me some Account of his intended Progress. "After taking Fort Duquesne," says he, "I am to proceed to Niagara; and having taken that, to Frontenac, if the Season will allow time; and I suppose it will; for Duquesne can hardly detain me above three or four Days; and then I see nothing that can obstruct my March to Niagara." Having before revolv'd in my Mind the long Line his Army must make in their March, by a very narrow Road to be cut for them thro' the Woods & Bushes; & also what I had read of a former Defeat of 1500 French who invaded the Iroquois Country, I had conceiv'd some Doubts & some Fears for the Event of the Campaign. But I ventur'd only to say, To be sure, Sir, if you arrive

well before Duquesne, with these fine Troops so well provided
with Artillery, that Place, not yet completely fortified, and as we
hear with no very strong Garrison, can probably make but a
short Resistance. The only Danger I apprehend of Obstruction
to your March, is from Ambuscades of Indians, who by constant Practice are dextrous in laying & executing them. And the
slender Line, near four Miles long, which your Army must
make, may expose it to be attack'd by Surprise in its Flanks,
and to be cut like a Thread into several Pieces, which from their
Distance cannot come up in time to support each other. He
smil'd at my Ignorance, & reply'd, "These Savages may indeed
be a formidable Enemy to your raw American Militia; but upon
the King's regular & disciplin'd Troops, Sir, it is impossible
they should make any Impression." I was conscious of an Impropriety in my Disputing with a military Man in Matters of
his Profession, and said no more—The Enemy however did not
take the Advantage of his Army which I apprehended its long
Line of March expos'd it to, but let it advance without Interruption till within 9 Miles of the Place; and then when more in
a Body, (for it had just pass'd a River where the Front had
halted till all were come over) & in a more open Part of the
Woods than any it had pass'd, attack'd its advanc'd Guard, by a
heavy Fire from behind Trees & Bushes; which was the first Intelligence the General had of an Enemy's being near him. This
Guard being disordered, the General hurried the Troops up to
their Assistance, which was done in great Confusion thro' Wagons, Baggage and Cattle; and presently the Fire came upon their
Flank; the Officers being on Horseback were more easily distinguish'd, pick'd out as Marks, and fell very fast; and the Soldiers
were crowded together in a Huddle, having or hearing no Orders, and standing to be shot at till two thirds of them were
killed, and then being seiz'd with a Panic the whole fled with
Precipitation. The Wagoners took each a Horse out of his
Team, and scamper'd; their Example was immediately follow'd
by others, so that all the Wagons, Provisions, Artillery and
Stores were left to the Enemy. The General being wounded was
brought off with Difficulty, his Secretary Mr Shirley was killed by

his Side, and out of 86 Officers 63 were killed or wounded, and 714 Men killed out of 1100. These 1100 had been picked Men, from the whole Army, the Rest had been left behind with Col. Dunbar, who was to follow with the heavier Part of the Stores, Provisions and Baggage. The Flyers, not being pursu'd, arriv'd at Dunbar's Camp, and the Panic they brought with them instantly seiz'd him and all his People. And tho' he had now above 1000 Men, and the Enemy who had beaten Braddock did not at most exceed 400, Indians and French together; instead of Proceeding and endeavoring to recover some of the lost Honor, he order'd all the Stores Ammunition, &c to be destroy'd, that he might have more Horses to assist his Flight towards the Settlements, and less Lumber to remove. He was there met with Requests from the Governors of Virginia, Maryland and Pennsylvania, that he would post his Troops on the Frontiers so as to afford some Protection to the Inhabitants; but he continu'd his hasty March thro' all the Country, not thinking himself safe till he arriv'd at Philadelphia, where the Inhabitants could protect him. This whole Transaction gave us Americans the first Suspicion that our exalted Ideas of the Prowess of British Regulars had not been well founded.

In their first March too, from their Landing till they got beyond the Settlements, they had plundered and stripped the Inhabitants, totally ruining some poor Families, besides insulting, abusing & confining the People if they remonstrated. This was enough to put us out of Conceit of such Defenders if we had really wanted any. How different was the Conduct of our French Friends in 1781, who during a March thro' the most inhabited Part of our Country, from Rhode Island to Virginia, near 700 Miles, occasion'd not the smallest Complaint, for the Loss of a Pig, a Chicken, or even an Apple!

Capt. Orme, who was one of the General's Aid de Camps, and being grievously wounded was brought off with him, and continu'd with him to his Death, which happen'd in a few Days, told me, that he was totally silent, all the first Day, and at Night only said, *Who'd have thought it?* that he was silent again the following Days, only saying at last, *We shall better*

know how to deal with them another time; and dy'd a few
Minutes after.

The Secretary's Papers with all the General's Orders, Instructions and Correspondence falling into the Enemy's Hands, they
selected and translated into French a Number of the Articles,
which they printed to prove the hostile Intentions of the British
Court before the Declaration of War. Among these I saw some
Letters of the General to the Ministry speaking highly of the
great Service I had rendered the Army, & recommending me to
their Notice. David Hume too, who was some Years after Secretary to Lord Harcourt when Minister in France, and afterwards to Genl Conway when Secretary of State, told me he had
seen among the Papers in that Office Letters from Braddock
highly recommending me. But the Expedition having been unfortunate, my Service it seems was not thought of much Value,
for those Recommendations were never of any Use to me.

As to Rewards from himself, I ask'd only one, which was,
that he would give Orders to his Officers not to enlist any more
of our bought Servants, and that he would discharge such as
had been already enlisted. This he readily granted, and several
were accordingly return'd to their Masters on my Application.
Dunbar, when the Command devolv'd on him, was not so generous. He Being at Philadelphia on his Retreat, or rather Flight,
I apply'd to him for the Discharge of the Servants of three poor
Farmers of Lancaster County that he had enlisted, reminding
him of the late General's Orders on that head. He promis'd me,
that if the Masters would come to him at Trenton, where he
should be in a few Days on his March to New York, he would
there deliver their Men to them. They accordingly were at the
Expense & Trouble of going to Trenton, and there he refus'd to
perform his Promise, to their great Loss & Disappointment.

As soon as the Loss of the Wagons and Horses was generally
known, all the Owners came upon me for the Valuation which
I had given Bond to pay. Their Demands gave me a great deal of
Trouble, my acquainting them that the Money was ready in the
Paymaster's Hands, but that Orders for paying it must first be
obtained from General Shirley, and my assuring them that I had

apply'd to that General by Letter, but he being at a Distance an Answer could not soon be receiv'd, and they must have Patience; all this was not sufficient to satisfy, and some began to sue me. General Shirley at length reliev'd me from this terrible Situation, by appointing Commissioners to examine the Claims and ordering Payment. They amounted to near twenty Thousand Pound, which to pay would have ruined me.

Before we had the News of this Defeat, the two Doctors Bond came to me with a Subscription Paper, for raising Money to defray the Expense of a grand Fire Work, which it was intended to exhibit at a Rejoicing on receipt of the News of our Taking Fort Duquesne. I looked grave and said "It would, I thought, be time enough to prepare for the Rejoicing when we knew we should have occasion to rejoice." They seem'd surpris'd that I did not immediately comply with their Proposal. "Why, the D———l," says one of them, "you surely don't suppose that the Fort will not be taken?" "I don't know that it will not be taken; but I know that the Events of War are subject to great Uncertainty." I gave them the reasons of my doubting. The Subscription was dropped, and the Projectors thereby miss'd the Mortification they would have undergone if the Firework had been prepared. Dr Bond on some other Occasions afterwards said, that he did not like Franklin's forebodings.

Governor Morris who had continually worried the Assembly with Message after Message before the Defeat of Braddock, to beat them into the making of Acts to raise Money for the Defense of the Province without Taxing among others the Proprietary Estates, and had rejected all their Bills for not having such an exempting Clause, now redoubled his Attacks, with more hope of Success, the Danger & Necessity being greater. The Assembly however continu'd firm, believing they had Justice on their side, and that it would be giving up an essential Right, if they suffered the Governor to amend their Money-Bills. In one of the last, indeed, which was for granting 50,000£ his propos'd Amendment was only of a single Word; the Bill express'd that all Estates real and personal were to be taxed, those of the Proprietaries *not* excepted. His Amendment was; for *not* read

only. A small but very material Alteration! However, when the
News of this Disaster reach'd England, our Friends there whom
we had taken care to furnish with all the Assembly's Answers
to the Governor's Messages, rais'd a Clamor against the Proprietaries for their Meanness & Injustice in giving their Governor
such Instructions, some going so far as to say that by obstructing the Defense of their Province, they forfeited their Right to
it. They were intimidated by this, and sent Orders to their Receiver General to add 5000£ of their Money to whatever Sum
might be given by the Assembly, for such Purpose. This being
notified to the House, was accepted in Lieu of their Share of
a general Tax, and a new Bill was form'd with an exempting
Clause which pass'd accordingly. By this Act I was appointed
one of the Commissioners for disposing of the Money, 60,000£.
I had been active in modelling it, and procuring its Passage; and
had at the same time drawn a Bill for establishing and disciplin-
ing a voluntary Militia, which I carried thro' the House without
much Difficulty, as Care was taken in it, to leave the Quakers at
their Liberty. To promote the Association necessary to form the
Militia, I wrote a Dialogue, stating and answering all the Objections I could think of to such a Militia, which was printed
& had as I thought great Effect. While the several Companies
in the City & Country were forming and learning their Exercise, the Governor prevail'd with me to take Charge of our
Northwestern Frontier, which was infested by the Enemy, and
provide for the Defense of the Inhabitants by raising Troops,
& building a Line of Forts. I undertook this military Business,
tho' I did not conceive myself well-qualified for it. He gave me
a Commission with full Powers and a Parcel of blank Commissions for Officers, to be given to whom I thought fit. I had but
little Difficulty in raising Men, having soon 560 under my
Command. My Son who had in the preceding War been an Officer in the Army rais'd against Canada, was my Aid de Camp,
and of great Use to me. The Indians had burnt Gnadenhut, a
Village settled by the Moravians, and massacred the Inhabitants, but the Place was thought a good Situation for one of
the Forts. In order to march thither, I assembled the Companies
at Bethlehem, the chief Establishment of those People. I was

surprised to find it in so good a Posture of Defense. The Destruction of Gnadenhut had made them apprehend Danger. The principal Buildings were defended by a Stockade. They had purchased a Quantity of Arms & Ammunition from New York, and had even plac'd Quantities of small Paving Stones between the Windows of their high Stone Houses, for their Women to throw down upon the Heads of any Indians that should attempt to force into them. The armed Brethren too, kept Watch, and reliev'd as methodically as in any Garrison Town. In Conversation with Bishop Spangenberg, I mention'd this my Surprise; for knowing they had obtain'd an Act of Parliament exempting them from military Duties in the Colonies, I had suppos'd they were conscientiously scrupulous of bearing arms. He answer'd me, "That it was not one of their establish'd Principles; but that at the time of their obtaining that Act, it was thought to be a Principle with many of their People. On this Occasion, however, they to their Surprise found it adopted by but a few." It seems they were either deceiv'd in themselves, or deceiv'd the Parliament. But Common Sense aided by present Danger, will sometimes be too strong for whimsical Opinions.

It was the Beginning of January when we set out upon this Business of Building Forts. I sent one Detachment towards the Minisinks, with Instructions to erect one for the Security of that upper Part of the Country; and another to the lower Part, with similar Instructions. And I concluded to go myself with the rest of my Force to Gnadenhut, where a Fort was tho't more immediately necessary. The Moravians procur'd me five Wagons for our Tools, Stores, Baggage, &c. Just before we left Bethlehem, Eleven Farmers who had been driven from their Plantations by the Indians, came to me requesting a supply of Fire Arms, that they might go back and fetch off their Cattle. I gave them each a Gun with suitable Ammunition. We had not march'd many Miles before it began to rain, and it continu'd raining all Day. There were no Habitations on the Road, to shelter us, till we arriv'd near Night, at the House of a German, where and in his Barn we were all huddled together as wet as Water could make us. It was well we were not attack'd in our

March, for Our Arms were of the most ordinary sort & our Men could not keep their Gunlocks dry. The Indians are dextrous in Contrivances for that purpose, which we had not. They met that Day the eleven poor Farmers abovementioned & kill'd Ten of them. The one who escap'd inform'd that his & his Companions' Guns would not go off, the Priming being wet with the Rain. The next Day being fair, we continued our March and arriv'd at the desolated Gnadenhut. There was a Saw Mill near, round which were left several Piles of Boards, with which we soon hutted ourselves; an Operation the more necessary at that inclement Season, as we had no Tents. Our first Work was to bury more effectually the Dead we found there, who had been half interr'd by the Country People. The next Morning our Fort was plann'd and mark'd out, the Circumference measuring 455 feet, which would require as many Palisades to be made of Trees one with another of a Foot Diameter each. Our Axes, of which we had 70, were immediately set to work, to cut down Trees; and our Men being dextrous in the Use of them, great Dispatch was made. Seeing the Trees fall so fast, I had the Curiosity to look at my Watch when two Men began to cut at a Pine. In 6 Minutes they had it upon the Ground; and I found it of 14 Inches Diameter. Each Pine made three Palisades of 18 Feet long, pointed at one End. While these were preparing, our other Men, dug a Trench all round of three feet deep in which the Palisades were to be planted, and our Wagons, the Body being taken off, and the fore and hind Wheels separated by taking out the Pin which united the two Parts of the Perch, we had 10 Carriages with two Horses each, to bring the Palisades from the Woods to the Spot. When they were set up, our Carpenters built a Stage of Boards all round within, about 6 Feet high, for the Men to stand on when to fire thro' the Loopholes. We had one swivel Gun which we mounted on one of the Angles; and fired it as soon as fix'd, to let the Indians know, if any were within hearing, that we had such Pieces. And thus our Fort, (if such a magnificent Name may be given to so miserable a Stockade) was finished in a Week, tho' it rain'd so hard every other Day that the Men could not work.

This gave me occasion to observe, that when Men are employ'd they are best contented. For on the Days they work'd
they were good-natur'd and cheerful; and with the consciousness of having done a good Day's work they spent the Evenings
jollily; but on the idle Days they were mutinous and quarrelsome, finding fault with their Pork, the Bread, &c. and in
continual ill-humor; which put me in mind of a Sea-Captain,
whose Rule it was to keep his Men constantly at Work; and
when his Mate once told him that they had done every thing,
and there was nothing farther to employ them about; O, says
he, *make them scour the Anchor.*

This kind of Fort, however contemptible, is a sufficient Defense against Indians who have no Cannon. Finding our selves
now posted securely, and having a Place to retreat to on Occasion, we ventur'd out in Parties to scour the adjacent Country.
We met with no Indians, but we found the Places on the neighboring Hills where they had lain to watch our Proceedings.
There was an Art in their Contrivance of those Places that
seems worth mention. It being Winter, a Fire was necessary for
them. But a common Fire on the Surface of the Ground would
by its Light have discover'd their Position at a Distance. They
had therefore dug Holes in the ground about three feet Diameter, and somewhat deeper. We saw where they had with their
Hatchets cut off the Charcoal from the Sides of burnt Logs lying in the Woods. With these Coals they had made small Fires
in the Bottom of the Holes, and we observ'd among the Weeds
& Grass the Prints of their Bodies made by their laying all
round with their Legs hanging down in the Holes to keep their
Feet warm, which with them is an essential Point. This kind
of Fire, so manag'd, could not discover them either by its Light,
Flame, Sparks or even Smoke. It appear'd that their Number
was not great, and it seems they saw we were too many to be attack'd by them with Prospect of Advantage.

We had for our Chaplain a zealous Presbyterian Minister, Mr
Beatty, who complain'd to me that the Men did not generally
attend his Prayers & Exhortations. When they enlisted, they
were promis'd, besides Pay & Provisions, a Gill of Rum a Day,
which was punctually serv'd out to them half in the Morning

and the other half in the Evening, and I observ'd they were as punctual in attending to receive it. Upon which I said to Mr Beatty, "It is perhaps below the Dignity of your Profession to act as Steward of the Rum. But if you were to deal it out, and only just after Prayers, you would have them all about you." He lik'd the Thought, undertook the Office, and with the help of a few hands to measure out the Liquor executed it to Satisfaction; and never were Prayers more generally & more punctually attended. So that I thought this Method preferable to the Punishments inflicted by some military Laws for Non-Attendance on Divine Service.

I had hardly finish'd this Business, and got my Fort well stor'd with Provisions, when I receiv'd a Letter from the Governor, acquainting me that he had called the Assembly, and wish'd my Attendance there, if the Posture of Affairs on the Frontiers was such that my remaining there was no longer necessary. My Friends too of the Assembly pressing me by their Letters to be if possible at the Meeting, and my three intended Forts being now completed, and the Inhabitants contented to remain on their Farms under that Protection, I resolved to return. The more willingly as a New England Officer, Col. Clapham, experienc'd in Indian War, being on a Visit to our Establishment, consented to accept the Command. I gave him a Commission, and parading the Garrison had it read before them, and introduc'd him to them as an Officer who from his Skill in Military Affairs, was much more fit to command them than myself; and giving them a little Exhortation took my Leave. I was escorted as far as Bethlehem, where I rested a few Days, to recover from the Fatigue I had undergone. The first Night being in a good Bed, I could hardly sleep, it was so different from my hard Lodging on the Floor of our Hut at Gnaden, wrapped only in a Blanket or two.

While at Bethlehem, I inquir'd a Little into the Practices of the Moravians. Some of them had accompanied me, and all were very kind to me. I found they work'd for a common Stock, eat at common Tables, and slept in common Dormitories, great Numbers together. In the Dormitories I observ'd Loopholes at certain Distances all along just under the Ceiling, which I thought judiciously plac'd for Change of Air. I was at their Church, where I was entertain'd with good Music, the Organ being accompanied with Violins, Hautboys, Flutes, Clarinets, &c. I understood that their Sermons were not usually preached to mix'd Congregations, of Men Women and Children, as is our common Practice; but that they assembled sometimes the married Men, at other times their Wives, then the Young Men, the young Women, and the little Children, each Division by itself. The Sermon I heard was to the latter, who came in and were plac'd in Rows on Benches, the Boys under the Conduct of a young Man their Tutor, and the Girls conducted by a young Woman. The Discourse seem'd well adapted to their Capacities, and was deliver'd in a pleasing familiar Manner, coaxing them as it were to be good. They behav'd very orderly, but look'd pale and unhealthy, which made me suspect they were kept too much within-doors, or not allow'd sufficient Exercise. I inquir'd concerning the Moravian Marriages, whether the Report was true that they were by Lot? I was told that Lots were us'd only in particular Cases. That generally when a young Man found himself dispos'd to marry, he inform'd the Elders of his Class, who consulted the Elder Ladies that govern'd the young Women. As these Elders of the different Sexes were well acquainted with the Tempers & Dispositions of their respective Pupils, they could best judge what Matches were suitable, and their Judgments were generally acquiese'd in. But if for example it should happen that two or three young Women were found to be *equally* proper for the young Man, the Lot was then recurr'd to. I objected, If the Matches are not made by the mutual Choice of the Parties, some of them may chance to be very unhappy. And so they may, answer'd my Informer, if you let the Parties choose for themselves.—Which indeed I could not deny.

Being return'd to Philadelphia, I found the Association went on swimmingly, the Inhabitants that were not Quakers having pretty generally come into it, form'd themselves into Companies, and chosen their Captains, Lieutenants and Ensigns according to the new Law. Dr B. visited me, and gave me an

Account of the Pains he had taken to spread a general good Liking to the Law, and ascrib'd much to those Endeavors. I had had the Vanity to ascribe all to my Dialogue; However, not knowing but that he might be in the right, I let him enjoy his Opinion, which I take to be generally the best way in such Cases. The Officers meeting chose me to be Colonel of the Regiment; which I this time accepted. I forget how many Companies we had, but we paraded about 1200 well looking Men, with a Company of Artillery who had been furnish'd with 6 brass Field Pieces, which they had become so expert in the Use of as to fire twelve times in a Minute. The first Time I review'd my Regiment, they accompanied me to my House, and would salute me with some Rounds fired before my Door, which shook down and broke several Glasses of my Electrical Apparatus. And my new Honor prov'd not much less brittle; for all our Commissions were soon after broke by a Repeal of the Law in England.

During the short time of my Colonelship, being about to set out on a Journey to Virginia, the Officers of my Regiment took it into their heads that it would be proper for them to escort me out of town as far as the Lower Ferry. Just as I was getting on Horseback, they came to my door, between 30 & 40, mounted, and all in their Uniforms. I had not been previously acquainted with the Project, or I should have prevented it, being naturally averse to the assuming of State on any Occasion; & I was a good deal chagrin'd at their Appearance, as I could not avoid their accompanying me. What made it worse, was, that as soon as we began to move, they drew their Swords, and rode with them naked all the way. Somebody wrote an Account of this to the Proprietor, and it gave him great Offense. No such Honor had been paid him when in the Province; nor to any of his Governors; and he said it was only proper to Princes of the Blood Royal; which may be true for aught I know, who was, and still am, ignorant of the Etiquette, in such Cases. This silly Affair however greatly increased his Rancor against me, which was before considerable, on account of my Conduct in the Assembly, respecting the Exemption of his Estate from Taxation, which I had always oppos'd very warmly, & not without severe

Reflections on his Meanness & Injustice in contending for it. He accus'd me to the Ministry as being the great Obstacle to the King's Service, preventing by my Influence in the House the proper Forming of the Bills for raising Money; and he instanc'd this Parade with my Officers as a Proof of my having an Intention to take the Government of the Province out of his Hands by Force. He also apply'd to Sir Everard Fauckener, then Post Master General, to deprive me of my Office. But this had no other Effect, than to procure from Sir Everard a gentle Admonition.

Notwithstanding the continual Wrangle between the Governor and the House, in which I as a Member had so large a Share, there still subsisted a civil Intercourse between that Gentleman & myself, and we never had any personal Difference. I have sometimes since thought that his little or no Resentment against me for the Answers it was known I drew up to his Messages, might be the Effect of professional Habit, and that, being bred a Lawyer, he might consider us both as merely Advocates for contending Clients in a Suit, he for the Proprietaries & I for the Assembly. He would therefore sometimes call in a friendly way to advise with me on difficult Points, and sometimes, tho' not often, take my Advice.

We acted in Concert to supply Braddock's Army with Provisions, and when the shocking News arriv'd of his Defeat, the Governor sent in haste for me, to consult with him on Measures for preventing the Desertion of the back Counties. I forget now the Advice I gave, but I think it was, that Dunbar should be written to and prevail'd with if possible to post his Troops on the Frontiers for their Protection, till by Reinforcements from the Colonies he might be able to proceed on the Expedition. And after my Return from the Frontier, he would have had me undertake the Conduct of such an Expedition with Provincial Troops, for the Reduction of Fort Duquesne, Dunbar & his Men being otherwise employ'd; and he propos'd to commission me as General. I had not so good an Opinion of my military Abilities as he profess'd to have; and I believe his Professions must have exceeded his real Sentiments: but probably he might think that my Popularity would facilitate the Raising of the Men, and my Influence in Assembly the Grant of Money to pay them; and that perhaps without taxing the Proprietary Estate. Finding me not so forward to engage as he expected, the Project was dropped: and he soon after left the Government, being superseded by Capt. Denny.

Before I proceed in relating the Part I had in public Affairs under this new Governor's Administration, it may not be amiss here to give some Account of the Rise & Progress of my Philosophical Reputation.

In 1746 being at Boston, I met there with a Dr Spence, who was lately arrived from Scotland, and show'd me some electric Experiments. They were imperfectly perform'd, as he was not very expert; but being on a Subject quite new to me, they equally surpris'd and pleas'd me. Soon after my Return to Philadelphia, our Library Company receiv'd from Mr Peter Collinson, F.R.S. of London a Present of a Glass Tube, with some Account of the Use of it in making such Experiments. I eagerly seized the Opportunity of repeating what I had seen at Boston, and by much Practice acquir'd great Readiness in performing those also which we had an Account of from England, adding a Number of new Ones. I say much Practice, for my House was continually full for some time, with People who came to see these new Wonders. To divide a little this Incumbrance among my Friends, I caused a Number of similar Tubes to be blown at our Glass-House, with which they furnish'd themselves, so that we had at length several Performers. Among these the principal was Mr Kinnersley, an ingenious Neighbor, who being out of Business, I encouraged to undertake showing the Experiments for Money, and drew up for him two Lectures, in which the Experiments were rang'd in such Order and accompanied with Explanations in such Method, as that the foregoing should assist in Comprehending the following. He procur'd an elegant Apparatus for the purpose, in which all the little Machines that I had roughly made for myself, were nicely form'd by Instrument-makers. His Lectures were well attended and gave great Satisfaction; and after some time he went thro' the Colonies exhibiting them in every capital Town, and pick'd up some Money. In the West India Islands indeed it was with

Difficulty the Experiments could be made, from the general Moisture of the Air.

Oblig'd as we were to Mr Collinson for his Present of the Tube, &c. I thought it right he should be inform'd of our Success in using it, and wrote him several Letters containing Accounts of our Experiments. He got them read in the Royal Society, where they were not at first thought worth so much Notice as to be printed in their Transactions. One Paper which I wrote for Mr Kinnersley, on the Sameness of Lightning with Electricity, I sent to Dr Mitchel, an Acquaintance of mine, and one of the Members also of that Society; who wrote me word that it had been read but was laughed at by the Connoisseurs: The Papers however being shown to Dr Fothergill, he thought them of too much value to be stifled, and advis'd the Printing of them. Mr Collinson then gave them to *Cave* for publication in his Gentleman's Magazine; but he chose to print them separately in a Pamphlet, and Dr Fothergill wrote the Preface. *Cave* it seems judg'd rightly for his Profit; for by the Additions that arriv'd afterwards they swell'd to a Quarto Volume, which has had five Editions, and cost him nothing for Copy-money.

It was however some time before those Papers were much taken Notice of in England. A Copy of them happening to fall into the Hands of the Count de Buffon, a Philosopher deservedly of great Reputation in France, and indeed all over Europe, he prevail'd with M. Dalibard to translate them into French, and they were printed at Paris. The Publication offended the Abbé Nollet, Preceptor in Natural Philosophy to the Royal Family, and an able Experimenter, who had form'd and publish'd a Theory of Electricity, which then had the general Vogue. He could not at first believe that such a Work came from America, & said it must have been fabricated by his Enemies at Paris, to decry his System. Afterwards having been assur'd that there really existed such a Person as Franklin of Philadelphia, which he had doubted, he wrote and published a Volume of Letters, chiefly address'd to me, defending his Theory, & denying the Verity of my Experiments and of the Positions deduc'd from them. I once purpos'd answering the Abbé, and actually began the Answer. But on Consideration that my Writings contain'd only a Description of Experiments, which any one might repeat & verify, and if not to be verify'd could not be defended; or of Observations, offer'd as Conjectures, & not delivered dogmatically, therefore not laying me under any Obligation to defend them; and reflecting that a Dispute between two Persons writing in different Languages might be lengthened greatly by mistranslations, and thence misconceptions of one another's Meaning, much of one of the Abbe's Letters being founded on an Error in the Translation; I concluded to let my Papers shift for themselves; believing it was better to spend what time I could spare from public Business in making new Experiments, than in Disputing about those already made. I therefore never answer'd M. Nollet; and the Event gave me no Cause to repent my Silence; for my friend M. le Roy, of the Royal Academy of Sciences, took up my Cause & refuted him, my Book was translated into the Italian, German and Latin Languages, and the Doctrine it contain'd was by degrees universally adopted by the Philosophers of Europe in preference to that of the Abbé, so that he liv'd to see himself the last of his Sect; except M^r B—his Eleve & immediate Disciple.

What gave my Book the more sudden and general Celebrity, was the Success of one of its propos'd Experiments, made by Messrs Dalibard & Delor at Marly, for drawing Lightning from the Clouds. This engag'd the public Attention every where. M. Delor, who had an Apparatus for experimental Philosophy, and lectur'd in that Branch of Science, undertook to repeat what he call'd the *Philadelphia Experiments*, and after they were performed before the King & Court, all the Curious of Paris flocked to see them. I will not swell this Narrative with an Account of that capital Experiment, nor of the infinite Pleasure I receiv'd in the Success of a similar one I made soon after with a Kite at Philadelphia, as both are to be found in the Histories of Electricity. Dr Wright, an English Physician then at Paris, wrote to a Friend who was of the Royal Society an Account of the high Esteem my Experiments were in among the Learned abroad, and of their Wonder that my Writings had been so little noticed in England. The Society on this resum'd the Consideration of the Letters that had been read to them, and the celebrated Dr Watson drew up a summary Account of them, & of all I had afterwards sent to England on the Subject, which he accompanied with some Praise of the Writer. This Summary was then printed in their Transactions: And some Members of the Society in London, particularly the very ingenious Mr Canton, having verified the Experiment of procuring Lightning from the Clouds by a Pointed Rod, and acquainting them with the Success, they soon made me more than Amends for the Slight with which they had before treated me. Without my having made any Application for that Honor, they chose me a Member, and voted that I should be excus'd the customary Payments, which would have amounted to twenty-five Guineas, and ever since have given me their Transactions gratis. They also presented me with the Gold Medal of Sir Godfrey Copley for the Year 1753, the Delivery of which was accompanied by a very handsome Speech of the President Lord Macclesfield, wherein I was highly honored.

Our new Governor, Capt. Denny, brought over for me the before mentioned Medal from the Royal Society, which he presented to me at an Entertainment given him by the City. He accompanied it with very polite Expressions of his Esteem for me, having, as he said been long acquainted with my Character. After Dinner, when the Company as was customary at that time, were engag'd in Drinking, he took me aside into another Room, and acquainted me that he had been advis'd by his Friends in England to cultivate a Friendship with me, as one who was capable of giving him the best Advice, & of contributing most effectually to the making his Administration easy. That he therefore desired of all things to have a good Understanding with me; and he begg'd me to be assur'd of his Readiness on all Occasions to render me every Service that might be in his Power. He said much to me also of the Proprietor's good Dispositions towards the Province, and of the Advantage it might be to us all, and to me in particular, if the Opposition that had been so long continu'd to his Measures, were dropped, and Harmony restor'd between him and the People, in effecting which it was thought no one could be more serviceable than myself, and I might depend on adequate Acknowledgements & Recompences, &c. &c. The Drinkers finding we did not return immediately to the Table, sent us a Decanter of Madeira, which the Governor made liberal Use of, and in proportion became more profuse of his Solicitations and Promises. My Answers were to this purpose, that my Circumstances, Thanks to God, were such as to make Proprietary Favors unnecessary to me; and that being a Member of the Assembly I could not possibly accept of any; that however I had no personal Enmity to the Proprietary, and that whenever the public Measures he propos'd should appear to be for the Good of the People, no one should espouse and forward them more zealously than myself, my past Opposition having been founded on this, that the Measures which had been urg'd were evidently intended to serve the Proprietary Interest with great Prejudice to that of the People. That I was much obliged to him (the Governor) for his Professions of Regard to me, and that he might rely on every thing in my Power to make his Administration as easy to him as possible, hoping at the same time that he had not brought with him the same unfortunate Instructions his Predecessor had been hamper'd with. On this he did not then explain himself. But when he afterwards came to do Business with the Assembly they appear'd again, the Disputes were renewed, and I was as active as ever in the Opposition, being the Penman first of the Request to have a Communication of the Instructions, and then of the Remarks upon them, which may be found in the Votes of the Time, and in the Historical Review I afterwards publish'd; but between us personally no Enmity arose; we were often together, he was a Man of Letters, had seen much of the World, and was very entertaining & pleasing in Conversation. He gave me the first Information that my old Friend Ja^s Ralph was still alive, that he was esteem'd one of the best political Writers in England, had been employ'd in the Dispute between Prince Frederic and the King, and had obtain'd a Pension of Three Hundred a Year; that his Reputation was indeed small as a Poet, *Pope* having damn'd his Poetry in the Dunciad, but his Prose was thought as good as any Man's.

The Assembly finally, finding the Proprietaries obstinately persisted in manacling their Deputies with Instructions inconsistent not only with the Privileges of the People, but with the Service of the Crown, resolv'd to petition the King against them, and appointed me their Agent to go over to England, to present & support the Petition. The House had sent up a Bill to the Governor granting a Sum of Sixty Thousand Pounds for the King's Use, (10,000£ of which was subjected to the Orders of the then General Lord Loudon,) which the Governor absolutely refus'd to pass in Compliance with his Instructions. I had agreed with Captain Morris of the Packet at New York for my Passage, and my Stores were put on board, when Lord Loudon arriv'd at Philadelphia, expressly, as he told me, to endeavor an Accommodation between the Governor and Assembly, that his Majesty's Service might not be obstructed by their Dissensions: Accordingly he desir'd the Governor & myself to meet him, that he might hear what was to be said on both sides. We met and discuss'd the Business. In behalf of the Assembly I urg'd all the Arguments that may be found in the public Papers of that Time, which were of my Writing, and are printed with the Minutes of the Assembly & the Governor pleaded his Instructions, the Bond he had given to observe them, and his Ruin if he disobey'd: Yet seem'd not unwilling to hazard himself if Lord Loudon would advise it. This his Lordship did not choose to do, tho' I once thought I had nearly prevail'd with him to do it; but finally he rather chose to urge the Compliance of the Assembly; and he entreated me to use my Endeavors with them for that purpose; declaring he could spare none of the King's Troops for the Defense of our Frontiers, and that if we did not continue to provide for that Defense ourselves they must remain expos'd to the Enemy. I acquainted the House with what had pass'd, and presenting them with a Set of Resolutions I had drawn up, declaring our Rights, & that we did not relinquish our Claim to those Rights but only suspended the Exercise of them on this Occasion thro' *Force,* against which we protested, they at length agreed to drop that Bill and frame another conformable to the Proprietary Instructions. This of course the Governor pass'd, and I was then at liberty to proceed on my Voyage: but in the meantime the Packet had sail'd with my Sea-Stores, which was some Loss to me, and my only Recompence was his Lordship's Thanks for my Service, all the Credit of obtaining the Accommodation falling to his Share.

He set out for New York before me; and as the Time for dispatching the Packet Boats, was in his Disposition, and there were two then remaining there, one of which he said was to sail very soon, I requested to know the precise time, that I might not miss her by any Delay of mine. His Answer was, I have given out that she is to sail on Saturday next, but I may let you know, *entre nous,* that if you are there by Monday morning you will be in time, but do not delay longer. By some Accidental Hindrance at a Ferry, it was Monday Noon before I arrived, and I was much afraid she might have sailed as the Wind was fair, but I was soon made easy by the Information that she was still in the Harbor, and would not move till the next Day.

One would imagine that I was now on the very point of Departing for Europe. I thought so; but I was not then so well acquainted with his Lordship's Character, of which *Indecision* was one of the Strongest Features. I shall give some Instances. It was about the Beginning of April that I came to New York, and I think it was near the End of June before we sail'd. There were then two of the Packet Boats which had been long in Port, but were detain'd for the General's Letters, which were always to be ready to-morrow. Another Packet arriv'd and she too was detain'd, and before we sail'd a fourth was expected. Ours was the first to be dispatch'd as having been there longest. Passengers were engag'd in all, & some extremely impatient to be gone, and the Merchants uneasy about their Letters, & the Orders they had given for Insurance, (it being Wartime) & for Fall Goods. But their Anxiety avail'd nothing; his Lordship's Letters were not ready. And yet whoever waited on him found him always at his Desk, Pen in hand, and concluded he must needs write abundantly. Going myself one Morning to pay my Respects, I found in his Antechamber one Innis, a Messenger of Philadelphia, who had come from thence express, with a Packet from Governor Denny for the General. He deliver'd to me some Letters from my Friends there, which occasion'd my inquiring when he was to return & where he lodg'd, that I might send some Letters by him. He told me he was order'd to call to-morrow at nine for the General's Answer to the Governor, and should set off immediately. I put my Letters into his Hands the same Day. A Fortnight after I met him again in the same Place. So you are soon return'd, Innis! *Return'd;* No, I am not *gone* yet.—How so?—I have call'd here by Order every Morning these two Weeks past for his Lordship's Letter, and it is not yet ready.—Is it possible, when he is so great a Writer, for I see him constantly at his Scritore. Yes, says Innis, but he is like St. George on the Signs, *always on horseback, and never rides on.* This Observation of the Messenger was it seems well founded; for when in England, I understood that Mr Pitt gave it as one Reason for Removing this General, and sending Amherst & Wolf, *that the Ministers never heard from him, and could not know what he was doing.*

This daily Expectation of Sailing, and all the three Packets going down to Sandy hook, to join the Fleet there, the Passengers thought it best to be on board, lest by a sudden Order the Ships should sail, and they be left behind. There if I remember right we were about Six Weeks, consuming our Sea Stores, and oblig'd to procure more. At length the Fleet sail'd, the General and all his Army on board, bound to Louisburg with Intent to besiege and take that Fortress; all the Packet Boats in Company, ordered to attend the General's Ship, ready to receive his Dispatches when those should be ready. We were out 5 Days before we got a Letter with Leave to part, and then our Ship quitted the Fleet and steered for England. The other two Packets he still detain'd, carry'd them with him to Halifax, where he stayed some time to exercise the Men in sham Attacks upon sham Forts, then alter'd his Mind as to besieging Louisburg, and return'd to New York with all his Troops, together with the two Packets abovementioned and all their Passengers. During his Absence the French and Savages had taken Fort George on the Frontier of that Province, and the Savages had massacred many of the Garrison after Capitulation. I saw afterwards in London, Capt. Bonnell, who commanded one of those Packets. He told me, that when he had been detain'd a Month, he acquainted his

Lordship that his Ship had grown foul, to a degree that must necessarily hinder her fast Sailing, a Point of consequence for a Packet Boat, and requested an Allowance of Time to heave her down and clean her Bottom. He was ask'd how long time that would require. He answer'd Three Days. The General reply'd, If you can do it in one Day, I give leave; otherwise not; for you must certainly sail the Day after to-morrow. So he never obtain'd leave tho' detain'd afterwards from day to day during full three Months. I saw also in London one of Bonnell's Passengers, who was so enrag'd against his Lordship for deceiving and detaining him so long at New York, and then carrying him to Halifax, and back again, that he swore he would sue him for Damages. Whether he did or not I never heard; but as he represented the Injury to his Affairs it was very considerable. On the whole I then wonder'd much, how such a Man came to be entrusted with so important a Business as the Conduct of a great Army: but having since seen more of the great World, and the means of obtaining & Motives for giving Places and employments, my Wonder is diminished. General Shirley, on whom the Command of the Army devolved upon the Death of Braddock, would in my Opinion if continued in Place, have made a much better Campaign than that of Loudon in 1757, which was frivolous, expensive and disgraceful to our Nation beyond Conception: For tho' Shirley was not a bred Soldier, he was sensible and sagacious in himself, and attentive to good Advice from others, capable of forming judicious Plans, quick and active in carrying them into Execution. Loudon, instead of defending the Colonies with his great Army, left them totaly expos'd while he paraded it idly at Halifax, by which means Fort George was lost; besides he derang'd all our mercantile Operations, & distress'd our Trade by a long Embargo on the Exportation of Provisions, on pretense of keeping Supplies from being obtain'd by the Enemy, but in reality for beating down their Price in Favor of the Contractors, in whose Profits it was said, perhaps from Suspicion only, he had a Share. And when at length the Embargo was taken off, by neglecting to send Notice of it to Charlestown the Carolina Fleet was detain'd near three Months longer, whereby their Bottoms were so much damag'd by the

Worm, that a great Part of them founder'd in the Passage home. Shirley was I believe sincerely glad of being reliev'd from so burdensome a Charge as the Conduct of an Army must be to a Man unacquainted with military Business. I was at the Entertainment given by the City of New York, to Lord Loudon on his taking upon him the Command. Shirley, tho' thereby superseded, was present also. There was a great Company of officers, Citizens and Strangers, and some Chairs having been borrowed in the Neighborhood, there was one among them very low which fell to the Lot of Mr Shirley. Perceiving it as I sat by him, I said, They have given you, Sir, too low a Seat. No Matter, says he, Mr Franklin; I find *a low Seat* the easiest!

While I was, as aforemention'd, detain'd at New York, I receiv'd all the Accounts of the Provisions, &c. that I had furnish'd to Braddock, some of which Accounts could not sooner be obtain'd from the different Persons I had employ'd to assist in the Business. I presented them to Lord Loudon, desiring to be paid the Balance. He caus'd them to be regularly examin'd by the proper Officer, who, after comparing every Article with its Voucher, certified them to be right, and the Balance due, for which his Lordship promis'd to give me an Order on the Paymaster. This, however, was put off from time to time, and tho' I called often for it by Appointment, I did not get it. At length, just before my Departure, he told me he had on better Consideration concluded not to mix his Accounts with those of his Predecessors. And you, says he, when in England, have only to exhibit your Accounts at the Treasury, and you will be paid immediately. I mention'd, but without Effect, the great & unexpected Expense I had been put to by being detain'd so long at New York, as a Reason for my desiring to be presently paid; and On my observing that it was not right I should be put to any farther Trouble or Delay in obtaining the Money I had advanc'd, as I charg'd no Commissions for my Service, O, Sir, says he, you must not think of persuading us that you are no Gainer. We understand better those Affairs, and know that every one concern'd in supplying the Army finds means in the doing it to fill his own Pockets. I assur'd him that was not my Case, and that I had not pocketed a Farthing: but he appear'd clearly not to believe me; and indeed I have since learned that immense Fortunes are often made in such Employment. As to my Balance, I am not paid it to this Day, of which more hereafter.

Our captain of the Packet had boasted much before we sail'd, of the Swiftness of his Ship. Unfortunately when we came to Sea, she proved the dullest of 96 Sail, to his no small Mortification. After many Conjectures respecting the Cause, when we were near another Ship almost as dull as ours, which however gain'd upon us, the Captain order'd all hands to come aft and stand as near the Ensign Staff as possible. We were, Passengers included, about forty Persons. While we stood there the Ship mended her Pace, and soon left our Neighbor far behind, which prov'd clearly what our Captain suspected, that she was loaded too much by the Head. The Casks of Water it seems had been all plac'd forward. These he therefore order'd to be remov'd farther aft; on which the Ship recover'd her Character, and prov'd the best Sailer in the Fleet. The Captain said she had once gone at the Rate of 13 Knots, which is accounted 13 Miles per hour. We had on board as a Passenger Captain Kennedy of the Navy, who contended that it was impossible, that no Ship ever sailed so fast, and that there must have been some Error in the Division of the Log-Line, or some Mistake in heaving the Log. A Wager ensu'd between the two Captains, to be decided when there should be sufficient Wind. Kennedy thereupon examin'd rigorously the Log-line, and being satisfy'd with that, he determin'd to throw the Log himself. Accordingly some Days after when the Wind blew very fair & fresh, and the Captain of the Packet (Lutwidge) said he believ'd she then went at the Rate of 13 Knots, Kennedy made the Experiment, and own'd his Wager lost. The above Fact I give for the sake of the following Observation. It has been remark'd as an Imperfection in the Art of Ship-building, that it can never be known 'till she is try'd, whether a new Ship will or will not be a good Sailer; for that the Model of a good sailing Ship has been exactly follow'd in the new One, which has prov'd on the contrary remarkably dull. I apprehend this may be partly occasion'd by the different Opinions of Seamen respecting the Modes of lading, rigging & sailing of a Ship. Each has his System. And the same Vessel

laden by the Judgment & Orders of one Captain shall sail better or worse than when by the Orders of another. Besides, it
scarce ever happens that a Ship is form'd, fitted for the Sea, &
sail'd by the same Person. One Man builds the Hull, another
riggs her, a third lades and sails her. No one of these has the Advantage of knowing all the Ideas & Experience of the others, &
therefore cannot draw just Conclusions from a Combination of
the whole. Even in the simple Operation of Sailing when at Sea,
I have often observ'd different Judgments in the Officers who
commanded the successive Watches, the Wind being the same.
One would have the Sails trimm'd sharper or flatter than another, so that they seem'd to have no certain Rule to govern by.
Yet I think a Set of Experiments might be instituted, first to determine the most proper Form of the Hull; for swift sailing; next
the best Dimensions & properest Place for the Masts; then the
Form & Quantity of Sails, and their Position as the Winds may
be; and lastly the Disposition of her Lading. This is the Age of
Experiments; and such a Set accurately made & combin'd would
be of great Use. I am therefore persuaded that erelong some ingenious Philosopher will undertake it; to whom I wish Success—

We were several times chas'd on our Passage, but outsail'd
every thing, and in thirty Days had Soundings. We had a good
Observation, and the Captain judg'd himself so near our Port,
(Falmouth) that if we made a good Run in the Night we might
be off the Mouth of that Harbor in the Morning, and by running in the Night might escape the Notice of the Enemy's Privateers, who often cruis'd near the Entrance of the Channel.
Accordingly all the Sail was set that we could possibly make,
and the Wind being very fresh & fair, we went right before it,
& made great Way. The Captain after his Observation, shap'd
his Course as he thought so as to pass wide of the Scilly Isles:
but it seems there is sometimes a strong Indraught setting up St.
George's Channel which deceives Seamen, and caus'd the Loss
of Sir Cloudsley Shovel's Squadron. This Indraught was probably the Cause of what happen'd to us. We had a Watchman
plac'd in the Bow to whom they often call'd, *Look well out before, there;* and he as often answer'd *Aye, Aye!* But perhaps had
his Eyes shut, and was half asleep at the time: they sometimes

answering as is said mechanically: For he did not see a Light just before us, which had been hid by the Studding Sails from the Man at Helm & from the rest of the Watch; but by an accidental Yaw of the Ship was discover'd, & occasion'd a great Alarm, we being very near it, the light appearing to me as big as a Cart Wheel. It was Midnight, & Our Captain fast asleep. But Capt. Kennedy jumping upon Deck, & seeing the Danger, ordered the Ship to wear round, all Sails standing. An Operation dangerous to the Masts, but it carried us clear, and we escap'd Shipwreck, for we were running right upon the Rocks on which the Lighthouse was erected. This Deliverance impress'd me strongly with the Utility of Lighthouses, and made me resolve to encourage the building more of them in America, if I should live to return there.

In the Morning it was found by the Soundings, &c. that we were near our Port, but a thick Fog hid the Land from our Sight. About 9 a Clock the Fog began to rise, and seem'd to be lifted up from the Water like the Curtain at a Play-house, discovering underneath the Town of Falmouth, the Vessels in its Harbour, & the Fields that surrounded it. A most pleasing Spectacle to those who had been so long without any other Prospects, than the uniform View of a vacant Ocean! And it gave us the more Pleasure, as we were now freed from the Anxieties which the State of War occasion'd.

I set out immediately, with my Son for London, and we only stopped a little by the Way to view Stonehenge on Salisbury Plain, and Lord Pembroke's House and Gardens, with his very curious Antiquities at Wilton.

We arriv'd in London the 27th of July 1757. As soon as I was settled in a Lodging Mr Charles had provided for me, I went to visit Dr Fothergill, to whom I was strongly recommended, and whose Counsel respecting my Proceedings I was advis'd to obtain. He was against an immediate Complaint to Government, and thought the Proprietaries should first be personally apply'd to, who might possibly be induc'd by the Interposition & Persuasion of some private Friends to accommodate Matters amicably. I then waited on my old Friend and Correspondent Mr Peter Collinson, who told me that John Hanbury, the great

Virginia Merchant, had requested to be informed when I should arrive, that he might carry me to Lord Granville's, who was then President of the Council, and wish'd to see me as soon as possible. I agreed to go with him the next Morning. Accordingly Mr Hanbury called for me and took me in his Carriage to that Nobleman's, who receiv'd me with great Civility; and after some Questions respecting the present State of Affairs in America, & Discourse thereupon, he said to me, "You Americans have wrong Ideas of the Nature of your Constitution; you contend that the King's Instructions to his Governors are not Laws, and think yourselves at Liberty to regard or disregard them at your own Discretion. But those Instructions are not like the Pocket Instructions given to a Minister going abroad, for regulating his Conduct in some trifling Point of Ceremony. They are first drawn up by Judges learned in the Laws; they are then considered, debated & perhaps amended in Council, after which they are signed by the King. They are then so far as relates to you, the *Law of the Land;* for THE KING IS THE LEGISLATOR OF THE COLONIES." I told his Lordship this was new Doctrine to me. I had always understood from our Charters, that our Laws were to be made by our Assemblies, to be presented indeed to the King for his Royal Assent, but that being once given the King could not repeal or alter them. And as the Assemblies could not make permanent Laws without his Assent, so neither could he make a Law for them without theirs. He assur'd me I was totally mistaken. I did not think so however. And his Lordship's Conversation having a little alarm'd me as to what might be the Sentiments of the Court concerning us, I wrote it down as soon as I return'd to my Lodgings. I recollected that about 20 Years before, a Clause in a Bill brought into Parliament by the Ministry, had propos'd to make the King's Instructions Laws in the Colonies; but the Clause was thrown out by the Commons, for which we ador'd them as our Friends & Friends of Liberty, till by their Conduct towards us in 1765, it seem'd that they had refus'd that Point of Sovereignty to the King, only that they might reserve it for themselves.

After some Days, Dr Fothergill having spoken to the Proprietaries, they agreed to a Meeting with me at Mr T. Penn's

House in Spring Garden. The Conversation at first consisted of mutual Declarations of Disposition to reasonable Accommodation; but I suppose each Party had its own Ideas of what should be meant by *reasonable*. We then went into Consideration of our several Points of Complaint which I enumerated. The Proprietaries justify'd their Conduct as well as they could, and I the Assembly's. We now appeared very wide, and so far from each other in our Opinions, as to discourage all Hope of Agreement. However, it was concluded that I should give them the Heads of our Complaints in Writing, and they promis'd then to consider them; I did so soon after; but they put the Paper into the Hands of their Solicitor Ferdinando John Paris, who manag'd for them all their Law Business in their great Suit with the neighboring Proprietary of Maryland, Lord Baltimore, which had subsisted 70 Years, and wrote for them all their Papers & Messages in their Dispute with the Assembly. He was a proud angry Man; and as I had occasionally in the Answers of the Assembly treated his Papers with some Severity, they being really weak in point of Argument, and haughty in Expression, he had conceiv'd a mortal Enmity to me, which discovering itself whenever we met, I declin'd the Proprietary's Proposal that he and I should discuss the Heads of Complaint between our two selves, and refus'd treating with any one but them. They then by his Advice put the Paper into the Hands of the Attorney and Solicitor General for their Opinion and Counsel upon it, where it lay unanswered a Year wanting eight Days, during which time I made frequent Demands of an Answer from the Proprietaries but without obtaining any other than that they had not yet receiv'd the Opinion of the Attorney & Solicitor General. What it was when they did receive it I never learned, for they did not communicate it to me, but sent a long Message to the Assembly drawn & signed by Paris reciting my Paper, complaining of its want of Formality as a Rudeness on my part, and giving a flimsy Justification of their Conduct, adding that they should be willing to accommodate Matters, if the Assembly would send over *some Person of Candor* to treat with them for that purpose, intimating thereby that I was not such.

The want of Formality or Rudeness, was probably my not having address'd the Paper to them with their assum'd Titles of true and absolute Proprietaries of the Province of Pennsylvania, which I omitted as not thinking it necessary in a Paper the Intention of which was only to reduce to a Certainty by writing what in Conversation I had delivered *viva voce*. But during this Delay, the Assembly having prevail'd with Gov\u2071 Denny to pass an Act taxing the Proprietary Estate in common with the Estates of the People, which was the grand Point in Dispute, they omitted answering the Message.

When this Act however came over, the Proprietaries counsell'd by Paris determin'd to oppose its receiving the Royal Assent. Accordingly they petition'd the King in Council, and a Hearing was appointed, in which two Lawyers were employ'd by them against the Act, and two by me in Support of it. They alleg'd that the Act was intended to load the Proprietary Estate in order to spare those of the People, and that if it were suffer'd to continue in force, & the Proprietaries who were in Odium with the People, left to their Mercy in proportioning the Taxes, they would inevitably be ruined. We reply'd that the Act had no such Intention and would have no such Effect. That the Assessors were honest & discreet Men, under an Oath to assess fairly & equitably, & that any Advantage each of them might expect in lessening his own Tax by augmenting that of the Proprietaries was too trifling to induce them to perjure themselves. This is the purport of what I remember as urg'd by both Sides, except that we insisted strongly on the mischievous Consequences that must attend a Repeal; for that the Money, 100,000£, being printed and given to the King's Use, expended in his Service, & now spread among the People, the Repeal would strike it dead in their Hands to the Ruin of many, & the total Discouragement of future Grants, and the Selfishness of the Proprietors in soliciting such a general Catastrophe, merely from a groundless Fear of their Estate being taxed too highly, was insisted on in the strongest Terms. On this Lord Mansfield, one of the Council, rose, & beckoning to me, took me into the Clerk's Chamber, while the Lawyers were pleading, and ask'd me if I was really of Opinion that no Injury would be done the Proprietary Estate in the Execution of the Act. I said, Certainly. Then says he, you can have little Objection to enter into an Engagement to assure that Point. I answer'd None at all. He then call'd in Paris, and after some Discourse his Lordship's Proposition was accepted on both Sides; a Paper to the purpose was drawn up by the Clerk of the Council, which I sign'd with Mr Charles, who was also an Agent of the Province for their ordinary Affairs; when Lord Mansfield return'd to the Council Chamber where finally the Law was allowed to pass. Some Changes were however recommended and we also engag'd they should be made by a subsequent Law; but the Assembly, did not think them necessary, For one Year's Tax having been levied by the Act, before the Order of Council arrived, they appointed a Committee to examine the Procedings of the Assessors, & On this Committee they put several particular Friends of the Proprietaries. After a full Inquiry they unanimously sign'd a Report that they found the Tax had been assess'd with perfect Equity. The Assembly look'd on my entering into the first Part of the Engagement as an essential Service to the Province, since it secur'd the Credit of the Paper Money then spread over all the Country; and they gave me their Thanks in form when I return'd. But the Proprietaries were enrag'd at Governor Denny for having pass'd the Act, & turn'd him out, with Threats of suing him for Breach of Instructions which he had given Bond to observe. He however having done it at the Instance of the General & for his Majesty's Service, and having some powerful Interest at Court, despis'd the Threats, and they were never put in Execution.

PART I

PRINTER, JOURNALIST, TRADESMAN (1722–1757)

THE DOGOOD PAPERS

THE NEW-ENGLAND COURANT.

From Monday March 26. to Monday April 2. 1722.

To the Author of the *New-England Courant.*

SIR,   No. I

It may not be improper in the first Place to inform your Readers, that I intend once a Fortnight to present them, by the Help of this Paper, with a short Epistle, which I presume will add somewhat to their Entertainment.

And since it is observed, that the Generality of People, now a days, are unwilling either to commend or dispraise what they read, until they are in some measure informed who or what the Author of it is, whether he be *poor* or *rich, old* or *young*, a *Scollar* or a *Leather Apron Man*, &c. and give their Opinion of the Performance, according to the Knowledge which they have of the Author's Circumstances, it may not be amiss to begin with a short Account of my past Life and present Condition, that the Reader may not be at a Loss to judge whether or no my Lucubrations are worth his reading.

At the time of my Birth, my Parents were on Ship-board in their Way from *London* to *N. England*. My Entrance into this troublesome World was attended with the Death of my Father, a Misfortune, which tho' I was not then capable of knowing, I shall never be able to forget; for as he, poor Man, stood upon the Deck rejoycing at my Birth, a merciless Wave entred the

Ship, and in one Moment carry'd him beyond Reprieve. Thus was the *first* Day which I saw, the *last* that was seen by my Father; and thus was my disconsolate Mother at once made both a *Parent* and a *Widow*.

When we arrived at *Boston* (which was not long after) I was put to Nurse in a Country Place, at a small Distance from the Town, where I went to School, and past my Infancy and Childhood in Vanity and Idleness, until I was bound out Apprentice, that I might no longer be a Charge to my Indigent Mother, who was put to hard Shifts for a Living.

My Master was a Country Minister, a pious good-natur'd young Man, & a Batchelor: He labour'd with all his Might to instil vertuous and godly Principles into my tender Soul, well knowing that it was the most suitable Time to make deep and lasting Impressions on the Mind, while it was yet untainted with Vice, free and unbiass'd. He endeavour'd that I might be instructed in all that Knowledge and Learning which is necessary for our Sex, and deny'd me no Accomplishment that could possibly be attained in a Country Place, such as all Sorts of Needle-Work, Writing, Arithmetick, &c. and observing that I took a more than ordinary Delight in reading ingenious Books, he gave me the free Use of his Library, which tho' it was but small, yet it was well chose, to inform the Understanding rightly and enable the Mind to frame great and noble Ideas.

Before I had liv'd quite two Years with this Reverend Gentleman, my indulgent Mother departed this Life, leaving me as it were by my self, having no Relation on Earth within my Knowledge.

I will not abuse your Patience with a tedious Recital of all the frivolous Accidents of my Life, that happened from this Time until I arrived to Years of Discretion, only inform you that I liv'd a chearful Country Life, spending my leisure Time either in some innocent Diversion with the neighbouring Females, or in some shady Retirement, with the best of Company, *Books*. Thus I past away the Time with a Mixture of Profit and Pleasure, having no Affliction but what was imaginary, and created in my own Fancy; as nothing is more common with us Women, than to be grieving for nothing, when we have nothing else to grieve for.

As I would not engross too much of your Paper at once, I will defer the Remainder of my Story until my next Letter, in the mean time desiring your Readers to exercise their Patience, and bear with my Humours now and then, because I shall trouble them but seldom. I am not insensible of the Impossibility of pleasing all, but I would not willingly displease any; and for those who will take Offence where none is intended, they are beneath the Notice of

Your Humble Servant,
SILENCE DOGOOD.

THE NEW-ENGLAND COURANT.

From Monday April 9. to Monday April 16. 1722.

To the Author of the *New-England Courant.*

SIR,   No. II

Histories of Lives are seldom entertaining unless they contain something either admirable or exemplar: And since there is little or nothing of this Nature in my own Adventures, I will not tire your Readers with tedious Particulars of no Consequence, but will briefly, and in as few Words as possible relate, the most material Occurrences of my Life, and according to my Promise, confine all to this Letter.

MY Reverend Master who had hitherto remained a Batchelor, (after much Meditation on the Eighteenth verse of the second Chapter of *Genesis,*) took up a Resolution to marry; and having made several unsuccessful fruitless Attempts on the more topping Sort of our Sex, and being tir'd with making troublesome Journeys and Visits to no Purpose, he began unexpectedly to cast a loving Eye upon Me, whom he had brought up cleverly to his Hand.

THERE is certainly scarce any Part of a Man's Life in which he appears more silly and ridiculous, than when he makes his first Onset in Courtship. The aukward Manner in which my Master first discover'd his Intentions, made me, in spite of my Reverence to his Person, burst out into an unmannerly Laughter: However, having ask'd his Pardon, and with much ado compos'd my Countenance, I promis'd him I would take his Proposal into serious Consideration, and speedily give him an Answer.

AS he had been a great Benefactor (and in a Manner a Father to me) I could not well deny his Request, when I once perceived he was in earnest. Whether it was Love, or Gratitude, or Pride, or all Three that made me consent, I know not; but it is certain, he found it no hard Matter, by the Help of his Rhetorick to conquer my Heart, and perswade me to marry him.

THIS unexpected Match was very astonishing to all the Country round about and served to furnish them with Discourse for a long Time after; some approving it, others disliking it, as they were led by their various Fancies and Inclinations.

WE lived happily together in the Heighth of conjugal Love and mutual Endearments, for near Seven Years in which Time we added Two likely Girls and a Boy to the Family of the *Dogoods:* But alas! When my Sun was in its meridian Altitude, inexorable unrelenting Death, as if he had envy'd my Happiness and Tranquility, and resolv'd to make me entirely miserable by the Loss of so good an Husband, hastened his Flight to the Heavenly World, by a sudden unexpected Departure from this.

I HAVE now remained in a State of Widowhood for several Years, but it is a State I never much admir'd, and I am apt to fancy that I could be easily perswaded to marry again, provided I was sure of a good-humour'd, sober, agreeable Companion: But one, even with these few good Qualities, being hard to find, I have lately relinquished all Thoughts of that Nature.

AT present I pass away my leisure Hours in Conversation, either with my honest Neighbour *Rusticus* and his Family, or with the ingenious Minister of our Town, who now lodges at my House, and by whose Assistance I intend now and then to beautify my Writings with a Sentence of two in the learned Languages, which will not only be fashionable, and pleasing to those who do not understand it, but will likewise be very ornamental.

I SHALL conclude this with my own Character, which (one would think) I should be best able to give. *Know then,* that I am an Enemy to Vice, and a Friend to Vertue. I am one of an extensive Charity, and a great Forgiver of *private* Injuries: A hearty Lover of the Clergy and all good Men, and a mortal Enemy to arbitrary Government & unlimited Power. I am naturally very jealous for the Rights and Liberties of my Country: & the least appearance of an Incroachment on those invaluable Priviledges, is apt to make my Blood boil exceedingly. I have likewise a natural Inclination to observe and reprove the Faults of others, at which I have an excellent Faculty. I speak this by Way of Warning to all such whose offences shall come under my Cognizance, for I never intend to wrap my Talent in a Napkin. To be brief; I am courteous and affable, good-humour'd (unless I am first provok'd,) and handsome, and sometimes witty, but always,

> SIR,   *Your Friend, and*
>   Humble Servant,
>   SILENCE DOGOOD.

THE NEW-ENGLAND COURANT.

From Monday May 7. to Monday May 14. 1722.

An sum etiam nunc vel Gracè loqui vel Latinè docendus?[1]
CICERO.

To the Author of the *New-England Courant.*

SIR,   No. IV

DISCOURSING the other Day at Dinner with my Reverend Boarder, formerly mention'd, (whom for Distinction sake we will call by the Name of *Clericus,*) concerning the Education of Children, I ask'd his Advice about my young Son *William,* whether or no I had best bestow upon him Academical Learning, or (as our Phrase is) *bring him up at our College:* He perswaded me to do it by all Means, using many weighty Arguments with me, and answering all the Objections that I could form against it; telling me withal, that he did not doubt but that the Lad would take his Learning very well, and not idle away his Time as too many there now-a-days do. These words of *Clericus* gave me a Curiosity to inquire a little more strictly into the present Circumstances of that famous Seminary of Learning; but the Information which he gave me, was neither pleasant, nor such as I expected.

AS soon as Dinner was over, I took a solitary Walk into my Orchard, still ruminating on *Clericus's* Discourse with much Consideration, until I came to my usual Place of Retirement under the *Great Apple-Tree;* where having seated my self, and carelesly laid my Head on a verdant Bank, I fell by Degrees into a soft and undisturbed Slumber. My waking Thoughts remained with me in my Sleep, and before I awak'd again, I dreamt the following DREAM.

I FANCY'D I was travelling over pleasant and delightful Fields and Meadows, and thro' many small Country Towns and Villages; and as I pass'd along, all Places resounded with the Fame of the Temple of LEARNING: Every Peasant, who had wherewithal, was preparing to send one of his Children at least to this famous Place; and in this Case most of them consulted their own Purses instead of their Childrens Capacities: So that I observed, a great many, yea, the most part of those who were travelling thither, were little better than Dunces and Block-heads. Alas! Alas!

AT length I entred upon a spacious Plain, in the Midst of which was erected a large and stately Edifice: It was to this that a great Company of Youths from all Parts of the Country were going; so stepping in among the Crowd, I passed on with them, and presently arrived at the Gate.

THE Passage was Kept by two sturdy Porters named *Riches* and *Poverty,* and the latter obstinately refused to give Entrance to any who had not first gain'd the Favour of the former; so that I observed, many who came even to the very Gate, were obliged to travel back again as ignorant as they came, for want of this necessary Qualification. However, as a Spectator I gain'd Admittance, and with the rest entred directly into the Temple.

IN the Middle of the great Hall stood a stately and magnificent Throne, which was ascending to by two high and difficult Steps. On the Top of it sat LEARNING in awful State; she was apparelled wholly in Black, and surrounded almost on every Side with innumerable Volumes in all Languages. She seem'd very busily employ'd in writing something on half a Sheet of Paper, and upon Enquiry, I understood she was preparing a Paper, call'd, *The New-England Courant.* On her Right Hand sat *English,* with a pleasant smiling Countenance, and handsomely attir'd; and on her left were seated several *Antique Figures* with their Faces vail'd. I was considerably puzzl'd to guess who they were, until one informed me, (who stood beside me,) that those Figures on her left Hand were *Latin, Greek, Hebrew,* &c. and that they were very much reserv'd, and seldom or never unvail'd their Faces here, and then to few or none, tho' most of those who have in this Place acquir'd so much Learning as to distinguish them from *English,* pretended to an intimate Acquaintance with them. I then enquir'd of him, what could be the Reason why they continued vail'd, in this Place especially: He pointed to the Foot of the Throne, where I saw *Idleness,* attended with *Ignorance,* and these (he informed me) were they, who first vail'd them, and still kept them so.

NOW I observed, that the whole Tribe who entred into the Temple with me, began to climb the Throne; but the Work proving troublesome and difficult to most of them, they withdrew their Hands from the Plow, and contented themselves to sit at the Foot, with Madam *Idleness* and her Maid *Ignorance,* until those who were assisted by Diligence and a docible Temper, had well nigh got up the first Step: But the Time drawing nigh in which they could no way avoid ascending, they were fain to crave the Assistance of those who had got up before them, and who, for the Reward perhaps of a *Pint of Milk,* or a *Piece of Plumb-Cake,* lent the Lubbers a helping Hand, and sat them in the Eye of the World, upon a Level with themselves.

THE other Step being in the same Manner ascended, and the usual Ceremonies at an End, every Beetle-Scull seem'd well satisfy'd with his own Portion of Learning, tho' perhaps he was *e'en just* as ignorant as ever. And now the Time of their Departure being come, they march'd out of Doors to make Room for another Company, who waited for Entrance: And I, having seen all that was to be seen, quitted the Hall likewise, and went to make my Observations on those who were just gone out before me.

SOME I perceiv'd took to Merchandizing, others to Travelling, some to one Thing, some to another, and some to Nothing; and many of them from henceforth, for want of Patrimony, liv'd as poor as church Mice, being unable to dig, and asham'd to beg, and to live by their Wits it was impossible. But the most Part of the Crowd went along a large beaten Path, which led to a Temple at the further End of the Plain, call'd, *The Temple of Theology.* The Business of those who were employ'd in this Temple being laborious and painful, I wonder'd exceedingly to see so many go towards it; but while I was pondering this Matter in my Mind, I spy'd *Pecunia* behind a Curtain, beckoning to them with her Hand, which Sight immediately satisfy'd me for whose Sake it was, that a great Part of them (I will not say all) travel'd that Road. In this Temple I saw nothing worth mentioning, except the ambitious and fraudulent Contrivances of *Plagius,* who (notwithstanding he had been severely reprehended for such Practices before) was diligently transcribing some eloquent Paragraphs out of *Tillotson's* Works, &c. to embellish his own.

NOW I bethought my self in my Sleep, that it was Time to be at Home, and as I fancy'd I was travelling back thither, I reflected in my Mind on the extream Folly of those Parents, who, blind to their Childrens Dulness, and insensible of the Solidity of their Skulls, because they think their Purses can afford it, will needs send them to the Temple of Learning, where, for want of a suitable Genius, they learn little more than how to carry themselves handsomely, and enter a Room genteely, (which might as well be acquir'd at a Dancing-School,) and from whence they return, after Abundance of Trouble and Charge, as great Blockheads as ever, only more proud and self-conceited.

WHILE I was in the midst of these unpleasant Reflections, *Clericus* (who with a Book in his Hand was walking under the Trees) accidentally awak'd me; to him I related my Dream with all its Particulars, and he, without much Study, presently interpreted it, assuring me, *That it was a lively Representation of* HARVARD COLLEGE, *Etcetera.*

I remain, Sir,
Your Humble Servant,
SILENCE DOGOOD.

THE NEW-ENGLAND COURANT.

June 18. to Monday June 25. 1722.

Give me the Muse, whose generous Force,
Impatient of the Reins,
Pursues an unattempted Course,
Breaks all the Cricks Iron Chains.
WATTS.

To the Author of the *New-England Courant.*

SIR,   No. VII

It has been the Complaint of many Ingenious Foreigners, who have travell'd amongst us, *That good Poetry is not to be expected in* New-England. I am apt to Fancy, the Reason is, not because our Countrymen are altogether void of a Poetical Genius, nor yet because we have not those Advantages of Education which other Countries have, but purely because we do not afford that Praise and Encouragement which is merited, when any thing extraordinary of this Kind is produc'd among us: Upon which Consideration I have determined, when I meet with a Good Piece of *New-England* Poetry, to give it a suitable Encomium, and thereby endeavour to discover to the World some of its Beautys, in order to encourage the Author to go on, and bless the World with more, and more Excellent Productions.

THERE has lately appear'd among us a most Excellent Piece of Poetry, entituled, *An Elegy upon the much Lamented Death of Mrs.* Mehitebell Kitel, *Wife of Mr.* John Kitel *of* Salem, *Etc.* It may justly be said in its Praise, without Flattery to the Author, that it is the most *Extraordinary* Piece that was ever wrote in *New-England.* The Language is so soft and Easy, the Expression so moving and pathetick, but above all, the Verse and Numbers so Charming and Natural, that it is almost beyond Comparison.

> The Muse *disdains*
> *Those Links and Chains,*
> *Measures and Rules of Vulgar Strains,*
> *And o'er the Laws of Harmony a Sovereign Queen she reigns.*

I FIND no English Author, Ancient or Modern, whose Elegies may be compar'd with this, in respect to the Elegance of Stile, or Smoothness of Rhime; and for the affecting Part, I will leave your Readers to judge, if ever they read any Lines, that would sooner make them *draw their Breath* and Sigh, if not shed Tears, than these following.

> *Come let us mourn, for we have lost a*
> *Wife, a Daughter, and a Sister,*
> *Who has lately taken Flight, and*
> *Greatly we have mist her.*

In another place,

> Some little Time *before she yielded up her Breath,*
> *She said, I ne'er shall hear one Sermon more on Earth.*
> *She kist her Husband* some little Time *before she expir'd,*
> *Then lean'd her Head the Pillow on, just out of Breath and tir'd.*

BUT the Threefold Appellation in the first Line

> *—a Wife, a Daughter, and a Sister,*

must not pass unobserved. That Line in the celebrated *Watts,*

GUNSTON *the Just, the Generous, and the Young,*

is nothing Comparable to it. The latter only mentions three Qualifications of *one* Person who was deceased, which therefore could raise Grief and Compassion but for *One.* Whereas the former, (*our most excellent Poet*) gives his Reader a Sort of an Idea of the Death of *Three Persons,* viz.

—*a Wife, a Daughter, and a Sister,*

which is *Three Times* as great a Loss as the Death of *One,* and consequently must raise *Three Times* as much Grief and Compassion in the Reader.

I SHOULD be very much straitened for Room, if I should attempt to discover even half the Excellencies of this Elegy which are obvious to me. Yet I cannot omit one Observation, which is, that the Author has (to his Honour) invented a new Species of Poetry, which wants a Name, and was never before known. His muse scorns to be confin'd to the old Measures and Limits, or to observe the dull Rules of Criticks;

Nor Rapin *gives her Rules to fly, nor* Purcell *Notes to Sing.*

Watts.

NOW 'tis Pity that such an Excellent Piece should not be dignify'd with a particular Name; and seeing it cannot justly be called, either *Epic, Sapphic, Lyric,* or *Pindaric,* nor any other Name yet invented, I presume it may, (in Honour and Remembrance of the Dead) be called the KITELIC. Thus much in the Praise of *Kitelic Poetry.*

IT is certain, that those Elegies which are of our own Growth, (and our Soil seldom produces any other sort of Poetry) are by far the greatest part, wretchedly Dull and Ridiculous. Now since it is imagin'd by many, that our Poets are honest, well-meaning Fellows, who do their best, and that if they had but some Instructions how to govern Fancy with Judgment, they would make indifferent good Elegies; I shall here subjoin a Receipt for that purpose, which was left me as a Legacy, (among other valuable Rarities) by my Reverend Husband. It is as follows,

A RECEIPT *to make a* New England
Funeral ELEGY.

For the Title of your Elegy. *Of these you may have enough ready made to your Hands; but if you should chuse to make it your self, you must be sure not to omit the words Ætatis Suæ, which will Beautify it exceedingly.*

For the Subject of your Elegy. *Take one of your Neighbours who has lately departed this Life; it is no great matter at what Age the Party dy'd, but it will be best if he went away suddenly, being* Kill'd, Drown'd, *or* Frose to Death.

Having chose the Person, take all his Virtues, Excellencies, &c. and if he have not enough, you may borrow some to make up a sufficient Quantity: To these add his last Words, dying Expressions, &c. if they are to be had; mix all these together, and be sure you strain them well. Then season all with a Handful or two of Melancholly Expressions, such as, Dreadful, Deadly, cruel cold Death, unhappy Fate, weeping Eyes, &c. *Have mixed all these Ingredients well, put them into the empty Scull of some* young Harvard; *(but in Case you have ne'er a One at Hand, you may use your own,) there let them Ferment for the Space of a Fortnight, and by that Time they will be incorporated into a Body, which take out, and having prepared a sufficient Quantity of double Rhimes, such as* Power, Flower; Quiver, Shiver; Grieve us, Leave us; tell you, excel you; Expeditions, Physicians; Fatigue him, Intrigue him; &c. *you must spread all upon Paper, and if you can procure a Scrap of Latin to put at the End, it will garnish it mightily; then having affixed your Name at the Bottom, with a* Mœstus Composuit,[2] *you will have an Excellent Elegy.*

N. B. *This Receipt will serve when a Female is the Subject of your Elegy, provided you borrow a greater Quantity of Virtues, Excellencies,* &c.

SIR,

Your Servant,

SILENCE DOGOOD.

P. S. I shall make no other Answer to *Hypercarpus's* Criticism on my last Letter than this, *Mater me genuit, peperit mox filia matrem.*[3]

EPITAPH[1]

The Body of
B. Franklin,
Printer;
Like the Cover of an old Book,
Its Contents torn out,
And stript of its Lettering and Gilding,
Lies here, Food for Worms.
But the Work shall not be wholly lost:
For it will, as he believ'd, appear once more,
In a new & more perfect Edition,
Corrected and amended
By the Author.
He was born Jan. 6. 1706.
Died   17

THE PRINTER TO
THE READER

The *Pennsylvania Gazette* being now to be carry'd on by other Hands, the Reader may expect some Account of the Method we design to proceed in.

Upon a View of *Chambers*'s great Dictionaries, from whence were taken the Materials of the *Universal Instructor in all Arts and Sciences,* which usually made the First Part of this Paper, we find that besides their containing many Things abstruse or insignificant to us, it will probably be fifty Years before the Whole can be gone thro' in this Manner of Publication. There are likewise in those Books continual References from Things under one Letter of the Alphabet to those under another, which relate to the same Subject, and are necessary to explain and compleat it; these taken in their Turn may perhaps be Ten Years distant; and since it is likely that they who desire to acquaint themselves with any particular Art or Science, would gladly have the whole before them in a much less Time, we believe our Readers will not think such a Method of communicating Knowledge to be a proper One.

However, tho' we do not intend to continue the Publication of those Dictionaries in a regular Alphabetical Method, as has hitherto been done; yet as several Things exhibited from them in the Course of these Papers, have been entertaining to such of the Curious, who never had and cannot have the Advantage of good Libraries; and as there are many Things still behind, which being in this Manner made generally known, may perhaps become of considerable Use, by giving such Hints to the excellent natural Genius's of our Country, as may contribute either to the Improvement of our present Manufactures, or towards the Invention of new Ones; we propose from Time to Time to communicate such particular Parts as appear to be of the most general Consequence.

As to the *Religious Courtship,* Part of which has been retal'd to the Publick in these Papers, the Reader may be inform'd, that the whole Book will probably in a little Time be printed and bound up by it self; and those who approve of it, will doubtless be better pleas'd to have it entire, than in this broken interrupted Manner.

There are many who have long desired to see a good NewsPaper in *Pennsylvania;* and we hope those Gentlemen who are able, will contribute towards the making This such. We ask Assistance, because we are fully sensible, that to publish a good News-Paper is not so easy an Undertaking as many People imagine it to be. The Author of a *Gazette* (in the Opinion of the Learned) ought to be qualified with an extensive Acquaintance with Languages, a great Easiness and Command of Writing and Relating Things cleanly and intelligibly, and in few Words; he should be able to speak of War both by Land and Sea; be well acquainted with Geography, with the History of the Time, with the several Interests of Princes and States, the Secrets of Courts, and the Manners and Customs of all Nations. Men thus accomplish'd are very rare in this remote Part of the World; and it would be well if the Writer of these Papers could make up among his Friends what is wanting in himself.

Upon the Whole, we may assure the Publick, that as far as the Encouragement we meet with will enable us, no Care and Pains shall be omitted, that may make the *Pennsylvania Gazette* as agreeable and useful an Entertainment as the Nature of the Thing will allow.

AN APOLOGY
FOR PRINTERS

BEING frequently censur'd and condemn'd by different Persons for printing Things which they say ought not to be printed, I have sometimes thought it might be necessary to make a standing Apology for my self, and publish it once a Year, to be read upon all Occasions of that Nature. Much Business has hitherto hindered the execution of this Design; but having very lately given extraordinary Offence by printing an Advertisement with a certain N. B. at the End of it, I find an Apology more particularly requisite at this Juncture, tho' it happens when I have not yet Leisure to write such a Thing in the proper Form, and can only in a loose manner throw those Considerations together which should have been the Substance of it.

I request all who are angry with me on the Account of printing things they don't like, calmly to consider these following Particulars.

1. That the Opinions of Men are almost as various as their Faces; an Observation general enough to become a common Proverb, *So many Men so many Minds.*

2. That the Business of Printing has chiefly to do with Mens Opinions; most things that are printed tending to promote some, or oppose others.

3. That hence arises the peculiar Unhappiness of that Business, which other Callings are no way liable to; they who follow Printing being scarce able to do any thing in their way of getting a Living, which shall not probably give Offence to some, and perhaps to many; whereas the Smith, the Shoemaker, the Carpenter, or the Man of any other Trade, may work indifferently for People of all Persuasions, without offending any of

them: and the Merchant may buy and sell with Jews, Turks, Hereticks and Infidels of all sorts, and get Money by every one of them, without giving Offence to the most orthodox, of any sort; or suffering the least Censure or Ill will on the Account from any Man whatever.

4. That it is as unreasonable in any one Man or Set of Men to expect to be pleas'd with every thing that is printed, as to think that nobody ought to be pleas'd but themselves.

5. Printers are educated in the Belief, that when Men differ in Opinion, both Sides ought equally to have the Advantage of being heard by the Publick; and that when Truth and Error have fair Play, the former is always an overmatch for the latter: Hence they chearfully serve all contending Writers that pay them well, without regarding on which side they are of the Question in Dispute.

6. Being thus continually employ'd in serving both Parties, Printers naturally acquire a vast Unconcernedness as to the right or wrong Opinions contain'd in what they print; regarding it only as the Matter of their daily labour: They print things full of Spleen and Animosity, with the utmost Calmness and Indifference, and without the least Ill-will to the Persons reflected on; who nevertheless unjustly think the Printer as much their Enemy as the Author, and join both together in their Resentment.

7. That it is unreasonable to imagine Printers approve of every thing they print, and to censure them on any particular thing accordingly; since in the way of their Business they print such great variety of things opposite and contradictory. It is likewise as unreasonable what some assert, "That Printers ought not to print any Thing but what they approve;" since if all of that Business should make such a Resolution, and abide by it, an End would thereby be put to Free Writing, and the World would afterwards have nothing to read but what happen'd to be the Opinions of Printers.

8. That if all Printers were determin'd not to print any thing till they were sure it would offend no body, there would be very little printed.

9. That if they sometimes print vicious or silly things not worth reading, it may not be because they approve such things

themselves, but because the People are so viciously and corruptly educated that good things are not encouraged. I have known a very numerous Impression of Robin Hood's Songs go off in this Province at 2s. per Book, in less than a Twelvemonth; when a small Quantity of David's Psalms (an excellent Version) have lain upon my Hands above twice the Time.

10. That notwithstanding what might be urg'd in behalf of a Man's being allow'd to do in the Way of his Business whatever he is paid for, yet Printers do continually discourage the Printing of great Numbers of bad things, and stifle them in the Birth. I my self have constantly refused to print anything that might countenance Vice, or promote Immorality; tho' by complying in such Cases with the corrupt Taste of the Majority I might have got much Money. I have also always refus'd to print such things as might do real Injury to any Person, how much soever I have been solicited, and tempted with Offers of Great Pay; and how much soever I have by refusing got the Ill-will of those who would have employ'd me. I have hitherto fallen under the Resentment of large Bodies of Men, for refusing absolutely to print any of their Party or Personal Reflections. In this Manner I have made my self many Enemies, and the constant Fatigue of denying is almost insupportable. But the Publick being unacquainted with all this, whenever the poor Printer happens either through Ignorance or much Persuasion, to do any thing that is generally thought worthy of Blame, he meets with no more Friendship or Favour on the above Account, than if there were no Merit in't at all. Thus, as Waller says,

> Poets lose half the Praise they would have got
> Were it but known what they discreetly blot;

Yet are censur'd for every bad Line found in their Works with the utmost Severity.

I come now to the Particular Case of the N. B. above mention'd, about which there has been more Clamour against me, than ever before on any other Account.—In the Hurry of other Business an Advertisement was brought to me to be printed; it signified that such a Ship lying at such a Wharff, would sail for

Barbadoes in such a Time, and that Freighters and Passengers might agree with the Captain at such a Place; so far is what's common: But at the Bottom this odd Thing was added, "N. B. No Sea Hens nor Black Gowns will be admitted on any Terms." I printed it, and receiv'd my Money; and the Advertisement was stuck up round the Town as usual. I had not so much Curiosity at that time as to enquire the Meaning of it, nor did I in the least imagine it would give so much Offence. Several good Men are very angry with me on this Occasion; they are pleas'd to say I have too much Sense to do such things ignorantly; that if they were Printers they would not have done such a thing on any Consideration; that it could proceed from nothing but my abundant Malice against Religion and the Clergy. They therefore declare they will not take any more of my Papers, nor have any farther Dealings with me; but will hinder me of all the Custom they can. All this is very hard!

I believe it had been better if I had refused to print the said Advertisement. However, 'tis done, and cannot be revok'd. I have only the following few Particulars to offer, some of them in my behalf, by way of Mitigation, and some not much to the Purpose; but I desire none of them may be read when the Reader is not in a very good Humour.

1. That I really did it without the least Malice, and imagin'd the N. B. was plac'd there only to make the Advertisement star'd at, and more generally read.

2. That I never saw the Word Sea-Hens before in my Life; nor have I yet ask'd the meaning of it; and tho' I had certainly known that Black Gowns in that place signified the Clergy of the Church of England, yet I have that confidence in the generous good Temper of such of them as I know, as to be well satisfied such a trifling mention of their Habit gives them no Disturbance.

3. That most of the Clergy in this and the neighbouring Provinces, are my Customers, and some of them my very good Friends; and I must be very malicious indeed, or very stupid, to print this thing for a small Profit, if I had thought it would have given them just Cause of Offence.

4. That if I had much Malice against the Clergy, and withal much Sense; 'tis strange I never write or talk against the Clergy myself. Some have observed that 'tis a fruitful Topic, and the easiest to be witty upon of all others; yet I appeal to the Publick that I am never guilty this way, and to all my Acquaintances as to my Conversation.

5. That if a Man of Sense had Malice enough to desire to injure the Clergy, this is the foolishest. Thing he could possibly contrive for that Purpose.

6. That I got Five Shillings by it.

7. That none who are angry with me would have given me so much to let it alone.

8. That if all the People of different Opinions in this Province would engage to give me as much for not printing things they don't like, as I can get by printing them, I should probably live a very easy Life; and if all Printers were everywhere so dealt by, there would be very little printed.

9. That I am oblig'd to all who take my Paper, and am willing to think they do it out of meer Friendship. I only desire they would think the same when I deal with them. I thank those who leave off, that they have taken it so long. But I beg they would not endeavour to dissuade others, for that will look like Malice.

10. That 'tis impossible any Man should know what he would do if he was a Printer.

11. That notwithstanding the Rashness and Inexperience of Youth, which is most likely to be prevail'd with to do things that ought not to be done; yet I have avoided printing such Things as usually give Offence either to Church or State, more than any Printer that has followed the Business in this Province before.

12. And lastly, That I have printed above a Thousand Advertisements which made not the least mention of *Sea-Hens* or *Black Gowns;* and this being the first Offence, I have the more Reason to expect Forgiveness.

I take leave to conclude with an old Fable, which some of my Readers have heard before, and some have not.

"A certain well-meaning Man and his Son, were travelling towards a Market Town, with an Ass which they had to sell.

The Road was bad; and the old Man therefore rid, but the Son went a-foot. The first Passenger they met, asked the Father if he was not ashamed to ride by himself, and suffer the poor Lad to wade along thro' the Mire; this induced him to take up his Son behind him: He had not travelled far, when he met others, who said, they are two unmerciful Lubbers to get both on the Back of that poor Ass, in such a deep Road. Upon this the old Man gets off, and let his Son ride alone. The next they met called the Lad a graceless, rascally young Jackanapes, to ride in that Manner thro' the Dirt, while his aged Father trudged along on Foot; and they said the old Man was a Fool, for suffering it. He then bid his Son come down, and walk with him, and they travell'd on leading the Ass by the Halter; 'till they met another Company, who called them a Couple of senseless Blockheads, for going both on Foot in such a dirty Way, when they had an empty Ass with them, which they might ride upon. The old Man could bear no longer; My Son, said he, it grieves me much that we cannot please all these People. Let me throw the Ass over the next Bridge, and be no further troubled with him."

Had the old Man been seen acting this last Resolution, he would probably have been called a Fool for troubling himself about the different Opinions of all that were pleas'd to find Fault with him: Therefore, tho' I have a Temper almost as complying as his, I intend not to imitate him in this last Particular. I consider the Variety of Humors among Men, and despair of pleasing every Body; yet I shall not therefore leave off Printing. I shall continue my Business. I shall not burn my Press and melt my Letters.

LETTER FROM
ANTHONY AFTERWIT

<small>Mr. Gazetteer,</small>

I am an honest Tradesman, who never meant Harm to any-Body. My Affairs went on smoothly while a Batchelor; but of late I have met with some Difficulties, of which I take the Freedom to give you an Account.

About the Time I first address'd my present Spouse, her Father gave out in Speeches, that if she married a Man he liked, he would give with her £200 on the Day of Marriage. 'Tis true he never said so to me, but he always receiv'd me very kindly at his House, and openly countenanc'd my Courtship. I form'd several fine Schemes what to do with this same £200, and in some Measure neglected my Business on that Account: But unluckily it came to pass, that when the old Gentleman saw I was pretty well engag'd, and that the Match was too far gone to be easily broke off; he, without any Reason given, grew very angry, forbid me the House, and told his Daughter, that if she married me he would not give her a Farthing. However, (as he foresaw) we were not to be disappointed in that Manner, but, having stole a Wedding, I took her home to my House, where we were not in quite so poor a Condition as the Couple describ'd in the Scotch Song, who had

> "Neither Pot nor Pan,
> But four bare Legs together,"

for I had a House tolerably furnished for an ordinary Man before. No thanks to Dad, who, I understand, was very much pleased with his politick Management. And I have since learn'd, that there are other old Curmudgeons (so called) besides him, who have this Trick to marry their Daughters, and yet keep what they might well spare, till they can keep it no longer; But this by way of Digression; a Word to the Wise is enough.

I soon saw, that with Care and Industry we might live tolerably easy and in Credit with our Neighbours; But my Wife had a strong Inclination to be a Gentlewoman. In Consequence of this, my old-fashioned Looking-Glass was one Day broke, as she said, *No Mortal could tell which way.* However, since we could not be without a Glass in the Room, "My Dear," says she, "we may as well buy a large fashionable One, that Mr. Such-a-one has to sell; It will cost but little more than a common Glass, and will be much handsomer and more creditable." Accordingly, the Glass was bought and hung against the Wall: But in a Week's time I was made sensible, by little and little, that *the Table was by no means suitable to such a Glass.* And a more proper Table being procur'd, my Spouse, who was an excellent Contriver, inform'd me where we might have very handsome Chairs *in the Way;* and thus by Degrees I found all my old Furniture stow'd up in the Garret, and every thing below alter'd for the better.

Had we stopp'd here, it might have done well enough; but my Wife being entertain'd with Tea by the Good Women she visited, we could do no less than the like when they visited us; and so we got a Tea-Table with all its Appurtenances of China and Silver. Then my Spouse unfortunately overwork'd herself in washing the House, so that we could do no longer without a Maid. Besides this, it happened frequently, that when I came home at One, the Dinner was but just put in the Pot, and *my Dear thought really it had been but Eleven:* At other Times, when I came at the same Hour, *She wondered I would stay so long, for Dinner was ready and had waited for me these two Hours.* These Irregularities occasioned by mistaking the Time, convinced me, that it was absolutely necessary *to buy a Clock,* which my Spouse observ'd was *a great Ornament to the Room!* And lastly, to my Grief, she was frequently troubled with some Ailment or other, and *nothing did her so much Good as Riding; And these Hackney Horses were such wretched ugly Creatures that—*I bought a very fine pacing Mare, which cost £20; and hereabouts Affairs have stood for some Months past.

I could see all along, that this Way of Living was utterly inconsistent with my Circumstances, but had not Resolution enough to help it. Till lately, receiving a very severe Dun, which mention'd the next Court, I began in earnest to project Relief. Last Monday, my Dear went over the River to see a Relation and stay a Fortnight, because she could not bear the Heat of the Town. In the Interim I have taken my Turn to make Alterations; viz, I have turn'd away the Maid, Bag and Baggage, (for what should we do with a Maid, who have except my Boy none but ourselves?) I have sold the fine Pacing Mare, and bought a good Milch Cow with £3 of the Money. I have dispos'd of the Tea Table, and put a Spinning-Wheel in its Place, which methinks looks very pretty: Nine empty Canisters I have stuff'd with Flax, and with some of the Money of the Tea-Furniture I have bought a Set of Knitting-Needles; for to tell you a truth, which I would have go no farther, *I begin to want Stockings.* The stately Clock I have transform'd into an Hour-Glass, by which I have gain'd a good round Sum, and one of the Pieces of the old Looking-Glass, squar'd and fram'd, supplies the Place of the Great One, which I have convey'd into a Closet, where it may possibly remain some Years. In short, the Face of Things is quite changed; and I am mightily pleased when I look at my Hour-Glass. What an Ornament it is to the Room! I have paid my Debts and find Money in my Pocket. I expect my Dame home next Friday, and, as your Paper is taken in at the House where she is, I hope the Reading of this will prepare her Mind for the above surprizing Revolutions. If she can conform to this new Scheme of Living, we shall be the happiest Couple perhaps in the Province, and by the Blessing of God may soon be in thriving Circumstances. I have reserv'd the great Glass, because I know her Heart is set upon it; I will allow her, when she comes in, to be taken suddenly ill with *the Head-ach, the Stomach-ach, Fainting Fits,* or whatever other Disorder she may think more proper, and she may retire to Bed as soon as she pleases: But, if I do not find her in perfect Health, both of Body and Mind, the next Morning, away goes the aforesaid Great Glass, with several other Trinkets I have no Occasion for, to the Vendue that very Day. Which is the irrevocable Resolution

Of, Sir, Her loving Husband, and

Your very humble Servant,

ANTHONY AFTERWIT.

Postscript. You know we can return to our former Way of Living, when we please, if Dad will be at the Expence of it.

LETTER FROM
CELIA SINGLE

Mr. Gazetteer,

I must needs tell you, that some of the Things you print do more Harm than Good; particularly I think so of my Neighbour the Tradesman's Letter, in one of your late Papers, which has broken the Peace of several Families, by causing Difference between Men and their Wives: I shall give you one Instance, of which I was an Eye and Ear Witness.

Happening last Wednesday Morning to be in at Mrs. C—ss's, when her Husband return'd from Market, among other Things which he had bought he show'd her some Balls of Thread. "My Dear," says he, "I like mightily those Stockings, which I yesterday saw Neighbour Afterwit knitting for her Husband, of Thread of her own Spinning. I should be glad to have some such stockins myself: I understand that your Maid Mary is a very good Knitter, and seeing this Thread in Market, I have bought it, that the Girl may make a Pair or two for me." Mrs. Careless was just then at the Glass, dressing her Head, and turning about with the Pins in her Mouth, "Lord, Child," says she, "are you crazy? What Time has Mary to knit? Who must do the Work, I wonder, if you set her to Knitting?" "Perhaps, my Dear," says he, "you have a mind to knit 'em yourself; I remember, when I courted you, I once heard you say, that you had learn'd to knit of your Mother." "I knit Stockins for you!" says she; "not I truly! There are poor Women enough in Town, that can knit; if you please, you may employ them." "Well, but my Dear," says he, "you know *a penny sav'd is a penny got,* A pin a day is a groat a year, every little makes a muckle, and there is neither Sin nor Shame in Knitting a pair of Stockins; why should you express such a mighty Aversion to it? As to *poor* Women, you know we are not People of Quality, we have no Income to maintain us but what arises from my Labour and Industry: Methinks you should not be at all displeas'd, if you have an Opportunity to get something as well as myself."

"I wonder," says she, "how you can propose such a thing to me; did not you always tell me you would maintain me like a Gentlewoman? If I had married Captain————, he would have scorn'd even to mention Knitting of Stockins" "Prithee," says he, (a little nettled,) "what do you tell me of your Captains? If you could have had him, I suppose you would, or perhaps you did not very well like him. If I did promise to maintain you like a Gentlewoman, I suppose 'tis time enough for that, when you know how to behave like one; Meanwhile 'tis your Duty to help make me able. How long, d'ye think, I can maintain you at your present Rate of Living?" "Pray," says she, (somewhat fiercely, and dashing the Puff into the Powder-Box,) "don't use me after this Manner, for I assure you I won't bear it. This is the Fruit of your poison Newspapers; there shall come no more here, I promise you." "Bless us," says he, "what an unaccountable thing is this? Must a Tradesman's Daughter, and the Wife of a Tradesman, necessarily and instantly be a Gentlewoman? You had no Portion; I am forc'd to work for a Living; you are too great to do the like; there's the Door, go and live upon your Estate, if you can find it; in short, I don't desire to be troubled w' ye."

What Answer she made, I cannot tell; for, knowing that a Man and his Wife are apt to quarrel more violently when before Strangers, than when by themselves, I got up and went out hastily: But I understood from Mary, who came to me of an Errand in the Evening, that they dined together pretty peaceably, (the Balls of Thread that had caused the Difference being thrown into the Kitchen Fire,) of which I was very glad to hear.

I have several times in your Paper seen severe Reflections upon us Women, for Idleness and Extravagance, but I do not remember to have once seen any such Animadversions upon the Men. If I were dispos'd to be censorious, I could furnish you with Instances enough. I might mention Mr. Billiard, who spends more than he earns at the Green Table, and would have been in Jail long since, were it not for his industrious Wife: Mr. Hussle-cap, who, often all day long, leaves his Business for the rattling of Half-pence, in a certain Alley: Mr. Finikin, who has seven different Suits of fine cloaths, and wears a Change every Day, while his Wife and Children sit at home half naked: Mr. Crown-him, who is always dreaming over the Chequer-Board, and cares not how the World goes, so he gets the game: Mr. T'other-pot, the Tavern-haunter; Mr. Bookish, the everlasting Reader; Mr. Toot-a-toot, and several others, who are mighty diligent at any thing beside their Business. I say, if I were disposed to be censorious, I might mention all these and more, but I hate to be thought a Scandalizer of my Neighbours, and therefore forbear; and for your part, I would advise you for the future to entertain your Readers with something else, besides People's Reflections upon one another; for remember, that there are Holes enough to be pick'd in your Coat, as well as others, and those that are affronted by the Satyrs you may publish, will not consider so much who *wrote* as who *printed:* Take not this Freedom amiss from

Your Friend and Reader,
CELIA SINGLE.

ADVICE TO A PRETTY
CREATURE AND REPLIES

Mr. *Franklin*,
   "Pray let the prettiest Creature in this Place know, (by publishing this) That if it was not for her Affectation, she would be absolutely irresistible."

The Pennsylvania Gazette, November 20, 1735

The little Epistle in our last, has produced, no less than six, which follow in the order we receiv'd 'em.

Mr. *Franklin*,
   'I cannot conceive who your Correspondent means by *the prettiest Creature* in this Place; but I can assure either him or her, that she who is truly so, has no Affectation at all.'

SIR,
   'Since your last Week's Paper I have look'd in my Glass a thousand Times, I believe, in one Day; and if it was not for the Charge of Affectation I might, without Partiality, believe myself the Person meant.'

Mr. *Franklin*,
   'I must own that several have told me, I am the prettiest Creature in this Place; but I believe I shou'd not have been tax'd with Affectation if I cou'd have thought as well of them as they do of themselves.'

SIR,

'Your Sex calls me pretty; my own affected. Is it from Judgment in the one, or Envy in the other?'

Mr. *Franklin,*

'They that call me affected are greatly mistaken; for I don't know that I ever refus'd a Kiss to any Body but a Fool.'

Friend Benjamin,

'I am not at all displeased at being charged with Affectation. Thou know'st the vain People call Decency of Behaviour by that Name.'

HINTS FOR THOSE THAT WOULD BE RICH

THE Use of Money is all the Advantage there is in having Money.

For £6 a Year you may have the Use of £100 if you are a Man of known Prudence and Honesty.

He that spends a Groat a day idly, spends idly above £6 a year, which is the Price of using £100.

He that wastes idly a Groat's worth of his Time per Day, one Day with another, wastes the Privilege of using £100 each Day.

He that idly loses 5s. worth of time, loses 5s. and might as prudently throw 5s. in the River.

He that loses 5s. not only loses that Sum, but all the Advantage that might be made by turning it in Dealing, which, by the time that a young Man becomes old, amounts to a comfortable Bag of Money.

Again, He that sells upon Credit, asks a Price for what he sells equivalent to the Principal and Interest of his Money for the Time he is like to be kept out of it: therefore He that buys upon Credit, pays Interest for what he buys. And he that pays ready Money, might let that Money out to Use; so that He that possesses any Thing he has bought, pays Interest for the Use of it.

Consider then when you are tempted to buy any unnecessary Householdstuff, or any superfluous thing, whether you will be willing to pay *Interest, and Interest upon Interest* for it as long as you live; and more if it grows worse by using.

Yet, in buying goods, 'tis best to pay Ready Money, because, He that sells upon Credit, expects to lose 5 *per Cent* by bad Debts; therefore he charges, on all he sells upon Credit, an Advance that shall make up that Deficiency.

Those who pay for what they buy upon Credit, pay their Share of this Advance.

He that pays ready Money, escapes or may escape that Charge.

> A Penny sav'd is Twopence clear,
> A Pin a Day is a Groat a Year.

A TRUE PROGNOSTICATION, FOR 1739

CourteouS ReaderS,

Having consider'd the infinite Abuses arising from the false Prognostications published among you, made under the shadow of a Pot of Drink, or so, I have here calculated one of the most sure and unerring that ever was seen in black and white, as hereafter you'll find. For doubtless it is a heinous, foul and crying Sin, to deceive the poor gaping World, greedy of the Knowledge of Futurity, as we Americans all are. Take Notice by the by, that having been at a great deal of pains in the Calculation, if you don't believe every Syllable, Jot and Tittle of it, you do me a great deal of wrong; for which either here or elsewhere, you may chance to be claw'd off with a Vengeance. A good Cowskin, Crabtree or Bull's pizzle may be plentifully bestow'd on your outward Man. You may snuff up your Noses as much as you please, 'tis all one for that.

Well however, come, suite your Noses my little Children; and you old doating Father Grey-Beards, pull out your best Eyes, on wi' your Barnacles, and carefully observe every Scruple of what I'm going to tell you.

OF THE GOLDEN NUMBER

The Golden Number, *non est inventus*. I cannot find it this Year by any Calculation I have made. I must content myself with a Number of Copper. No matter, go on.

Of the EClipSeS *this Year*

There are so many invisible Eclipses this Year, that I fear, not unjustly, our Pockets will suffer Inanition, be full empty, and our Feeling at a Loss. During the first visible Eclipse *Saturn* is retrograde: For which Reason the Crabs will go sidelong, and the Ropemakers backward. The Belly will wag before, and the A— shall sit down first. *Mercury* will have his share in these Affairs, and so confound the Speech of People, that when a *Pensilvanian* would say PANTHER he shall say PAINTER. When a *New Yorker* thinks to say (This) he shall say (Diss) and the people in *New England* and *Cape May* will not be able to say (Cow) for their Lives, but will be forc'd to say (Keow) by a certain involuntary Twist in the Root of their Tongues. No *Connecticut man* nor *Marylander* will be able to open his Mouth this Year but (Sir) shall be the first or last Syllable he pronounces, and sometimes both. Brutes shall speak in many Places, and there will be above seven and twenty irregular Verbs made this Year, if Grammar don't interpose.—Who can help these Misfortunes!

Of the DISEASES *This Year*

This Year the Stone-blind shall see but very little; the Deaf shall hear but poorly; and the Dumb sha'nt speak very plain. And it's much, if my Dame *Bridget* talks at all this Year.

Whole Flocks, Herds, and Droves of Sheep, Swine and Oxen, Cocks and Hens, Ducks and Drakes, Geese and Ganders shall go to Pot; but the Mortality will not be altogether so great among Cats, Dogs, and Horses. As for old Age, 'twill be incurable this Year, because of the Years past. And towards the Fall some People will be seiz'd with an unaccountable Inclination to roast and eat their own Ears: Should this be call'd Madness, Doctors? I think not. But the worst Disease of all will be a certain most horrid, dreadful, malignant, catching, perverse and odious Malady, almost epidemical, insomuch that many shall run mad upon it; I quake for very Fear when I think on't: for I assure you very few will escape this Disease, which is called by the learned Albumazar *Lacko'mony*.

Of the FRUITS of the EARTH

I find that this will be a plentiful Year of all manner of good Things, to those who have enough; but the Orange Trees in *Greenland,* will go near to fare the worse for the Cold. As for Oats, they'll be a great Help to Horses. I dare say there won't be much more Bacon than Swine. *Mercury* somewhat threatens our Parsley-beds, yet Parsly will be to be had for Money. Hemp will grow faster than the Children of this Age, and some will find there's but too much on't. As for Corn, Fruit, Cyder and Turnips, there never was such Plenty as will be now; if poor Folks may have their Wish.

Of the CONDITION of some COUNTRIES

I foresee an universal *Droughth* this Year thro' all the Northern Colonies. Hence there will be *dry* Rice in *Carolina, dry* Tobacco in *Virginia* and *Maryland, dry* Bread in *Pennsylvania* and *New York;* and in *New England dry* Fish and *dry* Doctrine. *Dry* Throats there will be everywhere; but then how pleasant it will be to drink cool Cyder! tho' some will tell you nothing is more contrary to Thirst. I believe it; and indeed, *Contraria contrariis curantur.*

R. SAUNDERS.

Poor RICHARD improved:

BEING AN

ALMANACK

AND

EPHEMERIS

OF THE

MOTIONS of the SUN and MOON;

THE TRUE

PLACES and ASPECTS of the PLANETS;

THE

RISING and *SETTING* of the *SUN*;

AND THE

Rifing, Setting *and* Southing *of the* Moon,

FOR THE

YEAR of our LORD 1753:

Being the Firft after LEAP-YEAR.

Containing alfo,

The Lunations, Conjunctions, Eclipfes, Judgment of the Weather, Rifing and Setting of the Planets, Length of Days and Nights, Fairs, Courts, Roads, &c. Together with ufeful Tables, chronological Obfervations, and entertaining Remarks.

Fitted to the Latitude of Forty Degrees, and a Meridian of near five Hours Weft from *London* ; but may, without fenfible Error, ferve all the NORTHERN COLONIES.

By *RICHARD SAUNDERS*, Philom.

PHILADELPHIA:

Printed and Sold by B. FRANKLIN, and D. HALL.

PREFACE TO POOR RICHARD IMPROVED

1753

Courteous Reader

This is the twentieth Time of my addressing thee in this Manner, and I have reason to flatter myself my Labours have not been unacceptable to the Publick. I am particularly pleas'd to understand that my *Predictions of the Weather* give such general Satisfaction; and indeed, such Care is taken in the Calculations, on which those Predictions are founded, that I could almost venture to say, there's not a single One of them, promising *Snow, Rain, Hail, Heat, Frost, Fogs, Wind,* or *Thunder,* but what comes to pass *punctually* and *precisely* on the very Day, in some Place or other on this little *diminutive* Globe of ours; (and when you consider the vast Distance of the Stars from whence we take our Aim, you must allow it no small Degree of Exactness to hit any Part of it) I say on this Globe; for tho' in other Matters I confine the Usefulness of my *Ephemeris* to the *Northern Colonies,* yet in that important matter of the Weather, which is of such *general Concern,* I would have it more extensively useful, and therefore take in both Hemispheres, and all Latitudes from *Hudson's Bay* to *Cape Horn.*

You will find this Almanack in my former Method, only conformable to the *New-stile*[1] established by the Act of Parliament, which I gave you in my last at length; the new Act since made for Amendment of that first Act, not affecting us in the least, being intended only to regulate some Corporation Matters in *England,* before unprovided for. I have only added a Column in the second Page of each Month, containing the Days of the *Old*

Stile opposite to their corresponding Days in the *New,* which may, in many Cases, be of Use; and so conclude (believing you will excuse a short Preface, when it is to make Room for something better).   Thy Friend and Servant

R. SAUNDERS.

A STRIKING SUN DIAL

How to make a STRIKING SUN DIAL, by which not only a Man's own Family, but all his Neighbours for ten Miles round, may know what a Clock it is, when the Sun shines, without seeing the Dial.

Chuse an open Place in your Yard or Garden, on which the Sun may shine all Day without any Impediment from Trees or Buildings.

On the Ground mark out your Hour Lines, as for a horizontal Dial, according to Art, taking Room enough for the Guns. On the Line for One o'Clock, place one Gun; on the Two o'Clock Line two Guns, and so of the rest. The Guns must all be charged with Powder, but Ball is unnecessary. Your Gnomon or Style must have twelve burning Glasses annex't to it, and be so placed that the Sun shining through the Glasses, one after the other, shall cause the Focus or burning Spot to fall on the Hour Line of One, for Example, at One a Clock, and there kindle a Train of Gunpowder that shall fire one Gun. At Two a Clock, a Focus shall fall on the Hour Line of Two, and kindle another Train that shall discharge two Guns successively: and so of the rest.

Note, There must be 78 Guns in all. Thirty-two Pounders will be best for this Use; but 18 Pounders may do, and will cost less, as well as use less Powder, for nine Pounds of Powder will do for one Charge of each eighteen Pounder, whereas the Thirty-two Pounders would require for each Gun 16 Pounds.

Note also, That the chief Expense will be the Powder, for the Cannon once bought, will, with Care, last 100 Years.

Note moreover, that there will be a great Saving of Powder in Cloudy Days.

Kind Reader, Methinks I hear thee say, That is indeed a good Thing to know how the Time passes, but this Kind of Dial, notwithstanding the mentioned Savings, would be very Expensive; and the Cost greater than the Advantage, Thou art wise, my Friend, to be so considerate beforehand; some Fools would not have found out so much, till they had made the Dial and try'd it. . . . Let all such learn that many a private and many a publick Project, are like this Striking Dial, great Cost for little Profit.

THE WAY TO WEALTH

Courteous Reader

I have heard that nothing gives an Author so great Pleasure, as to find his Works respectfully quoted by other learned Authors. This Pleasure I have seldom enjoyed; for tho' I have been, if I may say it without Vanity, an *eminent Author* of Almanacks annually now a full Quarter of a Century, my Brother Authors in the same Way, for what Reason I know not, have ever been very sparing in their Applauses, and no other Author has taken the least Notice of me, so that did not my Writings produce me some solid *Pudding,* the great Deficiency of *Praise* would have quite discouraged me.

I concluded at length, that the People were the best Judges of my Merit; for they buy my Works; and besides, in my Rambles, where I am not personally known, I have frequently heard one or other of my Adages repeated, with, *as Poor Richard says,* at the End on 't; this gave me some Satisfaction, as it showed not only that my Instructions were regarded, but discovered likewise some Respect for my Authority; and I own, that to encourage the Practice of remembering and repeating those wise Sentences, I have sometimes *quoted myself* with great Gravity.

Judge, then how much I must have been gratified by an Incident I am going to relate to you. I stopt my Horse lately where a great Number of People were collected at a Vendue of Merchant Goods. The Hour of Sale not being come, they were conversing on the Badness of the Times and one of the Company call'd to a plain clean old Man, with white Locks, "Pray, Father Abraham, what think you of the Times? Won't these heavy Taxes quite ruin the Country? How shall we be ever able to pay

them? What would you advise us to?" Father *Abraham* stood
up, and reply'd, "If you'd have my Advice, I'll give it you in
short, for *A Word to the Wise is enough,* and *many Words
won't fill a Bushel,* as *Poor Richard* says." They join'd in desiring him to speak his Mind, and gathering round him, he proceeded as follows;

"Friends," says he, and Neighbours, "the Taxes are indeed
very heavy, and if those laid on by the Government were the
only Ones we had to pay, we might more easily discharge them;
but we have many others, and much more grievous to some of
us. We are taxed twice as much by our *Idleness,* three times as
much by our *Pride,* and four times as much by our *Folly;* and
from these Taxes the Commissioners cannot ease or deliver us
by allowing an Abatement. However let us hearken to good Advice, and something may be done for us; *God helps them that
help themselves,* as *Poor Richard* says, in his Almanack of 1733.

It would be thought a hard Government that should tax its
People one-tenth Part of their *Time,* to be employed in its Service. But *Idleness* taxes many of us much more, if we reckon all
that is spent in absolute *Sloth,* or doing of nothing, with that
which is spent in idle Employments or Amusements, that amount
to nothing. *Sloth,* by bringing on Diseases, absolutely shortens
Life. *Sloth, like Rust, consumes faster than Labour wears;
while the used Key is always bright,* as *Poor Richard* says. *But
dost thou love Life, then do not squander Time, for that's
the stuff Life is made of,* as *Poor Richard* says. How much more
than is necessary do we spend in sleep, forgetting that *The
sleeping Fox catches no Poultry,* and that *There will be sleeping
enough in the Grave,* as *Poor Richard* says.

*If Time be of all Things the most precious, wasting Time
must be,* as *Poor Richard* says, *the greatest Prodigality;* since, as
he elsewhere tells us, *Lost Time is never found again; and what
we call Time enough, always proves little enough:* Let us then
up and be doing, and doing to the Purpose; so by Diligence
shall we do more with less Perplexity. *Sloth makes all Things
difficult, but Industry all easy,* as *Poor Richard* says; and
*He that riseth late must trot all Day, and shall scarce overtake
his Business at Night;* while *Laziness travels so slowly, that*

Poverty soon overtakes him, as we read in *Poor Richard,* who adds, *Drive thy Business, let not that drive thee;* and *Early to Bed, and early to rise, makes a Man healthy, wealthy, and wise.*

So what signifies *wishing* and *hoping* for better Times. We may make these Times better, if we bestir ourselves. *Industry need not wish,* as *Poor Richard* says, *and he that lives upon Hope will die fasting. There are no Gains without Pains; then Help Hands, for I have no Lands,* or if I have, they are smartly taxed. And, as *Poor Richard* likewise observes, *He that hath a Trade hath an Estate; and he that hath a Calling, hath an Office of Profit and Honour;* but then the *Trade* must be worked at, and the *Calling* well followed, or neither the *Estate* nor the *Office* will enable us to pay our Taxes. If we are industrious, we shall never starve; for, as *Poor Richard* says, *At the working Man's House Hunger looks in, but dares not enter.* Nor will the Bailiff or the Constable enter, for *Industry pays Debts, while Despair encreaseth them,* says *Poor Richard.* What though you have found no Treasure, nor has any rich Relation left you a Legacy, *Diligence is the Mother of Good-luck* as *Poor Richard* says *and God gives all Things to Industry. Then plough deep, while Sluggards sleep, and you shall have Corn to sell and to keep,* says *Poor Dick.* Work while it is called To-day, for you know not how much you may be hindered To-morrow, which makes *Poor Richard* say, *One to-day is worth two To-morrows,* and farther, *Have you somewhat to do To-morrow, do it To-day.* If you were a Servant, would you not be ashamed that a good Master should catch you idle? Are you then your own Master, *be ashamed to catch yourself idle,* as *Poor Dick* says. When there is so much to be done for yourself, your Family, your Country, and your gracious King, be up by Peep of Day; *Let not the Sun look down and say, Inglorious here he lies.* Handle your Tools without Mittens; remember that *The Cat in Gloves catches no Mice,* as *Poor Richard* says. 'Tis true there is much to be done, and perhaps you are weak-handed, but stick to it steadily; and you will see great Effects, for *Constant Dropping wears away Stones,* and by *Diligence and Patience the Mouse ate in two the Cable;* and *Little Strokes fell great Oaks,* as *Poor Richard* says in his Almanack, the Year I cannot just now remember.

Methinks I hear some of you say, *Must a Man afford himself no Leisure?* I will tell thee, my friend, what *Poor Richard* says, *Employ thy Time well, if thou meanest to gain Leisure; and, since thou art not sure of a Minute, throw not away an Hour.* Leisure, is Time for doing something useful; this Leisure the diligent Man will obtain, but the lazy Man never; so that, as *Poor Richard* says *A Life of Leisure and a Life of Laziness are two Things.* Do you imagine that Sloth will afford you more Comfort than Labour? No, for as *Poor Richard* says, *Trouble springs from Idleness, and grievous Toil from needless Ease. Many without Labour, would live by their Wits only, but they break for want of Stock.* Whereas Industry gives Comfort, and Plenty, and Respect: *Fly Pleasures, and they'll follow you. The diligent Spinner has a large Shift; and now I have a Sheep and a Cow, everyBody bids me good Morrow;* all which is well said by *Poor Richard.*

But with our Industry, we must likewise be *steady, settled,* and *careful,* and oversee our own Affairs *with our own Eyes,* and not trust too much to others; for, as *Poor Richard* says

> *I never saw an oft-removed Tree,*
> *Nor yet an oft-removed Family,*
> *That throve so well as those that settled be.*

And again, *Three Removes is as bad as a Fire;* and again, *Keep thy Shop, and thy Shop will keep thee;* and again, *If you would have your Business done, go; if not, send.* And again,

> *He that by the Plough would thrive,*
> *Himself must either hold or drive.*

And again, *The Eye of a Master will do more Work than both his Hands;* and again, *Want of Care does us more Damage than Want of Knowledge;* and again, *Not to oversee Workmen, is to leave them your Purse open.* Trusting too much to others' Care is the Ruin of many; for, as the Almanack says, *In the Affairs of this World, Men are saved, not by Faith, but by the Want of it;* but a Man's own Care is profitable; for, saith *Poor Dick, Learning is to the Studious,* and *Riches to the Careful,* as well as *Power to the Bold,* and *Heaven to the Virtuous,* And farther, *If you would have a faithful Servant, and one that you like, serve yourself.* And again, he adviseth to Circumspection and Care, even in the smallest Matters, because sometimes *A little Neglect may breed great Mischief;* adding, *for want of a Nail the Shoe was lost; for want of a Shoe the Horse was lost; and for want of a Horse the Rider was lost, being overtaken and slain by the Enemy; all for want of Care about a Horse-shoe Nail.*

So much for Industry, my Friends, and Attention to one's own Business; but to these we must add *Frugality,* if we would make our *Industry* more certainly successful. A Man may, if he knows not how to save as he gets, *keep his Nose all his Life to the Grindstone,* and die not worth a *Groat* at last. *A fat Kitchen makes a lean Will,* as *Poor Richard* says; and

> *Many Estates are spent in the Getting,*
> *Since Women for Tea forsook Spinning and Knitting,*
> *And Men for Punch forsook Hewing and Splitting.*

If you would be wealthy, says he, in another Almanack, *think of Saving as well as of Getting: The Indies have not made Spain rich, because her Outgoes are greater than her Incomes.*

Away then with your expensive Follies, and you will not then have so much Cause to complain of hard Times, heavy Taxes, and chargeable Families; for, as *Poor Dick* says,

> *Women and Wine, Game and Deceit,*
> *Make the Wealth small and the Wants great.*

And farther, *What maintains one Vice, would bring up two Children.* You may think perhaps, that a *little* Tea, or a *little* Punch now and then, Diet a *little* more costly, Clothes a *little* finer, and a *little* Entertainment now and then, can be no *great* Matter; but remember what *Poor Richard* says, *Many a Little makes a Mickle;* and farther, Beware of little *Expences; A small Leak will sink a great Ship;* and again, *Who Dainties love, shall Beggars prove;* and moreover, *Fools make Feasts, and wise Men eat them.*

Here you are all got together at this Vendue of *Fineries* and *Knicknacks.* You call them *Goods;* but if you do not take Care, they will prove *Evils* to some of you. You expect they will be sold *cheap,* and perhaps they may for less than they cost; but if you have no Occasion for them, they must be *dear* to you. Remember what *Poor Richard* says; *Buy what thou hast no Need of, and ere long thou shalt sell thy Necessaries.* And again, *At a great Pennyworth pause a while:* He means, that perhaps the Cheapness is *apparent* only, and not *Real;* or the bargain, by straitening thee in thy Business, may do thee more Harm than Good. For in another Place he says, *Many have been ruined by buying good Pennyworths.* Again, *Poor Richard* says, 'tis *foolish to lay out Money in a Purchase of Repentance;* and yet this Folly is practised every Day at Vendues, for want of minding the Almanack. *Wise Men,* as *Poor Dick* says, *learn by others Harms, Fools scarcely by their own;* but *felix quem faciunt aliena pericula cautum.* Many a one, for the Sake of Finery on the Back, have gone with a hungry Belly, and half-starved their Families. *Silks and Sattins, Scarlet and Velvets,* as *Poor Richard* says, *put out the Kitchen Fire.*

These are not the *Necessaries* of Life; they can scarcely be called the *Conveniences;* and yet only because they look pretty, how many *want* to *have* them! The *artificial* Wants of Mankind thus become more numerous than the *Natural;* and, as *Poor Dick* says, *for one poor Person, there are an hundred indigent.* By these, and other Extravagancies, the Genteel are reduced to poverty, and forced to borrow of those whom they formerly despised, but who through Industry and Frugality have maintained their Standing; in which Case it appears plainly, that *A Ploughman on his Legs is higher than a Gentleman on his Knees,* as *Poor Richard* says. Perhaps they have had a small Estate left them, which they knew not the Getting of; they think, *'tis Day, and will never be Night;* that a little to be spent out of *so much,* is not worth minding; *a Child and a Fool,* as *Poor*

Richard says, *imagine Twenty shillings and Twenty Years can never be spent* but, *always taking out of the Meal-tub, and never putting in, soon comes to the Bottom;* as *Poor Dick* says, *When the Well's dry, they know the Worth of Water.* But this they might have known before, if they had taken his Advice; *If you would know the Value of Money, go and try to borrow some; for, he that goes a borrowing goes a sorrowing;* and indeed so does he that lends to such People, when he goes *to get it in again. Poor Dick* farther advises, and says,

> *Fond Pride of Dress is sure a very Curse;*
> *E'er Fancy you consult, consult your Purse.*

And again, *Pride is as loud a Beggar as Want, and a great deal more saucy.* When you have bought one fine Thing, you must buy ten more, that your Appearance may be all of a Piece; but *Poor Dick* says, *'Tis easier to suppress the first Desire, than to satisfy all that follow it.* And 'tis as truly Folly for the Poor to ape the Rich, as for the Frog to swell, in order to equal the ox.

> *Great Estates may venture more,*
> *But little Boats should keep near Shore.*

'Tis, however, a Folly soon punished; for *Pride that dines on Vanity, sups on Contempt,* as *Poor Richard* says. And in another Place, *Pride breakfasted with Plenty, dined with Poverty, and supped with Infamy.* And after all, of what Use is this *Pride of Appearance,* for which so much is risked so much is suffered? It cannot promote Health, or ease Pain; it makes no Increase of Merit in the Person, it creates Envy, it hastens Misfortune.

> *What is a Butterfly? At best*
> *He's but a Caterpillar drest*
> *The gaudy Fop's his Picture just,*

as *Poor Richard* says.

But what Madness must it be to *run in Debt* for these Superfluities! We are offered, by the Terms of this Vendue, *Six*

Months' Credit; and that perhaps has induced some of us to attend it, because we cannot spare the ready Money, and hope now to be fine without it. But, ah, think what you do when you run in Debt; *you give to another Power over your Liberty.* If you cannot pay at the Time, you will be ashamed to see your Creditor; you will be in Fear when you speak to him; you will make poor pitiful sneaking Excuses, and by Degrees come to lose your Veracity, and sink into base downright lying; for, as Poor Richard says *The second Vice is Lying, the first is running in Debt.* And again, to the same Purpose, *Lying rides upon Debt's Back.* Whereas a free-born *Englishman* ought not to be ashamed or afraid to see or speak to any Man living. But Poverty often deprives a Man of all Spirit and Virtue: *'Tis hard for an empty Bag to stand upright,* as *Poor Richard* truly says.

What would you think of that Prince, or that Government, who should issue an Edict forbidding you to dress like a Gentleman or a Gentlewoman, on Pain of Imprisonment or Servitude? Would you not say, that you were free, have a Right to dress as you please, and that such an Edict would be a Breach of your Privileges, and such a Government tyrannical? And yet you are about to put yourself under that Tyranny, when you run in Debt for such Dress! Your Creditor has Authority, at his Pleasure to deprive you of your Liberty, by confining you in Goal for Life, or to sell you for a Servant, if you should not be able to pay him! When you have got your Bargain, you may, perhaps, think little of Payment; but *Creditors, Poor Richard* tells us, *have better Memories than Debtors;* and in another Place says, *Creditors are a superstitious Sect, great Observers of set Days and Times.* The Day comes round before you are aware, and the Demand is made before you are prepared to satisfy it, Or if you bear your Debt in Mind, the Term which at first seemed so long, will, as it lessens, appear extreamly short. *Time* will seem to have added Wings to his Heels as well as Shoulders. *Those have a short Lent,* saith *Poor Richard, who owe Money to be paid at Easter.* Then since, as he says, *The Borrower is a Slave to the Lender, and the Debtor to the Creditor,* disdain the Chain, preserve your Freedom; and maintain your Independency: Be *industrious* and *free;* be *frugal* and *free.*

At present, perhaps, you may think yourself in thriving Circumstances, and that you can bear a little Extravagance without Injury; but,

> For Age and Want, save while you may;
> No Morning Sun lasts a whole Day,

as *Poor Richard* says. Gain may be temporary and uncertain, but ever while you live, Expence is constant and certain; and *'tis easier to build two Chimnies, than to keep one in Fuel*, as *Poor Richard* says. So, *Rather go to Bed supperless than rise in Debt*.

> Get what you can, and what you get hold;
> 'Tis the Stone that will turn all your lead into Gold,

as *Poor Richard* says. And when you have got the Philosopher's Stone, sure you will no longer complain of bad Times, or the Difficulty of paying Taxes.

This Doctrine, my Friends, is *Reason* and *Wisdom*; but after all, do not depend too much upon your own *Industry*, and *Frugality*, and *Prudence*, though excellent Things, for they may all be blasted without the Blessing of Heaven; and therefore, ask that Blessing humbly, and be not uncharitable to those that at present seem to want it, but comfort and help them. Remember, *Job* suffered, and was afterwards prosperous.

And now to conclude, *Experience keeps a dear School, but Fools will learn in no other, and scarce in that*; for it is true, *we may give Advice, but we cannot give Conduct*, as *Poor Richard* says: However, remember this, *They that won't be counselled, can't be helped*, as *Poor Richard* says: and farther, That, *if you will not hear Reason, she'll surely rap your Knuckles*."

Thus the old Gentleman ended his Harangue. The People heard it, and approved the Doctrine, and immediately practised the contrary, just as if it had been a common Sermon; for the Vendue opened, and they began to buy extravagantly, notwithstanding, his Cautions and their own Fear of Taxes. I found the good Man had thoroughly studied my Almanacks, and digested all I had dropt on these Topicks during the Course of Five and twenty Years. The frequent Mention he made of me must have tired any one else, but my Vanity was wonderfully delighted with it, though I was conscious that not a tenth Part of the Wisdom was my own, which he ascribed to me, but rather the *Gleanings* I had made of the Sense of all Ages and Nations. However, I resolved to be the better for the Echo of it; and though I had at first determined to buy Stuff for a new Coat, I went away resolved to wear my old One a little longer. *Reader,* if thou wilt do the same, thy Profit will be as great as mine. I *am, as ever, thine to serve thee,*

RICHARD SAUNDERS.

PART II

THE BETTERMENT OF LIFE

A PROPOSAL

*For Promoting Useful Knowledge Among
the British Plantations in America*[1]

Philadelphia, May 14, 1743.

THE English are possessed of a long tract of continent, from Nova Scotia to Georgia, extending north and south through different climates, having different soils, producing different plants, mines, and minerals, and capable of different improvements, manufactures, &c.

The first drudgery of settling new colonies, which confines the attention of people to mere necessaries, is now pretty well over; and there are many in every province in circumstances that set them at ease, and afford leisure to cultivate the finer arts and improve the common stock of knowledge. To such of these who are men of speculation, many hints must from time to time arise, many observations occur, which if well examined, pursued, and improved, might produce discoveries to the advantage of some or all of the British plantations, or to the benefit of mankind in general.

But as from the extent of the country such persons are widely separated, and seldom can see and converse or be acquainted with each other, so that many useful particulars remain uncommunicated, die with the discoverers, and are lost to mankind; it is, to remedy this inconvenience for the future, proposed,

That one society be formed of *virtuosi* or ingenious men, residing in the several colonies, to be called *The American Philosophical Society,* who are to maintain a constant correspondence.

That Philadelphia, being the city nearest the centre of the continent colonies, communicating with all of them northward and southward by post, and with all the islands by sea, and having the advantage of a good growing library, be the centre of the Society.

That at Philadelphia there be always at least seven members, viz. a physician, a botanist, a mathematician, a chemist, a mechanician, a geographer, and a general natural philosopher, besides a president, treasurer, and secretary.

That these members meet once a month, or oftener, at their own expense, to communicate to each other their observations and experiments, to receive, read, and consider such letters, communications, or queries as shall be sent from distant members; to direct the dispersing of copies of such communications as are valuable, to other distant members, in order to procure their sentiments thereupon.

That the subjects of the correspondence be: all new-discovered plants, herbs, trees, roots, their virtues, uses, &c.; methods of propagating them, and making such as are useful, but particular to some plantations, more general; improvements of vegetable juices, as ciders, wines, &c.; new methods of curing or preventing diseases; all new-discovered fossils in different countries, as mines, minerals, and quarries; new and useful improvements in any branch of mathematics; new discoveries in chemistry, such as improvements in distillation, brewing, and assaying of ores; new mechanical inventions for saving labour, as mills and carriages, and for raising and conveying of water, draining of meadows, &c.; all new arts, trades, and manufactures, that may be proposed or thought of; surveys, maps, and charts of particular parts of the sea-coasts or inland countries; course and junction of rivers and great roads, situation of lakes and mountains, nature of the soil and productions; new methods of improving the breed of useful animals; introducing other sorts from foreign countries; new improvements in planting, gardening, and clearing land; and all philosophical experiments that let light into the nature of things, tend to increase the power of man over matter, and multiply the conveniences or pleasures of life.

That a correspondence, already begun by some intended members, shall be kept up by this Society with the ROYAL SOCIETY of London, and with the DUBLIN SOCIETY.

That every member shall have abstracts sent him quarterly, of every thing valuable communicated to the Society's Secretary at Philadelphia; free of all charge except the yearly payment hereafter mentioned.

That, by permission of the postmaster-general, such communications pass between the Secretary of the Society and the members, postage-free.

That, for defraying the expense of such experiments as the Society shall judge proper to cause to be made, and other contingent charges for the common good, every member send a piece of eight per annum to the treasurer, at Philadelphia, to form a common stock, to be disbursed by order of the President with the consent of the majority of the members that can conveniently be consulted thereupon, to such persons and places where and by whom the experiments are to be made, and otherwise as there shall be occasion; of which disbursements an exact account shall be kept, and communicated yearly to every member.

That, at the first meetings of the members at Philadelphia, such rules be formed for regulating their meetings and transactions for the general benefit, as shall be convenient and necessary; to be afterwards changed and improved as there shall be occasion, wherein due regard is to be had to the advice of distant members.

That, at the end of every year, collections be made and printed, of such experiments, discoveries, and improvements, as may be thought of public advantage; and that every member have a copy sent him.

That the business and duty of the Secretary be to receive all letters intended for the Society, and lay them before the President and members at their meetings; to abstract, correct, and methodize such papers as require it, and as he shall be directed to do by the President, after they have been considered, debated, and digested in the Society; to enter copies thereof in the Society's books, and make out copies for distant members; to answer their letters by direction of the President, and keep records of all material transactions of the Society.

Benjamin Franklin, the writer of this Proposal, offers himself to serve the Society as their secretary, till they shall be provided with one more capable.

PROPOSALS RELATING TO THE EDUCATION OF YOUTH IN PENSILVANIA. PHILADELPHIA: PRINTED IN THE YEAR, MDCCXLIX[1]

Advertisement to the Reader.

It has long been regretted as a Misfortune to the Youth of this Province, that we have no ACADEMY, in which they might receive the Accomplishments of a regular Education. The following Paper of Hints towards forming a Plan for that Purpose, is so far approv'd by some publick-spirited Gentlemen, to whom it has been privately communicated, that they have directed a Number of Copies to be made by the Press, and properly distributed, in order to obtain the Sentiments and Advice of Men of Learning, Understanding, and Experience in these Matters; and have determined to use their Interest and best Endeavours, to have the Scheme, when compleated, carried gradually into Execution; in which they have Reason to believe they shall have the hearty Concurrence and Assistance of many who are Wellwishers to their Country. Those who incline to favour the Design with their Advice, either as to the Parts of Learning to be taught, the Order of Study, the Method of Teaching, the Œconomy of the School, or any other Matter of Importance to the Success of the Undertaking, are desired to communicate their Sentiments as soon as may be, by Letter directed to B. FRANKLIN, *Printer,* in PHILADELPHIA.

PROPOSALS

The good Education of Youth has been esteemed by wise Men in all Ages, as the surest Foundation of the Happiness both of private Families and of Commonwealths. Almost all Governments have therefore made it a principal Object of their Attention, to establish and endow with proper Revenues, such Seminaries of Learning, as might supply the succeeding Age with Men qualified to serve the Publick with Honour to themselves, and to their Country.

Many of the first Settlers of these Provinces were Men who had received a good Education in *Europe,* and to their Wisdom and good Management we owe much of our present Prosperity. But their Hands were full, and they could not do all Things. The present Race are not thought to be generally of equal Ability: For though the *American* Youth are allow'd not to want Capacity; yet the best Capacities require Cultivation, it being truly with them, as with the best Ground, which unless well tilled and sowed with profitable Seed, produces only ranker Weeds.

That we may obtain the Advantages arising from an Increase of Knowledge, and prevent as much as may be the mischievous Consequences that would attend a general Ignorance among us, the following *Hints* are offered towards forming a Plan for the Education of the Youth of *Pennsylvania,* viz.

It is propos'd,

THAT some Persons of Leisure and publick Spirit apply for a CHARTER, by which they may be incorporated, with Power to erect an ACADEMY for the Education of Youth, to govern the same, provide Masters, make Rules, receive Donations, purchase Lands, etc., and to add to their Number, from Time to Time such other Persons as they shall judge suitable.

That the Members of the Corporation make it their Pleasure, and in some Degree their Business, to visit the Academy often, encourage and countenance the Youth, countenance and assist the Masters, and by all Means in their Power advance the Usefulness and Reputation of the Design; that they look on the Students as in some Sort their Children, treat them with Familiarity and Affection, and, when they have behav'd well, and gone through their Studies, and are to enter the World, zealously unite, and make all the Interest that can be made to establish them, whether in Business, Offices, Marriages, or any other Thing for their Advantage, preferably to all other Persons whatsoever even of equal Merit.

And if Men may, and frequently do, catch such a Taste for cultivating Flowers, for Planting, Grafting, Inoculating, and the like, as to despise all other Amusements for their Sake, why may not we expect they should acquire a Relish for that *more useful* Culture of young Minds. *Thompson* says,

> " 'T is Joy to see the human Blossoms blow,
>   When infant Reason grows apace, and calls
>   For the kind Hand of an assiduous Care.
>   Delightful Task! to rear the tender Thought,
>   To teach the young Idea how to shoot;
>   To pour the fresh Instruction o'er the Mind,
>   To breathe th' enliv'ning Spirit, and to fix
>   The generous Purpose in the glowing Breast."

That a House be provided for the ACADEMY, if not in the Town, not many Miles from it; the Situation high and dry, and if it may be, not far from a River, having a Garden, Orchard, Meadow, and a Field or two.

That the House be furnished with a Library (if in the Country, if in the Town, the Town Libraries may serve) with Maps of all Countries, Globes, some mathematical Instruments, an Apparatus for Experiments in Natural Philosophy, and for Mechanics; Prints, of all Kinds, Prospects, Buildings, Machines, &c.

That the Rector be a Man of good Understanding, good Morals, diligent and patient, learn'd in the Languages and Sciences, and a correct pure Speaker and Writer of the *English* Tongue; to have such Tutors under him as shall be necessary.

That the boarding Scholars diet together, plainly, temperately, and frugally.

That, to keep them in Health, and to strengthen and render

active their Bodies, they be frequently exercis'd in Running, Leaping, Wrestling, and Swimming, &c.

That they have peculiar Habits to distinguish them from other Youth, if the Academy be in or near the Town; for this, among other Reasons, that their Behaviour may be the better observed.

As to their STUDIES, it would be well if they could be taught *every Thing* that is useful, and *every Thing* that is ornamental: But Art is long, and their Time is short. It is therefore propos'd that they learn those Things that are likely to be *most useful* and *most ornamental*. Regard being had to the several Professions for which they are intended.

All should be taught to write a *fair Hand*, and swift, as that is useful to All. And with it may be learnt something of *Drawing*, by Imitation of Prints, and some of the first Principles of Perspective.

Arithmetick, Accounts, and some of the first Principles of *Geometry* and *Astronomy*.

The *English* Language might be taught by Grammar; in which some of our best Writers, as *Tillotson, Addison, Pope, Algernoon Sidney, Cato's Letters,* &c., should be Classicks: the *Stiles* principally to be cultivated, being the *clear* and the *concise*. Reading should also be taught, and pronouncing, properly, distinctly, emphatically; not with an even Tone, which *underdoes,* nor a theatrical, which *over-does* Nature.

To form their Stile they should be put on Writing Letters to each other, making Abstracts of what they read; or writing the same Things in their own Words; telling or writing Stories lately read, in their own Expressions. All to be revis'd and corrected by the Tutor, who should give his Reasons, and explain the Force and Import of Words, &c.

To form their Pronunciation, they may be put on making Declamations, repeating Speeches, delivering Orations &c.; The Tutor assisting at the Rehearsals, teaching, advising, correcting their Accent, &c.

But if History be made a constant Part of their Reading, such as the Translations of the *Greek* and *Roman* Historians, and the modern Histories of ancient *Greece* and *Rome,* &c. may

not almost all Kinds of useful Knowledge be that Way introduc'd to Advantage, and with Pleasure to the Student? As

GEOGRAPHY, by reading with Maps, and being required to
point out the Places *where* the greatest Actions were done, to
give their old and new Names, with the Bounds, Situation, Extent of the Countries concern'd, &c.

CHRONOLOGY, by the Help of *Helvicus* or some other Writer
of the Kind, who will enable them to tell *when* those Events
happened; what Princes were Cotemporaries, what States or famous Men flourish'd about that Time, &c. The several principal
Epochas to be first well fix'd in their Memories.

ANTIENT CUSTOMS, religious and civil, being frequently mentioned in History, will give Occasion for explaining them; in
which the Prints of Medals, Basso-Relievos, and antient Monu-
ments will greatly assist.

MORALITY, by descanting and making continual Observa-
tions on the Causes of the Rise or Fall of any Man's Character,
Fortune, Power &c. mention'd in History; the Advantages of
Temperance, Order, Frugality, Industry, Perseverance &c. &c.
Indeed the general natural Tendency of Reading good History
must be, to fix in the Minds of Youth deep Impressions of the
Beauty and Usefulness of Virtue of all Kinds, Publick Spirit,
Fortitude, &c.

History will show the wonderful Effects of ORATORY, in governing, turning and leading great Bodies of Mankind, Armies,
Cities, Nations. When the Minds of Youth are struck with Admiration at this, then is the Time to give them the Principles of
that Art, which they will study with Taste and Application. Then
they may be made acquainted with the best Models among the
antients, their Beauties being particularly pointed out to them.
Modern Political Oratory being chiefly performed by the Pen
and Press, its Advantages over the Antient in some Respects
are to be shown; as that its Effects are more extensive, more
lasting, &c.

History will also afford frequent Opportunities of showing
the Necessity of a *Publick Religion*, from its Usefulness to
the Publick; the Advantage of a Religious Character among
private Persons; the Mischiefs of Superstition, &c. and the

Excellency of the CHRISTIAN RELIGION above all others antient or modern.

History will also give Occasion to expatiate on the Advantage of Civil Orders and Constitutions; how Men and their Properties are protected by joining in Societies and establishing Government; their Industry encouraged and rewarded, Arts invented, and Life made more comfortable: The Advantages of *Liberty,* Mischiefs of *Licentiousness,* Benefits arising from good Laws and a due Execution of Justice, &c. Thus may the first Principles of sound *Politicks* be fix'd in the Minds of Youth.

On *Historical* Occasions, Questions of Right and Wrong, Justice and Injustice, will naturally arise, and may be put to Youth, which they may debate in Conversation and in Writing. When they ardently desire Victory, for the Sake of the Praise attending it, they will begin to feel the Want, and be sensible of the Use of *Logic,* or the Art of Reasoning to *discover* Truth, and of Arguing to *defend* it, and *convince* Adversaries. This would be the Time to acquaint them with the Principles of that Art. Grotius, Puffendorff, and some other Writers of the same Kind, may be used on these Occasions to decide their Disputes. Publick Disputes warm the Imagination, whet the Industry, and strengthen the natural Abilities.

When Youth are told, that the Great Men whose Lives and Actions they read in History, spoke two of the best Languages that ever were, the most expressive, copious, beautiful; and that the finest Writings, the most correct Compositions, the most perfect Productions of human Wit and Wisdom, are in those Languages, which have endured Ages, and will endure while there are Men; that no Translation can do them Justice, or give the Pleasure found in Reading the Originals; that those Languages contain all Science; that one of them is become almost universal, being the Language of Learned Men in all Countries; that to understand them is a distinguishing Ornament, &c. they may be thereby made desirous of learning those Languages, and their Industry sharpen'd in the Acquisition of them. All intended for Divinity, should be taught the *Latin* and *Greek;* for Physick, the *Latin, Greek,* and *French;* for Law, the *Latin* and

French; Merchants, the *French, German,* and *Spanish:* And though all should not be compell'd to learn *Latin, Greek,* or the modern foreign Languages; yet none that have an ardent Desire to learn them should be refused; their *English,* Arithmetick and other Studies absolutely necessary, being at the same Time not neglected.

If the new *Universal History* were also read, it would give a *connected* Idea of human Affairs, so far as it goes, which should be follow'd by the best modern Histories, particularly of our Mother Country; then of these Colonies; which should be accompanied with Observations on their Rise, Encrease, Use to *Great Britain,* Encouragements, Discouragements, etc. the Means to make them flourish, secure their Liberties, &c.

With the History of Men, Times, and Nations, should be read at proper Hours or Days, some of the best *Histories of Nature,* which would not only be delightful to Youth, and furnish them with Matter for their Letters, &c. as well as other History; but afterwards of great Use to them, whether they are Merchants, Handicrafts, or Divines; enabling the first the better to understand many Commodities, Drugs, &c.; the second to improve his Trade or Handicraft by new Mixtures, Materials, &c., and the last to adorn his Discourses by beautiful Comparisons, and strengthen them by new Proofs of Divine Providence. The Conversation of all will be improved by it, as Occasions frequently occur of making Natural Observations, which are instructive, agreeable, and entertaining in almost all Companies. *Natural History* will also afford Opportunities of introducing many Observations, relating to the Preservation of Health, which may be afterwards of great Use. *Arbuthnot* on Air and *Aliment, Sanctorius* on Perspiration, *Lemery* on Foods, and some others, may now be read, and a very little Explanation will make them sufficiently intelligible to Youth.

While they are reading Natural History, might not a little *Gardening, Planting, Grafting, Inoculating,* etc., be taught and practised; and now and then Excursions made to the neighbouring Plantations of the best Farmers, their Methods observ'd and reason'd upon for the Information of Youth? The

Improvement of Agriculture being useful to all, and Skill in it no Disparagement to any.

The History of *Commerce,* of the Invention of Arts, Rise of Manufactures, Progress of Trade, Change of its Seats, with the Reasons, Causes, &c., may also be made entertaining to Youth, and will be useful to all. And this, with the Accounts in other History of the prodigious Force and Effect of Engines and Machines used in War, will naturally introduce a Desire to be instructed in *Mechanicks,* and to be inform'd of the Principles of that Art by which weak Men perform such Wonders, Labour is sav'd, Manufactures expedited, &c. This will be the Time to show them Prints of antient and modern Machines, to explain them, to let them be copied, and to give Lectures in Mechanical Philosophy.

With the whole should be constantly inculcated and cultivated, that *Benignity of Mind,* which shows itself in *searching for* and *seizing* every Opportunity *to serve* and *to oblige;* and is the Foundation of what is called GOOD BREEDING; highly useful to the Possessor, and most agreeable to all.

The Idea of what is *true Merit* should also be often presented to Youth, explain'd and impress'd on their Minds, as consisting in an *Inclination* join'd with an *Ability* to serve Mankind, one's Country, Friends and Family; which *Ability* is (with the Blessing of God) to be acquir'd or greatly encreas'd by *true Learning;* and should indeed be the great *Aim* and *End* of all Learning.

TO MISS
MARY STEVENSON

I send my good Girl the Books I mention'd to her last Night. I beg her to accept them as a small Mark of my Esteem and Friendship. They are written in the familiar, easy Manner, for which the French are so remarkable; and afford a good deal of philosophic and practical Knowledge, unembarras'd with the dry Mathematics us'd by more exact Reasoners, but which is apt to discourage young Beginners.

I would advise you to read with a Pen in your Hand, and enter in a little Book short Hints of what you find that is curious, or that may be useful; for this will be the best Method of imprinting such Particulars in your Memory, where they will be ready, either for Practice on some future Occasion, if they are Matters of Utility, or at least to adorn and improve your Conversation, if they are rather Points of Curiosity. And, as many of the Terms of Science are such as you cannot have met with in your common Reading and may therefore be unacquainted with, I think it would be well for you to have a good Dictionary at hand, to consult immediately when you meet with a Word you do not comprehend the precise Meaning of. This may at first seem troublesome and interrupting; but 'tis a Trouble that will daily diminish, as you will daily find less and less Occasion for your Dictionary, as you become more acquainted with the Terms; and in the mean time you will read with more Satisfaction, because with more Understanding.

When any Point occurs, in which you would be glad to have farther Information than your Book affords you, I beg you would not in the least apprehend, that I should think it a Trouble to receive and answer your Questions. It will be a Pleasure, and no Trouble. For tho' I may not be able, out of my own little Stock of Knowledge, to afford you what you require, I can easily direct you to the Books, where it may most readily be found. Adieu, and believe me ever, my dear Friend, yours affectionately,

B. FRANKLIN.

TO MISS
MARY STEVENSON

Craven Street, June 11, 1760.

DEAR POLLY:

'Tis a very sensible Question you ask, how the Air can affect the Barometer, when its Opening appears covered with Wood? If indeed it was so closely covered as to admit of no Communication of the outward Air to the Surface of the Mercury, the Change of Weight in the Air could not possibly affect it. But the least Crevice is sufficient for the Purpose; a Pinhole will do the Business. And if you could look behind the Frame to which your Barometer is fixed, you would certainly find some small Opening.

There are indeed some Barometers in which the Body of Mercury at the lower End is contain'd in a close Leather Bag, and so the Air cannot come into immediate Contact with the Mercury; yet the same Effect is produc'd. For, the Leather being flexible, when the Bag is press'd by any additional Weight of Air, it contracts, and the Mercury is forced up into the Tube; when the Air becomes lighter, and its Pressure less, the Weight of the Mercury prevails, and it descends again into the Bag.

Your Observation on what you have lately read concerning Insects is very just and solid. Superficial Minds are apt to despise those who make that Part of the Creation their Study, as mere Triflers; but certainly the World has been much oblig'd to them. Under the Care and Management of Man, the Labours of the little Silkworm afford Employment and Subsistence to Thousands of Families, and become an immense Article of Commerce. The Bee, too, yields us its delicious Honey, and its

Wax useful to a Multitude of Purposes. Another Insect, it is said, produces the Cochineal, from whence we have our rich Scarlet Dye. The Usefulness of the Cantharides, or Spanish Flies, in Medicine, is known to all, and Thousands owe their Lives to that Knowledge. By human Industry and Observation, other Properties of other Insects may possibly be hereafter discovered, and of equal Utility. A thorough Acquaintance with the Nature of these little Creatures may also enable Mankind to prevent the Increase of such as are noxious, or secure us against the Mischiefs they occasion. These Things doubtless your Books make mention of: I can only add a particular late Instance which I had from a Swedish Gentleman of good Credit. In the green Timber, intended for Ship-building at the King's Yards in that Country, a kind of Worms were found, which every year became more numerous and more pernicious, so that the Ships were greatly damag'd before they came into Use. The King sent Linnæus, the great Naturalist, from Stockholm, to enquire into the Affair, and see if the Mischief was capable of any Remedy. He found, on Examination, that the Worm was produced from a small Egg, deposited in the little Roughnesses on the Surface of the Wood, by a particular kind of Fly or Beetle; from whence the Worm, as soon as it was hatched, began to eat into the Substance of the Wood, and after some time came out again a Fly of the Parent kind, and so the Species increased. The season in which this Fly laid its Eggs, Linnæus knew to be about a Fortnight (I think) in the Month of May, and at no other time of the Year. He therefore advis'd, that, some Days before that Season, all the green Timber should be thrown into the Water, and kept under Water till the Season was over. Which being done by the King's Order, the Flies missing their usual Nests, could not increase; and the Species was either destroy'd or went elsewhere; and the Wood was effectually preserved; for, after the first Year, it became too dry and hard for their purpose.

There is, however, a prudent Moderation to be used in Studies of this kind. The Knowledge of Nature may be ornamental, and it may be useful; but if, to attain an Eminence in that, we neglect the Knowledge and Practice of essential Duties, we

deserve Reprehension. For there is no Rank in Natural Knowledge of equal Dignity and Importance with that of being a good
Parent, a good Child, a good Husband or Wife, a good Neighbour or Friend, a good Subject or Citizen, that is, in short, a
good Christian. Nicholas Gimcrack, therefore, who neglected
the Care of his Family, to pursue Butterflies, was a just Object of
Ridicule, and we must give him up as fair Game to the satyrist.

Adieu, my dear Friend, and believe me ever

Yours affectionately,

B. FRANKLIN

TO MISS
MARY STEVENSON

Philad^a March 25, 1763.

MY DEAR POLLEY,

Your pleasing Favour of Nov. 11 is now before me. It found me as you suppos'd it would, happy with my American Friends and Family about me; and it made me more happy in showing me that I am not yet forgotten by the dear Friends I left in England. And indeed, why should I fear they will ever forget me, when I feel so strongly that I shall ever remember them!

I sympathise with you sincerely in your Grief at the Separation from your old Friend, Miss Pitt. The Reflection that she is going to be more happy, when she leaves you, might comfort you, if the Case was likely to be so circumstanc'd; but when the Country and Company she has been educated in, and those she is removing to, are compared, one cannot possibly expect it. I sympathize no less with you in your Joys. But it is not merely on your Account, that I rejoice at the Recovery of your dear Dolly's Health. I love that dear good Girl myself, and I love her other Friends. I am, therefore, made happy by what must contribute so much to the Happiness of them all. Remember me to her, and to every one of that worthy and amiable Family, most affectionately.

Remember me in the same manner to your and my good Doctor and Mrs. Hawkesworth. You have lately, you tell me, had the Pleasure of spending three Days with them at Mr. Stanley's. It was a sweet Society! I too, once partook of that same Pleasure, and can therefore feel what you must have felt. Remember me also to Mr. and Mrs. Stanley, and to Miss Arlond.

Of all the enviable Things England has, I envy it most its People. Why should that petty Island, which compar'd to America, is but like a stepping-Stone in a Brook, scarce enough of it above Water to keep one's Shoes dry; why, I say, should that little Island enjoy in almost every Neighbourhood, more sensible, virtuous, and elegant Minds, than we can collect in ranging 100 Leagues of our vast Forests? But 'tis said the Arts delight to travel Westward. You have effectually defended us in this glorious War, and in time you will improve us. After the first Cares for the Necessaries of Life are over, we shall come to think of the Embellishments. Already some of our young Geniuses begin to lisp Attempts at Painting, Poetry, and Musick. We have a young Painter now studying at Rome.[1] Some Specimens of our Poetry I send you, which if Dr. Hawkesworth's fine Taste cannot approve, his good Heart will at least excuse. The Manuscript Piece is by a young Friend of mine, and was occasion'd by the Loss of one of his Friends, who lately made a Voyage to Antigua to settle some Affairs, previous to an intended Marriage with an amiable young Lady here, but unfortunately died there. I send it to you, because the Author is a great Admirer of Mr. Stanley's musical Compositions, and has adapted this Piece to an Air in the 6th *Concerto* of that Gentleman, the sweetly solemn Movement of which he is quite in Raptures with. He has attempted to compose a *Recitativo* for it, but not being able to satisfy himself in the Bass, wishes I could get it supply'd. If Mr. Stanley would condescend to do that for him, thro' your Intercession, he would esteem it as one of the highest Honours, and it would make him excessively happy. You will say that a *Recitativo* can be but a poor Specimen of our Music. 'Tis the best and all I have at present, but you may see better hereafter.

I hope Mr. Ralph's Affairs are mended since you wrote. I know he had some Expectations, when I came away, from a Hand that would help him. He has Merit, and one would think ought not to be so unfortunate.

I do not wonder at the behaviour you mention of Dr. Smith[2] towards me, for I have long since known him thoroughly. I made that Man my Enemy by doing him too much Kindness. 'Tis the honestest Way of acquiring an Enemy. And, since 'tis convenient to have at least one Enemy, who by his Readiness to revile one on all Occasions, may make one careful of one's Conduct, I shall keep him an Enemy for that purpose; and shall observe your good Mother's Advice, never again to receive him as a Friend. She once admir'd the benevolent Spirit breath'd in his Sermons. She will now see the Justness of the Lines your Laureat White-head addresses to his Poets, and which I now address to her.

> "Full many a peevish, envious, slanderous Elf
> Is, in his Works, Benevolence itself.
> For all Mankind, unknown, his Bosom heaves;
> He only injures those, with whom he lives.
> Read then the Man;—does *Truth* his Actions guide,
> Exempt from *Petulance,* exempt from *Pride?*
> To social Duties does his Heart attend,
> As Son, as Father, Husband, Brother, *Friend?*
> *Do those, who know him, love him?* If they do,
> You 've *my* Permission : you may love him too."

Nothing can please me more than to see your philosophical Improvements when you have Leisure to communicate them to me. I still owe you a long Letter on that Subject, which I shall pay. I am vex'd with Mr. James, that he has been so dilatory in Mr. Maddison's *Armonica.* I was unlucky in both the Workmen, that I permitted to undertake making those Instruments. The first was fanciful, and never could work to the purpose, because he was ever conceiving some new Improvement, that answer'd no End. The other I doubt is absolutely idle. I have recommended a Number to him from hence, but must stop my hand.

Adieu, my dear Polly, and believe me as ever, with the sincerest Esteem and Regard, your truly affectionate Friend and humble Servant,

B. FRANKLIN.

P. S. My love to Mrs. Tickell and Mrs. Rooke, and to Pitty, when you write to her. Mrs. Franklin and Sally desire to be affectionately remember'd to you. I find the printed Poetry I intended to enclose will be too bulky to send per the Packet. I shall send it by a Ship, that goes shortly from hence.

TO OLIVER NEAVE

Dear SIR,

I cannot be of opinion with you that 'tis too late in life for you to learn to swim. The river near the bottom of your garden affords you a most convenient place for the purpose. And as your new employment requires your being often on the water, of which you have such a dread, I think you would do well to make the trial; nothing being so likely to remove those apprehensions as the consciousness of an ability to swim to the shore, in case of an accident, or of supporting yourself in the water till a boat could come to take you up.

I do not know how far corks or bladders may be useful in learning to swim, having never seen much trial of them. Possibly they may be of service in supporting the body while you are learning what is called the stroke, or that manner of drawing in and striking out the hands and feet that is necessary to produce progressive motion. But you will be no swimmer till you can place some confidence in the power of the water to support you; I would therefore advise the acquiring that confidence in the first place; especially as I have known several who by a little of the practice necessary for that purpose, have insensibly acquired the stroke, taught as it were by nature.

The practice I mean is this. Chusing a place where the water deepens gradually, walk coolly into it till it is up to your breast, then turn round, your face to the shore, and throw an egg into the water between you and the shore. It will sink to the bottom, and be easily seen there, as your water is clear. It must lie in water so deep as that you cannot reach it to take it up but by diving for it. To encourage yourself in undertaking to do this, reflect that your progress will be from deeper to shallower water, and that at any time you may by bringing your legs under you and standing on the bottom, raise your head far above the water. Then plunge under it with your eyes open, throwing yourself towards the egg, and endeavouring by the action of your hands and feet against the water to get forward till within reach of it. In this attempt you will find, that the water buoys you up against your inclination; that it is not so easy a thing to sink as you imagined; that you cannot, but by active force, get down to the egg. Thus you feel the power of the water to support you, and learn to confide in that power; while your endeavours to overcome it and to reach the egg, teach you the manner of acting on the water with your feet and hands, which action is afterwards used in swimming to support your head higher above water, or to go forward through it.

I would the more earnestly press you to the trial of this method, because, though I think I satisfyed you that your body is lighter than water, and that you might float in it a long time with your mouth free for breathing, if you would put yourself in a proper posture, and would be still and forbear struggling; yet till you have obtained this experimental confidence in the water, I cannot depend on your having the necessary presence of mind to recollect that posture and the directions I gave you relating to it. The surprize may put all out of your mind. For though we value ourselves on being reasonable knowing creatures, reason and knowledge seem on such occasions to be of little use to us; and the brutes to whom we allow scarce a glimmering of either, appear to have the advantage of us.

I will, however, take this opportunity of repeating those particulars to you, which I mentioned in our last conversation, as by perusing them at your leisure, you may possibly imprint them so in your memory as on occasion to be of some use to you.

1. That though the legs, arms and head, of a human body, being solid parts, are specifically something heavier than fresh water, yet the trunk, particularly the upper part from its hollowness, is so much lighter than water, as that the whole of the body taken together is too light to sink wholly under water, but some part will remain above, untill the lungs become filled with

water, which happens from drawing water into them instead of air, when a person in the fright attempts breathing while the mouth and nostrils are under water.

2. That the legs and arms are specifically lighter than salt-water, and will be supported by it, so that a human body would not sink in salt-water, though the lungs were filled as above, but from the greater specific gravity of the head.

3. That therefore a person throwing himself on his back in salt-water, and extending his arms, may easily lie so as to keep his mouth and nostrils free for breathing; and by a small motion of his hands may prevent turning, if he should perceive any tendency to it.

4. That in fresh water, if a man throws himself on his back, near the surface, he cannot long continue in that situation but by proper action of his hands on the water. If he uses no such action, the legs and lower part of the body will gradually sink till he comes into an upright position, in which he will continue suspended, the hollow of the breast keeping the head uppermost.

5. But if in this erect position, the head is kept upright above the shoulders, as when we stand on the ground, the immersion will, by the weight of that part of the head that is out of water, reach above the mouth and nostrils, perhaps a little above the eyes, so that a man cannot long remain suspended in water with his head in that position.

6. The body continuing suspended as before, and upright, if the head be leaned quite back, so that the face looks upwards, all the back part of the head being then under water, and its weight consequently in a great measure supported by it, the face will remain above water quite free for breathing, will rise an inch higher every inspiration, and sink as much every expiration, but never so low as that the water may come over the mouth.

7. If therefore a person unacquainted with swimming, and falling accidentally into the water, could have presence of mind sufficient to avoid struggling and plunging, and to let the body take this natural position, he might continue long safe from drowning till perhaps help would come. For as to the cloathes, their additional weight while immersed is very inconsiderable,

the water supporting it; though when he comes out of the water, he would find them very heavy indeed.

But, as I said before, I would not advise you or any one to depend on having this presence of mind on such an occasion, but learn fairly to swim; as I wish all men were taught to do in their youth; they would, on many occurrences, be the safer for having that skill, and on many more the happier, as freer from painful apprehensions of danger, to say nothing of the enjoyment in so delightful and wholesome an exercise. Soldiers particularly should, methinks, all be taught to swim; it might be of frequent use either in surprising an enemy, or saving themselves. And if I had now boys to educate, I should prefer those schools (other things being equal) where an opportunity was afforded for acquiring so advantageous an art, which once learnt is never forgotten.

I am, Sir, &c.

THE HANDSOME AND
DEFORMED LEG

THERE are two Sorts of People in the World, who with equal Degrees of Health, & Wealth, and the other Comforts of Life, become, the one happy, and the other miserable. This arises very much from the different Views in which they consider Things, Persons, and Events; and the Effect of those different Views upon their own Minds.

In whatever Situation Men can be plac'd, they may find Conveniencies & Inconveniencies: In whatever Company; they may find Persons & Conversation more or less pleasing. At whatever Table, they may meet with Meats & Drinks of better and worse Taste, Dishes better & worse dress'd: In whatever Climate they will find good and bad Weather: Under whatever Government, they may find good & bad Laws, and good & bad Administration of those Laws. In every Poem or Work of Genius they may see Faults and Beauties. In almost every Face & every Person, they may discover fine Features & Defects, good & bad Qualities.

Under these Circumstances, the two Sorts of People above mention'd fix their Attention, those who are to be happy, on the Conveniencies of Things, the pleasant Parts of Conversation, the well-dress'd Dishes, the Goodness of the Wines, the fine Weather; &c., and enjoy all with Chearfulness. Those who are to be unhappy, think & speak only of the contraries. Hence they are continually discontented themselves, and by their Remarks sour the Pleasures of Society, offend personally many People, and make themselves everywhere disagreable. If this Turn of Mind was founded in Nature, such unhappy Persons

would be the more to be pitied. But as the Disposition to criti-
cise, & be disgusted, is perhaps taken up originally by Imitation, and is unawares grown into a Habit, which tho' at present
strong may nevertheless be cured when those who have it are
convinc'd of its bad Effects on their Felicity; I hope this little
Admonition may be of Service to them, and put them on changing a Habit, which tho' in the Exercise it is chiefly an Act of
Imagination yet has serious Consequences in Life, as it brings
on real Griefs and Misfortunes. For as many are offended by, &
nobody well loves this Sort of People, no one shows them more
than the most common civility and respect, and scarcely that;
and this frequently puts them out of humour, and draws them
into disputes and contentions. If they aim at obtaining some advantage in rank or fortune, nobody wishes them success, or will
stir a step, or speak a word, to favour their pretensions. If they
incur public censure or disgrace, no one will defend or excuse,
and many join to aggravate their misconduct, and render them
completely odious. If these people will not change this bad habit,
and condescend to be pleased with what is pleasing, without
fretting themselves and others about the contraries, it is good
for others to avoid an acquaintance with them; which is always
disagreeable, and sometimes very inconvenient, especially when
one finds one's self entangled in their quarrels.

An old philosophical friend of mine was grown, from experience, very cautious in this particular, and carefully avoided any
intimacy with such people. He had, like other philosophers, a
thermometer to show him the heat of the weather, and a barometer to mark when it was likely to prove good or bad; but, there
being no instrument invented to discover, at first sight, this unpleasing disposition in a person, he for that purpose made use
of his legs; one of which was remarkably handsome, the other,
by some accident, crooked and deformed. If a Stranger, at the
first interview, regarded his ugly Leg more than his handsome
one, he doubted him. If he spoke of it, & took no notice of
the handsome Leg, that was sufficient to determine my Philosopher to have no further Acquaintance with him. Every body
has not this two-legged Instrument, but every one with a little

Attention, may observe Signs of that carping, fault-finding Disposition, & take the same Resolution of avoiding the Acquaintance of those infected with it. I therefore advise those critical, querulous, discontented, unhappy People, that if they wish to be respected and belov'd by others, & happy in themselves they should *leave off looking at the ugly Leg.*

TO RICHARD PRICE

Passy, March 18, 1785.

DEAR FRIEND,

My nephew, Mr. Williams, will have the honour of delivering you this line. It is to request from you a List of a few good Books, to the Value of about Twenty-five Pounds, such as are most proper to inculcate Principles of sound Religion and just Government. A New Town in the State of Massachusetts having done me the honour of naming itself after me, and proposing to build a Steeple to their meeting-house if I would give them a Bell, I have advis'd the sparing themselves the Expence of a Steeple, for the present, and that they would accept of Books instead of a Bell, Sense being preferable to Sound. These are therefore intended as the Commencement of a little Parochial Library for the Use of a Society of intelligent, respectable Farmers, such as our Country People generally consist of. Besides your own Works, I would only mention, on the Recommendation of my sister, "Stennet's *Discourses on Personal Religion,*" which may be one Book of the Number, if you know and approve of it.

With the highest Esteem and Respect, I am ever, my dear Friend, yours most affectionately,

B. FRANKLIN.

THE ART OF PROCURING PLEASANT DREAMS

Inscribed to Miss [Shipley], Being Written at her Request

As a great part of our life is spent in sleep during which we have sometimes pleasant and sometimes painful dreams, it becomes of some consequence to obtain the one kind and avoid the other; for whether real or imaginary, pain is pain and pleasure is pleasure. If we can sleep without dreaming, it is well that painful dreams are avoided. If while we sleep we can have any pleasing dream, it is, as the French say, *autant de gagné,* so much added to the pleasure of life.

To this end it is, in the first place, necessary to be careful in preserving health, by due exercise and great temperance; for, in sickness, the imagination is disturbed, and disagreeable, sometimes terrible, ideas are apt to present themselves. Exercise should precede meals, not immediately follow them; the first promotes, the latter, unless moderate, obstructs digestion. If, after exercise, we feed sparingly, the digestion will be easy and good, the body lightsome, the temper cheerful, and all the animal functions performed agreeably. Sleep, when it follows, will be natural and undisturbed; while indolence, with full feeding, occasions nightmares and horrors inexpressible; we fall from precipices, are assaulted by wild beasts, murderers, and demons, and experience every variety of distress. Observe, however, that the quantities of food and exercise are relative things; those who move much may, and indeed ought to eat more; those who use little exercise should eat little. In general, mankind, since the improvement of cookery, eat about twice as much as nature requires. Suppers are not bad, if we have not dined; but restless nights naturally follow hearty suppers after full dinners. Indeed, as there is a difference in constitutions, some rest well after these meals; it costs them only a frightful dream and an apoplexy, after which they sleep till doomsday. Nothing is more common in the newspapers, than instances of people who, after eating a hearty supper, are found dead abed in the morning.

Another means of preserving health, to be attended to, is the having a constant supply of fresh air in your bed-chamber. It has been a great mistake, the sleeping in rooms exactly closed, and in beds surrounded by curtains. No outward air that may come in to you is so unwholesome as the unchanged air, often breathed, of a close chamber. As boiling water does not grow hotter by longer boiling, if the particles that receive greater heat can escape; so living bodies do not putrefy, if the particles, so fast as they become putrid, can be thrown off. Nature expels them by the pores of the skin and the lungs, and in a free, open air they are carried off; but in a close room we receive them again and again, though they become more and more corrupt. A number of persons crowded into a small room thus spoil the air in a few minutes, and even render it mortal, as in the Black Hole at Calcutta. A single person is said to spoil only a gallon of air per minute, and therefore requires a longer time to spoil a chamber-full; but it is done, however, in proportion, and many putrid disorders hence have their origin. It is recorded of Methusalem, who, being the longest liver, may be supposed to have best preserved his health, that he slept always in the open air; for, when he had lived five hundred years, an angel said to him; "Arise, Methusalem, and build thee an house, for thou shalt live yet five hundred years longer." But Methusalem answered, and said, "If I am to live but five hundred years longer, it is not worth while to build me an house; I will sleep in the air, as I have been used to do." Physicians, after having for ages contended that the sick should not be indulged with fresh air, have at length discovered that it may do them good. It is therefore to be hoped, that they may in time discover likewise, that it is not hurtful to those who are in health, and that we may be then cured of the *aërophobia,* that at present distresses weak minds, and makes them choose to be stifled and poisoned, rather than leave open the window of a bed-chamber, or put down the glass of a coach.

Confined air, when saturated with perspirable matter, will not receive more; and that matter must remain in our bodies, and occasion diseases; but it gives some previous notice of its being about to be hurtful, by producing certain uneasiness, slight indeed at first, which as with regard to the lungs is a trifling sensation, and to the pores of the skin a kind of restlessness, which is difficult to describe, and few that feel it know the cause of it. But we may recollect, that sometimes on waking in the night, we have, if warmly covered, found it difficult to get asleep again. We turn often without finding repose in any position. This fidgettiness (to use a vulgar expression for want of a better) is occasioned wholly by an uneasiness in the skin, owing to the retention of the perspirable matter—the bed-clothes having received their quantity, and, being saturated, refusing to take any more. To become sensible of this by an experiment, let a person keep his position in the bed, but throw off the bed-clothes, and suffer fresh air to approach the part uncovered of his body; he will then feel that part suddenly refreshed; for the air will immediately relieve the skin, by receiving, licking up, and carrying off, the load of perspirable matter that incommoded it. For every portion of cool air that approaches the warm skin, in receiving its part of that vapour, receives therewith a degree of heat that rarefies and renders it lighter, when it will be pushed away with its burthen, by cooler and therefore heavier fresh air, which for a moment supplies its place, and then, being likewise changed and warmed, gives way to a succeeding quantity. This is the order of nature, to prevent animals being infected by their own perspiration. He will now be sensible of the difference between the part exposed to the air and that which, remaining sunk in the bed, denies the air access: for this part now manifests its uneasiness more distinctly by the comparison, and the seat of the uneasiness is more plainly perceived than when the whole surface of the body was affected by it.

Here, then, is one great and general cause of unpleasing dreams. For when the body is uneasy, the mind will be disturbed by it, and disagreeable ideas of various kinds will in sleep be the natural consequences. The remedies, preventive and curative, follow:

1. By eating moderately (as before advised for health's sake) less perspirable matter is produced in a given time; hence the bed-clothes receive it longer before they are saturated, and we may therefore sleep longer before we are made uneasy by their refusing to receive any more.

2. By using thinner and more porous bed-clothes, which will suffer the perspirable matter more easily to pass through them, we are less incommoded, such being longer tolerable.

3. When you are awakened by this uneasiness, and find you cannot easily sleep again, get out of bed, beat up and turn your pillow, shake the bed-clothes well, with at least twenty shakes, then throw the bed open and leave it to cool; in the meanwhile, continuing undrest, walk about your chamber till your skin has had time to discharge its load, which it will do sooner as the air may be dried and colder. When you begin to feel the cold air unpleasant, then return to your bed, and you will soon fall asleep, and your sleep will be sweet and pleasant. All the scenes presented to your fancy will be too of the pleasing kind. I am often as agreeably entertained with them, as by the scenery of an opera. If you happen to be too indolent to get out of bed, you may, instead of it, lift up your bed-clothes with one arm and leg, so as to draw in a good deal of fresh air, and by letting them fall force it out again. This, repeated twenty times, will so clear them of the perspirable matter they have imbibed, as to permit your sleeping well for some time afterwards. But this latter method is not equal to the former.

Those who do not love trouble, and can afford to have two beds, will find great luxury in rising, when they wake in a hot bed, and going into the cool one. Such shifting of beds would also be of great service to persons ill of a fever, as it refreshes and frequently procures sleep. A very large bed, that will admit a removal so distant from the first situation as to be cool and sweet, may in a degree answer the same end.

One or two observations more will conclude this little piece. Care must be taken, when you lie down, to dispose your pillow so as to suit your manner of placing your head, and to be perfectly easy; then place your limbs so as not to bear inconveniently hard upon one another, as, for instance, the joints of

your ankles; for, though a bad position may at first give but little pain and be hardly noticed, yet a continuance will render it
less tolerable, and the uneasiness may come on while you are
asleep, and disturb your imagination. These are the rules of the
art. But, though they will generally prove effectual in producing
the end intended, there is a case in which the most punctual ob-
servance of them will be totally fruitless. I need not mention the
case to you, my dear friend, but my account of the art would be
imperfect without it. The case is, when the person who desires
to have pleasant dreams has not taken care to preserve, what is
necessary above all things,

A Good Conscience.

TO CADWALLADER
COLDEN

Philadelphia, September 29, 1748.

SIR,

I received your favour of the 12th instant, which gave me the greater pleasure, as it was so long since I had heard from you. I congratulate you on your return to your beloved retirement. I, too, am taking the proper measures for obtaining leisure to enjoy life and my friends, more than heretofore, having put my printing-house under the care of my partner, David Hall, absolutely left off bookselling, and removed to a more quiet part of the town, where I am settling my old accounts, and hope soon to be quite master of my own time, and no longer, as the song has it, *at every one's call but my own.* If health continue, I hope to be able in another year to visit the most distant friend I have, without inconvenience.

With the same views I have refused engaging further in public affairs. The share I had in the late Association, &c., having given me a little present run of popularity, there was a pretty general intention of choosing me a representative of the city at the next election of Assembly men; but I have desired all my friends, who spoke to me about it, to discourage it, declaring that I should not serve, if chosen. Thus you see I am in a fair way of having no other tasks, than such as I shall like to give myself, and of enjoying what I look upon as a great happiness, leisure to read, study, make experiments, and converse at large with such ingenious and worthy men, as are pleased to honour me with their friendship or acquaintance, on such points as may produce something for the common benefit of mankind, uninterrupted by the little cares and fatigues of business. Among other pleasures I promise myself, that of corresponding more frequently and fully with Dr. Colden is none of the least. I shall only wish that what must be so agreeable to me may not prove troublesome to you.

I thank you for your kind recommending of me to Mr. Osborne. Mr. Read would readily have put the books into my hands, but, it being now out of my way to dispose of them, I propose to Mr. Hall the taking of them into his shop; but he, having looked over the invoice, says they are charged so extravagantly high, that he cannot sell them for any profit to himself, without hurting the character of his shop. He will, however, at my request, take the copies of the Indian History[1] and put them on sale; but the rest of the cargo must lie, I believe, for Mr. Osborne's further orders. I shall write to him by our next vessels.

I am glad you have had an opportunity of gaining the friendship of Governor Shirley, with whom though I have not the honour of being particularly acquainted, I take him to be a wise, good, and worthy man. He is now a fellow sufferer with you, in being made the subject of some public, virulent, and senseless libels. I hope they give him as little pain.

Mr. Bartram[2] continues well. Here is a Swedish gentleman,[3] a professor of botany, lately arrived, and I suppose will soon be your way, as he intends for Canada. Mr. Collinson and Dr. Mitchell recommend him to me as an ingenious man. Perhaps the enclosed (left at the post-office for you) may be from him. I have not seen him since the first day he came. I delivered yours to Mr. Evans; and, when I next see Mr. Bartram, I shall acquaint him with what you say.

I am, with great esteem and respect, dear Sir, &c.

B. FRANKLIN.

TO MRS. ABIAH FRANKLIN

Philad^a April 12, 1750

HONOURED MOTHER,

We received your kind Letter of the 2d Instant, and we are glad to hear you still enjoy such a Measure of Health, notwithstanding your great Age. We read your Writing very easily. I never met with a Word in your Letters but what I could readily understand; for, tho' the Hand is not always the best, the Sense makes every thing plain. My Leg, which you inquire after, is now quite well. I shall keep those Servants; but the Man not in my own house. I have hired him out to the Man, that takes care of my Dutch Printing-Office, who agrees to keep him in Victuals and Clothes, and to pay me a Dollar a Week for his Work. His wife, since that Affair, behaves exceeding well; but we conclude to sell them both the first good Opportunity, for we do not like Negro Servants. We got again about half what we lost.

As to your Grandchildren, Will is now nineteen years of age, a tall proper Youth, and much of a Beau. He acquired a Habit of Idleness on the Expedition but begins of late to apply himself to Business, and I hope will become an industrious Man. He imagin'd his Father had got enough for him, but I have assured him that I intend to spend what little I have myself, if it please God that I live long enough; and, as he by no means wants Sense, he can see by my going on, that I am like to be as good as my Word.

Sally grows a fine Girl, and is extreamly industrious with her Needle, and delights in her Book. She is of a most affectionate Temper, and perfectly dutiful and obliging to her Parents, and to all. Perhaps I flatter myself too much, but I have Hopes that she will prove an ingenious, sensible, notable, and worthy Woman, like her aunt Jenny. She goes now to the Dancing-School.

For my own Part, at present, I pass my Time agreably enough. I enjoy, thro' Mercy, a tolerable Share of Health. I read a great deal, ride a little, do a little Business for myself, more for others, retire when I can, and go into Company when I please; so the Years roll round, and the last will come; when I would rather have it said, *He lived Usefully,* than *He died Rich.*

Cousins Josiah and Sally are well, and I believe will do well, for they are an industrious saving young Couple; but they want a little more Stock to go on smoothly with their Business.

My Love to Brother and Sister Mecom, and their Children, and to all my Relations in general. I am your dutiful Son,

B. FRANKLIN.

TO MRS. DEBORAH
FRANKLIN

Gnadenhutten, January 25, 1756.

MY DEAR CHILD,

This day week we arrived here. I wrote to you the same day, and once since. We all continue well, thanks be to God. We have been hindered with bad weather, yet our fort is in a good defensible condition, and we have every day more convenient living. Two more are to be built, one on each side of this, at about fifteen miles' distance. I hope both will be done in a week or ten days, and then I purpose to bend my course homewards.

We have enjoyed your roast beef, and this day began on the roast veal. All agree that they are both the best that ever were of the kind. Your citizens, that have their dinners hot and hot, know nothing of good eating. We find it in much greater perfection when the kitchen is four score miles from the dining room.

The apples are extremely welcome, and do bravely to eat after our salt pork; the minced pies are not yet come to hand, but I suppose we shall find them among the things expected up from Bethlehem on Tuesday; the capillaire[1] is excellent, but none of us having taken cold as yet, we have only tasted it.

As to our lodging, it is on deal featherbeds, in warm blankets, and much more comfortable than when we lodged at our inn, the first night after we left home; for the woman being about to put very damp sheets on the bed, we desired her to air them first; half an hour afterwards, she told us the bed was ready, and the sheets *well aired*. I got into bed, but jumped out immediately, finding them as cold as death, and partly frozen. She had *aired* them indeed, but it was out upon the hedge. I was forced to wrap myself up in my great coat and woollen trowsers. Every thing else about the bed was shockingly dirty.

As I hope in a little time to be with you and my family, and chat things over, I now only add, that I am, dear Debby, your affectionate husband,

B. FRANKLIN.

TO MRS. DEBORAH
FRANKLIN

London, Feb. 19, 1758.

MY DEAR CHILD,

I have wrote you several long Letters lately; the last was by Mr. Ralphe, and at the same time I wrote to my dear Sally. Last Night I receiv'd yours of the 1st and 6th of January, which gave me the great Pleasure of hearing that you and my little Family were well. I hope you continue so, and that I shall have the Happiness to find you so. The Letter you mention to have sent me by Capt. Robinson is not come to hand; but that by Mr. Hunt I received and answered.

I regret the Loss of my Friend Parsons. Death begins to make Breaches in the little Junto of old Friends, that he had long forborne, and it must be expected he will now soon pick us all off one after another.

Your kind Advice about getting a Chariot, I had taken some time before; for I found that every time I walk'd out, I got fresh Cold; and the Hackney Coaches at this End of the Town, where most People keep their own, are the worst in the whole City, miserable, dirty, broken, shabby Things, unfit to go into when dress'd clean, and such as one would be asham'd to get out of at any Gentleman's Door. As to burning Wood, it would answer no End, unless one would furnish all one's Neighbours and the whole City with the same. The whole Town is one great smoaky House, and every Street a Chimney, the Air full of floating Sea Coal Soot, and you never get a sweet Breath of what is pure, without riding some Miles for it into the Country.

I am sorry to hear, that a storm has damag'd a House of my good Friend's Mr. Bartram's. Acquaint him that I have receiv'd the Seeds, and shall write to him shortly. I hope the Speaker is recovered of the Illness you mention. Peter behaves very well to me in general and begins to know the town so as to go any-where of Errands. My Shirts are always well air'd as you di-rected. Mrs. Stevenson takes care of that. I am much more tender than I us'd to be, and sleep in a short Callico Bedgown with close Sleeves, and Flannel close-footed Trousers; for with-out them I get no Warmth all Night. So it seems I grow older apace. But otherwise at present I am pretty well.

Give my Thanks to Dr. Bond for the Care he takes of you. I have wrote to him by this Vessel. Mr. Hunter and Polly talk of returning this Spring. He is wonderfully recruited. They both desire to be remembred to you. She receiv'd your Letter and an-swer'd it. Her Answer I enclos'd in one of mine to you. Her Daughter Rachel, who plays on the Harpsichord and sings pret-tily, sends Sally one of her Songs, that I fancy'd.

I send you by Capt. Budden a large Case, mark'd D.F. No. 1. and a small box DF N° 2. In the large Case is another small Box, containing some English China; viz. Melons and Leaves for a Desert of Fruit and Cream, or the like; a Bowl remarkable for the Neatness of the Figures, made at Bow, near this City; some Coffee Cups of the same; a Worcester Bowl, ordinary. To show the Difference of Workmanship, there is something from all the China Works in England; and one old true China Bason mended, of an odd Colour. The same Box contains 4 Silver Salt Ladles, newest, but ugliest, Fashion; a little Instrument to core Apples; another to make little Turnips out of great ones; six coarse diaper Breakfast Cloths; they are to spread on the Tea Table, for nobody breakfasts here on the naked Table, but on the Cloth set a large Tea Board with the Cups. There is also a little Basket, a Present from Mrs. Stevenson to Sally, and a Pair of Garters for you, which were knit by the young Lady, her Daughter, who favour'd me with a Pair of the same kind, the only ones I have been able to wear; as they need not be bound tight, the Ridges in them preventing their Slipping. We send them therefore as a Curiosity for the Form, more than for the

Value. Goody Smith may, if she pleases, make such for me here-after, and they will suit her own fat Knees. My Love to her.

In the great Case, besides the little Box, is contain'd some Carpeting for a best Room Floor. There is enough for one large or two small ones, it is to be sow'd together, the Edges being first fell'd down, and Care taken to make the Figures meet exactly: there is Bordering for the same. This was my Fancy. Also two large fine Flanders BedTicks, and two pair large superfine Blankets, 2 fine Damask TableCloths and Napkins, and 43 Ells of Ghentish Sheeting Holland; these you ordered. There is also 56 Yards of Cotton, printed curiously from Copper Plates, a new Invention, to make Bed and Window Curtains; and 7 yards Chair Bottoms, printed in the same Way, very neat. These were my Fancy; but Mrs. Stevenson tells me I did wrong not to buy both of the same Colour. Also 7 yards of printed Cotton, blue Ground, to make you a Gown. I bought it by Candlelight, and lik'd it then, but not so well afterwards. If you do not fancy it, send it as a Present from me to sister Jenny. There is a better Gown for you, of flower'd Tissue, 16 yards, of Mrs. Stevenson's Fancy, cost 9 Guineas; and I think it a great Beauty. There was no more of the Sort, or you should have had enough for a *Negligée* or Suit.

There is also Snuffers, SnuffStand, and Extinguisher, of Steel, which I send for the Beauty of the Work. The Extinguisher is for Spermaceti Candles only, and is of a new Contrivance, to preserve the Snuff upon the Candle. There is also some Musick Billy bought for his Sister, and some Pamphlets for the Speaker and for Susy Wright. A Mahogany and a little Shagrin Box, with Microscopes and other Optical Instruments loose, are for Mr. Allison, if he likes them; if not, put them in my Room till I return. I send the Invoice of them, and I wrote to him formerly the Reason of my exceeding his Orders. There are also two Sets of Books, a Present from me to Sally, *The World* and *The Connoisseur*. My love to her.

I forgot to mention another of my Fancyings, viz. a Pair of Silk Blankets, very fine. They are of a new kind, were just taken in a French Prize, and such were never seen in England before: they are called Blankets, but I think will be very neat to cover a

Summer Bed, instead of a Quilt or Counterpain. I had no Choice, so you will excuse the Soil on some of the Folds; your Neighbour Forster can get it off. I also forgot, among the China, to mention a large fine Jugg for Beer, to stand in the Cooler. I fell in Love with it at first Sight; for I thought it look'd like a fat jolly Dame, clean and tidy, with a neat blue and white Calico Gown on, good natur'd and lovely, and put me in mind of— Somebody. It has the Coffee Cups in its Belly, pack'd in best Chrystal Salt, of a peculiar nice Flavour, for the Table, not to be powder'd. N° 2. contains cut Table Glass of several Sorts. I am about buying a compleat Set of Table China, 2 Cases of silver handled Knives and Forks, and 2 pair Silver Candlesticks; but these shall keep to use here till my Return, as I am obliged sometimes to entertain polite Company.

I wrote you by former Letters everything relating to Mr. Ralph and other Friends and Affairs which I hope you have received.

I hope Sally applys herself closely to her French and Musick, and that I shall find she has made great Proficiency. The Harpsichord I was about, and which was to have cost me 40 Guineas, Mr. Stanley advises me not to buy, and we are looking out for another, one that has been some time in use, and is a try'd good one, there being not so much Dependance on a new One, tho' made by the best Hands. Sally's last Letter to her Brother is the best wrote that of late I have seen of hers. I only wish she was a little more careful of her Spelling. I hope she continues to love going to Church, and would have her read over and over again the *Whole Duty of Man,* and the *Lady's Library.*

Look at the Figures on the China Bowl and Coffee Cups, with your Spectacles on; they will bear Examining.

I have made your Compliments to Mrs. Stevenson. She is indeed very obliging, takes great Care of my Health, and is very diligent when I am any way indispos'd; but yet I have a thousand times wish'd you with me, and my little Sally with her ready Hands and Feet to do, and go, and come, and get what I wanted. There is a great Difference in Sickness between being nurs'd with that tender Attention, which proceeds from sincere Love; and[1]

TO WILLIAM STRAHAN

Philad^a Dec. 7, 1762.

DEAR FRIEND

I wrote to you some time since to acquaint you with my Arrival and the kind Reception I met with from my old and many new Friends, notwithstanding Dr. Smith's false Reports in London of my Interest as declining here. I could not wish for a more hearty Welcome, and I never experienc'd greater Cordiality. We had a long Passage near ten Weeks from Portsmouth to this Place, but it was a pleasant one; for we had ten sail in Company and a Man of War* to protect us; we had pleasant Weather and fair Winds, and frequently visited and dined from ship to ship; we call'd too at the delightful Island of Madeira, by way of half-way House, where we replenish'd our Stores and took in many Refreshments. It was the time of their Vintage, and we hung the Cieling of the Cabin with Bunches of fine Grapes, which serv'd as a Dissert at Dinner for some Weeks afterwards. The Reason of our being so long at Sea, was, that sailing with a Convoy, we could none of us go faster than the slowest, being oblig'd every day to shorten Sail or lay by till they came up; this was the only Inconvenience of our having Company, which was abundantly made up to us by the Sense of greater Safety, the mutual good Offices daily exchanged and the other Pleasures of Society. I have no Line from you yet but I hope there is a Letter on its way to me.

---

*It was the Scarborough, Capt. Stott, who took the greatest Care of his little Convoy that can be imagined, and brought us all safely to our several Ports. I wish you would mention this to his Honour in your Paper.—F.

My Son is not yet arrived, and I begin to think he will spend the Winter with you. Mr. Hall I suppose writes by this Ship. I mention'd what you desir'd in your Letter to me at Portsmouth; he informs me he has made some Remittances since I left England, and shall as fast as possible clear the Acc^t. He blames himself for ordering so large a Cargo at once, and will keep more within Bounds hereafter.

Mr. Hall sends you I believe, for Sale, some Poetic Pieces of our young Geniuses; it would encourage them greatly if their Performances could obtain any favourable Reception in England; I wish therefore you would take the proper Steps to get them recommended to the Notice of the Publick as far at least as you may find they deserve. I know that no one can do this better than yourself.

You have doubtless long since done Rejoicing on the Conquest of the Havana. It is indeed a Conquest of great Importance; but it has cost us dear, extreamly dear, when we consider the Havock made in our little brave Army by Sickness. I hope it will, in the Making of Peace, procure us some Advantages in Commerce or Possession that may in time countervail the heavy Loss we have sustained in that Enterprize.

I must joyn with David in petitioning that you would write us all the Politicks; you have an Opportunity of hearing them all, and no one that is not quite in the Secret of Affairs can judge better of them. I hope the crazy Heads that have been so long raving about Scotchmen and Scotland are by this time either broke or mended.

My dear Love to Mrs. Strahan and bid her be well for all our sakes. Remember me affectionately to Rachey and my little Wife and to your promising Sons my young Friends Billy, George, and Andrew. God bless you, and let me find you well and happy when I come again to England; happy England! My Respects to Mr. Johnson; I hope he has got the Armonica in order before this time, and that Rachey plays daily with more and more Boldness and Grace, to the absolute charming of all her Acquaintance.

In two Years at farthest I hope to settle all my Affairs in such a Manner, as that I *may* then conveniently remove to

England,—provided we can persuade the good Woman to cross the Seas. That will be the great Difficulty: but you can help me a little in removing it.

Present my Compliments to all enquiring Friends, and believe me Ever

My dear Friend
Yours most affectionately
B. FRANKLIN.

TO WILLIAM FRANKLIN

DEAR SON,

I received your Letter of the 22d past, and am glad to find that you desire to revive the affectionate Intercourse, that formerly existed between us.¹ It will be very agreable to me; indeed nothing has ever hurt me so much and affected me with such keen Sensations, as to find myself deserted in my old Age by my only Son; and not only deserted, but to find him taking up Arms against me, in a Cause, wherein my good Fame, Fortune and Life were all at Stake. You conceived, you say, that your Duty to your King and Regard for your Country requir'd this. I ought not to blame you for differing in Sentiment with me in Public Affairs. We are Men, all subject to Errors. Our Opinions are not in our own Power; they are form'd and govern'd much by Circumstances, that are often as inexplicable as they are irresistible. Your Situation was such that few would have censured your remaining Neuter, *tho' there are Natural Duties which precede political ones, and cannot be extinguish'd by them.*

This is a disagreable Subject. I drop it. And we will endeavour, as you propose mutually to forget what has happened relating to it, as well as we can. I send your Son over to pay his Duty to you. You will find him much improv'd. He is greatly esteem'd and belov'd in this Country, and will make his Way anywhere. It is my Desire, that he should study the Law, as a necessary Part of Knowledge for a public Man, and profitable if he should have occasion to practise it. I would have you therefore put into his hands those Law-books you have, viz.

Blackstone, Coke, Bacon, Viner, &c. He will inform you, that he received the Letter sent him by Mr. Galloway, and the Paper it enclosed, safe.

On my leaving America, I deposited with that Friend for you, a Chest of Papers, among which was a Manuscript of nine or ten Volumes, relating to Manufactures, Agriculture, Commerce, Finance, etc., which cost me in England about 70 Guineas; eight Quire Books, containing the Rough Drafts of all my Letters while I liv'd in London. These are missing. I hope you have got them, if not, they are lost. Mr. Vaughan has publish'd in London a Volume of what he calls my Political Works. He proposes a second Edition; but, as the first was very incompleat, and you had many Things that were omitted; (for I used to send you sometimes the Rough Drafts, and sometimes the printed Pieces I wrote in London,) I have directed him to apply to you for what may be in your Power to furnish him with, or to delay his Publication till I can be at home again, if that may ever happen.

I did intend returning this year; but the Congress, instead of giving me Leave to do so, have sent me another Commission, which will keep me here at least a Year longer; and perhaps I may then be too old and feeble to bear the Voyage. I am here among a People that love and respect me, a most amiable Nation to live with; and perhaps I may conclude to die among them; for my Friends in America are dying off, one after another, and I have been so long abroad, that I should now be almost a Stranger in my own Country.

I shall be glad to see you when convenient, but would not have you come here at present. You may confide to your son[2] the Family Affairs you wished to confer upon with me, for he is discreet. And I trust, that you will prudently avoid introducing him to Company, that it may be improper for him to be seen with. I shall hear from you by him and any letters to me afterwards, will come safe under Cover directed to Mr. Ferdinand Grand, Banker at Paris. Wishing you Health, and more Happiness than it seems you have lately experienced, I remain your affectionate father,

B. FRANKLIN.

CODICIL TO THE LAST WILL AND TESTAMENT[1]

I, Benjamin Franklin, in the foregoing or annexed last will and testament named, having further considered the same, do think proper to make and publish the following codicil or addition thereto.

It having long been a fixed political opinion of mine, that in a democratical state there ought to be no offices of profit, for the reasons I had given in an article of my drawing in our constitution, it was my intention when I accepted the office of President, to devote the appointed salary to some public uses. Accordingly, I had already, before I made my will in July last, given large sums of it to colleges, schools, building of churches, etc.; and in that will I bequeathed two thousand pounds more to the State for the purpose of making the Schuylkill navigable. But understanding since that such a sum will do but little towards accomplishing such a work, and that the project is not likely to be undertaken for many years to come, and having entertained another idea, that I hope may be more extensively useful, I do hereby revoke and annul that bequest, and direct that the certificates I have for what remains due to me of that salary be sold, towards raising the sum of two thousand pounds sterling, to be disposed of as I am now about to order.

It has been an opinion, that he who receives an estate from his ancestors is under some kind of obligation to transmit the same to their posterity. This obligation does not lie on me, who never inherited a shilling from any ancestor or relation. I shall, however, if it is not diminished by some accident before my death, leave a considerable estate among my descendants and relations. The above observation is made merely as some apology to my family for making bequests that do not appear to have any immediate relation to their advantage.

I was born in Boston, New England, and owe my first instructions in literature to the free grammar-schools established there. I have, therefore, already considered these schools in my will. But I am also under obligations to the State of Massachusetts for having, unasked, appointed me formerly their agent in England, with a handsome salary, which continued some years; and although I accidentally lost in their service, by transmitting Governor Hutchinson's letters, much more than the amount of what they gave me, I do not think that ought in the least to diminish my gratitude.

I have considered that, among artisans, good apprentices are most likely to make good citizens, and, having myself been bred to a manual art, printing, in my native town, and afterwards assisted to set up my business in Philadelphia by kind loans of money from two friends there, which was the foundation of my fortune, and of all the utility in life that may be ascribed to me, I wish to be useful even after my death, if possible, in forming and advancing other young men, that may be serviceable to their country in both these towns. To this end, I devote two thousand pounds sterling, of which I give one thousand thereof to the inhabitants of the town of Boston, in Massachusetts, and the other thousand to the inhabitants of the city of Philadelphia, in trust, to and for the uses, intents, and purposes hereinafter mentioned and declared.

The said sum of one thousand pounds sterling, if accepted by the inhabitants of the town of Boston, shall be managed under the direction of the selectmen, united with the ministers of the oldest Episcopalian, Congregational, and Presbyterian churches in that town, who are to let out the sum upon interest, at five per cent. per annum, to such young married artificers, under the age of twenty-five years, as have served an apprenticeship in the said town, and faithfully fulfilled the duties required in their indentures, so as to obtain a good moral character from at least two respectable citizens, who are willing to become their sureties, in a bond with the applicants, for the repayment of the moneys so lent, with interest, according to the terms hereinafter prescribed; all which bonds are to be taken for Spanish milled dollars, or the value thereof in current gold coin; and the managers shall keep a bound book or books, wherein shall be entered the names of those who shall apply for and receive the benefits of this institution, and of their sureties, together with the sums lent, the dates, and other necessary and proper records respecting the business and concerns of this institution. And as these loans are intended to assist young married artificers in setting up their business, they are to be proportioned by the discretion of the managers, so as not to exceed sixty pounds sterling to one person, nor to be less than fifteen pounds; and if the number of appliers so entitled should be so large as that the sum will not suffice to afford to each as much as might otherwise not be improper, the proportion to each shall be diminished so as to afford to every one some assistance. These aids may, therefore, be small at first, but, as the capital increases by the accumulated interest, they will be more ample. And in order to serve as many as possible in their turn, as well as to make the repayment of the principal borrowed more easy, each borrower shall be obliged to pay, with the yearly interest, one tenth part of the principal, which sums of principal and interest, so paid in, shall be again let out to fresh borrowers.

And, as it is presumed that there will always be found in Boston virtuous and benevolent citizens, willing to bestow a part of their time in doing good to the rising generation, by superintending and managing this institution gratis, it is hoped that no part of the money will at any time be dead, or be diverted to other purposes, but be continually augmenting by the interest; in which case there may, in time, be more than the occasions in Boston shall require, and then some may be spared to the neighbouring or other towns in the said State of Massachusetts, who may desire to have it; such towns engaging to pay punctually the interest and the portions of the principal, annually, to the inhabitants of the town of Boston.

If this plan is executed, and succeeds as projected without interruption for one hundred years, the sum will then be one hundred and thirty-one thousand pounds; of which I would have the managers of the donation to the town of Boston then lay out, at their discretion, one hundred thousand pounds in public works, which may be judged of most general utility to the inhabitants, such as fortifications, bridges, aqueducts, public buildings, baths, pavements, or whatever may make living in the town more convenient to its people, and render it more agreeable to strangers resorting thither for health or a temporary residence. The remaining thirty-one thousand pounds I would have continued to be let out on interest, in the manner above directed, for another hundred years, as I hope it will have been found that the institution has had a good effect on the conduct of youth, and been of service to many worthy characters and useful citizens. At the end of this second term, if no unfortunate accident has prevented the operation, the sum will be four millions and sixty one thousand pounds sterling, of which I leave one million sixty one thousand pounds to the disposition of the inhabitants of the town of Boston, and three millions to the disposition of the government of the state, not presuming to carry my views farther.

All the directions herein given, respecting the disposition and management of the donation to the inhabitants of Boston, I would have observed respecting that to the inhabitants of Philadelphia, only, as Philadelphia is incorporated, I request the corporation of that city to undertake the management agreeably to the said directions; and I do hereby vest them with full and ample powers for that purpose. And, having considered that the covering a ground plot with buildings and pavements, which carry off most of the rain and prevent its soaking into the Earth and renewing and purifying the Springs, whence the water of wells must gradually grow worse, and in time be unfit for use, as I find has happened in all old cities, I recommend that at the end of the first hundred years, if not done before, the corporation of the city Employ a part of the hundred thousand pounds in bringing, by pipes, the water of Wissahickon Creek into the town, so as to supply the inhabitants, which I apprehend may be done without great difficulty, the level of the creek being much above that of the city, and may be made higher by a dam. I also recommend making the Schuylkill completely navigable. At the end of the second hundred years, I would have the disposition of the four million and sixty one thousand pounds divided between the inhabitants of the city of Philadelphia and the government of Pennsylvania, in the same manner as herein directed with respect to that of the inhabitants of Boston and the government of Massachusetts.

It is my desire that this institution should take place and begin to operate within one year after my decease, for which purpose due notice should be publickly given previous to the expiration of that year, that those for whose benefit this establishment is intended may make their respective applications. And I hereby direct my executors, the survivors or survivor of them, within six months after my decease, to pay over the said sum of two thousand pounds sterling to such persons as shall be duly appointed by the Selectmen of Boston and the corporation of Philadelphia, to receive and take charge of their respective sums, of one thousand pounds each, for the purposes aforesaid.

Considering the accidents to which all human affairs and projects are subject in such a length of time, I have, perhaps, too much flattered myself with a vain fancy that these dispositions, if carried into execution, will be continued without interruption and have the effects proposed. I hope, however, that if the inhabitants of the two cities should not think fit to undertake the execution, they will, at least, accept the offer of these donations as a mark of my good will, a token of my gratitude, and a testimony of my earnest desire to be useful to them after my departure.

I wish, indeed, that they may both undertake to endeavour the execution of the project, because I think that, though unforeseen difficulties may arise, expedients will be found to remove them, and the scheme be found practicable. If one of them accepts the money, with the conditions, and the other refuses, my will then is, that both Sums be given to the inhabitants of the city accepting the whole, to be applied to the same purposes, and under the same regulations directed for the separate parts; and, if both refuse, the money of course remains in the mass of my Estate, and is to be disposed of therewith according to my will made the Seventeenth day of July, 1788.

I wish to be buried by the side of my wife, if it may be, and that a marble stone, to be made by Chambers, six feet long, four feet wide, plain, with only a small moulding round the upper edge, and this inscription:

Benjamin
And   } Franklin
Deborah

178–

to be placed over us both. My fine crab-tree walking-stick, with a gold head curiously wrought in the form of the cap of liberty, I give to my friend, and the friend of mankind, *General Washington.* If it were a Sceptre, he has merited it, and would become it. It was a present to me from that excellent woman, Madame de Forbach, the dowager Duchess of Deux-Ponts, connected with some verses which should go with it. I give my gold watch to my son-in-law, *Richard Bache,* and also the gold watch chain of the Thirteen United States, which I have not yet worn. My timepiece, that stands in my library, I give to my grandson *William Temple Franklin.* I give him also my Chinese gong. To my dear old friend, *Mrs. Mary Hewson,* I give one of my silver tankards marked for her use during her life, and after her decease I give it to her daughter *Eliza.* I give to her son, *William Hewson,* who is my godson, my new quarto Bible, Oxford edition, to be for his family Bible, and also the botanic description of the plants in the Emperor's garden at Vienna, in folio, with coloured cuts.

And to her son, *Thomas Hewson,* I give a set of *Spectators, Tatlers,* and *Guardians* handsomely bound.

There is an error in my will, where the bond of William Temple Franklin is mentioned as being four thousand pounds sterling, whereas it is but for three thousand five hundred pounds.

I give to my *executors,* to be divided equally among those that act, the sum of sixty pounds sterling, as some compensation for their trouble in the execution of my will; and I request my friend, *Mr. Duffield,* to accept moreover my French wayweiser, a piece of clockwork in Brass, to be fixed to the wheel of any carriage; and that my friend, *Mr. Hill,* may also accept my silver cream pot, formerly given to me by the good Doctor Fothergill, with the motto, *Keep bright the Chain.* My reflecting telescope, made by Short, which was formerly Mr. Canton's, I give to my friend, *Mr. David Rittenhouse,* for the use of his observatory.

My picture, drawn by Martin, in 1767, I give to the *Supreme Executive Council of Pennsylvania,* if they shall be pleased to do me the honour of accepting it and placing it in their chamber. Since my will was made I have bought some more city lots, near the centre part of the estate of Joseph Dean. I would have them go with the other lots, disposed of in my will, and I do give the same to my Son-in-law, *Richard Bache,* to his heirs and assigns forever.

In addition to the annuity left to my sister in my will, of fifty pounds sterling during her life, I now add thereto ten pounds sterling more, in order to make the Sum sixty pounds. I give twenty guineas to my good friend and physician, *Dr. John Jones.*

With regard to the separate bequests made to my daughter *Sarah* in my will, my intention is, that the same shall be for her sole and separate use, notwithstanding her coverture, or whether she be covert or sole; and I do give my executors so much right and power therein as may be necessary to render my intention effectual in that respect only. This provision for my daughter is not made out of any disrespect I have for her husband.

And lastly, it is my desire that this, my present codicil, be annexed to, and considered as part of, my last will and testament to all intents and purposes.

In witness whereof, I have hereunto set my hand and Seal this twenty-third day of June, Anno [SEAL.] Domini one thousand Seven hundred and eighty nine.

B. FRANKLIN.

Signed, sealed, published, and declared by the above named Benjamin Franklin to be a codicil to his last will and testament, in the presence of us.

FRANCIS BAILEY,
THOMAS LANG,
ABRAHAM SHOEMAKER.

TO PETER COLLINSON[1]

[PHILADELPHIA,] July 11, 1747.

SIR,

In my last I informed you that, in pursuing our electrical en-quiries, we had observed some particular phænomena, which we looked upon to be new, and of which I promised to give you some account, though I apprehended they might possibly not be new to you, as so many hands are daily employed in electrical experiments on your side the water, some or other of which would probably hit on the same observations.

The first is the wonderful effect of pointed bodies, both in *drawing off* and *throwing off* the electrical fire. For example,

Place an iron shot of three or four inches diameter on the mouth of a clean dry glass bottle. By a fine silken thread from the cieling, right over the mouth of the bottle, suspend a small cork ball, about the bigness of a marble; the thread of such a length, as that the cork ball may rest against the side of the shot. Electrify the shot, and the ball will be repelled to the dis-tance of four or five inches, more or less, according to the quan-tity of Electricity. When in this state, if you present to the shot the point of a long slender sharp bodkin, at six or eight inches dis-tance, the repellency is instantly destroy'd, and the cork flies to the shot. A blunt body must be brought within an inch, and draw a spark, to produce the same effect. To prove that the electrical fire is *drawn off* by the point, if you take the blade of the bodkin out of the wooden handle, and fix it in a stick of sealing-wax, and then present it at the distance aforesaid, or if you bring it very near, no such effect follows; but sliding one finger along the wax till you touch the blade, and the ball flies to the shot immediately. If you present the point in the dark, you will see, sometimes at a foot distance, and more, a light gather upon it, like that of a fire-fly, or glow-worm; the less sharp the point, the nearer you must bring it to observe the light; and, at whatever distance you see the light, you may draw off the electrical fire, and destroy the repellency. If a cork ball so suspended be repelled by the tube, and a point be presented quick to it, tho' at a considerable distance, 'tis surprizing to see how suddenly it flies back to the tube. Points of wood will do near as well as those of iron, provided the wood is not dry; for perfectly dry wood will no more conduct Electricity than sealing-wax.

To shew that points will *throw off* as well as *draw off* the electrical fire; lay a long sharp needle upon the shot, and you cannot electrise the shot so as to make it repel the rock ball. Or fix a needle to the end of a suspended gun-barrel, or iron rod, so as to point beyond it like a little bayonet; and while it remains there, the gun-barrel, or rod, cannot by applying the tube to the other end be electrised so as to give a spark, the fire continually running out silently at the point. In the dark you may see it make the same appearance as it does in the case before mentioned.

The repellency between the cork ball and the shot is likewise destroyed. 1, by sifting fine sand on it; this does it gradually. 2, by breathing on it. 3, by making a smoke about it from burning wood. 4, by candle-light, even though the candle is at a foot distance: these do it suddenly. The light of a bright coal from a wood fire; and the light of red-hot iron do it likewise; but not at so great a distance. Smoke from dry rosin dropt on hot iron, does not destroy the repellency; but is attracted by both shot and cork ball, forming proportionable atmospheres round them, making them look beautifully, somewhat like some of the figures in *Burnet's* or *Whiston's Theory of the Earth*.

N. B. This experiment should be made in a closet, where the air is very still, or it will be apt to fail.

The light of the sun thrown strongly on both cork and shot by a looking-glass for a long time together, does not impair the repellency in the least. This difference between fire-light and sun-light is another thing that seems new and extraordinary to us.

We had for some time been of opinion, that the electrical fire was not created by friction, but collected, being really an element diffus'd among, and attracted by other matter, particularly by water and metals. We had even discovered and demonstrated its afflux to the electrical sphere, as well as its efflux, by means of little light windmill-wheels made of stiff paper vanes, fixed obliquely and turning freely on fine wire axes; also by little wheels of the same matter, but formed like water-wheels. Of the disposition and application of which wheels, and the various phænomena resulting, I could, if I had time, fill you a sheet. The impossibility of electrising one's self (though standing on wax) by rubbing the tube, and drawing the fire from it; and the manner of doing it, by passing the tube near a person or thing standing on the floor, &c., had also occurred to us some months before Mr. *Watson's* ingenious *Sequel* came to hand, and these were some of the new things I intended to have communicated to you. But now I need only mention some particulars not hinted in that piece, with our reasonings thereupon; though perhaps the latter might well enough be spared.

1. A person standing on wax, and rubbing the tube, and an-other person on wax drawing the fire, they will both of them, (provided they do not stand so as to touch one another) appear to be electrised, to a person standing on the floor; that is, he will perceive a spark on approaching each of them with his knuckle.

2. But, if the persons on wax touch one another during the exciting of the tube, neither of them will appear to be electrised.

3. If they touch one another after exciting the tube, and drawing the fire as aforesaid, there will be a stronger spark be-tween them, than was between either of them and the person on the floor.

4. After such strong spark, neither of them discover any electricity.

These appearances we attempt to account for thus: We sup-pose, as aforesaid, that electrical fire is a common element, of which every one of the three persons above mentioned has his equal share, before any operation is begun with the tube. *A,* who stands on wax and rubs the tube, collects the electrical fire from himself into the glass; and his communication with the common stock being cut off by the wax, his body is not again immediately supply'd. *B,* (who stands on wax likewise) passing his knuckle along near the tube, receives the fire which was collected by the glass from *A;* and his communication with the common stock being likewise cut off, he retains the additional quantity received. To *C,* standing on the floor, both appear to be electrised: for he having only the middle quantity of electrical fire, receives a spark upon approaching *B,* who has an over quantity; but gives one to *A,* who has an under quantity. If *A* and *B* approach to touch each other, the spark is stronger, because the difference between them is greater: After such touch there is no spark between either of them and *C,* because the electrical fire in all is reduced to the original equality. If they touch while electrising, the equality is never destroy'd, the fire only circulating. Hence have arisen some new terms among us: we say, *B,* (and bodies like circumstanced) is electrised *positively; A, negatively.*[2] Or rather, *B* is electrised *plus; A, minus.* And we daily in our experiments electrise bodies *plus or minus,* as we think proper. To electrise *plus* or *minus,* no more needs to be known than this, that the parts of the tube or sphere that are rubbed, do, in the instant of the friction, attract the electrical fire, and therefore take it from the thing rubbing: the same parts immediately, as the friction upon them ceases, are disposed to give the fire they have received, to any body that has less. Thus you may circulate it, as Mr. *Watson* has shewn; you may also accumulate or subtract it upon, or from any body, as you connect that body with the rubber or with the receiver, the communication with the common stock being cut off. We think that ingenious gentleman was deceived when he imagined (in his *Sequel*) that the electrical fire came down the wire from the cieling to the gun-barrel, thence to the sphere, and so electrised the machine and the man turning the wheel, &c. We suppose it was *driven off,* and not brought on through that wire; and that the machine and man, &c., were electrised *minus, i.e.* had less electrical fire in them than things in common.

As the vessel is just upon sailing, I cannot give you so large an account of *American* electricity as I intended: I shall only mention a few particulars more. We find granulated lead better to fill the phial with, than water, being easily warmed, and keeping warm and dry in damp air. We fire spirits with the wire of the phial. We light candles, just blown out, by drawing a spark among the smoke, between the wire and snuffers. We represent lightning, by passing the wire in the dark, over a China plate, that has gilt flowers, or applying it to gilt frames of looking-glasses, &c. We electrise a person twenty or more times running, with a touch of the finger on the wire, thus: He stands on wax. Give him the electrised bottle in his hand. Touch the wire with your finger, and then touch his hand or face; there are sparks every time. We increase the force of the electrical kiss vastly, thus: Let *A* and *B* stand on wax; or *A* on wax, and *B* on the floor; give one of them the electrised phial in hand; let the other take hold of the wire; there will be a small spark; but when their lips approach, they will be struck and shock'd. The same if another gentleman and lady, *C* and *D*, standing also on wax, and joining hands with *A* and *B*, salute or shake hands. We suspend by fine silk thread a counterfeit spider, made of a small piece of burnt cork, with legs of linnen thread, and a grain or two of lead stuck in him, to give him more weight. Upon the table, over which he hangs, we stick a wire upright, as high as the phial and wire, two or three inches from the spider: then we animate him, by setting the electrified phial at the same distance on the other side of him; he will immediately fly to the wire of the phial, bend his legs in touching it; then spring off, and fly to the wire on the table; thence again to the wire of the phial, playing with his legs against both, in a very entertaining manner, appearing perfectly alive to persons unacquainted. He will continue this motion an hour or more in dry weather. We electrify, upon wax in the dark, a book that has a double line of gold round upon the covers, and then apply a knuckle to the gilding; the fire appears everywhere upon the gold like a flash of lightning: not upon the leather, nor, if you touch the leather instead of the gold. We rub our tubes with buckskin, and observe always to keep the same side to the tube, and never to sully the tube by handling; thus they work readily and easily, without the least fatigue, especially if kept in tight pasteboard cases, lined with flannel, and sitting close to the tube. This I mention, because the *European* papers on Electricity, frequently speak of rubbing the tube, as a fatiguing exercise. Our spheres are fixed on iron axes, which pass through them. At one end of the axis there is a small handle, with which you turn the sphere like a common grindstone. This we find very commodious, as the machine takes up but little room, is portable, and may be enclosed in a tight box, when not in use. 'Tis true, the sphere does not turn so swift as when the great wheel is used: but swiftness we think of little importance, since a few turns will charge the phial, &c., sufficiently.

I am, &c.

B. FRANKLIN.

TO A FRIEND IN BOSTON

*Account of an Accident while Making
an Electrical Experiment*

Philadelphia, December 25, 1750.

I have lately made an experiment in electricity, that I desire never to repeat. Two nights ago, being about to kill a turkey by the shock from two large glass jars, containing as much electrical fire as forty common phials, I inadvertently took the whole through my own arms and body, by receiving the fire from the united top wires with one hand, while the other held a chain connected with the outsides of both jars. The company present (whose talking to me, and to one another, I suppose occasioned my inattention to what I was about) say, that the flash was very great, and the crack as loud as a pistol; yet, my senses being instantly gone, I neither saw the one nor heard the other; nor did I feel the stroke on my hand, though I afterwards found it raised a round swelling where the fire entered, as big as half a pistol-bullet; by which you may judge of the quickness of the electrical fire, which by this instance seems to be greater than that of sound, light, or animal sensation.

What I can remember of the matter is that I was about to try whether the bottles or jars were fully charged, by the strength and length of the stream issuing to my hand, as I commonly used to do, and which I might safely enough have done if I had not held the chain in the other hand. I then felt what I know not how well to describe; a universal blow throughout my whole body from head to foot, which seemed within as well as without; after which the first thing I took notice of was a violent quick shaking of my body, which gradually remitting, my sense as gradually returned, and then I thought the bottles must be discharged, but could not conceive how, till at last I perceived the chain in my hand, and recollected what I had been about to do. That part of my hand and fingers, which held the chain, was left white, as though the blood had been driven out, and remained so eight or ten minutes after, feeling like dead flesh; and I had a numbness in my arms and the back of my neck, which continued till the next morning, but wore off. Nothing remains now of this shock, but a soreness in my breast-bone, which feels as if it had been bruised. I did not fall, but suppose I should have been knocked down, if I had received the stroke in my head. The whole was over in less than a minute.

You may communicate this to Mr. Bowdoin, as a caution to him, but do not make it more public, for I am ashamed to have been guilty of so notorious a blunder; a match for that of the Irishman, whom my sister told me of, who, to divert his wife, poured the bottle of gunpowder on the live coal; or of that other, who, being about to steal powder, made a hole in the cask with a hot iron. I am yours, &c.

B. FRANKLIN.

P. S. The jars hold six gallons each.

TO PETER COLLINSON

Electrical Kite

[*Philadelphia*] *Oct. 19, 1752.*

Sir,

As frequent mention is made in public papers from *Europe* of the success of the *Philadelphia* experiment for drawing the electric fire from clouds by means of pointed rods of iron erected on high buildings, &c., it may be agreeable to the curious to be informed, that the same experiment has succeeded in *Philadelphia*, though made in a different and more easy manner, which is as follows:

Make a small cross of two light strips of cedar, the arms so long as to reach to the four corners of a large thin silk handkerchief when extended; tie the corners of the handkerchief to the extremities of the cross, so you have the body of a kite; which being properly accommodated with a tail, loop, and string, will rise in the air, like those made of paper; but this being of silk, is fitter to bear the wet and wind of a thunder-gust without tearing. To the top of the upright stick of the cross is to be fixed a very sharp-pointed wire, rising a foot or more above the wood. To the end of the twine, next the hand, is to be tied a silk ribbon, and where the silk and twine join, a key may be fastened. This kite is to be raised when a thunder-gust appears to be coming on, and the person who holds the string must stand within a door or window, or under some cover, so that the silk ribbon may not be wet; and care must be taken that the twine does not touch the frame of the door or window. As soon as any of the thunder-clouds come over the kite, the pointed wire will draw the electric fire from them, and the kite, with all the twine, will be electrified, and the loose filaments of the twine will stand out every way, and be attracted by an approaching finger. And when the rain has wet the kite and twine, so that it can conduct the electric fire freely, you will find it stream out plentifully from the key on the approach of your knuckle. At this key the phial may be charged; and from electric fire thus obtained, spirits may be kindled, and all the other electric experiments be performed, which are usually done by the help of a rubbed glass globe or tube, and thereby the sameness of the electric matter with that of lightning completely demonstrated.

B. FRANKLIN.

TO PETER COLLINSON

Philadelphia, Aug. 25, 1755.

DEAR SIR,—

As you have my former papers on Whirlwinds, &c., I now send you an account of one which I had lately an opportunity of seeing and examining myself.

Being in *Maryland,* riding with Colonel *Tasker,* and some other gentlemen to his country-seat, where I and my son were entertained by that amiable and worthy man with great hospitality and kindness, we saw in the vale below us, a small whirlwind beginning in the road, and shewing itself by the dust it raised and contained. It appeared in the form of a sugar-loaf, spinning on its point, moving up the hill towards us, and enlarging as it came forward. When it passed by us, its smaller part near the ground, appeared no bigger than a common barrel, but widening upwards, it seemed, at 40 or 50 feet high, to be 20 or 30 feet in diameter. The rest of the company stood looking after it, but my curiosity being stronger, I followed it, riding close by its side, and observed its licking up, in its progress, all the dust that was under its smaller part. As it is a common opinion that a shot, fired through a water-spout, will break it, I tried to break this little whirlwind, by striking my whip frequently through it, but without any effect. Soon after, it quitted the road and took into the woods, growing every moment larger and stronger, raising, instead of dust, the old dry leaves with which the ground was thick covered, and making a great noise with them and the branches of the trees, bending some tall trees round in a circle swiftly and very surprizingly, though the progressive motion of the whirl was not so swift but that a man on foot might have kept pace with it; but the circular motion was amazingly rapid. By the leaves it was now filled with, I could plainly perceive that the current of air they were driven by, moved upwards in a spiral line; and when I saw the trunks and bodies of large trees invelop'd in the passing whirl, which continued intire after it had left them I no longer wondered that my whip had no effect on it in its smaller state. I accompanied it about three quarters of a mile, till some limbs of dead trees, broken off by the whirl, flying about and falling near me, made me more apprehensive of danger; and then I stopped, looking at the top of it as it went on, which was visible, by means of the leaves contained in it, for a very great height above the trees. Many of the leaves, as they got loose from the upper and widest part, were scattered in the wind; but so great was their height in the air, that they appeared no bigger than flies. My son, who was by this time come up with me, followed the whirlwind till it left the woods, and crossed an old tobacco-field, where, finding neither dust nor leaves to take up, it gradually became invisible below as it went away over that field. The course of the general wind then blowing was along with us as we travelled, and the progressive motion of the whirlwind was in a direction nearly opposite, though it did not keep a strait line, nor was its progressive motion uniform, it making little sallies on either hand as it went, proceeding sometimes faster and sometimes slower, and seeming sometimes for a few seconds almost stationary, then starting forward pretty fast again. When we rejoined the company, they were admiring the vast height of the leaves now brought by the common wind, over our heads. These leaves accompanied us as we travelled, some falling now and then round about us, and some not reaching the ground till we had gone near three miles from the place where we first saw the whirlwind begin. Upon my asking Colonel *Tasker* if such whirlwinds were common in *Maryland,* he answered pleasantly, "No, not at all common; but we got this on purpose to treat Mr. Franklin." And a very high treat it was, to

Dear Sir,

Your affectionate friend and humble servant,

B. F[RANKLIN.]

TO JOHN PRINGLE

Craven-Street, Dec. 21, 1757.

Sir,

In compliance with your request, I send you the following account of what I can at present recollect relating to the effects of electricity in paralytic cases, which have fallen under my observation.

Some years since, when the news-papers made mention of great cures performed in *Italy* and *Germany,* by means of electricity, a number of paralytics were brought to me from different parts of *Pensylvania,* and the neighbouring provinces, to be electrised, which I did for them at their request. My method was, to place the patient first in a chair, on an electric stool, and draw a number of large strong sparks from all parts of the affected limb or side. Then I fully charged two six gallon glass jars, each of which had about three square feet of surface coated; and I sent the united shock of these through the affected limb or limbs, repeating the stroke commonly three times each day. The first thing observed, was an immediate greater sensible warmth in the lame limbs that had received the stroke, than in the others; and the next morning the patients usually related, that they had in the night felt a pricking sensation in the flesh of the paralytic limbs; and would sometimes shew a number of small red spots, which they supposed were occasioned by those prickings. The limbs, too, were found more capable of voluntary motion, and seemed to receive strength. A man, for instance, who could not the first day lift the lame hand from off his knee, would the next day raise it four or five inches, the third day higher; and on the fifth day was able, but with a feeble languid motion, to take off his hat. These appearances gave great spirits to the patients, and made them hope a perfect cure; but I do not remember that I ever saw any amendment after the fifth day; which the patients perceiving, and finding the shocks pretty severe, they became discouraged, went home, and in a short time relapsed; so that I never knew any advantage from electricity in palsies that was permanent. And how far the apparent temporary advantage might arise from the exercise in the patients' journey, and coming daily to my house, or from the spirits given by the hope of success, enabling them to exert more strength in moving their limbs, I will not pretend to say.

Perhaps some permanent advantage might have been obtained, if the electric shocks had been accompanied with proper medicine and regimen, under the direction of a skilful physician. It may be, too, that a few great strokes, as given in my method, may not be so proper as many small ones; since, by the account from *Scotland* of a case, in which two hundred shocks from a phial were given daily, it seems, that a perfect cure has been made. As to any uncommon strength supposed to be in the machine used in that case, I imagine it could have no share in the effect produced; since the strength of the shock from charged glass is in proportion to the quantity of surface of the glass coated; so that my shocks from those large jars must have been much greater than any that could be received from a phial held in the hand. I am, with great respect, Sir,

Your most obedient servant,

B. Franklin.

TO SIR ALEXANDER DICK

London, Jan. 21, 1762.

DEAR SIR,

It gives me Pleasure to learn, by yours of Nov. 12. that my young Friend M^r. Morgan has rendered himself agreable to you, and that your Health and Eyes are much better.

I sent some time since to Mr Dalrymple one of my Machines for your Chimney, who readily paid the Smith's Bill for the same.—But now, on discoursing with some Gentlemen from Edinburgh, I am in doubt whether it is what you intended and expected. If not, pray let me know, that I may endeavour to procure for you the Thing that you desire.

However let me tell you, that after more than 20 Years Experience of my own Contrivances and those of others, for the Warming of Rooms, and much Thought on the Subject, I am of Opinion, that this, all Circumstances considered, is by far the best for common Use. You will judge of it when I have explain'd the Manner of Fixing it up, and its Operation.

It is a thin Iron Plate sliding in a grooved Frame of Iron. The Opening of your Chimney I suppose is wider than this Plate with its Frame is long, and deeper than it is wide: In which Case your Mason is to contract the Opening, by raising within it two Jambs of Brickwork about 3 Feet high, and at such a Distance from each other, that the Frame & Plate being laid on them may rest firmly, and be fix'd by additional Brickwork above upon the Jambs, and across from Jamb to Jamb over the Frame, so as to close the Opening above the Frame. This new Brickwork may be fac'd with Dutch Tiles, Stone or Marble at your Pleasure. This

Work is to be plac'd so far back in the Chimney, that when the Plate is close thrust in, the Chimney is quite stopt up, so as to prevent all passage of Air up or down. Then when you make a Fire, the Plate is to be drawn out so far only as to admit a Passage for all the Smoke; which will be one, two, or three Inches, at different Times, according to the Coldness of the Weather, and the Strength of the Draft in your Chimney. If at any time, you would have the Fire speedily blown up, the Plate is to be drawn out as far as the Hinge and let down to hang perpendicular, which enlarging the Passage above the Fire, and contracting it before, produces the Effect by occasioning a stronger Current of Air where it is required for the purpose.

The Principles of this Construction are these. Chimney Funnels are made much larger than is necessary for Conveying the Smoke. In a large Funnel a great quantity of Air is continually ascending out of the Room, which must be supply'd thro' the Crevices of Doors, Windows, Floors, Wainscots, &c. This occasions a continual Current of cold Air from the extream Parts of the Room to the Chimney, which presses the Air warm'd by the direct rays of the Fire into the Chimney, and carries it off, thereby preventing its diffusing itself to warm the Room.—By contracting the Funnel with this Plate, the Draft of Air up the Chimney is greatly lessen'd, and the Introduction of cold Air thro' the Crevices to supply its Place is proportionally lessen'd. Hence the Room is more uniformly warm'd & with less Fire; and the Current of cold Air towards the Chimney being lessen'd it becomes much more comfortable Sitting before the Fire.—

That the Draft of cold Air into the Room is lessen'd by this Plate may be demonstrated by several easy Experiments. When you have a lively Fire burning, and the Plate as far in as it will bear to be without stopping the Smoak, set the Door open about ¼ an Inch, & hold your Hand against the Crevice; you will then feel the Cool Air coming in, but slowly & weakly compar'd with what you will feel, if, while your Hand continues so plac'd another Person suddenly draws out the Plate. The stronger pressure of the outward Air into the Room, will when the Plate is drawn out, push the Door more strongly; and being shut, the Rushing of the Air thro' Crevices make a louder Noise.—

Since I first us'd this Contrivance in the Chimneys of my Lodging here, many Hundreds have been set up in Imitation of it, in and about this City, and they have afforded general Satisfaction. Simplicity, Cheapness, and Easy Execution, have all contributed to recommend it.—Then it is no Obstruction to the Sweeping of the Chimney, is attended with no ill Smells, & in Summer serves the purpose of a Chimney Board, by closing the Chimney entirely.—

It has indeed been mistaken by some as intended for the Cure of Smoaky Chimneys. But that is not to be expected from it, except in two Cases, viz. where the Chimney smokes because the Opening is too large, or where the Room is so tight & the Funnel so big, that all the Crevices together do not admit Air enough to supply the Draft. In these Cases it is of Service. But Chimneys often smoke from other Causes, & must have other Remedies.

Possibly where a Chimney smokes from Wind sometimes blowing down, it may also be of some Service, the Push of the heated Air upwards being stronger in its narrow Passage. But in this Case I have had no Opportunity of seeing it try'd.

If you are desirous of obtaining still more Heat in your Room, from the same Fire, I would recommend lining your Jambs with coving Plates of polish'd Brass. They throw a vast deal of Heat into the Room by Reflection. I have done my Parlour Chimney in that Manner with very good Effect. The Plates are thin, & the Expence of the two, but about twenty-five Shillings.

Please to acquaint your Friend Dr Hope, that I am about returning to America this Summer, and will send him free of Charge for Postage in America any Letters containing Leaves of Plants or small Parcels of Seeds that shall be committed to my Care by any of his or your medical Friends there.—

My Son joins in best Wishes for you & your Children. Our Compliments to the eldest, who proves an excellent Secretary for you. Be so good as to present our cordial Regards to Lord Kaims when you see him. I shall write to him shortly, being much in his Debt.—With the greatest Esteem, I am,

Dear Sir,

Your most obedient

humble Servant

B. FRANKLIN

TO DAVID HUME

London, January 24, 1762.

DEAR SIR,

In compliance with my Lord Marischal's request, communicated to me by you, when I last had the pleasure of seeing you, I now send you what at present appears to me to be the shortest and simplest method of securing buildings, &c., from the mischiefs of lightning. Prepare a steel rod five or six feet long, half an inch thick at its biggest end, and tapering to a sharp point; which point should be gilt to prevent its rusting. Let the big end of the rod have a strong eye or ring of half an inch diameter: Fix this rod upright to the chimney or highest part of the house, by means of staples, so as it may be kept steady. Let the pointed end be upwards, and rise three or four feet above the chimney or building that the rod is fixed to. Drive into the ground an iron rod of about an inch diameter, and ten or twelve feet long, that has also an eye or ring in its upper end. It is best that the rod should be at some distance from the foundation of the building, not nearer than ten feet, if your ground will allow so much. Then take as much length of iron rod of about half an inch diameter, as will reach from the eye in the rod above, to that in the rod below; and fasten it securely to those rods, by passing its ends through the rings, and bending those ends till they likewise form rings.

This length of rod may either be in one or several pieces. If in several, let the ends of the pieces be also well hooked to each other. Then close and cover every joint with lead, which is easily done, by making a small bag of strong paper round the joint, tying it close below, and then pouring in the melted lead; it being of use in these junctures, that there should be a considerable quantity of metalline contact between piece and piece. For, if they were only hooked together and so touched each other but in points, the lightning, in passing through them, might melt and break them where they join. The lead will also prevent the weakening of the joints by rust. To prevent the shaking of this rod by the wind, you may secure it by a few staples to the building, till it comes down within ten feet of the ground, and thence carry it off to your ground rod; near to which should be planted a post, to support the iron conductor above the heads of people walking under it.

If the building be large and long, as an hundred feet or upwards, it may not be amiss to erect a pointed rod at each end, and form a communication by an iron rod between them. If there be a well near the house, so that you can by such a rod form a communication from your top rod to the water, it is rather better to do so than to use the ground rod above mentioned. It may also be proper to paint the iron, to render it more durable by preserving it from rust.

A building thus guarded, will not be damaged by lightning, nor any person or thing therein killed, hurt, or set on fire. For, either the explosion will be prevented by the operation of the point; or, if not prevented, then the whole quantity of lightning exploded near the house, whether passing from the cloud to the earth or from the earth to the cloud, will be conveyed in the rods. And, though the iron be crooked round the corner of the building, or make ever so many turns between the upper and lower rod, the lightning will follow it, and be guided by it, without affecting the building. I omit the philosophical reasons and experiments on which this practice is founded; for they are many, and would make a book. Besides they are already known to most of the learned throughout Europe. In the American British colonies, many houses have been, since the year 1752, guarded by these principles. Three facts have only come to my knowledge of the effects of lightning on such houses.

If I have not been explicit enough in my directions, I shall, on the least intimation, endeavour to supply the defect.

I am, &c.

B. FRANKLIN.

TO JOSEPH PRIESTLEY

Passy, Feb. 8. 1780.

DEAR SIR,

Your kind Letter of September 27 came to hand but very lately, the Bearer having staied long in Holland. I always rejoice to hear of your being still employ'd in experimental Researches into Nature, and of the Success you meet with. The rapid Progress *true* Science now makes, occasions my regretting sometimes that I was born so soon. It is impossible to imagine the Height to which may be carried, in a thousand years, the Power of Man over Matter. We may perhaps learn to deprive large Masses of their Gravity, and give them absolute Levity, for the sake of easy Transport. Agriculture may diminish its Labour and double its Produce; all Diseases may by sure means be prevented or cured, not excepting even that of Old Age, and our Lives lengthened at pleasure even beyond the antediluvian Standard. O that moral Science were in as fair a way of Improvement, that Men would cease to be Wolves to one another, and that human Beings would at length learn what they now improperly call Humanity!

I am glad my little Paper on the *Aurora Borealis* pleased. If it should occasion further Enquiry, and so produce a better Hypothesis, it will not be wholly useless. I am ever, with the greatest and most sincere Esteem, dear Sir, yours very affectionately

B. FRANKLIN.

TO SIR JOSEPH BANKS

Passy, Aug. 30. 1783.

Sir,

On Wednesday the 27th Instant, the new aerostatic Experiment, invented by Messrs. Mongolfier of Annonay was repeated by M^r. Charles; Professor of Experimental Philosophy at Paris.

A hollow Globe 12 feet diameter was formed of what is called in England Oiled Silk, here Taffetas *gommée,* the Silk being impregnated with a Solution of Gum-elastic in Lint-seed Oil, as is said. The Parts were sewed together while wet with the Gum, and some of it was afterwards passed over the Seams, to render it as tight as possible.

It was afterwards filled with the inflammable Air that is produced by pouring Oil of Vitriol upon Filings of Iron, when it was found to have a Tendency upwards so strong as to be capable of lifting a Weight of 39 Pounds, exclusive of its own weight which was 25 lb, and the Weight of the Air contain'd.

It was brought early in the Morning to the *Champ de Mars,* a Field in which Reviews are sometimes made, lying between the Military School and the River. There it was held down by a Cord, till 5 in the Afternoon, when it was to be let loose. Care was taken before the Hour to replace what Portion had been lost of the inflammable Air, or of its Force, by injecting more.

It is supposed that not less than 50,000 People were assembled to see the Experiment. The Champ de Mars being surrounded by Multitudes, and vast Numbers on the opposite Side of the River.

At 5 o Clock Notice was given to the Spectators by the Firing of two Cannon, that the Cord was about to be cut. And presently the Globe was seen to rise, and that as fast as a Body of 12 feet diameter with a force only of 39 pounds, could be suppos'd to move the resisting Air out of its way. There was some Wind, but not very strong. A little Rain had wet it, so that it shone, and made an agreable Appearance. It diminish'd in Apparent Magnitude as it rose, till it enter'd the Clouds, when it seem'd to me scarce bigger than an Orange, and soon after became invisible, the Clouds concealing it.

The Multitude separated, all well satisfied & much delighted with the Success of the Experiment, and amusing one another with Discourses of the various Uses it may possibly be apply'd to, among which many were very extravagant. But possibly it may pave the Way to some Discoveries in Natural Philosophy of which at present we have no Conception.

A Note secur'd from the Weather had been affix'd to the Globe, signifying the Time & Place of its Departure, and praying those who might happen to find it, to send an Account of its State to certain Persons at Paris. No News was heard of it till the next Day, when Information was receiv'd, that it fell a little after 6 o Clock at Gonesse, a Place about 4 Leagues distance; and that it was rent open, and some say had Ice in it. It is suppos'd to have burst by the Elasticity of the contain'd Air when no longer compress'd by so heavy an Atmosphere.

One of 38 feet Diameter is preparing by M. Mongolfier himself at the Expence of the Academy, which is to go up in a few Days. I am told it is constructed of Linen & Paper, and is to be filled with a different Air, not yet made public, but cheaper than that produc'd by the Oil of Vitriol of which 200 Paris Pints were consum'd in filling the other.

It is said that for some Days after its being fill'd, the Ball was found to lose an eighth Part of its Force of Levity in 24 Hours: Whether this was from Imperfection in the Tightness of the Ball, or a Change in the Nature of the Air, Experiments may easily discover.

I thought it my Duty, Sir, to send an early Account of this extraordinary Fact, to the Society which does me the honour to reckon me among its Members; and I will endeavour to make it more perfect, as I receive farther Information.

> With great Respect, I am, Sir,
>
> [B. FRANKLIN.]

P. S.

Since writing the above, I am favour'd with your kind Letter of the 25th. I am much oblig'd to you for the Care you have taken to forward the Transactions, as well as to the Council for so readily ordering them on Application.—Please to accept and present my Thanks.

I just now learn, that some Observers say, the Ball was 150 seconds in rising, from the Cutting of the Cord till hid in the Clouds; that its height was then about 500 Toises, but, mov'd out of the Perpendicular by the Wind, it had made a Slant so as to form a Triangle, whose base on the Earth was about 200 Toises. It is said the Country people who saw it fall were frightened, conceiv'd from its bounding a little when it touch'd the Ground, that there was some living Animal in it, and attack'd it with Stones and Knives, so that it was much mangled; but it is now brought to Town & will be repaired.—

The great one of M. Mongolfier, is to go up as is said, from Versailles, in about 8 or 10 Days. It is not a Globe but of a different form, more convenient for penetrating the Air. It contains 50,000 cubic Feet, and is supposed to have a Force of Levity equal to 1500 pounds weight. A Philosopher here, M. Pilatre de Rozier, has seriously apply'd to the Academy for Leave to go up with it, in order to make some Experiments. He was complimented on his Zeal and Courage for the Promotion of Science, but advis'd to wait till the Management of these Balls was made by Experience more certain & safe. They say the filling of it in M. Mongolfier's Way will not cost more than half a Crown. One is talk'd of to be 110 feet Diameter. Several Gentlemen have ordered small ones to be made for their Amusement; one has ordered four of 15 feet diameter each; I know not with what Purpose; but such is the present Enthusiasm for promoting & improving this Discovery, that probably we shall soon make considerable Progress in the Art of constructing and Using the Machines.—

Among the Pleasantries Conversation produces on this Subject, some suppose Flying to be now invented, and that since Men may be supported in the Air, nothing is wanted but some light handy Instruments to give and direct Motion. Some think Progressive Motion on the Earth may be advanc'd by it, and that a Running Footman or a Horse slung & suspended under such a Globe so as to leave no more of Weight pressing the Earth with their Feet, than perhaps 8 or 10 Pounds, might with a fair Wind run in a straight Line across Countries as fast as that Wind, and over Hedges, Ditches, & even Waters. It has been even fancied that in time People will keep such Globes anchored in the Air, to which by Pullies they may draw up Game to be preserved in the Cool, & Water to be frozen when Ice is wanted. And that to get Money, it will be contrived to give People an extensive view of the Country, by running them upon an Elbow Chair a Mile high for a Guinea, &c. &c.

[A Pamphlet is printing in which we are to have a full and perfect Account of the Experiments hitherto made, & I will send it to you. M. Mongolfier's Air to fill the Globe has hitherto been kept secret. Some suppose it to be only common Air heated by passing thro' the Flame of burning Straw, & thereby extreamly rarified. If so its Levity will soon be diminished by Condensation when it comes into the cooler Regions above.[1]

TO LA SABLIERE DE
LA CONDAMINE

Passy, March 19, 1784.

Sir,

I receiv'd the very obliging Letter you did me honour of writing to me the 8th Inst. with the epigram &c. for which please to accept my Thanks.

You desire my Sentiments concerning the Cures perform'd by Comus & Mesmer. I think that in general, Maladies caus'd by Obstructions may be treated by Electricity with Advantage. As to the Animal Magnetism, so much talk'd of, I am totally unacquainted with it, and must doubt its Existence till I can see or feel some Effect of it. None of the Cures said to be perform'd by it, have fallen under my Observation; and there being so many Disorders which cure themselves and such a Disposition in Mankind to deceive themselves and one another on these Occasions; and living long having given me frequent Opportunities of seeing certain Remedies cry'd up as curing everything, and yet soon after totally laid aside as useless, I cannot but fear that the Expectation of great Advantage from the new Method of treating Diseases, will prove a Delusion. That Delusion may however in some cases be of use while it lasts. There are in every great rich City a Number of Persons who are never in health, because they are fond of Medicines and always taking them, whereby they derange the natural Functions, and hurt their Constitutions. If these People can be persuaded to forbear their Drugs in Expectation of being cured by only the Physician's Finger or an

Iron Rod pointing at them, they may possibly find good Effects tho' they mistake the Cause. I have the honour to be, Sir, &c.

[B. FRANKLIN.]

TO GEORGE WHATLEY

DEAR OLD FRIEND,

I sent you a few lines the other day, with my medallion, when I should have written more, but was prevented by the coming in of a *bavard,* who worried me till evening. I bore with him, and now you are to bear with me; for I shall probably *bavarder* in answering your letter.

I am not acquainted with the saying of Alphonsus, which you allude to as a sanctification of your rigidity, in refusing to allow me the plea of old age, as an excuse for my want of exactness in correspondence. What was that saying? You do not, it seems, feel any occasion for such an excuse, though you are, as you say, rising seventy-five. But I am rising (perhaps more properly falling) eighty, and I leave the excuse with you till you arrive at that age; perhaps you may then be more sensible of its validity, and see fit to use it for yourself.

I must agree with you, that the gout is bad, and that the stone is worse. I am happy in not having them both together, and I join in your prayer, that you may live till you die without either. But I doubt the author of the epitaph you send me was a little mistaken, when he, speaking of the world, says, that

> "he ne'er cared a pin
> What they said or may say of the mortal within."

It is so natural to wish to be well spoken of, whether alive or dead, that I imagine he could not be quite exempt from that desire; and that at least he wished to be thought a wit, or he would not have given himself the trouble of writing so good an epitaph to leave behind him. Was it not as worthy of his care, that the world should say he was an honest and a good man? I like better the concluding sentiment in the old song, called *The Old Man's Wish,* wherein, after wishing for a warm house in a country town, an easy horse, some good authors, ingenious and cheerful companions, a pudding on Sundays, with stout ale, and a bottle of Burgundy, &c. &c., in separate stanzas, each ending with this burthen,

> "May I govern my passions with absolute sway,
>   Grow wiser and better as my strength wears away,
>   Without gout or stone, by a gentle decay ;"

he adds,

> "With a courage undaunted may I face my last day,
>   And, when I am gone, may the better sort say,
>   'In the morning when sober, in the evening when mellow,
>   He 's gone, and has not left behind him his fellow ;
>   For he governed his passions, &c.' "

But what signifies our wishing? Things happen, after all, as they will happen. I have sung that *wishing song* a thousand times, when I was young, and now find, at fourscore, that the three contraries have befallen me, being subject to the gout and the stone, and not being yet master of all my passions. Like the proud girl in my country, who wished and resolved not to marry a parson, nor a Presbyterian, nor an Irishman; and at length found herself married to an Irish Presbyterian parson.

You see I have some reason to wish, that, in a future state, I may not only be *as well as I was,* but a little better. And I hope it; for I, too, with your poet, *trust in God.* And when I observe, that there is great frugality, as well as wisdom, in his works, since he has been evidently sparing both of labor and materials; for by the various wonderful inventions of propagation, he has provided for the continual peopling his world with plants and animals, without being at the trouble of repeated new creations; and by the natural reduction of compound substances to their original elements, capable of being employed in new compositions, he has prevented the necessity of creating new matter; so that the earth, water, air, and perhaps fire, which being compounded form wood, do, when the wood is dissolved, return, and again become air, earth, fire, and water; I say, that, when I see nothing annihilated, and not even a drop of water wasted, I cannot suspect the annihilation of souls, or believe, that he will suffer the daily waste of millions of minds ready made that now exist, and put himself to the continual trouble of making new ones. Thus finding myself to exist in the world, I believe I shall, in some shape or other, always exist; and, with all the inconveniences human life is liable to, I shall not object to a new edition of mine; hoping, however, that the *errata* of the last may be corrected.

I return your note of children received in the Foundling Hospital at Paris, from 1741 to 1755, inclusive; and I have added the years succeeding, down to 1770. Those since that period I have not been able to obtain. I have noted in the margin the gradual increase, viz. from every tenth child so thrown upon the public, till it comes to every third! Fifteen years have passed since the last account, and probably it may now amount to one half. Is it right to encourage this monstrous deficiency of natural affection? A surgeon I met with here excused the women of Paris, by saying, seriously, that they *could not* give suck; *"Car,"* said he, *"elles n'ont point de tetons."* He assured me it was a fact, and bade me look at them, and observe how flat they were on the breast; "they have nothing more there," said he, "than I have upon the back of my hand." I have since thought that there might be some truth in his observation, and that, possibly, nature, finding they made no use of bubbies, has left off giving them any. Yet, since Rousseau pleaded, with admirable eloquence, for the rights of children to their mother's milk, the mode has changed a little; and some ladies of quality now suckle their infants and find milk enough. May the mode descend to the lower ranks, till it becomes no longer the custom to pack their infants away, as soon as born, to the *Enfans Trouvés,* with the careless observation, that the King is better able to maintain them.

I am credibly informed, that nine-tenths of them die there pretty soon, which is said to be a great relief to the institution, whose funds would not otherwise be sufficient to bring up the remainder. Except the few persons of quality above mentioned, and the multitude who send to the Hospital, the practice is to hire nurses in the country to carry out the children, and take care of them there. Here is an office for examining the health of nurses, and giving them licenses. They come to town on certain days of the week in companies to receive the children, and we often meet trains of them on the road returning to the neighbouring villages, with each a child in her arms. But those, who are good enough to try this way of raising their children, are often not able to pay the expense; so that the prisons of Paris are crowded with wretched fathers and mothers confined *pour mois de nourrice,* though it is laudably a favorite charity to pay for them, and set such prisoners at liberty. I wish success to the new project of assisting the poor to keep their children at home, because I think there is no nurse like a mother (or not many), and that, if parents did not immediately send their infants out of their sight, they would in a few days begin to love them, and thence be spurred to greater industry for their maintenance. This is a subject you understand better than I, and, therefore, having perhaps said too much, I drop it. I only add to the notes a remark, from the *History of the Academy of Sciences,* much in favor of the Foundling Institution.

The Philadelphia bank goes on, as I hear, very well. What you call the Cincinnati Institution is no institution of our government, but a private convention among the officers of our late army, and so universally disliked by the people, that it is supposed it will be dropped. It was considered as an attempt to establish something like an hereditary rank or nobility. I hold with you, that it was wrong; may I add, that all *descending* honors are wrong and absurd; that the honor of virtuous actions appertains only to him that performs them, and is in its nature incommunicable. If it were communicable by descent, it must also be divisible among the descendants; and the more ancient the family, the less would be found existing in any one branch of it; to say nothing of the greater chance of unlucky interruptions.

Our constitution seems not to be well understood with you. If the Congress were a permanent body, there would be more reason in being jealous of giving it powers. But its members are chosen annually, cannot be chosen more than three years successively, nor more than three years in seven; and any of them may be recalled at any time, whenever their constituents shall be dissatisfied with their conduct. They are of the people, and return again to mix with the people, having no more durable preëminence than the different grains of sand in an hourglass. Such an assembly cannot easily become dangerous to liberty. They are the servants of the people, sent together to do the people's business, and promote the public welfare; their powers must be sufficient, or their duties cannot be performed. They have no profitable appointments, but a mere payment of daily wages, such as are scarcely equivalent to their expenses; so that, having no chance for great places, and enormous salaries or pensions, as in some countries, there is no canvassing or bribing for elections.

I wish Old England were as happy in its government, but I do not see it. Your people, however, think their constitution the best in the world, and affect to despise ours. It is comfortable to have a good opinion of one's self, and of every thing that belongs to us; to think one's own religion, king, and wife, the best of all possible wives, kings, or religions. I remember three Greenlanders, who had travelled two years in Europe under the care of some Moravian missionaries, and had visited Germany, Denmark, Holland, and England. When I asked them at Philadelphia, where they were in their way home, whether, now they had seen how much more commodiously the white people lived by the help of the arts, they would not choose to remain among us; their answer was, that they were pleased with having had an opportunity of seeing so many fine things, *but they chose to* LIVE *in their own country*. Which country, by the way, consisted of rock only, for the Moravians were obliged to carry earth in their ship from New York, for the purpose of making a cabbage garden.

By Mr. Dollond's saying, that my double spectacles can only serve particular eyes, I doubt he has not been rightly informed of their construction. I imagine it will be found pretty generally true, that the same convexity of glass, through which a man sees clearest and best at the distance proper for reading, is not the best for greater distances. I therefore had formerly two pair of spectacles, which I shifted occasionally, as in travelling I sometimes read, and often wanted to regard the prospects. Finding this change troublesome, and not always sufficiently ready, I had the glasses cut, and half of each kind associated in the same circle, thus,

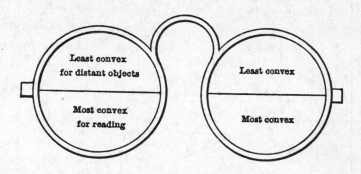

By this means, as I wear my spectacles constantly, I have only to move my eyes up or down, as I want to see distinctly far or near, the proper glasses being always ready. This I find more particularly convenient since my being in France, the glasses that serve me best at table to see what I eat, not being the best to see the faces of those on the other side of the table who speak to me; and when one's ears are not well accustomed to the sounds of a language, a sight of the movements in the features of him that speaks helps to explain; so that I understand French better by the help of my spectacles.

My intended translator of your piece, the only one I know who understands the *subject,* as well as the two languages, (which a translator ought to do, or he cannot make so good a translation,) is at present occupied in an affair that prevents his undertaking it; but that will soon be over. I thank you for the notes. I should be glad to have another of the printed pamphlets.

We shall always be ready to take your children, if you send them to us. I only wonder, that, since London draws to itself, and consumes such numbers of your country people, the country should not, to supply their places, want and willingly receive the children you have to dispose of. That circumstance, together with the multitude who voluntarily part with their freedom as men, to serve for a time as lackeys, or for life as soldiers, in consideration of small wages, seems to me proof that your island is over-peopled. And yet it is afraid of emigrations! Adieu, my dear friend, and believe me ever yours very affectionately,

B. FRANKLIN.

DESCRIPTION OF AN INSTRUMENT FOR TAKING DOWN BOOKS FROM HIGH SHELVES

January, 1786.

OLD men find it inconvenient to mount a ladder or steps for that purpose, their heads being sometimes subject to giddinesses, and their activity, with the steadiness of their joints, being abated by age; besides the trouble of removing the steps every time a book is wanted from a different part of their library.

For a remedy, I have lately made the following simple machine, which I call the *Long Arm*.

A B, the *Arm,* is a stick of pine, an inch square and 8 feet long. *C, D,* the *Thumb* and *Finger,* are two pieces of ash lath, an inch and half wide, and a quarter of an inch thick. These are fixed by wood screws on opposite sides of the end *A* of the arm *A B;* the finger *D* being longer and standing out an inch and half farther than the thumb *C*. The outside of the ends of these laths are pared off sloping and thin, that they may more easily enter between books that stand together on a shelf. Two small holes are bored through them at *i, k. E F,* the sinew, is a cord of the size of a small goosequill, with a loop at one end. When applied to the machine it passes through the two laths, and is stopped by a knot in its other end behind the longest at *k*. The hole at *i* is nearer the end of the arm than that at *k,* about an inch. A number of knots are also on the cord, distant three or four inches from each other.

To use this instrument; put one hand into the loop, and draw the sinew straight down the side of the arm; then enter the end of the finger between the book you would take down and that which is next to it. The laths being flexible, you may easily by a

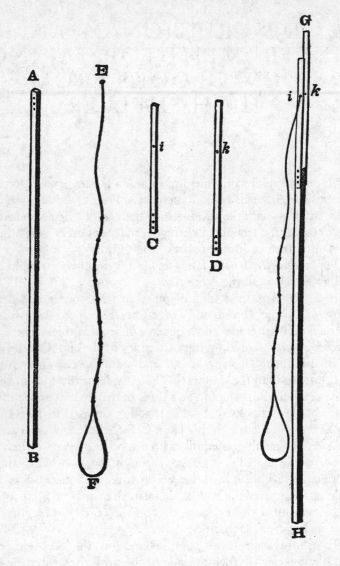

slight pressure sideways open them wider if the book is thick, or close them if it is thin by pulling the string, so as to enter the shorter lath or thumb between your book and that which is next to its other side, then push till the back of your book comes to touch the string. Then draw the string or sinew tight, which will cause the thumb and finger to pinch the book strongly, so that you may draw it out. As it leaves the other books, turn the instrument a *quarter* round, so that the book may lie flat and rest on its side upon the under lath or finger. The knots on the sinew will help you to keep it tight and close to the side of the arm as you take it down hand over hand, till the book comes to you; which would drop from between the thumb and finger if the sinew was let loose.

All new tools require some practice before we can become expert in the use of them. This requires very little.

Made in the proportions above given, it serves well for books in duodecimo or octavo. Quartos and folios are too heavy for it; but those are usually placed on the lower shelves within reach of hand.

The book taken down, may, when done with, be put up again into its place by the same machine.

TO BENJAMIN VAUGHAN

Philad^a, July 31, 1786.

DEAR FRIEND,

I recollect, that, when I had the great Pleasure of seeing you at Southampton, now a 12month since, we had some Conversation on the bad Effects of Lead taken inwardly; and that at your Request I promis'd to send you in writing a particular Account of several Facts I then mention'd to you, of which you thought some good use might be made. I now sit down to fulfil that Promise.

The first Thing I remember of this kind was a general Discourse in Boston, when I was a Boy, of a Complaint from North Carolina against New England Rum, that it poison'd their People, giving them the Dry Bellyach, with a Loss of the Use of their Limbs. The Distilleries being examin'd on the Occasion, it was found that several of them used leaden Still-heads and Worms, and the Physicians were of Opinion, that the Mischief was occasioned by that Use of Lead. The Legislature of the Massachusetts thereupon pass'd an Act, prohibiting under severe Penalties the Use of such Still-heads and Worms thereafter. Inclos'd I send you a Copy of the Acc^t, taken from my printed Law-book.

In 1724, being in London, I went to work in the Printing-House of Mr. Palmer, Bartholomew Close, as a Compositor. I there found a Practice, I had never seen before, of drying a Case of Types (which are wet in Distribution) by placing it sloping before the Fire. I found this had the additional Advantage, when the Types were not only dry'd but heated, of being comfortable to the Hands working over them in cold weather. I therefore sometimes heated my Case when the Types did not want drying. But an old Workman, observing it, advis'd me not to do so, telling me I might lose the Use of my Hands by it, as two of our Companions had nearly done, one of whom that us'd to earn his Guinea a Week, could not then make more than ten Shillings, and the other, who had the Dangles, but seven and sixpence. This, with a kind of obscure Pain, that I had sometimes felt, as it were in the Bones of my Hand when working over the Types made very hot, induced me to omit the Practice. But talking afterwards with Mr. James, a Letter-founder in the same Close, and asking him if his People, who work'd over the little Furnaces of melted Metal, were not subject to that Disorder; he made light of any danger from the effluvia, but ascribed it to Particles of the Metal swallow'd with their Food by slovenly Workmen, who went to their Meals after handling the Metal, without well washing their Fingers, so that some of the metalline Particles were taken off by their Bread and eaten with it. This appeared to have some Reason in it. But the Pain I had experienc'd made me still afraid of those Effluvia.

Being in Derbishire at some of the Furnaces for Smelting of Lead Ore, I was told, that the Smoke of those Furnaces was pernicious to the neighbouring Grass and other Vegetables; but I do not recollect to have heard any thing of the Effect of such Vegetables eaten by Animals. It may be well to make the Enquiry.

In America I have often observ'd, that on the Roofs of our shingled Houses, where Moss is apt to grow in northern Exposures, if there be any thing on the Roof painted with white Lead, such as Balusters, or Frames of dormant Windows, &c., there is constantly a Streak on the Shingles from such Paint down to the Eaves, on which no Moss will grow, but the wood remains constantly clean and free from it. We seldom drink RainWater that falls on our Houses; and if we did, perhaps the small Quantity of Lead, descending from such Paint, might not be sufficient to produce any sensible ill Effect on our Bodies. But I have been told of a Case in Europe, I forgot the Place, where a whole Family was afflicted with what we call the Dry Bellyach, or *Colica Pictonum,* by drinking RainWater. It was at a Country-Seat, which, being situated too high to have the Advantage of a Well, was supply'd with Water from a Tank, which received the Water from the leaded Roofs. This had been drunk several Years without Mischief; but some young Trees planted near the House growing up above the Roof, and shedding their Leaves upon it, it was suppos'd that an Acid in those Leaves had corroded the Lead they cover'd, and furnish'd the Water of that Year with its baneful Particles and Qualities.

When I was in Paris with Sir John Pringle in 1767, he visited *La Charité,* a Hospital particularly famous for the Cure of that Malady, and brought from thence a Pamphlet containing a List of the Names of Persons, specifying their Professions or Trades, who had been cured there. I had the Curiosity to examine that List, and found that all the Patients were of Trades, that, some way or other, use or work in Lead; such as Plumbers, Glaziers, Painters, &c., excepting only two kinds, Stonecutters and Soldiers. These I could not reconcile to my Notion, that Lead was the cause of that Disorder. But on my mentioning this Difficulty to a Physician of that Hospital, he inform'd me that the Stonecutters are continually using melted Lead to fix the Ends of Iron Balustrades in Stone; and that the Soldiers had been employ'd by Painters, as Labourers, in Grinding of Colours.

This, my dear Friend, is all I can at present recollect on the Subject. You will see by it, that the Opinion of this mischievous Effect from Lead is at least above Sixty Years old; and you will observe with Concern how long a useful Truth may be known and exist, before it is generally receiv'd and practis'd on.

I am, ever, yours most affectionately,

B. FRANKLIN.

PART III

POLITICS: THEORY AND PRACTICE

ON TRANSPORTED FELONS

The Pennsylvania Gazette, *April 11, 1751.*

From *Virginia* we hear, that six Convicts, who were transported for fourteen Years, and shipp'd at *Liverpool,* rose at Sea, shot the Captain, overcame and confin'd the Seamen, and kept Possession of the Vessel 19 Days; that coming in Sight of *Cape Hatteras,* they hoisted out the Boat to go on shore; when a Vessel passing by, a Boy they had not confin'd, hail'd her, and attempted to tell their Condition, but was prevented; and then the Villains drove a Spike up thro' his under and upper Jaws, and wound Spunyarn round the End that came out near his Nose, to prevent his getting it out. They then cut away the Sails from the Yards, left the Ship, and went ashore. But a *New-England* Sloop coming by soon after, and seeing a Ship driving in the Sea in that Manner, boarded her, found Things as above mentioned, and carried her into *North-Carolina;* from whence a Hue and Cry went after the Villains, who had stroll'd along to *Virginia;* they were taken at *Norfolk,* and one of them confess'd the Fact; upon which they were order'd up, about two Weeks since, to *Williamsburgh,* for Trial as Pyrates.

From *Maryland* we hear, that a Convict Servant, about three Weeks since, went into his Master's House, with an Ax in his Hand, determin'd to kill his Mistress; but changing his Purpose on seeing, as he expressed it, *how d——d innocent she look'd,* he laid his Left-hand on a Block, cut it off, and threw it at her, saying, *Now make me work, if you can.*

N. B. *'Tis said this desperate Villain is now begging in* Pennsylvania, *and 'tis thought has been seen in this City; he*

*pretends to have lost his Hand by an Accident: The Publick
are therefore caution'd to beware of him.*

From *Bucks* County we hear, that a Convict Servant, one
John McCaulefd, imported here last Fall, has broke open and
robb'd several Houses, of Goods to a considerable Value; but
being apprehended at a Ferry, is committed to Prison.

Yesterday the Trial of *Samuel Saunders,* for the Murder of
Simon Girtie, came on at the Supream Court, when the Jury return'd their Verdict *Manslaughter.*

"When we see our Papers fill'd continually with Accounts of
the most audacious Robberies, the most cruel Murders, and infinite other Villainies perpetrated by Convicts transported from
Europe, what melancholly, what terrible Reflections must it occasion! What will become of our Posterity!—These are some of
thy Favours, BRITAIN! Thou art called our MOTHER COUNTRY;
but what good *Mother* ever sent *Thieves* and *Villains* to accompany her *Children;* to corrupt some with their infectious Vices,
and murder the rest? What *Father* ever endeavour'd to spread
the *Plague* in his Family!—We do not ask Fish, but thou givest
us *Serpents,* and worse than Serpents!—In what can *Britain* show
a more Sovereign Contempt for us, than by emptying their *Jails*
into our Settlements; unless they would likewise empty their
Jakes on our Tables?—What must we think of that B——d,
which has advis'd the Repeal of every Law we have hitherto
made to prevent this Deluge of Wickedness overwhelming us;
and with this *cruel* Sarcasm, *That these Laws were against the*
Publick Utility, *for they tended to prevent the* IMPROVEMENT
and WELL-PEOPLING *of the Colonies!*—And what must we
think of those Merchants, who for the sake of a little paltry
Gain, will be concern'd in importing and disposing of these
abominable Cargoes?"

EXPORTING OF FELONS TO THE COLONIES

The Pennsylvania Gazette, *May 9, 1751.*

To the Printers of the Gazette

By a Passage in one of your late Papers, I understand that the Government at home will not suffer our mistaken Assemblies to make any Law for preventing or discouraging the Importation of Convicts from Great Britain, for this kind Reason, '*That such Laws are against the Publick Utility, as they tend to prevent the* IMPROVEMENT *and* WELL PEOPLING *of the Colonies.*'

Such a tender *parental* Concern in our *Mother Country* for the *Welfare* of her *Children,* calls aloud for the highest *Returns* of Gratitude and Duty. This every one must be sensible of: But 'tis said, that in our present Circumstances it is absolutely impossible for us to make *such* as are adequate to the Favour. I own it; but nevertheless let us do our Endeavour. 'Tis something to show a grateful Disposition.

In some of the uninhabited Parts of these Provinces, there are Numbers of these venomous Reptiles we call RATTLE-SNAKES; Felons-convict from the Beginning of the World: These, whenever we meet with them, we put to Death, by Virtue of an old Law, *Thou shalt bruise his Head.* But as this is a sanguinary Law, and may seem too cruel; and as however mischievous those Creatures are with us, they may possibly change their Natures, if they were to change the Climate; I would humbly propose, that this general Sentence of *Death* be changed for *Transportation.*

In the Spring of the Year, when they first creep out of their Holes, they are feeble, heavy, slow, and easily taken; and if a small Bounty were allow'd *per* Head, some Thousands might be collected annually, and *transported* to *Britain.* There I would propose to have them carefully distributed in *St. James's Park,* in the *Spring-Gardens* and other Places of Pleasure about *London;* in the Gardens of all the Nobility and Gentry throughout the Nation; but particularly in the Gardens of the *Prime Ministers,* the *Lords of Trade* and *Members of Parliament;* for to them we are *most particularly* obliged.

There is no human Scheme so perfect, but some Inconveniencies may be objected to it: Yet when the Conveniencies far exceed, the Scheme is judg'd rational, and fit to be executed. Thus Inconveniencies have been objected to that *good* and *wise* Act of Parliament, by virtue of which all the *Newgates* and *Dungeons* in *Britain* are emptied into the Colonies. It has been said, that these Thieves and Villains introduc'd among us, spoil the Morals of Youth in the Neighbourhoods that entertain them, and perpetrate many horrid Crimes: But let not *private Interests* obstruct *publick* Utility. Our *Mother* knows what is best for us. What is a little *Housebreaking, Shoplifting,* or *Highway Robbing;* what is a *Son* now and then *corrupted* and *hang'd,* a Daughter *debauch'd* and *pox'd,* a Wife *stabb'd,* a Husband's *Throat cut,* or a Child's *Brains beat out* with an Axe, compar'd with this 'IMPROVEMENT and WELL PEOPLING of the Colonies!'

Thus it may perhaps be objected to my Scheme, that the *Rattle-Snake* is a mischievous Creature, and that his changing his Nature with the Clime is a mere Supposition, not yet confirm'd by sufficient Facts. What then? Is not Example more prevalent than Precept? And may not the honest rough British Gentry, by a Familiarity with these Reptiles, learn to *creep,* and to *insinuate,* and to *slaver,* and to *wriggle* into Place (and perhaps to *poison* such as stand in their Way) Qualities of no small Advantage to Courtiers! In comparison of which 'IMPROVEMENT and PUBLICK UTILITY,' what is a *Child* now and then kill'd by their venomous Bite, . . . or even a favourite *Lap Dog?*

I would only add, that this exporting of Felons to the Colonies, may be consider'd as a *Trade,* as well as in the Light of a *Favour,* Now all Commerce implies Returns: Justice requires them: There can be no Trade without them. And *Rattle-Snakes* seem the most *suitable Returns* for the *Human Serpents* sent us by our *Mother* Country. In this, however, as in every other Branch of Trade, she will have the Advantage of us. She will reap *equal* Benefits without equal Risque of the Inconveniencies and Dangers. For the *Rattle-Snake* gives Warning before he attempts his Mischief; which the Convict does not. I am

Yours, &c.

AMERICANUS.

OBSERVATIONS CONCERNING THE INCREASE OF MANKIND, PEOPLING OF COUNTRIES, ETC.

Written in Pensilvania, 1751.

1. TABLES of the Proportion of Marriages to Births, of Deaths to Births, of Marriages to the Numbers of Inhabitants, &c., form'd on Observaions (sic) made upon the Bills of Mortality, Christnings, &c., of populous Cities, will not suit Countries; nor will Tables form'd on Observations made on full-settled old Countries, as *Europe,* suit new Countries, as *America.*

2. For People increase in Proportion to the Number of Marriages, and that is greater in Proportion to the Ease and Convenience of supporting a Family. When families can be easily supported, more Persons marry, and earlier in Life.

3. In Cities, where all Trades, Occupations, and Offices are full, many delay marrying till they can see how to bear the Charges of a Family; which Charges are greater in Cities, as Luxury is more common: many live single during Life, and continue Servants to Families, Journeymen to Trades; &c. hence Cities do not by natural Generation supply themselves with Inhabitants; the Deaths are more than the Births.

4. In Countries full settled, the Case must be nearly the same; all Lands being occupied and improved to the Heighth; those who cannot get Land, must Labour for others that have it; when Labourers are plenty, their Wages will be low; by low Wages a family is supported with Difficulty; this Difficulty deters many from Marriage, who therefore long continue Servants and single.

Only as the Cities take Supplies of People from the Country, and thereby make a little more Room in the Country; Marriage is a little more encourag'd there, and the Births exceed the Deaths.

5. *Europe* is generally full settled with Husbandmen, Manufacturers, &c., and therefore cannot now much increase in People: *America* is chiefly occupied by Indians, who subsist mostly by Hunting. But as the Hunter, of all Men, requires the greatest Quantity of Land from whence to draw his Subsistence, (the Husbandman subsisting on much less, the Gardner on still less, and the Manufacturer requiring least of all), the *Europeans* found *America* as fully settled as it well could be by Hunters; yet these, having large Tracks, were easily prevail'd on to part with Portions of Territory to the new Comers, who did not much interfere with the Natives in Hunting, and furnish'd them with many Things they wanted.

6. Land being thus plenty in *America,* and so cheap as that a labouring man, that understands Husbandry, can in a short Time save Money enough to purchase a Piece of new Land sufficient for a Plantation, whereon he may subsist a Family, such are not afraid to marry; for, if they even look far enough forward to consider how their Children, when grown up, are to be provided for, they see that more Land is to be had at rates equally easy, all Circumstances considered.

7. Hence Marriages in *America* are more general, and more generally early, than in *Europe*. And if it is reckoned there, that there is but one Marriage per Annum among 100 persons, perhaps we may here reckon two; and if in *Europe* they have but 4 Births to a Marriage (many of their Marriages being late), we may here reckon 8, of which if one half grow up, and our Marriages are made, reckoning one with another at 20 Years of Age, our People must at least be doubled every 20 Years.

8. But notwithstanding this Increase, so vast is the Territory of *North America,* that it will require many Ages to settle it fully; and, till it is fully settled, Labour will never be cheap here, where no Man continues long a Labourer for others, but gets a Plantation of his own, no Man continues long a Journeyman to a Trade, but goes among those new Settlers, and sets up for himself, &c. Hence Labour is no cheaper now in *Pennsylvania,*

than it was 30 Years ago, tho' so many Thousand labouring People have been imported.

9. The Danger therefore of these Colonies interfering with their Mother Country in Trades that depend on Labour, Manufactures, &c., is too remote to require the attention of *Great-Britain.*

10. But in Proportion to the Increase of the Colonies, a vast Demand is growing for British Manufactures, a glorious Market wholly in the Power of *Britain,* in which Foreigners cannot interfere, which will increase in a short Time even beyond her Power of supplying, tho' her whole Trade should be to her Colonies: Therefore *Britain* should not too much restrain Manufactures in her Colonies. A wise and good Mother will not do it. To distress, is to weaken, and weakening the Children weakens the whole Family.

11. Besides if the Manufactures of *Britain* (by reason of the *American* Demands) should rise too high in Price, Foreigners who can sell cheaper will drive her Merchants out of Foreign Markets; Foreign Manufactures will thereby be encouraged and increased, and consequently foreign Nations, perhaps her Rivals in Power, grow more populous and more powerful; while her own Colonies, kept too low, are unable to assist her, or add to her Strength.

12. 'Tis an ill-grounded Opinion that by the Labour of slaves, *America* may possibly vie in Cheapness of Manufactures with *Britain.* The Labour of Slaves can never be so cheap here as the Labour of working Men is in *Britain.* Any one may compute it. Interest of Money is in the Colonies from 6 to 10 per Cent. Slaves one with another cost 30£ Sterling per Head. Reckon then the Interest of the first Purchase of a Slave, the Insurance or Risque on his Life, his Cloathing and Diet, Expences in his Sickness and Loss of Time, Loss by his Neglect of Business (Neglect is natural to the Man who is not to be benefited by his own Care or Diligence), Expence of a Driver to keep him at Work, and his Pilfering from Time to Time, almost every Slave being *by Nature* a Thief, and compare the whole Amount with the Wages of a Manufacturer of Iron or Wool in *England,* you will see that Labour is much cheaper there than it ever can be by

Negroes here. Why then will *Americans* purchase Slaves? Because Slaves may be kept as long as a *Man* pleases, or has Occasion for their Labour; while hired Men are continually leaving their masters (often in the midst of his Business,) and setting up for themselves.—Sec. 8.

13. As the Increase of People depends on the Encouragement of Marriages, the following Things must diminish a Nation, viz. 1. *The being conquered;* for the Conquerors will engross as many Offices, and exact as much Tribute or Profit on the Labour of the conquered, as will maintain them in their new Establishment, and this diminishing the Subsistence of the Natives, discourages their Marriages, and so gradually diminishes them, while the foreigners increase. 2. *Loss of Territory.* Thus, the *Britons* being driven into *Wales,* and crowded together in a barren Country insufficient to support such great Numbers, diminished 'till the People bore a Proportion to the Produce, while the *Saxons* increas'd on their abandoned lands; till the Island became full of *English.* And, were the *English* now driven into *Wales* by some foreign Nation, there would in a few Years, be no more Englishmen in *Britain,* than there are now people in *Wales.* 3. *Loss of Trade.* Manufactures exported, draw Subsistence from Foreign Countries for Numbers; who are thereby enabled to marry and raise Families. If the Nation be deprived of any Branch of Trade, and no new Employment is found for the People occupy'd in that Branch, it will also be soon deprived of so many People. 4. *Loss of Food.* Suppose a Nation has a Fishery, which not only employs great Numbers, but makes the Food and Subsistence of the People cheaper. If another Nation becomes Master of the Seas, and prevents the Fishery, the People will diminish in Proportion as the Loss of Employ and Dearness of Provision, makes it more difficult to subsist a Family. 5. *Bad Government and insecure Property.* People not only leave such a Country, and settling Abroad incorporate with other Nations, lose their native Language, and become Foreigners, but, the Industry of those that remain being discourag'd, the Quantity of Subsistence in the Country is lessen'd, and the Support of a Family becomes more difficult. So heavy Taxes tend to diminish a People. 6. *The Introduction*

of Slaves. The Negroes brought into the *English* Sugar *Islands* have greatly diminish'd the Whites there; the Poor are by this Means deprived of Employment, while a few Families acquire vast Estates; which they spend on Foreign Luxuries, and educating their Children in the Habit of those Luxuries; the same Income is needed for the Support of one that might have maintain'd 100. The Whites who have Slaves, not labouring, are enfeebled, and therefore not so generally prolific; the Slaves being work'd too hard, and ill fed, their Constitutions are broken, and the Deaths among them are more than the Births; so that a continual Supply is needed from *Africa.* The Northern Colonies, having few Slaves, increase in Whites. Slaves also pejorate[1] the Families that use them; the white Children become proud, disgusted with Labour, and being educated in Idleness, are rendered unfit to get a Living by Industry.

14. Hence the Prince that acquires new Territory, if he finds it vacant, or removes the Natives to give his own People Room; the Legislator that makes effectual Laws for promoting of Trade, increasing Employment, improving Land by more or better Tillage, providing more Food by Fisheries; securing Property, &c. and the Man that invents new Trades, Arts, or Manufactures, or new Improvements in Husbandry, may be properly called *Fathers* of their Nation, as they are the Cause of the Generation of Multitudes, by the Encouragement they afford to Marriage.

15. As to Privileges granted to the married, (such as the *Jus trium Liberorum* among the *Romans,*) they may hasten the filling of a Country that has been thinned by War or Pestilence, or that has otherwise vacant Territory; but cannot increase a People beyond the Means provided for their Subsistence.

16. Foreign Luxuries and needless Manufactures, imported and used in a Nation, do, by the same Reasoning, increase the People of the Nation that furnishes them, and diminish the People of the Nation that uses them. Laws, therefore, that prevent such Importations, and on the contrary promote the Exportation of Manufactures to be consumed in Foreign Countries, may be called (with Respect to the People that make them) *generative Laws,* as, by increasing Subsistence they encourage Marriage.

Such Laws likewise strengthen a Country, doubly, by increasing its own People and diminishing its Neighbours.

17. Some *European* Nations prudently refuse to consume the Manufactures of *East-India:*—They should likewise forbid them to their Colonies; for the Gain to the Merchant is not to be compar'd with the Loss, by this Means, of People to the Nation.

18. Home Luxury in the Great increases the Nation's Manufacturers employ'd by it, who are many, and only tends to diminish the Families that indulge in it, who are few. The greater the common fashionable Expence of any Rank of People, the more cautious they are of Marriage. Therefore Luxury should never be suffer'd to become common.

19. The great Increase of Offspring in particular Families is not always owing to greater Fecundity of Nature, but sometimes to Examples of Industry in the Heads, and industrious Education; by which the Children are enabled to provide better for themselves, and their marrying early is encouraged from the Prospect of good Subsistence.

20. If there be a Sect, therefore, in our Nation, that regard Frugality and Industry as religious Duties, and educate their Children therein, more than others commonly do; such Sect must consequently increase more by natural Generation, than any other sect in *Britain*.

21. The Importation of Foreigners into a Country, that has as many Inhabitants as the present Employments and Provisions for Subsistence will bear, will be in the End no Increase of People; unless the New Comers have more Industry and Frugality than the Natives, and then they will provide more Subsistence, and increase in the Country; but they will gradually eat the Natives out. Nor is it necessary to bring in Foreigners to fill up any occasional Vacancy in a Country; for such Vacancy (if the Laws are good, sec. 14, 16,) will soon be filled by natural Generation. Who can now find the Vacancy made in *Sweden, France,* or other Warlike Nations, by the Plague of Heroism, 40 years ago; in *France,* by the Expulsion of the Protestants; in *England,* by the Settlement of her Colonies; or in *Guinea,* by 100 Years Exportation of Slaves, that has blacken'd half *America?* The thinness of Inhabitants in *Spain* is owing to National Pride and

Idleness, and other Causes, rather than to the Expulsion of the Moors, or to the making of new Settlements.

22. There is, in short, no Bound to the prolific Nature of Plants or Animals, but what is made by their crowding and interfering with each other's means of Subsistence. Was the Face of the Earth vacant of other Plants, it might be gradually sowed and overspread with one Kind only; as, for Instance, with Fennel; and were it empty of other Inhabitants, it might in a few Ages be replenish'd from one Nation only; as, for Instance, with *Englishmen*. Thus there are suppos'd to be now upwards of One Million *English* Souls in *North-America,* (tho' 'tis thought scarce 80,000 have been brought over Sea,) and yet perhaps there is not one the fewer in *Britain,* but rather many more, on Account of the Employment the Colonies afford to Manufacturers at Home. This Million doubling, suppose but once in 25 Years, will, in another Century, be more than the People of *England,* and the greatest Number of *Englishmen* will be on this Side the Water. What an Accession of Power to the *British* Empire by Sea as well as Land! What Increase of Trade and Navigation! What Numbers of Ships and Seamen! We have been here but little more than 100 years, and yet the Force of our Privateers in the late War, united, was greater, both in Men and Guns, than that of the whole *British* Navy in Queen *Elizabeth's* Time. How important an Affair then to *Britain* is the present Treaty for settling the Bounds between her Colonies and the *French,* and how careful should she be to secure Room enough, since on the Room depends so much the Increase of her People:

23. In fine, a Nation well regulated is like a Polypus; take away a Limb, its Place is soon supply'd; cut it in two, and each deficient Part shall speedily grow out of the Part remaining. Thus if you have Room and Subsistence enough, as you may by dividing, make ten Polypes out of one, you may of one make ten Nations, equally populous and powerful; or rather increase a Nation ten fold in Numbers and Strength.

And since Detachments of *English* from *Britain,* sent to *America,* will have their Places at Home so soon supply'd and increase so largely here; why should the *Palatine Boors*[2] be suffered to swarm into our Settlements and, by herding together, establish their Language and Manners, to the Exclusion of ours? Why should *Pennsylvania*, founded by the *English*, become a Colony of *Aliens*, who will shortly be so numerous as to Germanize us instead of our Anglifying them, and will never adopt our Language or Customs any more than they can acquire our Complexion?

24. Which leads me to add one Remark, that the Number of purely white People in the World is proportionably very small. All *Africa* is black or tawny; *Asia* chiefly tawny; *America* (exclusive of the new Comers) wholly so. And in *Europe*, the *Spaniards*, *Italians*, *French*, *Russians*, and *Swedes*, are generally of what we call a swarthy Complexion; as are the *Germans* also, the *Saxons* only excepted, who, with the *English*, make the principal Body of White People on the Face of the Earth. I could wish their Numbers were increased. And while we are, as I may call it, *Scouring* our Planet, by *clearing America* of Woods, and so making this Side of our Globe reflect a brighter Light to the Eyes of Inhabitants in *Mars* or *Venus*, why should we, in the Sight of Superior Beings, darken its People ? Why increase the Sons of *Africa*, by planting them in *America*, where we have so fair an Opportunity, by excluding all Blacks and Tawneys, of increasing the lovely White and Red? But perhaps I am partial to the Complexion of my Country, for such Kind of Partiality is natural to Mankind.

JOIN OR DIE

The Pennsylvania Gazette, *May 9, 1754.*

Friday last an Express arrived here from Major Washington, with Advice, that Mr. Ward, Ensign of Capt. Trent's Company, was compelled to surrender his small Fort in the Forks of Monongahela to the French, on the 17th past; who fell down from Venango with a Fleet of 360 Battoes and Canoes, upwards of 1000 Men, and 18 Pieces of Artillery, which they planted against the Fort; and Mr. Ward having but 44 Men, and no Cannon to make a proper Defence, was obliged to surrender on Summons, capitulating to march out with their Arms, &c. and they had accordingly joined Major Washington, who was advanced with three Companies of the Virginia Forces, as far as the New Store near the Allegheny Mountains, where the Men were employed in clearing a Road for the Cannon, which were every Day expected with Col. Fry, and the Remainder of the Regiment.—We hear farther, that some few of the English Traders on the Ohio escaped, but 'tis supposed the greatest Part are taken, with all their Goods, and Skins, to the Amount of near 20,000£. The Indian Chiefs, however, have dispatch'd Messages to Pennsylvania, and Virginia, desiring that the English would not be discouraged, but send out their Warriors to join them, and drive the French out of the Country before they fortify; otherwise the Trade will be lost, and, to their great Grief, an eternal Separation made between the Indians and their Brethren the English. 'Tis farther said, that besides the French that came down from

Venango, another Body of near 400, is coming up the Ohio; and that 600 French Indians, of the Chippaways and Ott-aways, are coming down Siota River, from the Lake, to join them; and many more French are expected from Canada; the Design being to establish themselves, settle their Indians, and build Forts just on the Back of our Settlements in all our Colonies; from which Forts, as they did from Crown-Point, they may send out their Parties to kill and scalp the Inhab-itants, and ruin the Frontier Counties. Accordingly we hear, that the Back Settlers in Virginia, are so terrify'd by the Murdering and Scalping of the Family last Winter, and the Taking of this Fort, that they begin already to abandon their Plantations, and remove to Places of more Safety.—The Con-fidence of the French in this Undertaking seems well-grounded on the present disunited State of the British Colonies, and the extreme Difficulty of bringing so many different Governments and Assemblies to agree in any speedy and effectual Mea-sures for our common Defence and Security; while our Enemies have the very great Advantage of being under one Direction, with one Council, and one Purse. Hence, and from the great Distance of Britain, they presume that they may with Im-punity violate the most solemn Treaties subsisting between the two Crowns, kill, seize and imprison our Traders, and confiscate their Effects at Pleasure (as they have done for several Years past) murder and scalp our Farmers, with their Wives and Children, and take an easy Possession of such Parts of the British Territory as they find most convenient for them; which if they are permitted to do, must end in the Destruction of the British Interest, Trade and Plantations in America.

THREE LETTERS TO GOVERNOR SHIRLEY

LETTER I.

Concerning the Voice of the People in Choosing
the Rulers by Whom Taxes Are Imposed.

Tuesday Morning. [December 17, 1754.]

SIR,

I return you the loose sheets of the plan, with thanks to your
Excellency for communicating them.

I apprehend, that excluding the *people* of the colonies from
all share in the choice of the grand council will give extreme
dissatisfaction, as well as the taxing them by act of Parliament,
where they have no representative. It is very possible, that this
general government might be as well and faithfully administered without the people, as with them; but where heavy burthens have been laid on them, it has been found useful to make
it, as much as possible, their own act; for they bear better when
they have, or think they have some share in the direction; and
when any public measures are generally grievous, or even distasteful to the people, the wheels of government move more
heavily.

LETTER II.

On the Imposition of Direct Taxes Upon the Colonies Without Their Consent.

Wednesday Morning. [December 18, 1754.]

SIR,

I mentioned it yesterday to your Excellency as my opinion, that excluding the *people* of the colonies from all share in the choice of the grand council, would probably give extreme dissatisfaction, as well as the taxing them by act of Parliament, where they have no representative. In matters of general concern to the people, and especially where burthens are to be laid upon them, it is of use to consider, as well what they will be apt to think and say, as what they ought to think; I shall therefore, as your Excellency requires it of me, briefly mention what of either kind occurs to me on this occasion.

First they will say, and perhaps with justice, that the body of the people in the colonies are as loyal, and as firmly attached to the present constitution, and reigning family, as any subjects in the king's dominions.

That there is no reason to doubt the readiness and willingness of the representatives they may choose, to grant from time to time such supplies for the defence of the country, as shall be judged necessary, so far as their abilities will allow.

That the people in the colonies, who are to feel the immediate mischiefs of invasion and conquest by an enemy in the loss of their estates, lives and liberties, are likely to be better judges of the quantity of forces necessary to be raised and maintained, forts to be built and supported, and of their own abilities to bear the expence, than the parliament of England at so great a distance.

That governors often come to the colonies merely to make fortunes, with which they intend to return to Britain; are not always men of the best abilities or integrity; have many of them no estates here, nor any natural connexions with us, that should make them heartily concerned for our welfare; and might possibly be fond of raising and keeping up more forces than necessary, from the profits accruing to themselves, and to make provision for their friends and dependants.

That the counsellors in most of the colonies being appointed by the crown, on the recommendation of governors, are often of small estates, frequently dependant on the governors for offices, and therefore too much under influence.

That there is therefore great reason to be jealous of a power in such governors and councils, to raise such sums as they shall judge necessary, by draft on the lords of the treasury, to be afterwards laid on the colonies by act of parliament, and paid by the people here; since they might abuse it by projecting useless expeditions, harassing the people, and taking them from their labour to execute such projects, merely to create offices and employments, and gratify their dependants, and divide profits.

That the parliament of England is at a great distance, subject to be misinformed and misled by such Governors and Councils, whose united interests might probably secure them against the effect of any complaint from hence.

That it is supposed an undoubted right of Englishmen, not to be taxed but by their own consent given through their representatives.

That the colonies have no representatives in parliament.

That to propose taxing them by parliament, and refuse them the liberty of choosing a representative council, to meet in the colonies, and consider and judge of the necessity of any general tax, and the quantum, shews suspicion of their loyalty to the crown, or of their regard for their country, or of their common sense and understanding, which they have not deserved.

That compelling the colonies to pay money without their consent, would be rather like raising contributions in an enemy's country, than taxing of Englishmen for their own public benefit.

That it would be treating them as a conquered people, and not as true British subjects.

That a tax laid by the representatives of the colonies might easily be lessened as the occasions should lessen, but being once laid by parliament under the influence of the representations made by Governors, would probably be kept up and continued for the benefit of Governors, to the grievous burthen and discouragement of the colonies, and prevention of their growth and increase.

That a power in Governors to march the inhabitants from one end of the British and French colonies to the other, being a country of at least 1500 square miles, without the approbation or the consent of their representatives first obtained, such expeditions might be grievous and ruinous to the people, and would put them on footing with the subjects of France in Canada, that now groan under such oppression from their Governor, who for two years past has harassed them with long and destructive marches to Ohio.

That if the colonies in a body may be well governed by governors and councils appointed by the crown, without representatives, particular colonies may as well or better be so governed; a tax may be laid upon them all by act of parliament for support of government, and their assemblies may be dismissed as an useless part of the constitution.

That the powers proposed by the Albany Plan of Union, to be vested in a grand council representative of the people, even with regard to military matters, are not so great as those the colonies of Rhode Island and Connecticut are entrusted with by their charters, and have never abused; for by this plan, the president-general is appointed by the crown, and controls all by his negative; but in those governments, the people choose the Governor, and yet allow him no negative.

That the British colonies bordering on the French are properly frontiers of the British empire; and the frontiers of an empire are properly defended at the joint expence of the body of the people in such empire: It would now be thought hard by act of parliament to oblige the Cinque Ports or seacoasts of Britain to maintain the whole navy, because they are more immediately defended by it, not allowing them at the same time a vote in choosing members of the parliament; and if the frontiers in America bear the expence of their own defence, it seems hard to allow them no share in voting the money, judging of the necessity and sum, or advising the measures.

That besides the taxes necessary for the defence of the frontiers, the colonies pay yearly great sums to the mother-country unnoticed: For taxes paid in Britain by the landholder or artificer, must enter into and increase the price of the produce of land and of manufactures made of it; and great part of this is paid by consumers in the colonies, who thereby pay a considerable part of the British taxes.

We are restrained in our trade with foreign nations, and where we could be supplied with any manufacture cheaper from them, but must buy the same dearer from Britain; the difference of price is a clear tax to Britain.

We are obliged to carry a great part of our produce directly to Britain; and where the duties laid upon it lessen its price to the planter, or it sells for less than it would in foreign markets; the difference is a tax paid to Britain.

Some manufactures we could make, but are forbidden, and must take them of British merchants; the whole price is a tax paid to Britain.

By our greatly increasing the demand and consumption of British manufactures, their price is considerably raised of late years; the advantage is clear profit to Britain, and enables its people better to pay great taxes; and much of it being paid by us, is clear tax to Britain.

In short, as we are not suffered to regulate our trade, and restrain the importation and consumption of British superfluities (as Britain can the consumption of foreign superfluities) our whole wealth centers finally amongst the merchants and inhabitants of Britain, and if we make them richer, and enable them better to pay their taxes, it is nearly the same as being taxed ourselves, and equally beneficial to the crown.

These kind of secondary taxes, however, we do not complain of, though we have no share in the laying, or disposing of them; but to pay immediate heavy taxes, in the laying, appropriation, and disposition of which we have no part, and which perhaps we may know to be as unnecessary, as grievous, must seem hard measure to Englishmen, who cannot conceive, that by hazarding their lives and fortunes, in subduing and settling new countries, extending the dominion, and increasing the commerce of the mother nation, they have forfeited the native rights of Britons, which they think ought rather to be given to them, as due to such merit, if they had been before in a state of slavery.

These, and such kind of things as these, I apprehend, will be thought and said by the people, if the proposed alteration of the Albany plan should take place. Then the administration of the board of governors and councils so appointed, not having any representative body of the people to approve and unite in its measures, and conciliate the minds of the people to them, will probably become suspected and odious; dangerous animosities and feuds will arise between the governors and governed; and every thing go into confusion.

Perhaps I am too apprehensive in this matter; but having freely given my opinion and reasons, your Excellency can judge better than I whether there be any weight in them, and the shortness of the time allowed me, will, I hope, in some degree excuse the imperfections of this scrawl.

With the greatest respect, and fidelity, I have the honour to be,
Your Excellency's most obedient,
and most humble servant,
B. FRANKLIN.[1]

LETTER III.

On the Subject of Uniting the Colonies More Intimately with Great Britain, by Allowing Them Representatives in Parliament.

Boston, Dec. 22, 1754.

SIR,

Since the conversation your Excellency was pleased to honour me with, on the subject of *uniting the colonies* more intimately with Great Britain, by allowing them *representatives in parliament,* I have something further considered that matter, and am of opinion, that such a union would be very acceptable to the colonies, provided they had a reasonable number of representatives allowed them; and that all the old acts of Parliament restraining the trade or cramping the manufactures of the colonies be at the same time repealed, and the British subjects *on this side the water* put, in those respects, on the same footing with those in Great Britain, till the new Parliament, representing the whole, shall think it for the interest of the whole to reënact some or all of them. It is not that I imagine so many representatives will be allowed the colonies, as to have any great weight by their numbers; but I think there might be sufficient to occasion those laws to be better and more impartially considered, and perhaps to overcome the interest of a petty corporation, or of any particular set of artificers or traders in England, who heretofore seem, in some instances, to have been more regarded than all the colonies, or than was consistent with the general interest, or best national good. I think too, that the government of the colonies by a parliament, in which they are fairly represented, would be vastly more agreeable to the people, than the method lately attempted to be introduced by royal instructions, as well as more agreeable to the nature of an English constitution, and to English liberty; and that such laws as now seem to bear hard on the colonies, would (when judged by such a Parliament for the best interest of the whole) be more cheerfully submitted to, and more easily executed.

I should hope too, that by such a union, the people of Great Britain, and the people of the colonies, would learn to consider themselves, as not belonging to a different community with different interests, but to one community with one interest; which I imagine would contribute to strengthen the whole, and greatly lessen the danger of future separations.

It is, I suppose, agreed to be the general interest of any state, that its people be numerous and rich; men enough to fight in its defence, and enough to pay sufficient taxes to defray the charge; for these circumstances tend to the security of the state, and its protection from foreign power: But it seems not of so much importance, whether the fighting be done by John or Thomas, or the tax paid by William or Charles. The iron manufacture employs and enriches British subjects, but is it of any importance to the state, whether the manufacturers live at Birmingham, or Sheffield, or both, since they are still within its bounds, and their wealth and persons still at its command? Could the Goodwin Sands be laid dry by banks, and land equal to a large country thereby gained to England, and presently filled with English inhabitants, would it be right to deprive such inhabitants of the common privileges enjoyed by other Englishmen, the right of vending their produce in the same ports, or of making their own shoes, because a merchant or a shoemaker, living on the old land, might fancy it more for his advantage to trade or make shoes for them? Would this be right, even if the land were gained at the expence of the state? And would it not seem less right, if the charge and labour of gaining the additional territory to Britain had been borne by the settlers themselves? And would not the hardship appear yet greater, if the people of the new country should be allowed no representatives in the parliament enacting such impositions?

Now I look on the colonies as so many counties gained to Great Britain, and more advantageous to it than if they had been gained out of the seas around its coasts, and joined to its land: For being in different climates, they afford greater variety of produce, and being separated by the ocean, they increase much more its shipping and seamen; and since they are all included in the British empire, which has only extended itself by their means; and the strength and wealth of the parts are the strength and wealth of the whole; what imports it to the general state, whether a merchant, a smith, or a hatter, grow rich in Old or New England? And if, through increase of people, two smiths are wanted for one employed before, why may not the *new* smith be allowed to live and thrive in the *new* country, as well as the *old* one in the *old*? In fine, why should the countenance of a state be *partially* afforded to its people, unless it be most in favour of those who have most merit? And if there be any difference, those who have most contributed to enlarge Britain's empire and commerce, increase her strength, her wealth, and the numbers of her people, at the risk of their own lives and private fortunes in new and strange countries, methinks ought rather to expect some preference. With the greatest respect and esteem, I have the honour to be

Your Excellency's most obedient
and most humble servant,
B. FRANKLIN.

TO ISAAC NORRIS

Sɪʀ,

It is now six Years, since, in obedience to the Order of the House, I undertook a Voyage to England, to transact their Affairs there.

Fifteen Hundred Pounds of the Public Money was at different Times put into my Hands, for which I ought to account.

The following Articles are vouch'd by the Receipts inclos'd, viz

1758	Jan. 26.	Paid Robert Charles Esqr for the Province 26 *Guineas*	27 ″ 6 ″ 0
	April 20.	Paid Richard Partridge Esq for Ditto	40 ″ 0 . 0
	May 2.	Paid D° for D°	30 ″ 0 ″ 0
	Sept. 27.	Paid T. Osborne for 3 Vols Journals House of Commons	10 ″ 10 ′ 0
		And for Indexes to the whole	1 ″ 1 ′ 0
1759	Dec. 31.	Paid Accounts for Printing sundry Pieces in Defence of the Province	213 ″ 13 . 0
1760	Dec. 2.	Paid the Solicitor's Bill	470 ″ 8 . 8
			£ 792 ″ 18 ″ 8
		Deduct ⅛ᵗʰ of the Solicitor's Bill it being charg'd in the Trustees Acct	78 ″ 8 . 1
			£ 714 : 10 : 7

I made many other Disbursements for which I have no Receipts; such as for Postage of Letters and Pacquets, which were often very heavy, containing Bills and Duplicates &c. under the

Great Seal, brought by Post to London from the Out-Ports, which to compute moderately could not, I think, fall short of 15 £ per Annum. Also for customary New Year's Gifts, and Christmas Presents to Door-keepers & Clerks of the Public Offices, Tavern Dinners for the Lawyers and our other Friends at Hearings, Coach Hire, &c. for which I know not what to reckon, having kept no Account of such things. —

I therefore can make no Claim of Allowance for them.

The House will therefore please to consider the remainder of the 1500 £ put into my Hands, so unaccounted for, as now in their Disposition; for as to any Compensation for my Time & Pains in their Service, tho' I am conscious of having done faithfully every thing in my Power for the Public Good, according to the best of my Abilities, yet as the House, when they appointed me their Agent at first, and afterwards from Year to Year, did not vote any particular Sum as my Salary, I am therefore not warranted to charge any thing, but do now, with the same Confidence I have ever had in the Justice & Goodness of the House, chearfully submit the same to their present Discretion.

With the greatest Respect & Esteem I am,

Sir,   Your most obedient
                                  & most humble Servant
                                       B FRANKLIN

TO PETER COLLINSON

Philadᵃ, April 30, 1764.

DEAR FRIEND

I have before me your kind Notices of Feb. 3. and Feb. 10. Those you enclos'd for our Friend Bartram were carefully deliver'd. I have not yet seen the Squib you mention against your People, in the Supplement to the Magazine; but I think it impossible they should be worse us'd there than they have lately been here; where sundry inflammatory Pamphlets are printed and spread about to excite a mad armed Mob to massacre them. And it is my Opinion they are still in some Danger, more than they themselves seem to apprehend, as our Government has neither Goodwill nor Authority enough to protect them.

By the enclos'd Papers you will see that we are all to pieces again; and the general Wish seems to be a King's Government. If that is not to be obtain'd, many talk of quitting the Province, and among them your old Friend, who is tired of these Contentions, & longs for philosophic Ease and Leisure.

I suppose by this Time the Wisdom of your Parliament has determin'd in the Points you mention, of Trade, Duties, Troops and Fortifications in America.

Our Opinions or Inclinations, if they had been known, would perhaps have weigh'd but little among you. We are in your Hands as Clay in the Hands of the Potter; and so in one more Particular than is generally consider'd: for as the Potter cannot waste or spoil his Clay without injuring himself, so I think there is scarce anything you can do that may be hurtful to us, but what will be as much or more so to you. This must be our chief Security; for Interest with you we have but little. The West Indians vastly outweigh us of the Northern Colonies. What we get above a Subsistence we lay out with you for your Manufactures.

Therefore what you get from us in Taxes you must lose in Trade. The Cat can yield but her skin. And as you must have the whole Hide, if you first cut Thongs out of it, 'tis at your own Expence. The same in regard to our Trade with the foreign West India Islands. If you restrain it in any Degree, you restrain in the same Proportion our Power of making Remittances to you & of course our Demand for your Goods; for you will not clothe us out of Charity, tho' to receive 100 per cent for it in Heaven. In time perhaps Mankind may be wise enough to let Trade take its own Course, find its own Channels, and regulate its own Proportions, etc. At present, most of the Edicts of Princes, Placaerts, Laws & Ordinances of Kingdoms & States for that purpose, prove political Blunders. The Advantages they produce not being *general* for the Commonwealth; but *particular*, to private Persons or Bodies in the State who procur'd them, and *at the Expence of the rest of the People*. Does no body see, that if you confine us in America to your own Sugar Islands for that Commodity, it must raise the Price of it upon you in England? Just so much as the Price advances, so much is every Englishman tax'd to the West Indians.

Apropos, Now we are on the Subject of Trade and Manufactures, let me tell you a Piece of News, that though it might displease a very respectable Body among you, the Button-makers, will be agreable to yourself as a Virtuoso: It is, that we have discover'd a Beach in a Bay several Miles round, the Pebbles of which are all in the Form of Buttons, whence it is called *Button-mold Bay;* where thousands of Tons may be had for fetching; and as the Sea washes down the slaty Cliff, more are continually manufacturing out of the Fragments by the Surge. I send you a Specimen of Coat, Wastecoat & Sleeve Buttons; just as Nature has turn'd them. But I think I must not mention the Place, lest some Englishman get a Patent for this *Button-mine*, as one did for the *Coalmine* at Louisburgh, and by neither suffering others to work it, nor working it himself, deprive us of the Advantage God & Nature seem to have intended us. As we have now got Buttons, 'tis something towards our Cloathing; and who knows but in time we may find out where to get Cloth?—for as to our being always supply'd by you, 'tis folly to expect it. Only consider *the rate of our Increase,* and tell me if you can increase your Wooll in that Proportion, and where, in your little Island you can feed the Sheep. Nature has put Bounds to your Abilities, tho' none to your Desires. Britain would, if she could, manufacture & trade for all the World; England for all Britain;—London for all England;—and every Londoner for all London. So selfish is the human Mind! But 'tis well there is One above that rules these Matters with a more equal Hand. He that is pleas'd to feed the Ravens, will undoubtedly take care to prevent a Monopoly of the Carrion. Adieu, my dear Friend, & believe me ever

Yours most affectionately
B. FRANKLIN

ON THE PRICE OF CORN, AND MANAGEMENT OF THE POOR

TO THE PUBLIC.

I AM one of that class of people, that feeds you all, and at present is abused by you all; in short I am a *farmer*.

By your newspapers we are told, that God had sent a very short harvest to some other countries of Europe. I thought this might be in favour of Old England; and that now we should get a good price for our grain, which would bring millions among us, and make us flow in money; that to be sure is scarce enough.

But the wisdom of government forbade the exportation.

"Well," says I, "then we must be content with the market price at home."

"No;" say my lords the mob, "you sha'nt have that. Bring your corn to market if you dare; we'll sell it for you for less money, or take it for nothing."

Being thus attacked by both ends *of the constitution,* the head and tail *of government,* what am I to do?

Must I keep my corn in the barn, to feed and increase the breed of rats? Be it so; they cannot be less thankful than those I have been used to feed.

Are we farmers the only people to be grudged the profits of our honest labour? And why? One of the late scribblers against us gives a bill of fare of the provisions at my daughter's wedding, and proclaims to all the world, that we had the insolence to eat beef and pudding! Has he not read the precept in the good Book, *Thou shalt not muzzle the mouth of the ox that treadeth out the corn;* or does he think us less worthy of good living than our oxen?

"O, but the manufacturers! the manufacturers! they are to be favoured, and they must have bread at a cheap rate!"

Hark ye, Mr. Oaf; the farmers live splendidly, you say. And pray, would you have them hoard the money they get? Their fine clothes and furniture, do they make them themselves, or for one another, and so keep the money among them? Or do they employ these your darling manufacturers, and so scatter it again all over the nation?

The wool would produce me a better price, if it were suffered to go to foreign markets; but that, Messieurs the Public, your laws will not permit. It must be kept all at home, that our *dear* manufacturers may have it the cheaper. And then, having yourselves thus lessened our encouragement for raising sheep, you curse us for the scarcity of mutton!

I have heard my grandfather say, that the farmers submitted to the prohibition on the exportation of wool, being made to expect and believe, that, when the manufacturer bought his wool cheaper, they should also have their cloth cheaper. But the deuce a bit. It has been growing dearer and dearer from that day to this. How so? Why, truly, the cloth is exported; and that keeps up the price.

Now, if it be a good principle, that the exportation of a commodity is to be restrained, that so our people at home may have it the cheaper, stick to that principle, and go thorough-stitch with it. Prohibit the exportation of your cloth, your leather, and shoes, your iron ware, and your manufactures of all sorts, to make them all cheaper at home. And cheap enough they will be, I will warrant you; till people leave off making them.

Some folks seem to think they ought never to be easy till England becomes another Lubberland, where it is fancied that streets are paved with penny-rolls, the houses tiled with pancakes, and chickens, ready roasted, cry, "Come eat me."

I say, when you are sure you have got a good principle, stick to it, and carry it through. I hear it is said, that though it was *necessary and right* for the ministry to advise a prohibition of the exportation of corn, yet it was *contrary to law;* and also, that though it was *contrary to law* for the mob to obstruct wagons, yet it was *necessary and right.* Just the same thing to a tittle. Now they tell me, an act of indemnity ought to pass in favour of the ministry, to secure them from the consequences of having acted illegally. If so, pass another in favour of the mob. Others say, some of the mob ought to be hanged, by way of example. If so,—but I say no more than I have said before, *when you are sure that you have a good principle, go through with it.*

You say, poor labourers cannot afford to buy bread at a high price, unless they had higher wages. Possibly. But how shall we farmers be able to afford our labourers higher wages, if you will not allow us to get, when we might have it, a higher price for our corn?

By all that I can learn, we should at least have had a guinea a quarter more, if the exportation had been allowed. And this money England would have got from foreigners.

But, it seems, we farmers must take so much less, that the poor may have it so much cheaper.

This operates, then, as a tax for the maintenance of the poor. A very good thing you will say. But I ask, Why a partial tax? why laid on us farmers only? If it be a good thing, pray, Messieurs the Public, take your share of it, by indemnifying us a little out of your public treasury. In doing a good thing, there is both honour and pleasure; you are welcome to your share of both.

For my own part, I am not so well satisfied of the goodness of this thing. I am for doing good to the poor, but I differ in opinion about the means. I think the best way of doing good to the poor, is, not making them easy *in* poverty, but leading or driving them *out* of it. In my youth, I travelled much, and I observed in different countries, that the more public provisions were made for the poor, the less they provided for themselves, and of course became poorer. And, on the contrary, the less was done for them, the more they did for themselves, and became richer. There is no country in the world where so many provisions are established for them; so many hospitals to receive them when they are sick or lame, founded and maintained by voluntary charities; so many almshouses for the aged of both sexes, together with a solemn general law made by the rich to subject their estates to a heavy tax for the support of the poor. Under all these obligations, are our poor modest, humble, and thankful? And do they use their best endeavours to maintain themselves, and lighten our shoulders of this burthen? On the contrary, I affirm, that there is no country in the world in which the poor are more idle, dissolute, drunken, and insolent. The day you passed that act, you took away from before their eyes the greatest of all inducements to industry, frugality, and sobriety, by giving them a dependence on somewhat else than a careful accumulation during youth and health, for support in age or sickness.

In short, you offered a premium for the encouragement of idleness, and you should not now wonder, that it has had its effect in the increase of poverty. Repeal that law, and you will soon see a change in their manners. *Saint Monday* and *Saint Tuesday* will soon cease to be holidays. Six *days shalt thou labour,* though one of the old commandments long treated as out of date, will again be looked upon as a respectable precept; industry will increase, and with it plenty among the lower people; their circumstances will mend, and more will be done for their happiness by inuring them to provide for themselves, than could be done by dividing all your estates among them.

Excuse me, Messieurs the Public, if, upon this *interesting* subject, I put you to the trouble of reading a little of *my* nonsense. I am sure I have lately read a great deal of *yours,* and therefore from you (at least from those of you who are writers) I deserve a little indulgence.

I am yours, &c. ARATOR.

RULES BY WHICH A GREAT EMPIRE MAY BE REDUCED TO A SMALL ONE;

Presented to a Late Minister,
When He Entered Upon His Administration.

An ancient Sage boasted, that, tho' he could not fiddle, he knew how to make a *great city* of a *little one*. The science that I, a modern simpleton, am about to communicate, is the very reverse.

I address myself to all ministers who have the management of extensive dominions, which from their very greatness are become troublesome to govern, because the multiplicity of their affairs leaves no time for *fiddling*.

I. In the first place, gentlemen, you are to consider, that a great empire, like a great cake, is most easily diminished at the edges. Turn your attention, therefore, first to your *remotest* provinces; that, as you get rid of them, the next may follow in order.

II. That the possibility of this separation may always exist, take special care the provinces are never incorporated with the mother country; that they do not enjoy the same common rights, the same privileges in commerce; and that they are governed by *severer* laws, all of *your enacting,* without allowing them any share in the choice of the legislators. By carefully making and preserving such distinctions, you will (to keep to my simile of the cake) act like a wise gingerbread-baker, who, to facilitate a division, cuts his dough half through in those places where, when baked, he would have it *broken to pieces*.

III. Those remote provinces have perhaps been acquired, purchased, or conquered, at the *sole expence* of the settlers, or their ancestors, without the aid of the mother country. If this should happen to increase her *strength,* by their growing numbers, ready to join in her wars; her *commerce,* by their growing demand for her manufactures; or her *naval power,* by greater employment for her ships and seamen, they may probably suppose some merit in this, and that it entitles them to some favour; you are therefore to *forget it all, or resent it,* as if they had done you injury. If they happen to be zealous whigs, friends of liberty, nurtured in revolution principles, *remember all that* to their prejudice, and resolve to punish it; for such principles, after a revolution is thoroughly established, are of *no more use;* they are even *odious* and *abominable.*

IV. However peaceably your colonies have submitted to your government, shewn their affection to your interests, and patiently borne their grievances; you are to *suppose* them always inclined to revolt, and treat them accordingly. Quarter troops among them, who by their insolence may *provoke* the rising of mobs, and by their bullets and bayonets *suppress* them. By this means, like the husband who uses his wife ill *from suspicion,* you may in time convert your *suspicions* into *realities.*

V. Remote provinces must have *Governors* and *Judges,* to represent the Royal Person, and execute everywhere the delegated parts of his office and authority. You ministers know, that much of the strength of government depends on the *opinion* of the people; and much of that opinion on the *choice of rulers* placed immediately over them. If you send them wise and good men for governors, who study the interest of the colonists, and advance their prosperity, they will think their King wise and good, and that he wishes the welfare of his subjects. If you send them learned and upright men for Judges, they will think him a lover of justice. This may attach your provinces more to his government. You are therefore to be careful whom you recommend for those offices. If you can find prodigals, who have ruined their fortunes, broken gamesters or stockjobbers, these may do well as *governors;* for they will probably be rapacious, and provoke the people by their extortions. Wrangling proctors and pettifogging lawyers, too, are not amiss; for they will be for ever disputing and quarrelling with their little parliaments. If withal they should be ignorant, wrongheaded, and insolent, so much the better. Attornies' clerks and Newgate solicitors will do for *Chief Justices,* especially if they hold their places *during your pleasure;* and all will contribute to impress those ideas of your government, that are proper for a people *you would wish to renounce it.*

VI. To confirm these impressions, and strike them deeper, whenever the injured come to the capital with complaints of mal-administration, oppression, or injustice, punish such suitors with long delay, enormous expence, and a final judgment in favour of the oppressor. This will have an admirable effect every way. The trouble of future complaints will be prevented, and Governors and Judges will be encouraged to farther acts of oppression and injustice; and thence the people may become more disaffected, and at length desperate.

VII. When such Governors have crammed their coffers, and made themselves so odious to the people that they can no longer remain among them, with safety to their persons, *recall and reward* them with pensions. You may make them *baronets* too, if that respectable order should not think fit to resent it. All will contribute to encourage new governors in the same practice, and make the supreme government, *detestable.*

VIII. If, when you are engaged in war, your colonies should vie in liberal aids of men and money against the common enemy, upon your simple requisition, and give far beyond their abilities, reflect that a penny taken from them by your power is more honourable to you, than a pound presented by their benevolence; despise therefore their voluntary grants, and resolve to harass them with novel taxes. They will probably complain to your parliaments, that they are taxed by a body in which they have no representative, and that this is contrary to common right. They will petition for redress. Let the Parliaments flout their claims, reject their petitions, refuse even to suffer the reading of them, and treat the petitioners with the utmost contempt. Nothing can have a better effect in producing the alienation proposed; for though many can forgive injuries, *none ever forgave contempt.*

IX. In laying these taxes, never regard the heavy burthens those remote people already undergo, in defending their own frontiers, supporting their own provincial governments, making new roads, building bridges, churches, and other public edifices, which in old countries have been done to your hands by your ancestors, but which occasion constant calls and demands on the purses of a new people. Forget the *restraints* you lay on their trade for *your own* benefit, and the advantage a *monopoly* of this trade gives your exacting merchants. Think nothing of the wealth those merchants and your manufacturers acquire by the colony commerce; their encreased ability thereby to pay taxes at home; their accumulating, in the price of their commodities, most of those taxes, and so levying them from their consuming customers; all this, and the employment and support of thousands of your poor by the colonists, you are *intirely to forget.* But remember to make your arbitrary tax more grievous to your provinces, by public declarations importing that your power of taxing them has *no limits;* so that when you take from them without their consent one shilling in the pound, you have a clear right to the other nineteen. This will probably weaken every idea of *security in their property,* and convince them, that under such a government they *have nothing they can call their own;* which can scarce fail of producing the *happiest consequences!*

X. Possibly, indeed, some of them might still comfort themselves, and say, "Though we have no property, we have yet *something* left that is valuable; we have constitutional *liberty,* both of person and of conscience. This King, these Lords, and these Commons, who it seems are too remote from us to know us, and feel for us, cannot take from us our *Habeas Corpus* right, or our right of trial *by a jury of our neighbours;* they cannot deprive us of the exercise of our religion, alter our ecclesiastical constitution, and compel us to be Papists, if they please, or Mahometans." To annihilate this comfort, begin by laws to perplex their commerce with infinite regulations, impossible to be remembered and observed; ordain seizures of their property for every failure; take away the trial of such property by Jury, and give it to arbitrary Judges of your own appointing, and of the lowest characters in the country, whose salaries and emoluments are to arise out of the duties or condemnations, and whose appointments are *during pleasure*. Then let there be a formal declaration of both Houses, that opposition to your edicts is *treason,* and that any person suspected of treason in the provinces may, according to some obsolete law, be seized and sent to the metropolis of the empire for trial; and pass an act, that those there charged with certain other offences, shall be sent away in chains from their friends and country to be tried in the same manner for felony. Then erect a new Court of Inquisition among them, accompanied by an armed force, with instructions to transport all such suspected persons; to be ruined by the expence, if they bring over evidences to prove their innocence, or be found guilty and hanged, if they cannot afford it. And, lest the people should think you cannot possibly go any farther, pass another solemn declaratory act, "that King, Lords, Commons had, hath, and of right ought to have, full power and authority to make statutes of sufficient force and validity to bind the unrepresented provinces IN ALL CASES WHATSOEVER." This will include *spiritual* with temporal, and, taken together, must operate wonderfully to your purpose; by convincing them, that they are at present under a power something like that spoken of in the scriptures, which can not only *kill their bodies,* but *damn their souls* to all eternity, by compelling them, if it pleases, *to worship the Devil.*

XI. To make your taxes more odious, and more likely to procure resistance, send from the capital a board of officers to superintend the collection, composed of the most *indiscreet, ill-bred,* and *insolent* you can find. Let these have large salaries out of the extorted revenue, and live in open, grating luxury upon the sweat and blood of the industrious; whom they are to worry continually with groundless and expensive prosecutions before the abovementioned arbitrary revenue Judges; *all at the cost of the party prosecuted,* tho' acquitted, because *the King is to pay no costs.* Let these men, *by your order,* be exempted from all the common taxes and burthens of the province, though they and their property are protected by its laws. If any revenue officers are *suspected* of the least tenderness for the people, discard them. If others are justly complained of, protect and reward them. If any of the under officers behave so as to provoke the people to drub them, promote those to better offices: this will encourage others to procure for themselves such profitable drubbings, by multiplying and enlarging such provocations, and *all will work towards the end you aim at.*

XII. Another way to make your tax odious, is to misapply the produce of it. If it was originally appropriated for the *defence* of the provinces, the better support of government, and the administration of justice, where it may be *necessary,* then apply none of it to that *defence,* but bestow it where it is *not necessary,* in augmented salaries or pensions to every governor, who has distinguished himself by his enmity to the people, and by calumniating them to their sovereign. This will make them pay it more unwillingly, and be more apt to quarrel with those that collect it and those that imposed it, who will quarrel again with them, and all shall contribute to your *main purpose,* of making them *weary of your government.*

XIII. If the people of any province have been accustomed to support their own Governors and Judges to satisfaction, you are to apprehend that such Governors and Judges may be thereby influenced to treat the people kindly, and to do them justice. This is another reason for applying part of that revenue in larger salaries to such Governors and Judges, given, as their commissions are, *during your pleasure* only; forbidding them to take any salaries from their provinces; that thus the people may no longer hope any kindness from their Governors, or (in Crown cases) any justice from their Judges. And, as the money thus misapplied in one province is extorted from all, probably *all will resent the misapplication.*

XIV. If the parliaments of your provinces should dare to claim rights, or complain of your administration, order them to be harassed with *repeated dissolutions.* If the same men are continually returned by new elections, adjourn their meetings to some country village, where they cannot be accommodated, and there keep them *during pleasure;* for this, you know, is your PREROGATIVE; and an excellent one it is, as you may manage it to promote discontents among the people, diminish their respect, and *increase their disaffection*.

XV. Convert the brave, honest officers of your *navy* into pimping tide-waiters and colony officers of the *customs*. Let those, who in time of war fought gallantly in defence of the commerce of their countrymen, in peace be taught to prey upon it. Let them learn to be corrupted by great and real smugglers; but (to shew their diligence) scour with armed boats every bay, harbour, river, creek, cove, or nook throughout the coast of your colonies; stop and detain every coaster, every wood-boat, every fisherman, tumble their cargoes and even their ballast inside out and upside down; and, if a penn'orth of pins is found un-entered, let the whole be seized and confiscated. Thus shall the trade of your colonists suffer more from their friends in time of peace, than it did from their enemies in war. Then let these boats crews land upon every farm in their way, rob the orchards, steal the pigs and the poultry, and insult the inhabitants. If the injured and exasperated farmers, unable to procure other justice, should attack the aggressors, drub them, and burn their boats; you are to call this *high treason and rebellion*, order fleets and armies into their country, and threaten to carry all the offenders three thousand miles to be hanged, drawn, and quartered. *O! this will work admirably!*

XVI. If you are told of discontents in your colonies, never believe that they are general, or that you have given occasion for them; therefore do not think of applying any remedy, or of changing any offensive measure. Redress no grievance, lest they should be encouraged to demand the redress of some other grievance. Grant no request that is just and reasonable, lest they should make another that is unreasonable. Take all your informations of the state of the colonies from your Governors and officers in enmity with them. Encourage and reward these *leasing-makers;* secrete their lying accusations, lest they should be confuted; but act upon them as the clearest evidence; and believe nothing you hear from the friends of the people: suppose all *their* complaints to be invented and promoted by a few factious demagogues, whom if you could catch and hang, all would be quiet. Catch and hang a few of them accordingly; and the *blood of the Martyrs* shall *work miracles* in favour of your purpose.

XVII. If you see *rival nations* rejoicing at the prospect of your disunion with your provinces, and endeavouring to promote it; if they translate, publish, and applaud all the complaints of your discontented colonists, at the same time privately stimulating you to severer measures, let not that *alarm* or offend you. Why should it, since you all mean *the same thing?*

XVIII. If any colony should at their own charge erect a fortress to secure their port against the fleets of a foreign enemy, get your Governor to betray that fortress into your hands. Never think of paying what it cost the country, for that would look, at least, like some regard for justice; but turn it into a citadel to awe the inhabitants and curb their commerce. If they should have lodged in such fortress the very arms they bought and used to aid you in your conquests, seize them all; it will provoke like *ingratitude* added to *robbery*. One admirable effect of these operations will be, to discourage every other colony from erecting such defences, and so your enemies may more easily invade them; to the great disgrace of your government, and of course *the furtherance of your project.*

XIX. Send armies into their country under pretence of protecting the inhabitants; but, instead of garrisoning the forts on their frontiers with those troops, to prevent incursions, demolish those forts, and order the troops into the heart of the country, that the savages may be encouraged to attack the frontiers, and that the troops may be protected by the inhabitants. This will seem to proceed from your ill will or your ignorance, and contribute farther to produce and strengthen an opinion among them, *that you are no longer fit to govern them.*

XX. Lastly, invest the General of your army in the provinces, with great and unconstitutional powers, and free him from the controul of even your own Civil Governors. Let him have troops enow under his command, with all the fortresses in his possession; and who knows but (like some provincial Generals in the Roman empire, and encouraged by the universal discontent you have produced) he may take it into his head to set up for himself? If he should, and you have carefully practised these few *excellent rules* of mine, take my word for it, all the provinces will immediately join him; and you will that day (if you have not done it sooner) get rid of the trouble of governing them, and all the *plagues* attending their *commerce* and connection from henceforth and for ever.

Q. E. D.

AN EDICT BY THE KING
OF PRUSSIA

Dantzic, Sept. 5, [1773.]

WE have long wondered here at the supineness of the English nation, under the Prussian impositions upon its trade entering our port. We did not, till lately, know the claims, ancient and modern, that hang over that nation; and therefore could not suspect that it might submit to those impositions from a sense of duty or from principles of equity. The following Edict, just made publick, may, if serious, throw some light upon this matter.

"FREDERIC, by the grace of God, King of Prussia, &c. &c. &c., to all present and to come, (*à tous présens et à venir,*) Health. The peace now enjoyed throughout our dominions, having afforded us leisure to apply ourselves to the regulation of commerce, the improvement of our finances, and at the same time the easing our domestic subjects in their taxes: For these causes, and other good considerations us thereunto moving, we hereby make known, that, after having deliberated these affairs in our council, present our dear brothers, and other great officers of the state, members of the same, we, of our certain knowledge, full power, and authority royal, have made and issued this present Edict, viz.

"Whereas it is well known to all the world, that the first German settlements made in the Island of Britain, were by colonies of people, subject to our renowned ducal ancestors, and drawn from their dominions, under the conduct of Hengist, Horsa, Hella, Uff, Cerdicus, Ida, and others; and that the said colonies have flourished under the protection of our august house for ages past; have never been emancipated therefrom; and yet have hitherto yielded little profit to the same: And whereas we our-self have in the last war fought for and defended the said colonies, against the power of France, and thereby enabled them to make conquests from the said power in America, for which we have not yet received adequate compensation: And whereas it is just and expedient that a revenue should be raised from the said colonies in Britain, towards our indemnification; and that those who are descendants of our ancient subjects, and thence still owe us due obedience, should contribute to the re-plenishing of our royal coffers as they must have done, had their ancestors remained in the territories now to us appertain-ing: We do therefore hereby ordain and command, that, from and after the date of these presents, there shall be levied and paid to our officers of the *customs,* on all goods, wares, and merchandizes, and on all grain and other produce of the earth, exported from the said Island of Britain, and on all goods of whatever kind imported into the same, a duty of four and a half per cent *ad valorem,* for the use of us and our successors. And that the said duty may more effectually be collected, we do hereby ordain, that all ships or vessels bound from Great Britain to any other part of the world, or from any other part of the world to Great Britain, shall in their respective voyages touch at our port of Koningsberg, there to be unladen, searched, and charged with the said duties.

"And whereas there hath been from time to time discovered in the said island of Great Britain, by our colonists there, many mines or beds of iron-stone; and sundry subjects, of our ancient dominion, skilful in converting the said stone into metal, have in time past transported themselves thither, carrying with them and communicating that art; and the inhabitants of the said is-land, presuming that they had a natural right to make the best use they could of the natural productions of their country for their own benefit, have not only built furnaces for smelting the said stone into iron, but have erected plating-forges, slitting-mills, and steel-furnaces, for the more convenient manufactur-ing of the same; thereby endangering a diminution of the said manufacture in our ancient dominion;—we do therefore hereby farther ordain, that, from and after the date hereof, no mill or other engine for slitting or rolling of iron, or any plating-forge to work with a tilt-hammer, or any furnace for making steel, shall be erected or continued in the said island of Great Britain: And the Lord Lieutenant of every county in the said island is hereby commanded, on information of any such erection within his county, to order and by force to cause the same to be abated and destroyed; as he shall answer the neglect thereof to us at his peril. But we are nevertheless graciously pleased to permit the inhabitants of the said island to transport their iron into Prussia, there to be manufactured, and to them returned; they paying our Prussian subjects for the workmanship, with all the costs of commission, freight, and risk, coming and returning; any thing herein contained to the contrary notwithstanding.

"We do not, however, think fit to extend this our indulgence to the article of wool; but, meaning to encourage, not only the manufacturing of woollen cloth, but also the raising of wool, in our ancient dominions, and to prevent both, as much as may be, in our said island, we do hereby absolutely forbid the transportation of wool from thence, even to the mother country, Prussia; and that those islanders may be farther and more effectually restrained in making any advantage of their own wool in the way of manufacture, we command that none shall be carried out of one county into another; nor shall any worsted, bay, or woollen yarn, cloth, says, bays, kerseys, serges, frizes, druggets, cloth-serges, shalloons, or any other drapery stuffs, or woollen manufactures whatsoever, made up or mixed with wool in any of the said counties, be carried into any other county, or be waterborne even across the smallest river or creek, on penalty of forfeiture of the same, together with the boats, carriages, horses, &c., that shall be employed in removing them. Nevertheless, our loving subjects there are hereby permitted (if they think proper) to use all their wool as manure for the improvement of their lands.

"And whereas the art and mystery of making hats hath arrived at great perfection in Prussia, and the making of hats by our remoter subjects ought to be as much as possible restrained: And forasmuch as the islanders before mentioned, being in possession of wool, beaver and other furs, have presumptuously conceived they had a right to make some advantage thereof, by manufacturing the same into hats, to the prejudice of our domestic manufacture: We do therefore hereby strictly command and ordain, that no hats or felts whatsoever, dyed or undyed, finished or unfinished, shall be loaded or put into or upon any vessel, cart, carriage, or horse, to be transported or conveyed out of one county in the said island into another county, or to any other place whatsoever, by any person or persons whatsoever; on pain of forfeiting the same, with a penalty of five hundred pounds sterling for every offence. Nor shall any hat-maker, in any of the said counties, employ more than two apprentices, on penalty of five pounds sterling per month; we intending hereby, that such hatmakers, being so restrained, both in the production and sale of their commodity, may find no advantage in continuing their business. But, lest the said islanders should suffer inconveniency by the want of hats, we are farther graciously pleased to permit them to send their beaver furs to Prussia; and we also permit hats made thereof to be exported from Prussia to Britain; the people thus favoured to pay all costs and charges of manufacturing, interest, commission to our merchants, insurance and freight going and returning, as in the case of iron.

"And, lastly, being willing farther to favour our said colonies in Britain, we do hereby also ordain and command, that all the *thieves,* highway and street robbers, housebreakers, forgerers, murderers, s—d—tes, and villains of every denomination, who have forfeited their lives to the law in Prussia; but whom we, in our great clemency, do not think fit here to hang, shall be emptied out of our gaols into the said island of Great Britain, for the better peopling of that country.

"We flatter ourselves, that these our royal regulations and commands will be thought just and reasonable by our much-favoured colonists in England; the said regulations being copied from their statutes of 10 and 11 William III. c. 10, 5 Geo. II. c. 22, 23 Geo. II. c. 29, 4 Geo. I. c. 11, and from other equitable laws made by their parliaments; or from instructions given by their Princes; or from resolutions of both Houses, entered into for the good government of their *own colonies in Ireland and America.*

"And all persons in the said island are hereby cautioned not to oppose in any wise the execution of this our Edict, or any part thereof, such opposition being high treason; of which all who are suspected shall be transported in fetters from Britain to Prussia, there to be tried and executed according to the Prussian law.

"Such is our pleasure.

"Given at Potsdam, this twenty-fifth day of the month of August, one thousand seven hundred and seventy-three, and in the thirty-third year of our reign.
"By the King, in his Council.

"RECHTMAESSIG, *Sec.*"

Some take this Edict to be merely one of the King's *Jeux d'Esprit:* others suppose it serious, and that he means a quarrel with England; but all here think the assertion it concludes with, "that these regulations are copied from acts of the English parliament respecting their colonies," a very injurious one; it being impossible to believe, that a people distinguished for their love of liberty, a nation so wise, so liberal in its sentiments, so just and equitable towards its neighbours, should, from mean and injudicious views of petty immediate profit, treat its own children in a manner so arbitrary and tyrannical!

TO WILLIAM FRANKLIN

DEAR SON,

I wrote to you the 1st of last month, since which I have received yours of July 29, from New York. I know not what letters of mine Governor H[utchinson] could mean, as advising the people to insist on their independency. But whatever they were, I suppose he has sent copies of them hither, having heard some whisperings about them. I shall however, be able at any time to justify every thing I have written; the purport being uniformly this, that they should carefully avoid all tumults and every violent measure, and content themselves with verbally keeping up their claims, and holding forth their rights whenever occasion requires; secure, that, from the growing importance of America, those claims will ere long be attended to and acknowledged.

From a long and thorough consideration of the subject, I am indeed of opinion, that the parliament has no right to make any law whatever, binding on the colonies; that the king, and not the king, lords, and commons collectively, is their sovereign; and that the king, with their respective parliaments, is their only legislator. I know your sentiments differ from mine on these subjects. You are a thorough government man, which I do not wonder at, nor do I aim at converting you. I only wish you to act uprightly and steadily, avoiding that duplicity, which in Hutchinson, adds contempt to indignation. If you can promote the prosperity of your people, and leave them happier than you found them, whatever your political principles are, your memory will be honoured.

I have written two pieces here lately for the *Public Advertiser,* on American affairs, designed to expose the conduct of this country towards the colonies in a short, comprehensive, and striking view, and stated, therefore, in out-of-the-way forms, as most likely to take the general attention. The first was called *"Rules by which a Great Empire may be reduced to a small one;"* the second, *"An Edict of the King of Prussia."* I sent you one of the first, but could not get enough of the second to spare you one, though my clerk went the next morning to the printer's, and wherever they were sold. They were all gone but two. In my own mind I preferred the first, as a composition for the quantity and variety of the matter contained, and a kind of spirited ending of each paragraph. But I find that others here generally prefer the second.

I am not suspected as the author, except by one or two friends; and have heard the latter spoken of in the highest terms, as the keenest and severest piece that has appeared here for a long time. Lord Mansfield, I hear, said of it, that it *was very* ABLE *and very* ARTFUL *indeed;* and would do mischief by giving here a bad impression of the measures of government; and in the colonies, by encouraging them in their contumacy. It is reprinted in the *Chronicle,* where you will see it, but stripped of all the capitaling and italicing, that intimate the allusions and mark the emphasis of written discourses, to bring them as near as possible to those spoken: printing such a piece all in one even small character, seems to me like repeating one of Whitefield's sermons in the monotony of a schoolboy.

What made it the more noticed here was, that people in reading it were, as the phrase is, *taken in,* till they had got half through it, and imagined it a real edict, to which mistake I suppose the King of Prussia's *character* must have contributed. I was down at Lord Le Despencer's, when the post brought that day's papers. Mr. Whitehead was there, too, (Paul Whitehead, the author of "Manners,") who runs early through all the papers, and tells the company what he finds remarkable. He had them in another room, and we were chatting in the breakfast parlour, when he came running in to us, out of breath, with the paper in his hand. Here! says he, here's news for ye! *Here's the*

King of Prussia, claiming a right to this kingdom! All stared, and I as much as anybody; and he went on to read it. When he had read two or three paragraphs, a gentleman present said, *Damn his impudence, I dare say, we shall hear by next post that he is upon his march with one hundred thousand men to back this.* Whitehead, who is very shrewd, soon after began to smoke it, and looking in my face said, *I'll be hanged if this is not some of your American jokes upon us.* The reading went on, and ended with abundance of laughing, and a general verdict that it was a fair hit: and the piece was cut out of the paper and preserved in my Lord's collection.

I do not wonder that Hutchinson should be dejected. It must be an uncomfortable thing to live among people who he is conscious universally detest him. Yet I fancy he will not have leave to come home, both because they know not well what to do with him, and because they do not very well like his conduct. I am ever your affectionate father,

B. FRANKLIN.

TO WILLIAM STRAHAN[1]

Philad^a July 5, 1775

MR. STRAHAN,

You are a Member of Parliament, and one of that Majority which has doomed my Country to Destruction.—You have begun to burn our Towns, and murder our People.—Look upon your Hands! They are stained with the Blood of your Relations!—You and I were long Friends:—You are now my Enemy,—and I am

Yours,

B. FRANKLIN

TO JOSEPH PRIESTLEY

Philadelphia, July 7, 1775.

DEAR FRIEND,

The Congress met at a time when all minds were so exasperated by the perfidy of General Gage, and his attack on the country people, that propositions of attempting an accommodation were not much relished; and it has been with difficulty that we have carried another humble petition to the crown, to give Britain one more chance, one opportunity more, of recovering the friendship of the colonies; which, however, I think she has not sense enough to embrace, and so I conclude she has lost them for ever.

She has begun to burn our seaport towns; secure, I suppose, that we shall never be able to return the outrage in kind. She may doubtless destroy them all; but, if she wishes to recover our commerce, are these the probable means? She must certainly be distracted; for no tradesman out of Bedlam ever thought of encreasing the number of his customers, by knocking them on the head; or of enabling them to pay their debts, by burning their houses. If she wishes to have us subjects, and that we should submit to her as our compound sovereign, she is now giving us such miserable specimens of her government, that we shall ever detest and avoid it, as a complication of robbery, murder, famine, fire, and pestilence.

You will have heard, before this reaches you, of the treacherous conduct [of General Gage] to the remaining people in Boston, in detaining their *goods,* after stipulating to let them go out with their *effects,* on pretence that merchants' goods were not effects; the defeat of a great body of his troops by the country people at Lexington; some other small advantages gained in skirmishes with their troops; and the action at Bunker's Hill, in which they were twice repulsed, and the third time gained a dear victory. Enough has happened, one would think, to convince your ministers, that the Americans will fight, and that this is a harder nut to crack than they imagined.

We have not yet applied to any foreign power for assistance, nor offered our commerce for their friendship. Perhaps we never may; yet it is natural to think of it, if we are pressed. We have now an army on our establishment, which still holds yours besieged. My time was never more fully employed. In the morning at six, I am at the Committee of Safety, appointed by the Assembly to put the province in a state of defence; which committee holds till near nine, when I am at the Congress, and that sits till after four in the afternoon. Both these bodies proceed with the greatest unanimity, and their meetings are well attended. It will scarce be credited in Britain, that men can be as diligent with us from zeal for the public good, as with you for thousands per annum. Such is the difference between uncorrupted new states, and corrupted old ones.

Great frugality and great industry are now become fashionable here. Gentlemen, who used to entertain with two or three courses, pride themselves now in treating with simple beef and pudding. By these means, and the stoppage of our consumptive trade with Britain, we shall be better able to pay our voluntary taxes for the support of our troops. Our savings in the article of trade amount to near five millions sterling per annum.

I shall communicate your letter to Mr. Winthrop; but the camp is at Cambridge, and he has as little leisure for philosophy as myself. Believe me ever with sincere esteem, my dear friend, yours most affectionately,

B. FRANKLIN.

TO A FRIEND
IN ENGLAND

Philadelphia, Oct. 3, 1775.

DEAR SIR,

I wish as ardently as you can do for peace, and should rejoice exceedingly in coöperating with you to that end. But every ship from Britain brings some intelligence of new measures that tend more and more to exasperate; and it seems to me, that until you have found by dear experience the reducing us by force impracticable, you will think of nothing fair and reasonable.

We have as yet resolved only on defensive measures. If you would recall your forces and stay at home, we should meditate nothing to injure you. A little time so given for cooling on both sides would have excellent effects. But you will goad and provoke us. You despise us too much; and you are insensible of the Italian adage, that there is no *little enemy*. I am persuaded that the body of the British people are our friends; but they are changeable, and by your lying Gazettes may soon be made our enemies. Our respect for them will proportionably diminish, and I see clearly we are on the high road to mutual Enmity hatred and detestation. A separation of course will be inevitable. 'Tis a million of pities so fair a plan as we have hitherto been engaged in, for increasing strength and empire with *public felicity,* should be destroyed by the mangling hands of a few blundering ministers. It will not be destroyed; God will protect and prosper it, you will only exclude yourselves from any share in it. We hear, that more ships and troops are coming out. We know, that you may do us a great deal of mischief, and are determined to bear it patiently as long as we can. But, if you flatter yourselves with beating us into submission, you know neither the people nor the country. The Congress are still sitting, and will wait the result of their *last* petition.

Yours, &c.
B. FRANKLIN.

TO LORD HOWE

MY LORD,

I receiv'd safe the Letters your Lordship so kindly forwarded to me, and beg you to accept my thanks.

The official dispatches, to which you refer me, contain nothing more than what we had seen in the Act of Parliament, viz. Offers of Pardon upon Submission, which I was sorry to find, as it must give your Lordship Pain to be sent upon so fruitless a Business.

Directing Pardons to be offered to the Colonies, who are the very Parties injured, expresses indeed that Opinion of our Ignorance, Baseness, and Insensibility, which your uninform'd and proud Nation has long been pleased to entertain of us; but it can have no other effect than that of increasing our Resentments. It is impossible we should think of Submission to a Government, that has with the most wanton Barbarity and Cruelty burnt our defenceless Towns in the midst of Winter, excited the Savages to massacre our Peacefull Farmers, and our Slaves to murder their Masters, and is even now bringing foreign Mercenaries to deluge our Settlements with Blood. These atrocious Injuries have extinguished every remaining Spark of Affection for that Parent Country we once held so dear; but, were it possible for *us* to forget and forgive them, it is not possible for *you* (I mean the British Nation) to forgive the People you have so heavily injured. You can never confide again in those as Fellow Subjects, and permit them to enjoy equal Freedom, to whom you know you have given such just Cause of lasting Enmity.

And this must impel you, were we again under your Government, to endeavour the breaking our Spirit by the severest Tyranny, and obstructing, by every Means in your Power, our growing Strength and Prosperity.

But your Lordship mentions "the King's paternal solicitude for promoting the Establishment of lasting *Peace* and Union with the Colonies." If by Peace is here meant a Peace to be entered into between Britain and America, as distinct States now at War, and his Majesty has given your Lordship Powers to treat with us of such a Peace, I may venture to say, though without Authority, that I think a Treaty for that purpose not yet quite impracticable, before we enter into foreign Alliances. But I am persuaded you have no such Powers. Your nation, though, by punishing those American Governors, who have fomented the Discord, rebuilding our burnt Towns, and repairing as far as possible the mischiefs done us, might yet recover a great Share of our Regard, and the greatest Part of our growing Commerce, with all the Advantage of that additional Strength to be derived from a Friendship with us; but I know too well her abounding Pride and deficient Wisdom, to believe she will ever take such salutary Measures. Her Fondness for Conquest, as a warlike Nation, her lust of Dominion, as an ambitious one, and her wish for a gainful Monopoly, as a commercial One, (none of them legitimate Causes of war,) will all join to hide from her Eyes every view of her true Interests, and continually goad her on in those ruinous distant Expeditions, so destructive both of Lives and Treasure, that must prove as pernicious to her in the End, as the Crusades formerly were to most of the Nations in Europe.

I have not the Vanity, my Lord, to think of intimidating by thus predicting the Effects of this War; for I know it will in England have the Fate of all my former Predictions, not to be believed till the Event shall verify it.

Long did I endeavour, with unfeigned and unwearied Zeal, to preserve from breaking that fine and noble China Vase, the British Empire; for I knew, that, being once broken, the separate Parts could not retain even their Shares of the Strength and Value that existed in the Whole, and that a perfect Reunion of those Parts could scarce ever be hoped for. Your Lordship may possibly remember the tears of Joy that wet my Cheek, when, at your good Sister's in London, you once gave me Expectations that a Reconciliation might soon take Place. I had the Misfortune to find those Expectations disappointed, and to be treated as the Cause of the Mischief I was laboring to prevent. My Consolation under that groundless and malevolent Treatment was, that I retained the Friendship of many wise and good Men in that country, and, among the rest, some Share in the Regard of Lord Howe.

The well-founded Esteem, and, permit me to say, Affection, which I shall always have for your Lordship, makes it Painful to me to see you engaged in conducting a War, the great Ground of which, as expressed in your Letter, is "the necessity of preventing the American trade from passing into foreign Channels." To me it seems, that neither the Obtaining or Retaining of any trade, how valuable soever, is an Object for which men may justly spill each other's Blood; that the true and sure Means of extending and securing Commerce is the goodness and Cheapness of Commodities; and that the profit of no trade can ever be equal to the Expence of compelling it, and of holding it, by Fleets and Armies.

I consider this War against us, therefore, as both unjust and unwise; and I am persuaded, that cool, dispassionate Posterity will condemn to Infamy those who advised it; and that even Success will not save from some Degree of Dishonor those, who voluntarily engaged to Conduct it. I know your great motive in coming hither was the hope of being Instrumental in a Reconciliation; and I believe, when you find *that* to be impossible on any Terms given you to propose, you will relinquish so odious a Command, and return to a more honourable private Station.

With the greatest and most sincere Respect, I have the Honour to be, my Lord, your Lordship's most obedient humble Servant,   B. FRANKLIN.

ANECDOTE RECALLED
BY JEFFERSON

When the Declaration of Independence was under the consideration of Congress, there were two or three unlucky expressions in it which gave offence to some members. The words "Scotch and other foreign auxiliaries" excited the ire of a gentleman or two of that country. Severe strictures on the conduct of the British king, in negotiating our repeated repeals of the law which permitted the importation of slaves, were disapproved by some Southern gentlemen, whose reflections were not yet matured to the full abhorrence of that traffic. Although the offensive expressions were immediately yielded these gentlemen continued their depredations on other parts of the instrument. I was sitting by Dr. Franklin, who perceived that I was not insensible to these mutilations. "I have made it a rule," said he, "whenever in my power, to avoid becoming the draughtsmen of papers to be reviewed by a public body. I took my lesson from an incident which I will relate to you. When I was a journeyman printer, one of my companions, an apprentice hatter, having served out his time, was about to open shop for himself. His first concern was to have a handsome sign-board, with a proper inscription, He composed it in these words, 'John Thompson, *Hatter, makes* and *sells hats* for ready money,' with a figure of a hat subjoined; but he thought he would submit it to his friends for their amendments. The first he showed it to thought the word *'Hatter'* tautologous, because followed by the words 'makes hats,' which show he was a hatter. It was struck out. The next observed that the word *'makes'* might as well be omitted, because his customers would not care who made the hats. If good and to their mind, they would buy, by whomsoever made. He struck it out. A third said he though the words *'for ready money'* were useless, as it was not the custom of the place to sell on credit. Every one who purchased expected to pay. They were parted with, and the inscription now stood, 'John Thompson sells hats.' *'Sells hats!'* says his next friend. Why nobody will expect you to give them away, what then is the use of that word? It was stricken out, and *'hats'* followed it, the rather as there was one painted on the board. So the inscription was reduced ultimately to 'John Thompson' with the figure of a hat subjoined."

TO MRS. MARY HEWSON

MY DEAR, DEAR POLLY,

Figure to yourself an old Man, with grey Hair Appearing under a Martin Fur Cap, among the Powder'd Heads of Paris. It is this odd Figure that salutes you, with handfuls of Blessings on you and your dear little ones.

On my Arrival here, Mlle. Biheron gave me great Pleasure in the Perusal of a Letter from you to her. It acquainted me that you and yours were well in August last. I have with me here my young Grandson, Benja. Franklin Bache, a special good Boy. I give him a little French Language and Address, and then send him over to pay his Respects to Miss Hewson. My Love to all that love you, particularly to dear Polly. I am ever, my dear Friend, your affectionate

B. FRANKLIN.

P. S. Temple, who attends me here, presents his Respects. I must contrive to get you to America. I want all my Friends out of that wicked Country. I have just seen in the Papers 7 Paragraphs about me, of which 6 were Lies.

THE SALE OF THE HESSIANS

*From the Count de Schaumbergh to
the Baron Hohendorf, Commanding
the Hessian Troops in America.*

Rome, February 18, 1777.

MONSIEUR LE BARON:—On my return from Naples, I received at Rome your letter of the 27th December of last year. I have learned with unspeakable pleasure the courage our troops exhibited at Trenton, and you cannot imagine my joy on being told that of the 1,950 Hessians engaged in the fight, but 345 escaped. There were just 1,605 men killed, and I cannot sufficiently commend your prudence in sending an exact list of the dead to my minister in London. This precaution was the more necessary, as the report sent to the English ministry does not give but 1,455 dead. This would make 483,450 florins instead of 643,500 which I am entitled to demand under our convention. You will comprehend the prejudice which such an error would work in my finances, and I do not doubt you will take the necessary pains to prove that Lord North's list is false and yours correct.

The court of London objects that there were a hundred wounded who ought not to be included in the list, nor paid for as dead; but I trust you will not overlook my instructions to you on quitting Cassel, and that you will not have tried by human succor to recall the life of the unfortunates whose days could not be lengthened but by the loss of a leg or an arm. That would be making them a pernicious present, and I am sure they would rather die than live in a condition no longer fit for my service. I do not mean by this that you should assassinate them; we should be humane, my dear Baron, but you may insinuate to the surgeons with entire propriety that a crippled man is a reproach to their profession, and that there is no wiser course than to let every one of them die when he ceases to be fit to fight.

I am about to send to you some new recruits. Don't economize them. Remember glory before all things. Glory is true wealth. There is nothing degrades the soldier like the love of money. He must care only for honour and reputation, but this reputation must be acquired in the midst of dangers. A battle gained without costing the conqueror any blood is an inglorious success, while the conquered cover themselves with glory by perishing with their arms in their hands. Do you remember that of the 300 Lacedæmonians who defended the defile of Thermopylæ, not one returned? How happy should I be could I say the same of my brave Hessians!

It is true that their king, Leonidas, perished with them: but things have changed, and it is no longer the custom for princes of the empire to go and fight in America for a cause with which they have no concern. And besides, to whom should they pay the thirty guineas per man if I did not stay in Europe to receive them? Then, it is necessary also that I be ready to send recruits to replace the men you lose. For this purpose I must return to Hesse. It is true, grown men are becoming scarce there, but I will send you boys. Besides, the scarcer the commodity the higher the price. I am assured that the women and little girls have begun to till our lands, and they get on not badly. You did right to send back to Europe that Dr. Crumerus who was so successful in curing dysentery. Don't bother with a man who is subject to looseness of the bowels. That disease makes bad soldiers. One coward will do more mischief in an engagement than ten brave men will do good. Better that they burst in their barracks than fly in a battle, and tarnish the glory of our arms. Besides, you know that they pay me as killed for all who die from disease, and I don't get a farthing for runaways. My trip to Italy, which has cost me enormously, makes it desirable that there should be a great mortality among them. You will therefore promise promotion to all who expose themselves; you will exhort them to seek glory in the midst of dangers; you will say to Major Maundorff that I am not at all content with his saving the 345 men who escaped the massacre of Trenton. Through the whole campaign he has not had ten men killed in consequence of his orders. Finally, let it be your principal object to prolong the war and avoid a decisive engagement on either side, for I have made arrangements for a grand Italian opera, and I do not wish to be obliged to give it up. Meantime I pray God, my dear Baron de Hohendorf, to have you in his holy and gracious keeping.

TO A FRIEND

Passy, [1777?]

You know, my dear Friend, that I am not capable of refusing you any Thing in my Power, which would be a real Kindness to you, or any Friend of yours: but when I am certain that what you request would be directly the contrary, I ought to refuse it. I know that Officers going to America for Employment will probably be disappointed; that our Armies are full; that there are a Number of Expectants unemployed, and starving for want of Subsistence; that my Recommendation will not make Vacancies, nor can it fill them, to the Prejudice of those who have a better Claim; that some of those officers I have been Prevail'd on to recommend have, by their Conduct, given no favourable Impression of my Judgment in military Merit; and then the Voyage is long, the Passage very expensive, and the Hazard of being taken and imprison'd by the English very considerable. If, after all, no Place can be found affording a livelihood for the Gentleman in question, he will perhaps be distressed in a strange Country, and ready to blaspheme his Friends, who, by their Solicitations, procured for him so unhappy a Situation.

Permit me to mention to you, that, in my Opinion, the natural complaisance of this Country often carries People too far in the Article of *Recommendations.* You give them with too much Facility to Persons of whose real Characters you know nothing, and sometimes at the request of others of whom you know as little. Frequently, if a man has no useful Talents, is good for

nothing and burdensome to his Relations, or is indiscreet, prof-
ligate, and extravagant, they are glad to get rid of him by sending him to the other End of the World; and for that purpose
scruple not to recommend him to those they wish should recommend him to others, as *"un bon sujet, plein de mérite,"* &c.
&c. In consequence of my crediting such Recommendations,
my own are out of Credit, and I cannot advise anybody to have
the least Dependence on them. If, after knowing this, you persist in desiring my Recommendation for this Person, who is
known neither to *me* nor to *you*, I will give it, tho', as I said before, I ought to refuse it.

These Applications are my perpetual Torment. People will
believe, notwithstanding my continually repeated Declarations
to the Contrary, that I am sent hither to engage Officers. In
Truth, I never had any such Orders. It was never so much as intimated to me, that it would be agreable to my constituents. I
have even received for what I have done of the kind, not indeed
an absolute Rebuke, but some pretty strong *hints* of Disapprobation. Not a day passes in which I have not a Number of soliciting Visits, besides Letters. If I could gratify them all, or any
of them, it would be a Pleasure. I might, indeed, give them the
Recommendation and the Promises they desire, and thereby
please them for the present; but, when the certain Disappointment of the Expectations with which they will so obstinately
flatter themselves shall arrive, they must curse me for complying with their mad Requests, and not undeceiving them; and
will become so many Enemies to our Cause and Country.

You can have no Conception how I am harass'd. All my
Friends are sought out and teiz'd to teaze me. Great Officers of
all Ranks, in all Departments; Ladies, great and small, besides
professed Sollicitors, worry me from Morning to Night. The
Noise of every coach now that enters my Court terrifies me. I am
afraid to accept an Invitation to dine abroad, being almost sure
of meeting with some Officer or Officer's Friend, who, as soon
as I am put in good Humour by a Glass or two of Champaign,
begins his Attack upon me. Luckily I do not often in my sleep
dream myself in these vexatious Situations, or I should be afraid

of what are now my only Hours of Comfort. If, therefore, you
have the least remaining Kindness for me, if you would not help
to drive me out of France, for God's sake, my dear friend, let this
your 23^d Application be your last. Yours, &c.

B. FRANKLIN.

MODEL OF A LETTER OF RECOMMENDATION

Paris, April 2, 1777.

SIR:— The bearer of this, who is going to America, presses me to give him a Letter of Recommendation, tho' I know nothing of him, not even his Name. This may seem extraordinary, but I assure you it is not uncommon here. Sometimes, indeed one unknown Person brings another equally unknown, to recommend him; and sometimes they recommend one another! As to this Gentleman, I must refer you to himself for his Character and Merits, with which he is certainly better acquainted than I can possibly be. I recommend him however to those Civilities, which every Stranger, of whom one knows no Harm, has a Right to; and I request you will do him all the good Offices, and show him all the Favour that, on further Acquaintance, you shall find him to deserve. I have the Honour to be, etc.   [B. F.]

TO CHARLES
DE WEISSENSTEIN

Passy, July 1, 1778.

SIR,

I received your letter, dated at Brussels the 16th past. My vanity might possibly be flattered by your expressions of compliment to my understanding, if your *proposals* did not more clearly manifest a mean opinion of it.

You conjure me, in the name of the omniscient and just God, before whom I must appear, and by my hopes of future fame, to consider if some expedient cannot be found to put a stop to the desolation of America, and prevent the miseries of a general war. As I am conscious of having taken every step in my power to prevent the breach, and no one to widen it, I can appear cheerfully before that God, fearing nothing from his justice in this particular, though I have much occasion for his mercy in many others. As to my future fame, I am content to rest it on my past and present conduct, without seeking an addition to it in the crooked, dark paths, you propose to me, where I should most certainly lose it. This your solemn address would therefore have been more properly made to your sovereign and his venal Parliament. He and they, who wickedly began, and madly continue, a war for the desolation of America, are alone accountable for the consequences.

You endeavour to impress me with a bad opinion of French faith; but the instances of their friendly endeavours to serve a race of weak princes, who, by their own imprudence, defeated every attempt to promote their interest, weigh but little with me, when I consider the steady friendship of France to the Thirteen

United States of Switzerland, which has now continued invio-
late two hundred years. You tell me, that she will certainly cheat
us, and that she despises us already. I do not believe that she
will cheat us, and I am not certain that she despises us; but I see
clearly that you are endeavouring to cheat us by your conciliatory bills; that you actually despised our understandings, when
you flattered yourselves those artifices would succeed; and that
not only France, but all Europe, yourselves included, most certainly and for ever would despise us, if we were weak enough to
accept your insidious propositions.

Our expectations of the future grandeur of America are not
so magnificent, and therefore not so vain or visionary, as you
represent them to be. The body of our people are not merchants, but humble husbandmen, who delight in the cultivation
of their lands, which, from their fertility and the variety of our
climates, are capable of furnishing all the necessaries and conveniences of life without external commerce; and we have too
much land to have the least temptation to extend our territory
by conquest from peaceable neighbours, as well as too much
justice to think of it. Our militia, you find by experience, are
sufficient to defend our lands from invasion; and the commerce
with us will be defended by all the nations who find an advantage in it. We, therefore, have not the occasion you imagine, of
fleets or standing armies, but may leave those expensive machines to be maintained for the pomp of princes, and the wealth
of ancient states. We propose, if possible, to live in peace with
all mankind; and after you have been convinced, to your cost,
that there is nothing to be got by attacking us, we have reason
to hope, that no other power will judge it prudent to quarrel
with us, lest they divert us from our own quiet industry, and
turn us into corsairs preying upon theirs. The weight therefore
of an independent empire, which you seem certain of our inability to bear, will not be so great as you imagine. The expense
of our civil government we have always borne, and can easily
bear, because it is small. A virtuous and laborious people may
be cheaply governed. Determining, as we do, to have no offices
of profit, nor any sinecures or useless appointments, so common in ancient or corrupted states, we can govern ourselves a

year, for the sum you pay in a single department, or for what
one jobbing contractor, by the favour of a minister, can cheat
you out of in a single article.

You think we flatter ourselves, and are deceived into an opinion that England *must* acknowledge our independency. We, on
the other hand, think you flatter yourselves in imagining such
an acknowledgment a vast boon, which we strongly desire, and
which you may gain some great advantage by granting or with-
holding. We have never asked it of you; we only tell you, that
you can have no treaty with us but as an independent state;
and you may please yourselves and your children with the rattle
of your right to govern us, as long as you have done with that of
your King's being King of France, without giving us the least
concern, if you do not attempt to exercise it. That this pretended right is indisputable, as you say, we utterly deny. Your
Parliament never had a right to govern us, and your King has
forfeited it by his bloody tyranny. But I thank you for letting me
know a little of your mind, that, even if the Parliament should
acknowledge our independency, the act would not be binding to
posterity, and that your nation would resume and prosecute the
claim as soon as they found it convenient from the influence of
your passions, and your present malice against us. We suspected
before, that you would not be actually bound by your conciliatory acts, longer than till they had served their purpose of in-
ducing us to disband our forces; but we were not certain, that
you were knaves by principle, and that we ought not to have the
least confidence in your offers, promises, or treaties, though
confirmed by Parliament.

I now indeed recollect my being informed, long since, when
in England, that a certain very great personage, then young,
studied much a certain book, called *Arcana Imperii*. I had the
curiosity to procure the book and read it. There are sensible
and good things in it, but some bad ones; for, if I remember
rightly, a particular king is applauded for his politically exciting a rebellion among his subjects, at a time when they had not
strength to support it, that he might, in subduing them, take
away their privileges, which were troublesome to him; and a
question is formally stated and discussed, *Whether a prince,*

who, to appease a revolt, makes promises of indemnity to the revolters, is obliged to fulfil those promises. Honest and good men would say, Ay; but this politician says, as you say, No. And he gives this pretty reason, that, though it was right to make the promises, because otherwise the revolt would not be suppressed, yet it would be wrong to keep them, because revolters ought to be punished to deter from future revolts.

If these are the principles of your nation, no confidence can be placed in you; it is in vain to treat with you; and the wars can only end in being reduced to an utter inability of continuing them.

One main drift of your letter seems to be, to impress me with an idea of your own impartiality, by just censures of your ministers and measures, and to draw from me propositions of peace, or approbations of those you have enclosed to me which you intimate may by your means be conveyed to the King directly, without the intervention of those ministers. You would have me give them to, or drop them for, a stranger, whom I may find next Monday in the church of Notre Dame, to be known by a rose in his hat. You yourself, Sir, are quite unknown to me; you have not trusted me with your true name. Our taking the least step towards a treaty with England through you, might, if you are an enemy, be made use of to ruin us with our new and good friends. I may be indiscreet enough in many things; but certainly, if I were disposed to make propositions (which I cannot do, having none committed to me to make), I should never think of delivering them to the Lord knows who, to be carried to the Lord knows where, to serve no one knows what purposes. Being at this time one of the most remarkable figures in Paris, even my appearance in the church of Notre Dame, where I cannot have any conceivable business, and especially being seen to leave or drop any letter to any person there, would be a matter of some speculation, and might, from the suspicions it must naturally give, have very mischievous consequences to our credit here.

The very proposing of a correspondence so to be managed, in a manner not necessary where fair dealing is intended, gives just reason to suppose you intend the contrary. Besides, as your court has sent Commissioners to treat with the Congress, with all the powers that could be given them by the crown under the act of Parliament, what good purpose can be served by privately obtaining propositions from us? Before those Commissioners went, we might have treated in virtue of our general powers, (with the knowledge, advice, and approbation of our friends), upon any propositions made to us. But, under the present circumstances, for us to make propositions, while a treaty is supposed to be actually on foot with the Congress, would be extremely improper, highly presumptuous with regard to our constituents, and answer no good end whatever.

I write this letter to you, notwithstanding; (which I think I can convey in a less mysterious manner, and guess it may come to your hands;) I write it because I would let you know our sense of your procedure, which appears as insidious as that of your conciliatory bills. Your true way to obtain peace, if your ministers desire it, is, to propose openly to the Congress fair and equal terms, and you may possibly come sooner to such a resolution, when you find, that personal flatteries, general cajolings, and panegyrics on our *virtue* and *wisdom* are not likely to have the effect you seem to expect; the persuading us to act basely and foolishly, in betraying our country and posterity into the hands of our most bitter enemies, giving up or selling our arms and warlike stores, dismissing our ships of war and troops, and putting those enemies in possession of our forts and ports.

This proposition of delivering ourselves, bound and gagged, ready for hanging, without even a right to complain, and without a friend to be found afterwards among all mankind, you would have us embrace upon the faith of an act of Parliament! Good God! an act of your Parliament! This demonstrates that you do not yet know us, and that you fancy we do not know you; but it is not merely this flimsy faith, that we are to act upon; you offer us *hope,* the hope of PLACES, PENSIONS, and PEERAGES. These, judging from yourselves, you think are motives irresistible. This offer to corrupt us, Sir, is with me your credential, and convinces me that you are not a private volunteer in your application. It bears the stamp of British court character. It is even the signature of your King. But think for a moment in what light it must be viewed in America. By PLACES, you mean places among us, for you take care by a special article to secure your own to yourselves. We must then pay the salaries in order to enrich ourselves with these places. But you will give us PENSIONS, probably to be paid too out of your expected American revenue, and which none of us can accept without deserving, and perhaps obtaining, a SUS-*pension*. PEERAGES! alas! Sir, our long observation of the vast servile majority of your peers, voting constantly for every measure proposed by a minister, however weak or wicked, leaves us small respect for that title. We consider it as a sort of *tar-and-feather* honour, or a mixture of foulness and folly, which every man among us, who should accept it from your King, would be obliged to renounce, or exchange for that conferred by the mobs of their own country, or wear it with everlasting infamy. I am, Sir, your humble servant,

B. FRANKLIN.

PASSPORT FOR CAPTAIN COOK

To all Captains and Commanders of armed Ships acting by Commission from the Congress of the United States of America, now in war with Great Britain.

Gentlemen,

A Ship having been fitted out from England before the Commencement of this War, to make Discoveries of new Countries in Unknown Seas, under the Conduct of that most celebrated Navigator and Discoverer Captain Cook; an Undertaking truly laudable in itself, as the Increase of Geographical Knowledge facilitates the Communication between distant Nations, in the Exchange of useful Products and Manufactures, and the Extension of Arts, whereby the common Enjoyments of human Life are multiply'd and augmented, and Science of other kinds increased to the benefit of Mankind in general; this is, therefore, most earnestly to recommend to every one of you, that, in case the said Ship, which is now expected to be soon in the European Seas on her Return, should happen to fall into your Hands, you would not consider her as an Enemy, nor suffer any Plunder to be made of the Effects contain'd in her, nor obstruct her immediate Return to England, by detaining her or sending her into any other Part of Europe or to America, but that you would treat the said Captain Cook and his People with all Civility and Kindness, affording them, as common Friends to Mankind, all the Assistance in your Power, which they may happen to stand in need of. In so doing you will not only gratify the Generosity of your own Dispositions, but there is no doubt of your obtaining the Approbation of the Congress, and your other American Owners. I have the honour to be, Gentlemen, your most obedient humble Servant.

[Given] at Passy, near Paris, this 10th day of March, 1779.

B. FRANKLIN,
Plenipotentiary from the Congress of the
United States to the Court of France.

THE LEVÉE

IN the first chapter of Job we have an account of a transaction said to have arisen in the court, or at the *levée,* of the best of all possible princes, or of governments by a single person, viz. that of God himself.

At this *levée,* in which the sons of God were assembled, Satan also appeared.

It is probable the writer of that ancient book took his idea of this *levée* from those of the eastern monarchs of the age he lived in.

It is to this day usual at the *levées* of princes, to have persons assembled who are enemies to each other, who seek to obtain favor by whispering calumny and detraction, and thereby ruining those that distinguish themselves by their virtue and merit. And kings frequently ask a familiar question or two, of every one in the circle, merely to show their benignity. These circumstances are particularly exemplified in this relation.

If a modern king, for instance, finds a person in the circle who has not lately been there, he naturally asks him how he has passed his time since he last had the pleasure of seeing him? the gentleman perhaps replies that he has been in the country to view his estates, and visit some friends. Thus Satan being asked whence he cometh? answers, "From going to and fro in the earth, and walking up and down in it." And being further asked, whether he had considered the uprightness and fidelity of the prince's servant Job, he immediately displays all the malignance of the designing courtier, by answering with another question: "Doth Job serve God for naught? Hast thou not given him immense wealth, and protected him in the possession of it?

Deprive him of that, and he will curse thee to thy face." In modern phrase, Take away his places and his pensions, and your Majesty will soon find him in the opposition.

This whisper against Job had its effect. He was delivered into the power of his adversary, who deprived him of his fortune, destroyed his family, and completely ruined him.

The book of Job is called by divines a sacred poem, and, with the rest of the Holy Scriptures, is understood to be written for our instruction.

What then is the instruction to be gathered from this supposed transaction?

Trust not a single person with the government of your state. For if the Deity himself, being the monarch may for a time give way to calumny, and suffer it to operate the destruction of the best of subjects; what mischief may you not expect from such power in a mere man, though the best of men, from whom the truth is often industriously hidden, and to whom falsehood is often presented in its place, by artful, interested, and malicious courtiers?

And be cautious in trusting him even with limited powers, lest sooner or later he sap and destroy those limits, and render himself absolute.

For by the disposal of places, he attaches to himself all the placeholders, with their numerous connexions, and also all the expecters and hopers of places, which will form a strong party in promoting his views. By various political engagements for the interest of neighbouring states or princes, he procures their aid in establishing his own personal power. So that, through the hopes of emolument in one part of his subjects, and the fear of his resentment in the other, all opposition falls before him.

TO GEORGE WASHINGTON

SIR,

I have received but lately the Letter your Excellency did me the honour of writing to me in Recommendation of the Marquis de la Fayette. His modesty detained it long in his own Hands. We became acquainted, however, from the time of his Arrival at Paris; and his Zeal for the Honour of our Country, his Activity in our Affairs here, and his firm Attachment to our Cause and to you, impress'd me with the same Regard and Esteem for him that your Excellency's Letter would have done, had it been immediately delivered to me.

Should peace arrive after another Campaign or two, and afford us a little Leisure, I should be happy to see your Excellency in Europe, and to accompany you, if my Age and Strength would permit, in visiting some of its ancient and most famous Kingdoms. You would, on this side of the Sea, enjoy the great Reputation you have acquir'd, pure and free from those little Shades that the Jealousy and Envy of a Man's Countrymen and Cotemporaries are ever endeavouring to cast over living Merit. Here you would know, and enjoy, what Posterity will say of Washington. For 1000 Leagues have nearly the same Effect with 1000 Years. The feeble Voice of those grovelling Passions cannot extend so far either in Time or Distance. At present I enjoy that Pleasure for you, as I frequently hear the old Generals of this martial Country, (who study the Maps of America, and mark upon them all your Operations,) speak with sincere Approbation and great Applause of your conduct; and join in giving you the Character of one of the greatest Captains of the Age.

I must soon quit the Scene, but you may live to see our Country flourish, as it will amazingly and rapidly after the War is over. Like a Field of young Indian Corn, which long Fair weather and Sunshine had enfeebled and discolored, and which in that weak State, by a Thunder Gust, of violent Wind, Hail, and Rain, seem'd to be threaten'd with absolute Destruction; yet the Storm being past, it recovers fresh Verdure, shoots up with double Vigour, and delights the Eye, not of its Owner only, but of every observing Traveller.

The best Wishes that can be form'd for your Health, Honour, and Happiness, ever attend you from your Excellency's most obedient and most humble servant

B. F.

TO JAMES HUTTON

Passy, July 7, 1782.

My old and dear Friend,

A Letter written by you to M. Bertin, *Ministre d'Etat,* containing an Account of the abominable Murders committed by some of the frontier People on the poor Moravian Indians, has given me infinite Pain and Vexation. The Dispensations of Providence in this World puzzle my weak Reason. I cannot comprehend why cruel Men should have been permitted thus to destroy their Fellow Creatures. Some of the Indians may be suppos'd to have committed Sins, but one cannot think the little Children had committed any worthy of Death. Why has a single Man in England, who happens to love Blood and to hate Americans, been permitted to gratify that bad Temper by hiring German Murderers, and joining them with his own, to destroy in a continued Course of bloody Years near 100,000 human Creatures, many of them possessed of useful Talents, Virtues and Abilities to which he has no Pretension! It is he who has furnished the Savages with Hatchets and Scalping Knives, and engages them to fall upon our defenceless Farmers, and murder them with their Wives and Children, paying for their Scalps, of which the account kept in America already amounts, as I have heard, to near *two Thousand!*

Perhaps the people of the frontiers, exasperated by the Cruelties of the Indians, have been induced to kill all Indians that fall into their Hands without Distinction; so that even these horrid Murders of our poor Moravians may be laid to his Charge. And yet this Man lives, enjoys all the good Things this World can afford, and is surrounded by Flatterers, who keep even his Conscience quiet by telling him he is the best of Princes! I wonder at this, but I cannot therefore part with the comfortable Belief of a Divine Providence; and the more I see the Impossibility, from the number & extent of his Crimes, of giving equivalent Punishment to a wicked Man in this Life, the more I am convinc'd of a future State, in which all that here appears to be wrong shall be set right, all that is crooked made straight. In this Faith let you & I, my dear Friend, comfort ourselves; it is the only Comfort, in the present dark Scene of Things, that is allow'd us.

I shall not fail to write to the Government of America, urging that effectual Care may be taken to protect & save the Remainder of those unhappy People.

Since writing the above, I have received a Philadelphia Paper, containing some Account of the same horrid Transaction, a little different, and some Circumstances alledged as Excuses or Palliations, but extreamly weak & insufficient. I send it to you inclos'd. With great and sincere Esteem, I am ever, my dear Friend, yours most affectionately,

B. FRANKLIN.

APOLOGUE

LION, king of a certain forest, had among his subjects a body of faithful dogs, in principle and affection strongly attached to his person and government, but through whose assistance he had extended his dominions, and had become the terror of his enemies.

Lion, however, influenced by evil counsellors, took an aversion to the dogs, condemned them unheard, and ordered his tigers, leopards, and panthers to attack and destroy them.

The dogs petitioned humbly, but their petitions were rejected haughtily; and they were forced to defend themselves, which they did with bravery.

A few among them, of a mongrel race, derived from a mixture with wolves and foxes, corrupted by royal promises of great rewards, deserted the honest dogs and joined their enemies.

The dogs were finally victorious: a treaty of peace was made, in which Lion acknowledged them to be free, and disclaimed all future authority over them.

The mongrels not being permitted to return among them, claimed of the royalists the reward that had been promised.

A council of the beasts was held to consider their demand.

The wolves and the foxes agreed unanimously that the demand was just, that royal promises ought to be kept, and that every loyal subject should contribute freely to enable his majesty to fulfil them.

The horse alone, with a boldness and freedom that became the nobleness of his nature, delivered a contrary opinion.

"The King," said he, "has been misled, by bad ministers, to war unjustly upon his faithful subjects. Royal promises, when

made to encourage us to act for the public good, should indeed
be honourably acquitted; but if to encourage us to betray and
destroy each other, they are wicked and void from the beginning. The advisers of such promises, and those who murdered
in consequence of them, instead of being recompensed, should be
severely punished. Consider how greatly our common strength
is already diminished by our loss of the dogs. If you enable the
King to reward those fratricides, you will establish a precedent
that may justify a future tyrant to make like promises; and
every example of such an unnatural brute rewarded will give
them additional weight. Horses and bulls, as well as dogs, may
thus be divided against their own kind, and civil wars produced
at pleasure, till we are so weakened that neither liberty nor
safety is any longer to be found in the forest, and nothing remains but abject submission to the will of a despot, who may
devour us as he pleases."

The council had sense enough to resolve—that the demand be
rejected.

TO SIR JOSEPH BANKS

DEAR SIR,

I have just received the very kind friendly Letter you were so good as to write to me by Dr. Broussonnet. Be assured, that I long earnestly for a Return of those peaceful Times, when I could sit down in sweet Society with my English philosophic Friends, communicating to each other new Discoveries, and proposing Improvements of old ones; all tending to extend the Power of Man over Matter, avert or diminish the Evils he is subject to, or augment the Number of his Enjoyments. Much more happy should I be thus employ'd in your most desirable Company, than in that of all the Grandees of the Earth projecting Plans of Mischief, however necessary they may be supposed for obtaining greater Good.

I am glad to learn by the D^r that your great Work goes on. I admire your Magnanimity in the Undertaking, and the Perseverance with which you have prosecuted it.

I join with you most perfectly in the charming Wish you so well express, "that such Measures may be taken by both Parties as may tend to the Elevation of both, rather than the Destruction of either." If any thing has happened endangering one of them, my Comfort is, that I endeavour'd earnestly to prevent it, and gave honest, faithful Advice, which, if it had been regarded, would have been effectual. And still, if proper Means are us'd to produce, not only a Peace, but what is much more interesting, a thorough Reconciliation, a few Years may heal the Wounds that have been made in our Happiness, and produce a Degree of Prosperity of which at present we can hardly form a Conception. With great and sincere Esteem and Respect, I am, dear Sir, &c.

B. FRANKLIN.

INFORMATION TO THOSE
WHO WOULD REMOVE
TO AMERICA

MANY Persons in Europe, having directly or by Letters, express'd to the Writer of this, who is well acquainted with North America, their Desire of transporting and establishing themselves in that Country; but who appear to have formed, thro' Ignorance, mistaken Ideas and Expectations of what is to be obtained there; he thinks it may be useful, and prevent inconvenient, expensive, and fruitless Removals and Voyages of improper Persons, if he gives some clearer and truer Notions of that part of the World, than appear to have hitherto prevailed.

He finds it is imagined by Numbers, that the Inhabitants of North America are rich, capable of rewarding, and dispos'd to reward, all sorts of Ingenuity; that they are at the same time ignorant of all the Sciences, and, consequently, that Strangers, possessing Talents in the Belles-Lettres, fine Arts, &c., must be highly esteemed, and so well paid, as to become easily rich themselves; that there are also abundance of profitable Offices to be disposed of, which the Natives are not qualified to fill; and that, having few Persons of Family among them, Strangers of Birth must be greatly respected, and of course easily obtain the best of those Offices, which will make all their Fortunes; that the Governments too, to encourage Emigrations from Europe, not only pay the Expense of personal Transportation, but give Lands gratis to Strangers, with Negroes to work for them, Utensils of Husbandry, and Stocks of Cattle. These are all wild Imaginations; and those who go to America with Expectations founded upon them will surely find themselves disappointed.

The Truth is, that though there are in that Country few People so miserable as the Poor of Europe, there are also very few that in Europe would be called rich; it is rather a general happy Mediocrity that prevails. There are few great Proprietors of the Soil, and few Tenants; most People cultivate their own Lands, or follow some Handicraft or Merchandise; very few rich enough to live idly upon their Rents or Incomes, or to pay the high Prices given in Europe for Paintings, Statues, Architecture, and the other Works of Art, that are more curious than useful. Hence the natural Geniuses, that have arisen in America with such Talents, have uniformly quitted that Country for Europe, where they can be more suitably rewarded. It is true, that Letters and Mathematical Knowledge are in Esteem there, but they are at the same time more common than is apprehended; there being already existing nine Colleges or Universities, viz. four in New England, and one in each of the Provinces of New York, New Jersey, Pensilvania, Maryland, and Virginia, all furnish'd with learned Professors; besides a number of smaller Academies; these educate many of their Youth in the Languages, and those Sciences that qualify men for the Professions of Divinity, Law, or Physick. Strangers indeed are by no means excluded from exercising those Professions; and the quick Increase of Inhabitants everywhere gives them a Chance of Employ, which they have in common with the Natives. Of civil Offices, or Employments, there are few; no superfluous Ones, as in Europe; and it is a Rule establish'd in some of the States, that no Office should be so profitable as to make it desirable. The 36th Article of the Constitution of Pennsilvania, runs expressly in these Words; "As every Freeman, to preserve his Independence, (if he has not a sufficient Estate) ought to have some Profession, Calling, Trade, or Farm, whereby he may honestly subsist, there can be no Necessity for, nor Use in, establishing Offices of Profit; the usual Effects of which are Dependence and Servility, unbecoming Freemen, in the Possessors and Expectants; Faction, Contention, Corruption, and Disorder among the People. Wherefore, whenever an Office, thro' Increase of Fees or otherwise, becomes so profitable, as to occasion many to apply for it, the Profits ought to be lessened by the Lagislature."

These Ideas prevailing more or less in all the United States, it cannot be worth any Man's while, who has a means of Living at home, to expatriate himself, in hopes of obtaining a profitable civil Office in America; and, as to military Offices, they are at an End with the War, the Armies being disbanded. Much less is it adviseable for a Person to go thither, who has no other Quality to recommend him but his Birth. In Europe it has indeed its Value; but it is a Commodity that cannot be carried to a worse Market than that of America, where people do not inquire concerning a Stranger, *What is he?* but, *What can he do?* If he has any useful Art, he is welcome; and if he exercises it, and behaves well, he will be respected by all that know him; but a mere Man of Quality, who, on that Account, wants to live upon the Public, by some Office or Salary, will be despis'd and disregarded. The Husbandman is in honor there, and even the Mechanic, because their Employments are useful. The People have a saying, that God Almighty is himself a Mechanic, the greatest in the Univers; and he is respected and admired more for the Variety, Ingenuity, and Utility of his Handyworks, than for the Antiquity of his Family. They are pleas'd with the Observation of a Negro, and frequently mention it, that *Boccarorra* (meaning the White men) *make de black man workee, make de Horse workee, make de Ox workee, make ebery ting workee; only de Hog. He, de hog, no workee; he eat, he drink, he walk about, he go to sleep when he please, he libb like a Gentleman.* According to these Opinions of the Americans, one of them would think himself more oblig'd to a Genealogist, who could prove for him that his Ancestors and Relations for ten Generations had been Ploughmen, Smiths, Carpenters, Turners, Weavers, Tanners, or even Shoemakers, and consequently that they were useful Members of Society; than if he could only prove that they were Gentlemen, doing nothing of Value, but living idly on the Labour of others, mere *fruges consumere nati,** and otherwise *good for nothing,* till by their Death their Estates, like the Carcass of the Negro's Gentleman-Hog, come to be *cut up.*

With regard to Encouragements for Strangers from Government, they are really only what are derived from good Laws

---

*". . . . . . born / Merely to eat up the corn." —WATTS.

and Liberty. Strangers are welcome, because there is room enough for them all, and therefore the old Inhabitants are not jealous of them; the Laws protect them sufficiently, so that they have no need of the Patronage of Great Men; and every one will enjoy securely the Profits of his Industry. But, if he does not bring a Fortune with him, he must work and be industrious to live. One or two Years' residence gives him all the Rights of a Citizen; but the government does not at present, whatever it may have done in former times, hire People to become Settlers, by Paying their Passages, giving Land, Negroes, Utensils, Stock, or any other kind of Emolument whatsoever. In short, America is the Land of Labour, and by no means what the English call *Lubberland,* and the French *Pays de Cocagne,* where the streets are said to be pav'd with half-peck Loaves, the Houses til'd with Pancakes, and where the Fowls fly about ready roasted, crying, *Come eat me!*

Who then are the kind of Persons to whom an Emigration to America may be advantageous? And what are the Advantages they may reasonably expect?

Land being cheap in that Country, from the vast Forests still void of Inhabitants, and not likely to be occupied in an Age to come, insomuch that the Propriety of an hundred Acres of fertile Soil full of Wood may be obtained near the Frontiers, in many Places, for Eight or Ten Guineas, hearty young Labouring Men, who understand the Husbandry of Corn and Cattle, which is nearly the same in that Country as in Europe, may easily establish themselves there. A little Money sav'd of the good Wages they receive there, while they work for others, enables them to buy the Land and begin their Plantation, in which they are assisted by the Good-Will of their Neighbours, and some Credit. Multitudes of poor People from England, Ireland, Scotland, and Germany, have by this means in a few years become wealthy Farmers, who, in their own Countries, where all the Lands are fully occupied, and the Wages of Labour low, could never have emerged from the poor Condition wherein they were born.

From the salubrity of the Air, the healthiness of the Climate, the plenty of good Provisions, and the Encouragement to early

Marriages by the certainty of Subsistence in cultivating the Earth, the Increase of Inhabitants by natural Generation is very rapid in America, and becomes still more so by the Accession of Strangers; hence there is a continual Demand for more Artisans of all the necessary and useful kinds, to supply those Cultivators of the Earth with Houses, and with Furniture and Utensils of the grosser sorts, which cannot so well be brought from Europe. Tolerably good Workmen in any of those mechanic Arts are sure to find Employ, and to be well paid for their Work, there being no Restraints preventing Strangers from exercising any Art they understand, nor any Permission necessary. If they are poor, they begin first as Servants or Journeymen; and if they are sober, industrious, and frugal, they soon become Masters, establish themselves in Business, marry, raise Families, and become respectable Citizens.

Also, Persons of moderate Fortunes and Capitals, who, having a Number of Children to provide for, are desirous of bringing them up to Industry, and to secure Estates for their Posterity, have Opportunities of doing it in America, which Europe does not afford. There they may be taught and practise profitable mechanic Arts, without incurring Disgrace on that Account, but on the contrary acquiring Respect by such Abilities. There small Capitals laid out in Lands, which daily become more valuable by the Increase of People, afford a solid Prospect of ample Fortunes thereafter for those Children. The Writer of this has known several Instances of large Tracts of Land, bought, on what was then the Frontier of Pensilvania, for Ten Pounds per hundred Acres, which after 20 years, when the Settlements had been extended far beyond them, sold readily, without any Improvement made upon them, for three Pounds per Acre. The Acre in America is the same with the English Acre, or the Acre of Normandy.

Those, who desire to understand the State of Government in America, would do well to read the Constitutions of the several States, and the Articles of Confederation that bind the whole together for general Purposes, under the Direction of one Assembly, called the Congress. These Constitutions have been printed, by order of Congress, in America; two Editions of them have also been printed in London; and a good Translation of them into French has lately been published at Paris.

Several of the Princes of Europe having of late years, from an Opinion of Advantage to arise by producing all Commodities and Manufactures within their own Dominions, so as to diminish or render useless their Importations, have endeavoured to entice Workmen from other Countries by high Salaries, Privileges, &c. Many Persons, pretending to be skilled in various great Manufactures, imagining that America must be in Want of them, and that the Congress would probably be dispos'd to imitate the Princes above mentioned, have proposed to go over, on Condition of having their Passages paid, Lands given, Salaries appointed, exclusive Privileges for Terms of years, &c. Such Persons, on reading the Articles of Confederation, will find, that the Congress have no Power committed to them, or Money put into their Hands, for such purposes; and that if any such Encouragement is given, it must be by the Government of some separate State. This, however, has rarely been done in America; and, when it has been done, it has rarely succeeded, so as to establish a Manufacture, which the Country was not yet so ripe for as to encourage private Persons to set it up; Labour being generally too dear there, and Hands difficult to be kept together, every one desiring to be a Master, and the Cheapness of Lands inclining many to leave Trades for Agriculture. Some indeed have met with Success, and are carried on to Advantage; but they are generally such as require only a few Hands, or wherein great Part of the Work is performed by Machines. Things that are bulky, and of so small Value as not well to bear the Expence of Freight, may often be made cheaper in the Country than they can be imported; and the Manufacture of such Things will be profitable wherever there is a sufficient Demand. The Farmers in America produce indeed a good deal of Wool and Flax; and none is exported, it is all work'd up; but it is in the Way of domestic Manufacture, for the Use of the Family. The buying up Quantities of Wool and Flax, with the Design to employ Spinners, Weavers, &c., and form great Establishments, producing Quantities of Linen and Woollen Goods for Sale, has been several times attempted in different

Provinces; but those Projects have generally failed, goods of equal Value being imported cheaper. And when the Governments have been solicited to support such Schemes by Encouragements, in Money, or by imposing Duties on Importation of such Goods, it has been generally refused, on this Principle, that, if the Country is ripe for the Manufacture, it may be carried on by private Persons to Advantage; and if not, it is a Folly to think of forcing Nature. Great Establishments of Manufacture require great Numbers of Poor to do the Work for small Wages; these Poor are to be found in Europe, but will not be found in America, till the Lands are all taken up and cultivated, and the Excess of People, who cannot get Land, want Employment. The Manufacture of Silk, they say, is natural in France, as that of Cloth in England, because each Country produces in Plenty the first Material; but if England will have a Manufacture of Silk as well as that of Cloth, and France one of Cloth as well as that of Silk, these unnatural Operations must be supported by mutual Prohibitions, or high Duties on the Importation of each other's Goods; by which means the Workmen are enabled to tax the home Consumer by greater Prices, while the higher Wages they receive makes them neither happier nor richer, since they only drink more and work less. Therefore the Governments in America do nothing to encourage such Projects. The People, by this Means, are not impos'd on, either by the Merchant or Mechanic. If the Merchant demands too much Profit on imported Shoes, they buy of the Shoemaker; and if he asks too high a Price, they take them of the Merchant; thus the two Professions are checks on each other. The Shoemaker, however, has, on the whole, a considerable Profit upon his Labour in America, beyond what he had in Europe, as he can add to his Price a Sum nearly equal to all the Expences of Freight and Commission, Risque or Insurance, &c., necessarily charged by the Merchant. And the Case is the same with the Workmen in every other Mechanic Art. Hence it is, that Artisans generally live better and more easily in America than in Europe; and such as are good Œconomists make a comfortable Provision for Age, and for their Children. Such may, therefore, remove with Advantage to America.

In the long-settled Countries of Europe, all Arts, Trades, Professions, Farms, &c., are so full, that it is difficult for a poor Man, who has Children, to place them where they may gain, or learn to gain, a decent Livelihood. The Artisans, who fear creating future Rivals in Business, refuse to take Apprentices, but upon Conditions of Money, Maintenance, or the like, which the Parents are unable to comply with. Hence the Youth are dragg'd up in Ignorance of every gainful Art, and oblig'd to become Soldiers, or Servants, or Thieves, for a Subsistence. In America, the rapid Increase of Inhabitants takes away that Fear of Rivalship, and Artisans willingly receive Apprentices from the hope of Profit by their Labour, during the Remainder of the Time stipulated, after they shall be instructed. Hence it is easy for poor Families to get their Children instructed; for the Artisans are so desirous of Apprentices, that many of them will even give Money to the Parents, to have Boys from Ten to Fifteen Years of Age bound Apprentices to them till the Age of Twenty-one; and many poor Parents have, by that means, on their Arrival in the Country, raised Money enough to buy Land sufficient to establish themselves, and to subsist the rest of their Family by Agriculture. These Contracts for Apprentices are made before a Magistrate, who regulates the Agreement according to Reason and Justice, and, having in view the Formation of a future useful Citizen, obliges the Master to engage by a written Indenture, not only that, during the time of Service stipulated, the Apprentice shall be duly provided with Meat, Drink, Apparel, washing, and Lodging, and, at its Expiration, with a compleat new Suit of Cloaths, but also that he shall be taught to read, write, and cast Accompts; and that he shall be well instructed in the Art or Profession of his Master, or some other, by which he may afterwards gain a Livelihood, and be able in his turn to raise a Family. A Copy of this Indenture is given to the Apprentice or his Friends, and the Magistrate keeps a Record of it, to which recourse may be had, in case of Failure by the Master in any Point of Performance. This desire among the Masters, to have more Hands employ'd in working for them, induces them to pay the Passages of young Persons, of both Sexes, who, on their Arrival, agree to serve them one, two, three, or four Years; those, who have already learnt a Trade, agreeing for a shorter Term, in proportion to their Skill, and the consequent immediate Value of their Service; and those, who have none, agreeing for a longer Term, in consideration of being taught an Art their Poverty would not permit them to acquire in their own Country.

The almost general Mediocrity of Fortune that prevails in America obliging its People to follow some Business for subsistence, those Vices, that arise usually from Idleness, are in a great measure prevented. Industry and constant Employment are great preservatives of the Morals and Virtue of a Nation. Hence bad Examples to Youth are more rare in America, which must be a comfortable Consideration to Parents. To this may be truly added, that serious Religion, under its various Denominations, is not only tolerated, but respected and practised. Atheism is unknown there; Infidelity rare and secret; so that persons may live to a great Age in that Country, without having their Piety shocked by meeting with either an Atheist or an Infidel. And the Divine Being seems to have manifested his Approbation of the mutual Forbearance and Kindness with which the different Sects treat each other, by the remarkable Prosperity with which He has been pleased to favour the whole Country.

TO SIR JOSEPH BANKS

DEAR SIR,

I received your very kind letter by Dr. Blagden, and esteem myself much honoured by your friendly Remembrance. I have been too much and too closely engaged in public Affairs, since his being here, to enjoy all the Benefit of his Conversation you were so good as to intend me. I hope soon to have more Leisure, and to spend a part of it in those Studies, that are much more agreable to me than political Operations.

I join with you most cordially in rejoicing at the return of Peace. I hope it will be lasting, and that Mankind will at length, as they call themselves reasonable Creatures, have Reason and Sense enough to settle their Differences without cutting Throats; for, in my opinion, *there never was a good War, or a bad Peace.* What vast additions to the Conveniences and Comforts of Living might Mankind have acquired, if the Money spent in Wars had been employed in Works of public utility! What an extension of Agriculture, even to the Tops of our Mountains: what Rivers rendered navigable, or joined by Canals: what Bridges, Aqueducts, new Roads, and other public Works, Edifices, and Improvements, rendering England a compleat Paradise, might have been obtained by spending those Millions in doing good, which in the last War have been spent in doing Mischief; in bringing Misery into thousands of Families, and destroying the Lives of so many thousands of working people, who might have performed the useful labour!

I am pleased with the late astronomical Discoveries made by

our Society. Furnished as all Europe now is with Academies of Science, with nice Instruments and the Spirit of Experiment, the progress of human knowledge will be rapid, and discoveries made, of which we have at present no Conception. I begin to be almost sorry I was born so soon, since I cannot have the happiness of knowing what will be known 100 years hence.

I wish continued success to the Labours of the Royal Society, and that you may long adorn their Chair; being, with the highest esteem, dear Sir, &c.

B. FRANKLIN.

P. S. Dr. Blagden will acquaint you with the experiment of a vast Globe sent up into the Air, much talked of here, and which, if prosecuted, may furnish means of new knowledge.

TO MRS. SARAH BACHE

Passy, Jan. 26, 1784.

My dear Child,

Your Care in sending me the Newspapers is very agreable to me. I received by Capt. Barney those relating to the *Cincinnati*. My Opinion of the Institution cannot be of much Importance; I only wonder that, when the united Wisdom of our Nation had, in the Articles of Confederation, manifested their Dislike of establishing Ranks of Nobility, by Authority either of the Congress or of any particular State, a Number of private Persons should think proper to distinguish themselves and their Posterity, from their fellow Citizens, and form an Order of *hereditary Knights,* in direct Opposition to the solemnly declared Sense of their Country! I imagine it must be likewise contrary to the Good Sense of most of those drawn into it by the Persuasion of its Projectors, who have been too much struck with the Ribbands and Crosses they have seen among them hanging to the Buttonholes of Foreign Officers. And I suppose those, who disapprove of it, have not hitherto given it much Opposition, from a Principle somewhat like that of your good Mother, relating to punctilious Persons, who are always exacting little Observances of Respect; that, *"if People can be pleased with small Matters, it is a pity but they should have them."*

In this View, perhaps, I should not myself, if my Advice had been ask'd, have objected to their wearing their Ribband and Badge according to their Fancy, tho' I certainly should to the entailing it as an Honour on their Posterity. For Honour, worthily obtain'd (as for Example that of our Officers), is in its Nature a *personal* Thing, and incommunicable to any but those who had some Share in obtaining it. Thus among the Chinese, the most ancient, and from long Experience the wisest of Nations, honour does not *descend,* but *ascends.* If a man from his Learning, his Wisdom, or his Valour, is promoted by the Emperor to the Rank of Mandarin, his Parents are immediately entitled to all the same Ceremonies of Respect from the People, that are establish'd as due to the Mandarin himself; on the supposition that it must have been owing to the Education, Instruction, and good Example afforded him by his Parents, that he was rendered capable of serving the Publick.

This *ascending* Honour is therefore useful to the State, as it encourages Parents to give their Children a good and virtuous Education. But the *descending Honour,* to Posterity who could have no Share in obtaining it, is not only groundless and absurd, but often hurtful to that Posterity, since it is apt to make them proud, disdaining to be employ'd in useful Arts, and thence falling into Poverty, and all the Meannesses, Servility, and Wretchedness attending it; which is the present case with much of what is called the *Noblesse* in Europe. Or if, to keep up the Dignity of the Family, Estates are entailed entire on the Eldest male heir, another Pest to Industry and Improvement of the Country is introduc'd, which will be followed by all the odious mixture of pride and Beggary, and idleness, that have half depopulated and *decultivated* Spain; occasioning continual Extinction of Families by the Discouragements of Marriage and neglect in the improvement of estates.

I wish, therefore, that the Cincinnati, if they must go on with their Project, would direct the Badges of their Order to be worn by their Parents, instead of handing them down to their Children. It would be a good Precedent, and might have good Effects. It would also be a kind of Obedience to the Fourth Commandment, in which God enjoins us to *honour* our Father and Mother, but has nowhere directed us to honour our

Children. And certainly no mode of honouring those immediate Authors of our Being can be more effectual, than that of doing praiseworthy Actions, which reflect Honour on those who gave us our Education; or more becoming, than that of manifesting, by some public Expression or Token, that it is to their Instruction and Example we ascribe the Merit of those Actions.

But the Absurdity of *descending Honours* is not a mere Matter of philosophical Opinion; it is capable of mathematical Demonstration. A Man's Son, for instance, is but half of his Family, the other half belonging to the Family of his Wife. His Son, too, marrying into another Family, his Share in the Grandson is but a fourth; in the Great Grandson, by the same Process, it is but an Eighth; in the next Generation a Sixteenth; the next a Thirty-second; the next a Sixty-fourth; the next an Hundred and twenty-eighth; the next a Two hundred and Fifty-sixth; and the next a Five hundred and twelfth; thus in nine Generations, which will not require more than 300 years (no very great Antiquity for a Family), our present Chevalier of the Order of Cincinnatus's Share in the then existing Knight, will be but a 512th part; which, allowing the present certain Fidelity of American Wives to be insur'd down through all those Nine Generations, is so small a Consideration, that methinks no reasonable Man would hazard for the sake of it the disagreable Consequences of the Jealousy, Envy, and Ill will of his Countrymen.

Let us go back with our Calculation from this young Noble, the 512th part of the present Knight, thro' his nine Generations, till we return to the year of the Institution. He must have had a Father and Mother, they are two. Each of them had a father and Mother, they are four. Those of the next preceding Generation will be eight, the next Sixteen, the next thirty-two, the next sixty-four, the next one hundred and Twenty-eight, the next Two hundred and fifty-six, and the ninth in this Retrocession Five hundred and twelve, who must be now existing, and all contribute their Proportion of this future *Chevalier de Cincinnatus*. These, with the rest, make together as follows:

$$
\begin{array}{r}
2 \\
4 \\
8 \\
16 \\
32 \\
64 \\
128 \\
256 \\
512 \\
\hline
\text{Total} \quad 1022
\end{array}
$$

One Thousand and Twenty-two Men and Women, contributors to the formation of one Knight. And, if we are to have a Thousand of these future knights, there must be now and hereafter existing One million and Twenty-two Thousand Fathers and Mothers, who are to contribute to their Production, unless a Part of the Number are employ'd in making more Knights than One. Let us strike off then the 22,000, on the Supposition of this double Employ, and then consider whether, after a reasonable Estimation of the Number of Rogues, and Fools, and Royalists and Scoundrels and Prostitutes, that are mix'd with, and help to make up necessarily their Million of Predecessors, Posterity will have much reason to boast of the noble Blood of the then existing Set of Chevaliers de Cincinnatus. The future genealogists, too, of these Chevaliers, in proving the lineal descent of their honour through so many generations (even supposing honour capable in its nature of descending), will only prove the small share of this honour, which can be justly claimed by any one of them; since the above simple process in arithmetic makes it quite plain and clear that, in proportion as the antiquity of the family shall augment, the right to the honour of the ancestor will diminish; and a few generations more would reduce it to something so small as to be very near an absolute nullity. I hope, therefore, that the Order will drop this part of their project, and content themselves, as the Knights of the Garter, Bath, Thistle, St. Louis, and other Orders of Europe do, with a Life Enjoyment of their little Badge and Ribband, and let the Distinction die with those who have merited it. This I imagine will give no offence. For my own part, I shall think it a Convenience, when I go into a Company where there may be Faces unknown to me, if I discover, by this Badge, the Persons who merit some particular Expression of my Respect; and it will save modest Virtue the Trouble of calling for our Regard, by awkward roundabout Intimations of having been heretofore employ'd in the Continental Service.

The Gentleman, who made the Voyage to France to provide the Ribands and Medals, has executed his Commission. To me they seem tolerably done; but all such Things are criticis'd. Some find Fault with the Latin, as wanting classic Elegance and Correctness; and, since our Nine Universities were not able to furnish better Latin, it was pity, they say, that the Mottos had not been in English. Others object to the Title, as not properly assumable by any but Gen. Washington, and a few others who serv'd without Pay. Others object to the *Bald Eagle* as looking too much like a *Dindon,* or Turkey. For my own part, I wish the Bald Eagle had not been chosen as the Representative of our Country; he is a Bird of bad moral Character; he does not get his living honestly; you may have seen him perch'd on some dead Tree, near the River where, too lazy to fish for himself, he watches the Labour of the Fishing-Hawk; and, when that diligent Bird has at length taken a Fish, and is bearing it to his Nest for the support of his Mate and young ones, the Bald Eagle pursues him, and takes it from him. With all this Injustice he is never in good Case; but, like those among Men who live by Sharping and Robbing, he is generally poor, and often very lousy. Besides, he is a rank Coward; the little *KingBird,* not bigger than a Sparrow, attacks him boldly and drives him out of the District. He is therefore by no means a proper emblem for the brave and honest Cincinnati of America, who have driven all the *Kingbirds* from our Country; though exactly fit for that Order of Knights, which the French call *Chevaliers d'Industrie.*

I am, on this account, not displeas'd that the Figure is not known as a Bald Eagle, but looks more like a Turk'y. For in Truth, the Turk'y is in comparison a much more respectable Bird, and withal a true original Native of America. Eagles have been found in all Countries, but the Turk'y was peculiar to ours; the first of the Species seen in Europe being brought to France by the Jesuits from Canada, and serv'd up at the Wedding Table of Charles the Ninth. He is, though a little vain and silly, it is true, but not the worse emblem for that, a Bird of Courage, and would not hesitate to attack a Grenadier of the British Guards, who should presume to invade his FarmYard with a *red* Coat on.

I shall not enter into the Criticisms made upon their Latin. The gallant officers of America may [not have the merit of being] be no great scholars, but they undoubtedly merit much, [as brave soldiers,] from their Country, which should therefore not leave them merely to *Fame* for their *"Virtutis Premium,"* which is one of their Latin Mottos. Their *"Esto perpetua,"* another, is an excellent Wish, if they meant it for their Country; bad, if intended for their Order. The States should not only restore to them the *Omnia* of their first Motto, which many of them have left and lost, but pay them justly, and reward them generously. They should not be suffered to remain, with all their new-created Chivalry, *entirely* in the Situation of the Gentleman in the Story, which their *omnia reliquit* reminds me of. You know every thing makes me recollect some Story. He had built a very fine House, and thereby much impair'd his Fortune. He had a Pride, however, in showing it to his Acquaintance. One of them, after viewing it all, remark'd a Motto over the Door, "ŌIA VANITAS." "What," says he, "is the Meaning of this ŌIA? it is a word I don't understand." "I will tell you," said the Gentleman; "I had a mind to have the Motto cut on a Piece of smooth Marble, but there was not room for it between the Ornaments, to be put in Characters large enough to be read. I therefore made use of a Contraction antiently very common in Latin Manuscripts, by which the *m*'s and *n*'s in Words are omitted, and the Omission noted by a little Dash above, which you may see there; so that the Word is *omnia*, OMNIA VANITAS." "O," says his Friend, "I now comprehend the Meaning of your motto, it relates to your Edifice; and signifies, that, if you have abridged your *Omnia,* you have, nevertheless, left your VANITAS legible at full length." I am, as ever, your affectionate father,   B. FRANKLIN.

SPEECH IN THE CONSTITUTIONAL CONVENTION ON THE SUBJECT OF SALARIES

June 2, 1787

SIR,

It is with Reluctance that I rise to express a Disapprobation of any one Article of the Plan, for which we are so much obliged to the honourable Gentleman who laid it before us. From its first Reading, I have borne a good Will to it, and, in general, wish'd it Success. In this Particular of Salaries to the Executive Branch, I happen to differ; and, as my Opinion may appear new and chimerical, it is only from a Persuasion that it is right, and from a Sense of Duty, that I hazard it. The Committee will judge of my Reasons when they have heard them, and their judgment may possibly change mine. I think I see Inconveniences in the Appointment of Salaries; I see none in refusing them, but on the contrary great Advantages.

Sir, there are two Passions which have a powerful Influence in the Affairs of Men. These are *Ambition* and *Avarice;* the Love of Power and the Love of Money. Separately, each of these has great Force in prompting Men to Action; but when united in View of the same Object, they have in many Minds the most violent Effects. Place before the Eyes of such Men a Post of *Honour,* that shall at the same time be a Place of *Profit,* and they will move Heaven and Earth to obtain it. The vast Number of such Places it is that renders the British Government so tempestuous. The Struggles for them are the true Source of all those Factions which are perpetually dividing the Nation, distracting its Councils, hurrying it sometimes into fruitless and mischievous Wars, and often compelling a Submission to dishonourable Terms of Peace.

And of what kind are the men that will strive for this profitable Preëminence, thro' all the Bustle of Cabal, the Heat of Contention, the infinite mutual Abuse of Parties, tearing to Pieces the best of Characters? It will not be the wise and moderate, the Lovers of Peace and good Order, the men fittest for the Trust. It will be the Bold and the Violent, the men of strong Passions and indefatigable Activity in their selfish Pursuits. These will thrust themselves into your Government, and be your Rulers. And these, too, will be mistaken in the expected Happiness of their Situation; for their vanquish'd competitors, of the same Spirit, and from the same Motives, will perpetually be endeavouring to distress their Administration, thwart their Measures, and render them odious to the People.

Besides these Evils, Sir, tho' we may set out in the Beginning with moderate Salaries, we shall find, that such will not be of long Continuance. Reasons will never be wanting for propos'd Augmentations; and there will always be a Party for giving more to the Rulers, that the Rulers may be able in Return to give more to them. Hence, as all History informs us, there has been in every State and Kingdom a constant kind of Warfare between the Governing and the Governed; the one striving to obtain more for its Support, and the other to pay less. And this has alone occasion'd great Convulsions, actual civil Wars, ending either in dethroning of the Princes or enslaving of the People. Generally, indeed, the Ruling Power carries its Point, and we see the Revenues of Princes constantly increasing, and we see that they are never satisfied, but always in want of more. The more the People are discontented with the Oppression of Taxes, the greater Need the Prince has of Money to distribute among his Partisans, and pay the Troops that are to suppress all Resistance, and enable him to plunder at Pleasure. There is scarce a King in a hundred, who would not, if he could, follow the Example of Pharaoh,—get first all the People's Money, then all their Lands, and then make them and their Children Servants for ever. It will be said, that we do not propose to establish Kings. I know it. But there is a natural Inclination in Mankind to kingly Government. It sometimes relieves them from Aristocratic Domination. They had rather have one Tyrant than 500. It gives more of the Appearance of Equality among Citizens; and that they like. I am apprehensive, therefore,—perhaps too apprehensive,— that the Government of these States may in future times end in a Monarchy. But this Catastrophe, I think, may be long delay'd, if in our propos'd System we do not sow the Seeds of Contention, Faction, and Tumult, by making our Posts of Honour Places of Profit. If we do, I fear, that, tho' we employ at first a Number and not a single Person, the Number will in time be set aside; it will only nourish the Fœtus of a King (as the honourable Gentleman from Virg^a very aptly express'd it), and a King will the sooner be set over us.

It may be imagined by some, that this is an Utopian Idea, and that we can never find Men to serve us in the Executive Department, without paying them well for their Services. I conceive this to be a Mistake. Some existing Facts present themselves to me, which incline me to a contrary Opinion. The High Sheriff of a County in England is an honourable Office, but it is not a profitable one. It is rather expensive, and therefore not sought for. But yet it is executed, and well executed, and usually by some of the principal Gentlemen of the County. In France, the Office of Counsellor, or Member of their judiciary Parliaments, is more honourable. It is therefore purchas'd at a high Price; there are indeed Fees on the Law Proceedings, which are divided among them, but these Fees do not amount to more than three per cent on the Sum paid for the Place. Therefore, as legal Interest is there at five per cent, they in fact pay two per cent for being allow'd to do the Judiciary Business of the Nation, which is at the same time entirely exempt from the Burthen of paying them any Salaries for their Services. I do not, however, mean to recommend this as an eligible Mode for our judiciary Department. I only bring the Instance to show, that the Pleasure of doing Good and serving their Country, and the Respect such Conduct entitles them to, are sufficient Motives with some Minds, to give up a great Portion of their Time to the Public, without the mean Inducement of pecuniary Satisfaction.

Another Instance is that of a respectable Society, who have made the Experiment, and practis'd it with Success, now more than a hundred years. I mean the Quakers. It is an establish'd

Rule with them that they are not to go to law, but in their Controversies they must apply to their Monthly, Quarterly, and Yearly Meetings. Committees of these sit with Patience to hear the Parties, and spend much time in composing their Differences. In doing this, they are supported by a Sense of Duty, and the Respect paid to Usefulness. It is honourable to be so employ'd, but it was never made profitable by Salaries, Fees, or Perquisites. And indeed, in all Cases of public Service, the less the Profit the greater the Honour.

To bring the Matter nearer home, have we not seen the greatest and most important of our Offices, that of General of our Armies, executed for Eight Years together, without the smallest Salary, by a patriot whom I will not now offend by any other Praise; and this, thro' Fatigues and Distresses, in common with the other brave Men, his military Friends and Companions, and the constant Anxieties peculiar to his Station? And shall we doubt finding three or four Men in all the United States, with public Spirit enough to bear sitting in peaceful Council, for perhaps an equal Term, merely to preside over our civil Concerns, and see that our Laws are duly executed? Sir, I have a better opinion of our Country. I think we shall never be without a sufficient Number of wise and good Men to undertake, and execute well and faithfully, the Office in question.

Sir, the Saving of the Salaries, that may at first be propos'd, is not an object with me. The subsequent Mischiefs of proposing them are what I apprehend. And therefore it is that I move the Amendment. If it is not seconded or accepted, I must be contented with the Satisfaction of having delivered my Opinion frankly, and done my Duty.

SPEECH IN THE CONSTITUTIONAL CONVENTION AT THE CONCLUSION OF ITS DELIBERATIONS

I confess that I do not entirely approve of this Constitution at present, but Sir, I am not sure I shall never approve it: For having lived long, I have experienced many Instances of being oblig'd, by better Information or fuller Consideration, to change Opinions even on important Subjects, which I once thought right, but found to be otherwise. It is therefore that the older I grow the more apt I am to doubt my own Judgment and to pay more Respect to the Judgment of others. Most Men indeed as well as most Sects in Religion, think themselves in Possession of all Truth, and that wherever others differ from them it is so far Error. Steele, a Protestant, in a Dedication tells the Pope, that the only Difference between our two Churches in their Opinions of the Certainty of their Doctrine, is, the Romish Church is infallible, and the Church of England is never in the Wrong. But tho' many private Persons think almost as highly of their own Infallibility, as that of their Sect, few express it so naturally as a certain French lady, who in a little Dispute with her Sister, said, I don't know how it happens, Sister, but I meet with no body but myself that's *always* in the right. *Il n'y a que moi qui a toujours raison.*

In these Sentiments, Sir, I agree to this Constitution, with all its Faults, if they are such: because I think a General Government necessary for us, and there is no *Form* of Government but what may be a Blessing to the People if well administred; and I believe farther that this is likely to be well administred for a Course of Years, and can only end in Despotism as other Forms have done before it, when the People shall become so corrupted as to need Despotic Government, being incapable of any other. I doubt too whether any other Convention we can obtain, may be able to make a better Constitution: For when you assemble a Number of Men to have the Advantage of their joint Wisdom, you inevitably assemble with those Men all their Prejudices, their Passions, their Errors of Opinion, their local Interests, and their selfish Views. From such an Assembly can a perfect Production be expected? It therefore astonishes me, Sir, to find this System approaching so near to Perfection as it does; and I think it will astonish our Enemies, who are waiting with Confidence to hear that our Councils are confounded, like those of the Builders of Babel, and that our States are on the Point of Separation, only to meet hereafter for the Purpose of cutting one another's Throats. Thus I consent, Sir, to this Constitution because I expect no better, and because I am not sure that it is not the best. The Opinions I have had of its Errors, I sacrifice to the Public Good. I have never whisper'd a Syllable of them abroad. Within these Walls they were born, & here they shall die. If every one of us in returning to our Constituents were to report the Objections he has had to it, and endeavour to gain Partizans in support of them, we might prevent its being generally received, and thereby lose all the salutary Effects & great Advantages resulting naturally in our favour among foreign Nations, as well as among ourselves, from our real or apparent Unanimity. Much of the Strength and Efficiency of any Government, in procuring & securing Happiness to the People depends on Opinion, on the general Opinion of the Goodness of that Government as well as of the Wisdom & Integrity of its Governors. I hope therefore that for our own Sakes, as a Part of the People, and for the Sake of our Posterity, we shall act heartily & unanimously in recommending this Constitution, wherever our Influence may extend, and turn our future Thoughts and Endeavours to the Means of having it well administred.—

On the whole, Sir, I cannot help expressing a Wish, that every Member of the Convention, who may still have Objections to it, would with me on this Occasion doubt a little of his own Infallibility, and to make *manifest* our *Unanimity,* put his Name to this Instrument.—

Then the Motion was made for adding the last Formula, viz Done in Convention by the unanimous Consent &c— which was agreed to and added—accordingly.

ON THE ABUSE OF THE PRESS

TO THE EDITORS OF THE
PENNSYLVANIA GAZETTE:

MESSRS. HALL AND SELLERS,

I lately heard a remark, that on examination of *The Pennsylvania Gazette* for fifty years, from its commencement, it appeared, that, during that long period, scarce one libellous piece had ever appeared in it. This generally chaste conduct of your paper is much to its reputation; for it has long been the opinion of sober, judicious people, that nothing is more likely to endanger the liberty of the press, than the abuse of that liberty, by employing it in personal accusation, detraction, and calumny. The excesses some of our papers have been guilty of in this particular, have set this State in a bad light abroad, as appears by the following letter, which I wish you to publish, not merely to show your own disapprobation of the practice, but as a caution to others of the profession throughout the United States. For I have seen a European newspaper, in which the editor, who had been charged with frequently calumniating the Americans, justifies himself by saying, "that he had published nothing disgraceful to us, which he had not taken from our own printed papers." I am, &c.

A. B.

New York, March 30, 1788.

"DEAR FRIEND,

"My Gout has at length left me, after five Months' painful Confinement. It afforded me, however, the Leisure to read, or hear read, all the Packets of your various Newspapers, which you so kindly sent for my Amusement.

"Mrs. W. has partaken of it; she likes to read the Advertisements; but she remarks some kind of Inconsistency in the announcing so many Diversions for almost every Evening of the Week, and such Quantities to be sold of expensive Superfluities, Fineries, and Luxuries *just imported,* in a Country, that at the same time fills its Papers with Complaints of *Hard Times,* and Want of Money. I tell her, that such Complaints are common to all Times and all Countries, and were made even in Solomon's Time; when, as we are told, Silver was as plenty in Jerusalem as the Stones in the Street; and yet, even then, there were People who grumbled, so as to incur this Censure from that knowing Prince. *'Say not thou that the former Times were better than these; for thou dost not enquire rightly concerning that matter.'*

"But the Inconsistence that strikes me the most is, that between the Name of your City, Philadelphia, (*Brotherly Love,*) and the Spirit of Rancour, Malice, and *Hatred* that breathes in its NewsPapers. For I learn from those Papers, that your State is divided into Parties, that each Party ascribes all the public Operations of the other to vicious Motives; that they do not even suspect one another of the smallest Degree of Honesty; that the antifederalists are such, merely from the Fear of losing Power, Places, or Emoluments, which they have in Possession or in Expectation; that the Federalists are a set of *Conspirators,* who aim at establishing a Tyranny over the Persons and Property of their Countrymen, and to live in Splendor on the Plunder of the People. I learn, too, that your Justices of the Peace, tho' chosen by their Neighbours, make a villainous Trade of their Office, and promote Discord to augment Fees, and fleece their Electors; and that this would not be mended by placing the Choice in the Executive Council, who, with interested or party Views, are continually making as improper Appointments; witness a *'petty Fidler, Sycophant, and Scoundrel,'* appointed Judge of the Admiralty; *'an old Woman and Fomenter of Sedition'* to be another of the Judges, and *'a Jeffries'* Chief Justice, &c. &c.; with *'two Harpies'* the Comptroller and Naval Officers, to prey upon the Merchants and deprive them of their Property by Force of Arms, &c.

"I am inform'd also by these Papers, that your General Assembly, tho' the annual choice of the People, shows no Regard to their Rights, but from sinister Views or Ignorance makes Laws in direct Violation of the Constitution, to divest the Inhabitants of their Property and give it to Strangers and Intruders; and that the Council, either fearing the Resentment of their Constituents, or plotting to enslave them, had projected to disarm them, and given Orders for that purpose; and finally, that your President, the unanimous joint choice of the Council and Assembly, is 'an old Rogue,' who gave his Assent to the federal Constitution merely to avoid refunding Money he had purloin'd from the United States.

"There is, indeed, a good deal of manifest *Inconsistency* in all this, and yet a Stranger, seeing it in your own Prints, tho' he does not believe it all, may probably believe enough of it to conclude, that Pennsylvania is peopled by a Set of the most unprincipled, wicked, rascally, and quarrelsome Scoundrels upon the Face of the Globe. I have sometimes, indeed, suspected, that those Papers are the Manufacture of foreign Enemies among you, who write with a view of disgracing your Country, and making you appear contemptible and detestable all the World over; but then I wonder at the Indiscretion of your Printers in publishing such Writings! There is, however, one of your *Inconsistencies* that consoles me a little, which is, that tho' *living,* you give one another the characters of Devils; *dead,* you are all Angels! It is delightful, when any of you die, to read what good Husbands, good Fathers, good Friends, good Citizens, and good Christians you were, concluding with a Scrap of Poetry that places you, with certainty, every one in Heaven. So that I think Pennsylvania a good country *to dye in,* though a very bad one to *live in.*"

AN ADDRESS
TO THE PUBLIC;

*From the Pennsylvania Society for Promoting
the Abolition of Slavery, and the Relief
of Free Negroes Unlawfully Held in Bondage.*

Philadelphia, 9th of November, 1789.

It is with peculiar satisfaction we assure the friends of human-ity, that, in prosecuting the design of our association, our en-deavours have proved successful, far beyond our most sanguine expectations.

Encouraged by this success, and by the daily progress of that luminous and benign spirit of liberty, which is diffusing itself throughout the world, and humbly hoping for the continu-ance of the divine blessing on our labours, we have ventured to make an important addition to our original plan, and do there-fore earnestly solicit the support and assistance of all who can feel the tender emotions of sympathy and compassion, or relish the exalted pleasure of beneficence.

Slavery is such an atrocious debasement of human nature, that its very extirpation, if not performed with solicitous care, may sometimes open a source of serious evils.

The unhappy man, who has long been treated as a brute ani-mal, too frequently sinks beneath the common standard of the human species. The galling chains, that bind his body, do also fetter his intellectual faculties, and impair the social affections of his heart. Accustomed to move like a mere machine, by the will of a master, reflection is suspended; he has not the power of choice; and reason and conscience have but little influence over his conduct, because he is chiefly governed by the passion of fear. He is poor and friendless; perhaps worn out by extreme labour, age, and disease.

Under such circumstances, freedom may often prove a misfortune to himself, and prejudicial to society.

Attention to emancipated black people, it is therefore to be hoped, will become a branch of our national policy; but, as far as we contribute to promote this emancipation, so far that attention is evidently a serious duty incumbent on us, and which we mean to discharge to the best of our judgment and abilities.

To instruct, to advise, to qualify those, who have been restored to freedom, for the exercise and enjoyment of civil liberty, to promote in them habits of industry, to furnish them with employments suited to their age, sex, talents, and other circumstances, and to procure their children an education calculated for their future situation in life; these are the great outlines of the annexed plan, which we have adopted, and which we conceive will essentially promote the public good, and the happiness of these our hitherto too much neglected fellow-creatures.

A plan so extensive cannot be carried into execution without considerable pecuniary resources, beyond the present ordinary funds of the Society. We hope much from the generosity of enlightened and benevolent freemen, and will gratefully receive any donations or subscriptions for this purpose, which may be made to our treasurer, James Starr, or to James Pemberton, chairman of our committee of correspondence.

Signed, by order of the Society,

B. FRANKLIN, *President.*

PLAN FOR IMPROVING
THE CONDITION OF
THE FREE BLACKS

THE business relative to free blacks shall be transacted by a committee of twenty-four persons, annually elected by ballot, at the meeting of this Society, in the month called April; and, in order to perform the different services with expedition, regularity, and energy, this committee shall resolve itself into the following sub-committees, viz.

I. A Committee of Inspection, who shall superintend the morals, general conduct, and ordinary situation of the free negroes, and afford them advice and instruction, protection from wrongs, and other friendly offices.

II. A Committee of Guardians, who shall place out children and young people with suitable persons, that they may (during a moderate time of apprenticeship or servitude) learn some trade or other business of subsistence. The committee may effect this partly by a persuasive influence on parents and the persons concerned, and partly by coöperating with the laws, which are, or may be, enacted for this and similar purposes. In forming contracts on these occasions, the committee shall secure to the Society, as far as may be practicable, the right of guardianship over the persons so bound.

III. A Committee of Education, who shall superintend the school instruction of the children and youth of the free blacks. They may either influence them to attend regularly the schools already established in this city, or form others with this view; they shall, in either case, provide, that the pupils may receive such learning as is necessary for their future situation in life, and especially a deep impression of the most important and generally acknowledged moral and religious principles. They shall also procure and preserve a regular record of the marriages, births, and manumissions of all free blacks.

IV. A Committee of Employ, who shall endeavour to procure constant employment for those free negroes who are able to work; as the want of this would occasion poverty, idleness, and many vicious habits. This committee will, by sedulous inquiry, be enabled to find common labour for a great number; they will also provide, that such as indicate proper talents may learn various trades, which may be done by prevailing upon them to bind themselves for such a term of years as shall compensate their masters for the expense and trouble of instruction and maintenance. The committee may attempt the institution of some useful and simple manufactures, which require but little skill, and also may assist, in commencing business, such as appear to be qualified for it.

Whenever the committee of inspection shall find persons of any particular description requiring attention, they shall immediately direct them to the committee of whose care they are the proper objects.

In matters of a mixed nature, the committees shall confer, and, if necessary, act in concert. Affairs of great importance shall be referred to the whole committee.

The expense, incurred by the prosecution of this plan, shall be defrayed by a fund, to be formed by donations or subscriptions for these particular purposes, and to be kept separate from the other funds of this Society.

The committee shall make a report of their proceedings, and of the state of their stock, to the Society, at their quarterly meetings, in the months called April and October.

SIDI MEHEMET IBRAHIM ON THE SLAVE TRADE

TO THE EDITOR OF THE
FEDERAL GAZETTE

March 23d, 1790.

Sir,

Reading last night in your excellent Paper the speech of Mr. Jackson in Congress against their meddling with the Affair of Slavery, or attempting to mend the Condition of the Slaves, it put me in mind of a similar One made about 100 Years since by Sidi Mehemet Ibrahim, a member of the Divan of Algiers, which may be seen in Martin's Account of his Consulship, anno 1687. It was against granting the Petition of the Sect called *Erika,* or Purists, who pray'd for the Abolition of Piracy and Slavery as being unjust. Mr. Jackson does not quote it; perhaps he has not seen it. If, therefore, some of its Reasonings are to be found in his eloquent Speech, it may only show that men's Interests and Intellects operate and are operated on with surprising similarity in all Countries and Climates, when under similar Circumstances. The African's Speech, as translated, is as follows.

> *"Allah Bismillah, &c.*
> *God is great, and Mahomet is his Prophet.*

"Have these *Erika* considered the Consequences of granting their Petition? If we cease our Cruises against the Christians, how shall we be furnished with the Commodities their Countries produce, and which are so necessary for us? If we forbear to make Slaves of their People, who in this hot Climate are to cultivate our Lands? Who are to perform the common Labours of our City, and in our Families? Must we not then be our own Slaves? And is there not more Compassion and more Favour due to us as Mussulmen, than to these Christian Dogs? We have now above 50,000 Slaves in and near Algiers. This Number, if not kept up by fresh Supplies, will soon diminish, and be gradually annihilated. If we then cease taking and plundering the Infidel Ships, and making Slaves of the Seamen and Passengers, our Lands will become of no Value for want of Cultivation; the Rents of Houses in the City will sink one half; and the Revenues of Government arising from its Share of Prizes be totally destroy'd! And for what? To gratify the whims of a whimsical Sect, who would have us, not only forbear making more Slaves, but even to manumit those we have.

"But who is to indemnify their Masters for the Loss? Will the State do it? Is our Treasury sufficient? Will the *Erika* do it? Can they do it? Or would they, to do what they think Justice to the Slaves, do a greater Injustice to the Owners? And if we set our Slaves free, what is to be done with them? Few of them will return to their Countries; they know too well the greater Hardships they must there be subject to; they will not embrace our holy Religion; they will not adopt our Manners; our People will not pollute themselves by intermarrying with them. Must we maintain them as Beggars in our Streets, or suffer our Properties to be the Prey of their Pillage? For Men long accustom'd to Slavery will not work for a Livelihood when not compell'd. And what is there so pitiable in their present Condition? Were they not Slaves in their own Countries?

"Are not Spain, Portugal, France, and the Italian states govern'd by Despots, who hold all their Subjects in Slavery, without Exception? Even England treats its Sailors as Slaves; for they are, whenever the Government pleases, seiz'd, and confin'd in Ships of War, condemn'd not only to work, but to fight, for small Wages, or a mere Subsistence, not better than our Slaves are allow'd by us. Is their Condition then made worse by their falling into our Hands? No; they have only exchanged one Slavery for another, and I may say a better; for here they are brought into a Land where the Sun of Islamism gives forth its Light, and shines in full Splendor, and they have an Opportunity of making themselves acquainted with the true Doctrine, and thereby saving their immortal Souls. Those who remain at home have not that Happiness. Sending the Slaves home then would be sending them out of Light into Darkness.

"I repeat the Question, What is to be done with them? I have heard it suggested, that they may be planted in the Wilderness, where there is plenty of Land for them to subsist on, and where they may flourish as a free State; but they are, I doubt, too little dispos'd to labour without Compulsion, as well as too ignorant to establish a good government, and the wild Arabs would soon molest and destroy or again enslave them. While serving us, we take care to provide them with every thing, and they are treated with Humanity. The Labourers in their own Country are, as I am well informed, worse fed, lodged, and cloathed. The Condition of most of them is therefore already mended, and requires no further Improvement. Here their Lives are in Safety. They are not liable to be impress'd for Soldiers, and forc'd to cut one another's Christian Throats, as in the Wars of their own Countries. If some of the religious mad Bigots, who now teaze us with their silly Petitions, have in a Fit of blind Zeal freed their Slaves, it was not Generosity, it was not Humanity, that mov'd them to the Action; it was from the conscious Burthen of a Load of Sins, and Hope, from the supposed Merits of so good a Work, to be excus'd Damnation.

"How grossly are they mistaken in imagining Slavery to be disallow'd by the Alcoran! Are not the two Precepts, to quote no more, *'Masters, treat your Slaves with kindness; Slaves, serve your Masters with Cheerfulness and Fidelity,'* clear Proofs to the contrary? Nor can the Plundering of Infidels be in that sacred Book forbidden, since it is well known from it, that God has given the World, and all that it contains, to his faithful Mussulmen, who are to enjoy it of Right as fast as they conquer it. Let us then hear no more of this detestable Proposition, the Manumission of Christian Slaves, the Adoption of which

would, by depreciating our Lands and Houses, and thereby depriving so many good Citizens of their Properties, create universal Discontent, and provoke Insurrections, to the endangering of
Government and producing general Confusion. I have therefore
no doubt, but this wise Council will prefer the Comfort and
Happiness of a whole Nation of true Believers to the Whim of a
few *Erika,* and dismiss their Petition."

The Result was, as Martin tells us, that the Divan came to this
Resolution; "The Doctrine, that Plundering and Enslaving the
Christians is unjust, is at best *problematical;* but that it is the Interest of this State to continue the Practice, is clear; therefore let
the Petition be rejected."

And it was rejected accordingly.

And since like Motives are apt to produce in the Minds of
Men like Opinions and Resolutions, may we not, Mr. Brown,
venture to predict, from this Account, that the Petitions to the
Parliament of England for abolishing the Slave-Trade, to say
nothing of other Legislatures, and the Debates upon them, will
have a similar Conclusion? I am, Sir, your constant Reader and
humble Servant,

HISTORICUS.

PART IV

RELIGION: BELIEF
AND CRITIQUE

A DISSERTATION ON LIBERTY AND NECESSITY, PLEASURE AND PAIN[1]

Whatever is, is in its Causes just
Since all Things are by Fate; but purblind Man
Sees but a part o' th' Chain, the nearest Link,
His Eyes not carrying to the equal Beam
That poises all above.

Dryd.

TO MR. *J. R.*

London, 1725

SIR,

I have here, according to your Request, given you my *present* Thoughts of the *general State of Things* in the Universe. Such as they are, you have them, and are welcome to 'em; and if they yield you any Pleasure or Satisfaction, I shall think my Trouble sufficiently compensated. I know my Scheme will be liable to many Objections from a less discerning Reader than your self; but it is not design'd for those who can't understand it. I need not give you any Caution to distinguish the hypothetical Parts of the Argument from the conclusive: You will easily perceive what I design for Demonstration, and what for Probability only. The whole I leave entirely to you, and shall value my self more or less on this account, in proportion to your Esteem and Approbation.

SECT. I. *Of* Liberty *and* Necessity.

I. *There is said to be a* First Mover, *who is called* GOD, *Maker of the Universe.*

II. *He is said to be all-wise, all-good, all powerful.*

These two Propositions being allow'd and asserted by People of almost every Sect and Opinion; I have here suppos'd them granted, and laid them down as the Foundation of my Argument; What follows then, being a Chain of Consequences truly drawn from them, will stand or fall as they are true or false.

III. *If He is all-good, whatsoever He doth must be good.*

IV. *If He is all-wise, whatsoever He doth must be wise.*

The Truth of these Propositions, with relation to the two first, I think may be justly call'd evident; since, either that infinite Goodness will act what is ill, or infinite Wisdom what is not wise, is too glaring a Contradiction not to be perceiv'd by any Man of common Sense, and deny'd as soon as understood.

V. *If He is all-powerful, there can be nothing either existing or acting in the Universe against or without his Consent; and what He consents to must be good, because He is good; therefore Evil doth not exist.*

Unde Malum? has been long a Question, and many of the Learned have perplex'd themselves and Readers to little Purpose in Answer to it. That there are both Things and Actions to which we give the Name of *Evil,* is not here deny'd, as *Pain, Sickness, Want, Theft, Murder,* &c. but that these and the like are not in reality *Evils, Ills,* or *Defects* in the Order of the Universe, is demonstrated in the next Section, as well as by this and the following Proposition. Indeed, to suppose any Thing to exist or be done, *contrary* to the Will of the Almighty, is to suppose him not almighty; or that Something (the Cause of *Evil*) is more mighty than the Almighty; an Inconsistence that I think no One will defend: And to deny any Thing or Action, which he consents to the existence of, to be good, is entirely to destroy his two Attributes of *Wisdom* and *Goodness.*

There is nothing done in the Universe, say the Philosophers, *but what God either does, or* permits *to be done.* This, as He is Almighty, is certainly true: But what need of this Distinction between *doing* and *permitting?* Why, first they take it for granted that many Things in the Universe exist in such a Manner as is not for the best, and that many Actions are done which ought not to be done, or would be better undone; these Things or Actions they cannot ascribe to God as His, because they have already attributed to Him infinite Wisdom and Goodness; Here then is the Use of the Word *Permit;* He *permits* them to be done, *say they.* But we will reason thus: If God permits an Action to be done, it is because he wants either *Power* or *Inclination* to hinder it; in saying he wants *Power,* we deny Him to be *almighty;* and if we say He wants *Inclination* or *Will,* it must be, either because He is not Good, or the Action is not *evil,* (for all Evil is contrary to the Essence of *infinite Goodness.*) The former is inconsistent with his before-given Attribute of Goodness, therefore the latter must be true.

It will be said, perhaps, that *God permits evil Actions to be done, for* wise *Ends and Purposes.* But this Objection destroys itself; for whatever an infinitely good God hath wise Ends in suffering to *be,* must be good, is thereby made good, and cannot be otherwise.

VI. *If a Creature is made by God, it must depend upon God, and receive all its Power from Him; with which Power the Creature can do nothing contrary to the Will of God, because God is Almighty; what is not contrary to His Will, must be agreeable to it; what is agreeable to it, must be good, because He is Good; therefore a Creature can do nothing but what is good.*

This Proposition is much to the same Purpose with the former, but more particular; and its Conclusion is as just and evident. Tho' a Creature may do many Actions which by his Fellow Creatures will be nam'd *Evil,* and which will naturally and necessarily cause or bring upon the Doer, certain *Pains* (which will likewise be call'd *Punishments;*) yet this Proposition proves, that he cannot act what will be in itself really Ill, or displeasing to God. And that the painful Consequences of his evil Actions (*so call'd*) are not, as indeed they ought not to be, *Punishments* or Unhappinesses, will be shewn hereafter.

Nevertheless, the late learned Author of *The Religion of Nature,* (which I send you herewith) has given us a Rule or Scheme, whereby to discover which of our Actions ought to be esteem'd and denominated *good,* and which *evil*: It is in short this, "Every Action which is done according to *Truth,* is good; and every Action contrary to Truth, is evil: To act according to Truth is to use and esteem every Thing as what it is, *&c.* Thus if *A* steals a Horse from *B,* and rides away upon him, he uses him not as what he is in Truth, *viz.* the Property of another, but as his own, which is contrary to Truth, and therefore *evil*". But, as this Gentleman himself says, (Sect. I. Prop. VI.) "In order to judge rightly what any Thing is, it must be consider'd, not only what it is in one Respect, but also what it may be in any other Respect; and the whole Description of the Thing ought to be taken in:" So in this Case it ought to be consider'd, that *A* is naturally a *covetous* Being, feeling an Uneasiness in the want of *B*'s Horse, which produces an Inclination for stealing him, stronger than his Fear of Punishment for so doing. This is *Truth* likewise, and *A* acts according to it when he steals the Horse. Besides, if it is prov'd to be a *Truth,* that *A* has not Power over his own Actions, it will be indisputable that he acts according to Truth, and impossible he should do otherwise.

I would not be understood by this to encourage or defend Theft; 'tis only for the sake of the Argument, and will certainly have no *ill Effect*. The Order and Course of Things will not be affected by Reasoning of this Kind; and 'tis as just and necessary, and as much according to Truth, for *B* to dislike and punish the Theft of his Horse, as it is for *A* to steal him.

VII. *If the Creature is thus limited in his Actions, being able to do only such Things as God would have him to do, and not being able to refuse doing what God would have done; then he can have no such Thing as Liberty, Free-will or Power to do or refrain an Action.*

By *Liberty* is sometimes understood the Absence of Opposition; and in this Sense, indeed, all our Actions may be said to be the Effects of our Liberty: But it is a Liberty of the same Nature with the Fall of a heavy Body to the Ground; it has Liberty to fall, that is, it meets with nothing to hinder its Fall, but at the same Time it is necessitated to fall, and has no Power or Liberty to remain suspended.

But let us take the Argument in another View, and suppose ourselves to be, in the common sense of the Word, *Free Agents.* As Man is a Part of this great Machine, the Universe, his regular Acting is requisite to the regular moving of the whole. Among the many Things which lie before him to be done, he may, as he is at Liberty and his Choice influenc'd by nothing, (for so it must be, or he is not at Liberty) chuse any one, and refuse the rest. Now there is every Moment something *best* to be done, which is alone then *good,* and with respect to which, every Thing else is at that Time *evil.* In order to know which is best to be done, and which not, it is requisite that we should have at one View all the intricate Consequences of every Action with respect to the general Order and Scheme of the Universe, both present and future; but they are innumerable and incomprehensible by any Thing but Omniscience. As we cannot know these, we have but as one Chance to ten thousand, to hit on the right Action; we should then be perpetually blundering about in the Dark, and putting the Scheme in Disorder; for every wrong Action of a Part, is a Defect or Blemish in the Order of the Whole. Is it not necessary then, that our Actions should be over-rul'd and govern'd by an all-wise Providence?—How exact and regular is every Thing in the *natural* World! How wisely in every Part contriv'd! We cannot here find the least Defect! Those who have study'd the mere animal and vegetable Creation, demonstrate that nothing can be more harmonious and beautiful! All the heavenly Bodies, the Stars and Planets, are regulated with the utmost Wisdom! And can we suppose less Care to be taken in the Order of the *moral* than in the *natural* System? It is as if an ingenious Artificer, having fram'd a curious Machine or Clock, and put its many intricate Wheels and Powers in such a Dependance on one another, that the whole might move in the most exact Order and Regularity, had nevertheless plac'd in it several other Wheels endu'd with an independent *Self-Motion*, but ignorant of the general Interest of the Clock; and these would every now and then be moving wrong, disordering the true Movement, and making continual Work for the Mender; which might better be prevented, by depriving them of that Power of Self-Motion, and placing them in a Dependance on the regular Part of the Clock.

VIII. *If there is no such Thing as Free-Will in Creatures, there can be neither Merit nor Demerit in Creatures.*

IX. *And therefore every Creature must be equally esteem'd by the Creator.*

These Propositions appear to be the necessary Consequences of the former. And certainly no Reason can be given, why the Creator should prefer in his Esteem one Part of His Works to another, if with equal Wisdom and Goodness he design'd and created them all, since all Ill or Defect, as contrary to his Nature, is excluded by his Power. We will sum up the Argument thus, When the Creator first design'd the Universe, either it was His Will and Intention that all Things should exist and be in the Manner they are at this Time; or it was his Will they should *be* otherwise *i.e.* in a different Manner: To say it was His Will Things should be otherwise than they are, is to say Somewhat hath contradicted His Will, and broken His Measures, which is impossible because inconsistent with his Power; therefore we must allow that all Things exist now in a Manner agreeable to His Will, and in consequence of that are all equally Good, and therefore equally esteem'd by Him.

I proceed now to shew, that as all the Works of the Creator are equally esteem'd by Him, so they are, as in Justice they ought to be, equally us'd.

Sect. II. *Of* Pleasure *and* Pain.

I. *When a Creature is form'd and endu'd with Life, 'tis suppos'd to receive a Capacity of the Sensation of* Uneasiness *or* Pain.

It is this distinguishes Life and Consciousness from unactive unconscious Matter. To know or be sensible of Suffering or being acted upon is *to live;* and whatsoever is not so, among created Things, is properly and truly *dead.*

All *Pain* and *Uneasiness* proceeds at first from and is caus'd by Somewhat without and distinct from the Mind itself. The Soul must first be acted upon before it can re-act. In the Beginning of Infancy it is as if it were not; it is not conscious of its own Existence, till it has receiv'd the first Sensation of *Pain;* then, and not before, it begins to feel itself, is rous'd, and put into Action; then it discovers its Powers and Faculties, and exerts them to expel the Uneasiness. Thus is the Machine set on work; this is Life. We are first mov'd by *Pain,* and the whole succeeding Course of our Lives is but one continu'd Series of Action with a View to be freed from it. As fast as we have excluded one Uneasiness another appears, otherwise the Motion would cease. If a continual Weight is not apply'd, the Clock will stop. And as soon as the Avenues of Uneasiness to the Soul are choak'd up or cut off, we are dead, we think and act no more.

II. *This Uneasiness, whenever felt, produces* Desire *to be freed from it, great in exact proportion to the Uneasiness.*

Thus is *Uneasiness* the first Spring and Cause of all Action; for till we are uneasy in Rest, we can have no Desire to move, and without Desire of moving there can be no voluntary Motion. The Experience of every Man who has observ'd his own Actions will evince the Truth of this; and I think nothing need be said to prove that the *Desire* will be equal to the *Uneasiness,* for the very Thing implies as much: It is not *Uneasiness* unless we desire to be freed from it, nor a great *Uneasiness* unless the consequent Desire is great.

I might here observe, how necessary a Thing in the Order and Design of the Universe this *Pain* or *Uneasiness* is, and how beautiful in its Place! Let us but suppose it just now banish'd the World entirely, and consider the Consequence of it: All the Animal Creation would immediately stand stock still, exactly in the Posture they were in the Moment Uneasiness departed; not a Limb, not a Finger would henceforth move; we should all be reduc'd to the Condition of Statues, dull and unactive: Here I should continue to sit motionless with the Pen in my Hand thus —— and neither leave my Seat nor write one Letter more. This may appear odd at first View, but a little Consideration will make it evident; for 'tis impossible to assign any other Cause for the voluntary Motion of an Animal than its *uneasiness* in Rest. What a different Appearance then would the Face of Nature make, without it! How necessary is it! And how unlikely that the Inhabitants of the World ever were, or that the Creator ever design'd they should be, exempt from it!

I would likewise observe here, that the VIIIth Proposition in the preceding Section, viz. *That there is neither Merit nor Demerit,* &c. is here again demonstrated, as infallibly, tho' in another manner: For since *Freedom from Uneasiness* is the End of all our Actions, how is it possible for us to do any Thing disinterested?—How can any Action be meritorious of Praise or Dispraise, Reward or Punishment, when the natural Principle of *Self-Love* is the only and the irresistible Motive to it?

III. *This* Desire *is always fulfill'd or satisfy'd,*

In the *Design* or *End* of it, tho' not in the *Manner:* The first is requisite, the latter not. To exemplify this, let us make a Supposition; A Person is confin'd in a House which appears to be in imminent Danger of Falling, this, as soon as perceiv'd, creates a violent *Uneasiness,* and that instantly produces an equal strong *Desire,* the *End* of which is *freedom from the Uneasiness,* and the *Manner* or Way propos'd to gain this *End,* is *to get out of the House.* Now if he is convinc'd by any Means, that he is mistaken, and the House is not likely to fall, he is immediately freed from his *Uneasiness,* and the *End* of his Desire is attain'd as well as if it had been in the *Manner* desir'd, viz. *leaving the House.*

All our different Desires and Passions proceed from and are reducible to this one Point, *Uneasiness,* tho' the Means we propose to ourselves for expelling of it are infinite. One proposes *Fame,* another *Wealth,* a third *Power,* &c. as the Means to gain this *End;* but tho' these are never attain'd, if the Uneasiness be remov'd by some other Means, the *Desire* is satisfy'd. Now during the Course of Life we are ourselves continually removing successive Uneasinesses as they arise, and the *last* we suffer is remov'd by the *sweet Sleep* of Death.

IV. *The fulfilling or Satisfaction of this* Desire, *produces the Sensation of* Pleasure, *great or small in exact proportion to the* Desire.

Pleasure is that Satisfaction which arises in the Mind upon, and is caus'd by, the accomplishment of our *Desires,* and by no other Means at all; and those Desires being above shewn to be caus'd by our *Pains* or *Uneasinesses,* it follows that *Pleasure* is wholly caus'd by *Pain,* and by no other Thing at all.

V. *Therefore the Sensation of* Pleasure *is equal, or in exact proportion to the Sensation of* Pain.

As the *Desire* of being freed from Uneasiness is equal to the *Uneasiness,* and the *Pleasure* of satisfying that Desire equal to the *Desire,* the *Pleasure* thereby produc'd must necessarily be equal to the *Uneasiness* or *Pain* which produces it: Of three Lines, *A, B,* and *C,* if *A* is equal to *B,* and *B* to *C, C* must be equal to *A.* And as our *Uneasinesses* are always remov'd by some Means or other, it follows that *Pleasure* and *Pain* are in their Nature inseparable: So many Degrees as one Scale of the Ballance descends, so many exactly the other ascends; and one cannot rise or fall without the Fall or Rise of the other: 'Tis impossible to taste of *Pleasure,* without feeling its preceding proportionate *Pain;* or to be sensible of *Pain,* without having its necessary Consequent *Pleasure:* The *highest Pleasure* is only

Consciousness of Freedom from the *deepest Pain,* and Pain is not Pain to us unless we ourselves are sensible of it. They go Hand in Hand; they cannot be divided.

You have a View of the whole Argument in a few familiar Examples: The *Pain* of Abstinence from Food, as it is greater or less, produces a greater of less *Desire* of Eating, the Accomplishment of this *Desire* produces a greater or less *Pleasure* proportionate to it. The *Pain* of Confinement causes the *Desire* of Liberty, which accomplish'd, yields a *Pleasure* equal to that *Pain* of Confinement. The *Pain* of Labour and Fatigue causes the *Pleasure* of Rest, equal to that *Pain.* The *Pain* of Absence from Friends, produces the *Pleasure* of Meeting in exact proportion. *&c.*

This is the *fixt Nature* of Pleasure and Pain, and will always be found to be so by those who examine it.

One of the most common Arguments for the future Existence of the Soul, is taken from the generally suppos'd Inequality of Pain and Pleasure in the present; and this, notwithstanding the Difficulty by outward Appearances to make a Judgment of another's Happiness, has been look'd upon as almost unanswerable: but since *Pain* naturally and infallibly produces a *Pleasure* in proportion to it, every individual Creature must, in any State of *Life,* have an equal Quantity of each, so that there is not, on that Account, any Occasion for a future Adjustment.

Thus are all the Works of the Creator *equally* us'd by him; And no Condition of Life or Being is in itself better or preferable to another: The Monarch is not more happy than the Slave, nor the Beggar more miserable than *Crœsus.* Suppose *A, B,* and *C,* three distinct Beings; *A* and *B,* animate, capable of *Pleasure* and *Pain, C* an inanimate Piece of Matter, insensible of either. *A* receives ten Degrees of *Pain,* which are necessarily succeeded by ten Degrees of *Pleasure: B* receives fifteen of *Pain,* and the consequent equal Number of *Pleasure: C* all the while lies unconcern'd, and as he has not suffer'd the former, has no right to the latter. What can be more equal and just than this? When the Accounts come to be adjusted, *A* has no Reason to complain that his Portion of *Pleasure* was five Degrees less than

that of *B,* for his Portion of *Pain* was five Degrees less likewise:
Nor has *B* any Reason to boast that his *Pleasure* was five Degrees greater than that of *A,* for his *Pain* was proportionate:
They are then both on the same Foot with *C,* that is, they are
neither Gainers nor Losers.

It will possibly be objected here, that even common Experience shews us, there is not in Fact this Equality: "Some we see
hearty, brisk and chearful perpetually, while others are constantly burden'd with a heavy Load of Maladies and Misfortunes, remaining for Years perhaps in Poverty, Disgrace, or
Pain, and die at last without any Appearance of Recompence."
Now tho' 'tis not necessary, when a Proposition is demonstrated to be a general Truth, to shew in what manner it agrees
with the particular Circumstances of Persons, and indeed ought
not to be requir'd; yet, as this is a common Objection, some
Notice may be taken of it: And here let it be observ'd, that we
cannot be proper Judges of the good or bad Fortune of Others;
we are apt to imagine, that what would give us a great Uneasiness or a great Satisfaction, has the same Effect upon others: we
think, for Instance, those unhappy, who must depend upon
Charity for a mean Subsistence, who go in Rags, fare hardly,
and are despis'd and scorn'd by all; not considering that Custom renders all these Things easy, familiar, and even pleasant.
When we see Riches, Grandeur and a chearful Countenance, we
easily imagine Happiness accompanies them, when oftentimes
'tis quite otherwise: Nor is a constantly sorrowful Look, attended with continual Complaints, an infallible Indication of
Unhappiness. In short, we can judge by nothing but Appearances, and they are very apt to deceive us. Some put on a gay
chearful Outside, and appear to the World perfectly at Ease,
tho' even then, some inward Sting, some secret Pain imbitters
all their Joys, and makes the Ballance even: Others appear continually dejected and full of Sorrow; but even Grief itself is
sometimes *pleasant,* and Tears are not always without their
Sweetness: Besides, Some take a Satisfaction in being thought
unhappy, (as others take a Pride in being thought humble,)
these will paint their Misfortunes to others in the strongest
Colours, and leave no Means unus'd to make you think them

thoroughly miserable; so great a *Pleasure* it is to them *to be pitied;* Others retain the Form and outside Shew of Sorrow, long after the Thing itself, with its Cause, is remov'd from the Mind; it is a Habit they have acquir'd and cannot leave. These, with many others that might be given, are Reasons why we cannot make a true Estimate of the *Equality* of the Happiness and Unhappiness of others; and unless we could, Matter of Fact cannot be opposed to this Hypothesis. Indeed, we are sometimes apt to think, that the Uneasinesses we ourselves have had, outweigh our Pleasures; but the Reason is this, the Mind takes no Account of the latter, they slip away un-remark'd, when the former leave more lasting Impressions on the Memory. But suppose we pass the greatest part of Life in Pain and Sorrow, suppose we die by Torments and *think no more,* 'tis no Diminution to the Truth of what is here advanc'd; for the *Pain,* tho' exquisite, is not so to the *last* Moments of Life, the Senses are soon benumm'd, and render'd incapable of transmitting it so sharply to the Soul as at first; She perceives it cannot hold long, and 'tis an *exquisite Pleasure* to behold the immediate Approaches of Rest. This makes an Equivalent tho' Annihilation should follow: For the Quantity of *Pleasure* and *Pain* is not to be measur'd by its Duration, any more than the Quantity of Matter by its Extension; and as one cubic Inch may be made to contain, by Condensation, as much Matter as would fill ten thousand cubic Feet, being more expanded, so one single Moment of *Pleasure* may outweigh and compensate an Age of *Pain.*

It was owing to their Ignorance of the Nature of Pleasure and Pain that the Antient Heathens believ'd the idle Fable of their *Elizium,* that State of uninterrupted Ease and Happiness! The Thing is intirely impossible in Nature! Are not the Pleasures of the Spring made such by the Disagreeableness of the Winter? Is not the Pleasure of fair Weather owing to the Unpleasantness of foul? Certainly. Were it then always Spring, were the Fields always green and flourishing, and the Weather constantly serene and fair, the Pleasure would pall and die upon our Hands; it would cease to be Pleasure to us, when it is not usher'd in by Uneasiness. Could the Philosopher visit, in reality, every Star and Planet with as much Ease and Swiftness as he can now visit their Ideas, and pass from one to another of them in the Imagination; it would be a *Pleasure* I grant; but it would be only in proportion to the *Desire* of accomplishing it, and that would be no greater than the *Uneasiness* suffer'd in the Want of it. The Accomplishment of a long and difficult Journey yields a great *Pleasure;* but if we could take a Trip to the Moon and back again, as frequently and with as much Ease as we can go and come from Market, the Satisfaction would be just the same.

The *Immateriality* of the Soul has been frequently made use of as an Argument for its *Immortality;* but let us consider, that tho' it should be allow'd to be immaterial, and consequently its Parts incapable of Separation or Destruction by any Thing material, yet by Experience we find, that it is not incapable of Cessation of *Thought,* which is its Action. When the Body is but a little indispos'd it has an evident Effect upon the Mind; and a right Disposition of the Organs is requisite to a right Manner of Thinking. In a sound Sleep sometimes, or in a Swoon, we cease to think at all; tho' the Soul is not therefore then annihilated, but *exists* all the while tho' it does not *act;* and may not this probably be the Case after Death? All our Ideas are first admitted by the Senses and imprinted on the Brain, increasing in Number by Observation and Experience; there they become the Subjects of the Soul's Action. The Soul is a mere Power or Faculty of *contemplating* on, and *comparing* those Ideas when it has them; hence springs Reason: But as it can *think* on nothing but Ideas, it must have them before it can *think* at all. Therefore as it may exist before it has receiv'd any Ideas, it may exist before it *thinks*. To remember a Thing, is to have the Idea of it still plainly imprinted on the Brain, which the Soul can turn to and contemplate on Occasion. To forget a Thing, is to have the Idea of it defac'd and destroy'd by some Accident, or the crouding in and imprinting of great variety of other Ideas upon it, so that the Soul cannot find out its Traces and distinguish it. When we have thus lost the Idea of any one Thing, we can *think* no more, or *cease to think,* on that Thing; and as we can lose the Idea of one Thing, so we may of ten, twenty, a hundred, *&c.* and even of all Things, because they are not in their Nature permanent; and often during Life we see that some Men, (by an Accident or Distemper affecting the

Brain,) lose the greatest Part of their Ideas, and remember very little of their past Actions and Circumstances. Now upon *Death*, and the Destruction of the Body, the Ideas contain'd in the Brain, (which are alone the Subjects of the Soul's Action) being then likewise necessarily destroy'd, the Soul, tho' incapable of Destruction itself, must then necessarily *cease to think* or *act*, having nothing left to think or act upon. It is reduc'd to its first inconscious State before it receiv'd any Ideas. And to cease to *think* is but little different from *ceasing to be*.

Nevertheless, 'tis not impossible that this same *Faculty* of contemplating Ideas may be hereafter united to a new Body, and receive a new Set of Ideas; but that will no way concern us who are now living; for the Identity will be lost, it is no longer that same *Self* but a new Being.

I shall here subjoin a short Recapitulation of the Whole, that it may with all its Parts be comprehended at one View.

1. *It is suppos'd that God the Maker and Governour of the Universe, is infinitely wise, good, and powerful.*

2. *In consequence of His infinite Wisdom and Goodness, it is asserted, that whatever He doth must be infinitely wise and good;*

3. *Unless He be interrupted, and His Measures broken by some other Being, which is impossible because He is Almighty.*

4. *In consequence of His infinite Power, it is asserted, that nothing can exist or be done in the Universe which is not agreeable to His Will, and therefore good.*

5. *Evil is hereby excluded, with all Merit and Demerit; and likewise all preference in the Esteem of God, of one Part of the Creation to another.* This is the Summary of the first Part.

Now our common Notions of Justice will tell us, that if all created Things are equally esteem'd by the Creator, they ought to be equally us'd by Him; and that they are therefore equally us'd, we might embrace for Truth upon the Credit, and as the true consequence of the foregoing Argument. Nevertheless we proceed to confirm it, by shewing *how* they are equally us'd, and that in the following Manner.

1. *A Creature when endu'd with Life or Consciousness, is made capable of Uneasiness or Pain.*

2. *This Pain produces Desire to be freed from it, in exact proportion to itself.*

3. *The Accomplishment of this Desire produces an equal Pleasure.*

4. *Pleasure is consequently equal to Pain.*

From these Propositions it is observ'd,

1. *That every Creature hath as much Pleasure as Pain.*

2. *That Life is not preferable to Insensibility; for Pleasure and Pain destroy one another: That Being which has ten Degrees of Pain subtracted from ten of Pleasure, has nothing remaining, and is upon an equality with that Being which is insensible of both.*

3. *As the first Part proves that all Things must be equally us'd by the Creator because equally esteem'd; so this second Part demonstrates that they are equally esteem'd because equally us'd.*

4. *Since every Action is the Effect of Self-Uneasiness, the Distinction of Virtue and Vice is excluded; and* Prop. VIII. *in* Sect. I. *again demonstrated.*

5. *No State of Life can be happier than the present, because Pleasure and Pain are inseparable.*

Thus both Parts of this Argument agree with and confirm one another, and the Demonstration is reciprocal.

I am sensible that the Doctrine here advanc'd, if it were to be publish'd, would meet with but an indifferent Reception. Mankind naturally and generally love to be flatter'd: Whatever sooths our Pride, and tends to exalt our Species above the rest of the Creation, we are pleas'd with and easily believe, when ungrateful Truths shall be with the utmost Indignation rejected. "What! bring ourselves down to an Equality with the Beasts of the Field! with the *meanest* part of the Creation! 'Tis insufferable!" But, (to use a Piece of *common* Sense) our *Geese* are but *Geese* tho' we may think 'em *Swans;* and Truth will be Truth tho' it sometimes prove mortifying and distasteful.

TO JOSIAH FRANKLIN

HONOURED FATHER,

I have your favours of the 21st of March, in which you both seem concerned lest I have imbibed some erroneous opinions. Doubtless I have my share; and when the natural weakness and imperfection of human understanding is considered, the unavoidable influence of education, custom, books, and company upon our ways of thinking, I imagine a man must have a good deal of vanity who believes, and a good deal of boldness who affirms, that all the doctrines he holds are true, and all he rejects are false. And perhaps the same may be justly said of every sect, church, and society of men, when they assume to themselves that infallibility, which they deny to the Pope and councils.

I think opinions should be judged of by their influences and effects; and, if a man holds none that tend to make him less virtuous or more vicious, it may be concluded he holds none that are dangerous; which I hope is the case with me.

I am sorry you should have any uneasiness on my account; and if it were a thing possible for one to alter his opinions in order to please another, I know none whom I ought more willingly to oblige in that respect than yourselves. But, since it is no more in a man's power to *think* than to *look* like another, methinks all that should be expected from me is to keep my mind open to conviction, to hear patiently and examine attentively, whatever is offered me for that end; and, if after all I continue in the same errors, I believe your usual charity will induce you to rather pity and excuse, than blame me. In the mean time your care and concern for me is what I am very thankful for.

My mother grieves, that one of her sons is an Arian, another an Arminian. What an Arminian or an Arian is, I cannot say that I very well know. The truth is, I make such distinctions very little my study. I think vital religion has always suffered, when orthodoxy is more regarded than virtue; and the Scriptures assure me, that at the last day we shall not be examined what we *thought,* but what we *did;* and our recommendation will not be, that we said, *Lord! Lord!* but that we did good to our fellow creatures. See Matt. xxv.

As to the freemasons, I know no way of giving my mother a better account of them than she seems to have at present, since it is not allowed that women should be admitted into that secret society. She has, I must confess, on that account some reason to be displeased with it; but for any thing else, I must entreat her to suspend her judgment till she is better informed, unless she will believe me, when I assure her that they are in general a very harmless sort of people, and have no principles or practices that are inconsistent with religion and good manners.

We have had great rains here lately, which, with the thawing of snow on the mountains back of our country, have made vast floods in our rivers, and, by carrying away bridges, boats, &c., made travelling almost impracticable for a week past; so that our post has entirely missed making one trip.

I hear nothing of Dr. Crook, nor can I learn any such person has ever been here.

I hope my sister Jenny's child is by this time recovered. I am your dutiful son.

B. FRANKLIN.

TO JOSEPH HUEY

Philadelphia, June 6, 1753.

SIR,

    I received your kind Letter of the 2d inst., and am glad to hear that you increase in Strength; I hope you will continue mending, 'till you recover your former Health and firmness. Let me know whether you still use the Cold Bath, and what Effect it has.

    As to the Kindness you mention, I wish it could have been of more Service to you. But if it had, the only Thanks I should desire is, that you would always be equally ready to serve any other Person that may need your Assistance, and so let good Offices go round, for Mankind are all of a Family.

    For my own Part, when I am employed in serving others, I do not look upon myself as conferring Favours, but as paying Debts. In my Travels, and since my Settlement, I have received much Kindness from Men, to whom I shall never have any Opportunity of making the least direct Return. And numberless Mercies from God, who is infinitely above being benefited by our Services. Those Kindnesses from Men, I can therefore only Return on their Fellow Men; and I can only shew my Gratitude for these mercies from God, by a readiness to help his other Children and my Brethren. For I do not think that Thanks and Compliments, tho' repeated weekly, can discharge our real Obligations to each other, and much less those to our Creator. You will see in this my Notion of good Works, that I am far from expecting to merit Heaven by them. By Heaven we understand a State of Happiness, infinite in Degree, and eternal in

Duration: I can do nothing to deserve such rewards: He that for giving a Draught of Water to a thirsty Person, should expect to be paid with a good Plantation, would be modest in his Demands, compar'd with those who think they deserve Heaven for the little good they do on Earth. Even the mix'd imperfect Pleasures we enjoy in this World, are rather from God's Goodness than our Merit; how much more such Happiness of Heaven. For my own part I have not the Vanity to think I deserve it, the Folly to expect it, nor the Ambition to desire it; but content myself in submitting to the Will and Disposal of that God who made me, who has hitherto preserv'd and bless'd me, and in whose Fatherly Goodness I may well confide, that he will never make me miserable, and that even the Afflictions I may at any time suffer shall tend to my Benefit.

The Faith you mention has doubtless its use in the World. I do not desire to see it diminished, nor would I endeavour to lessen it in any Man. But I wish it were more productive of good Works, than I have generally seen it: I mean real good Works, Works of Kindness, Charity, Mercy, and Publick Spirit; not Holiday-keeping, Sermon-Reading or Hearing; performing Church Ceremonies, or making long Prayers, filled with Flatteries and Compliments, despis'd even by wise Men, and much less capable of pleasing the Deity. The worship of God is a Duty; the hearing and reading of Sermons may be useful; but, if Men rest in Hearing and Praying, as too many do, it is as if a Tree should Value itself on being water'd and putting forth Leaves, tho' it never produc'd any Fruit.

Your great Master tho't much less of these outward Appearances and Professions than many of his modern Disciples. He prefer'd the *Doers* of the Word, to the meer *Hearers;* the Son that seemingly refus'd to obey his Father, and yet perform'd his Commands, to him that profess'd his Readiness, but neglected the Work; the heretical but charitable Samaritan, to the uncharitable tho' orthodox Priest and sanctified Levite; & those who gave Food to the hungry, Drink to the Thirsty, Raiment to the Naked, Entertainment to the Stranger, and Relief to the Sick, tho' they never heard of his Name, he declares shall in the last Day be accepted, when those who cry Lord! Lord! who value themselves on their Faith, tho' great enough to perform Miracles, but have neglected good Works, shall be rejected. He profess'd, that he came not to call the Righteous but Sinners to repentance; which imply'd his modest Opinion, that there were some in his Time so good, that they need not hear even him for Improvement; but now-a-days we have scarce a little Parson, that does not think it the Duty of every Man within his Reach to sit under his petty Ministrations; and that whoever omits them offends God. I wish to such more humility, and to you health and happiness, being your friend and servant,

B. FRANKLIN.

TO JARED INGERSOLL

Philadelphia, December 11, 1762.

DEAR SIR: — I thank you for your kind congratulations. It gives me pleasure to hear from an old friend; it will give me much more pleasure to see him. I hope, therefore, nothing will prevent the journey you propose for next summer and the favour you intend me of a visit. I believe I must make a journey early in the spring to Virginia, but purpose being back again before the hot weather. You will be kind enough to let me know beforehand what time you expect to be here, that I may not be out of the way, for that would mortify me exceedingly.

I should be glad to know what it is that distinguishes Connecticut religion from common religion. Communicate, if you please, some of these particulars that you think will amuse me as a virtuoso. When I travelled in Flanders, I thought of your excessively strict observation of Sunday; and that a man could hardly travel on that day among you upon his lawful occasions without hazard of punishment; while, where I was, every one travelled, if he pleased, or diverted himself in any other way; and in the afternoon both high and low went to the play or the opera, where there was plenty of singing, fiddling and dancing. I looked around for God's judgments, but saw no signs of them. The cities were well built and full of inhabitants, the markets filled with plenty, the people well favoured and well clothed, the fields well tilled, the cattle fat and strong, the fences, houses, and windows all in repair, and no Old Tenor anywhere in the country; which would almost make one suspect that the Deity is not so angry at that offence as a New England Justice.

I left our friend Mr. Jackson well, and I had the great pleasure of finding my little family well when I came home, and my friends as cordial and more numerous than ever. May every prosperity attend you and yours. I am, dear friend, yours affectionately,

B. FRANKLIN.

CONTE

There was once an Officer, a worthy man, named Montrésor, who was very ill. His parish Priest, thinking he would die, advised him to make his Peace with God, so that he would be received into Paradise. "I don't feel much Uneasiness on that Score," said Montrésor; "for last Night I had a Vision which set me entirely at rest." "What Vision did you have?" asked the good Priest. "I was," he said, "at the Gate of Paradise with a Crowd of People who wanted to enter. And St. Peter asked each of them what Religion he belonged to. One answered, 'I am a Roman Catholic.' 'Very well,' said St. Peter; 'come in, & take your Place over there among the Catholics.' Another said he belonged to the Anglican Church. 'Very well,' said St. Peter; 'come in, & take your Place over there among the Anglicans.' Another said he was a Quaker. 'Come in,' said St. Peter, 'and take a Place among the Quakers.' Finally, my turn having arrived, he asked me what my Religion was. 'Alas!' I replied, 'unfortunately, poor Jacques Montrésor belongs to none at all.' 'That's a pity,' said the Saint. 'I don't know where to put you; but come in anyway; just find a Place for yourself wherever you can.' "

TO RICHARD PRICE

Passy, Oct. 9, 1780.

DEAR SIR,

Besides the Pleasure of their Company, I had the great Satisfaction of hearing by your two valuable Friends, and learning from your Letter, that you enjoy a good State of Health. May God continue it, as well for the Good of Mankind as for your Comfort. I thank you much for the second Edition of your excellent Pamphlet. I forwarded that you sent to Mr. Dana, he being in Holland. I wish also to see the Piece you have written (as Mr. Jones tells me) on Toleration. I do not expect that your new Parliament will be either wiser or honester than the last. All Projects to procure an honest one, by Place Bills, &c., appear to me vain and Impracticable. The true Cure, I imagine, is to be found only in rendring all Places unprofitable, and the King too poor to give Bribes and Pensions. Till this is done, which can only be by a Revolution (and I think you have not Virtue enough left to procure one), your Nation will always be plundered, and obliged to pay by Taxes the Plunderers for Plundering and Ruining. Liberty and Virtue therefore join in the call, COME OUT OF HER, MY PEOPLE!

I am fully of your Opinion respecting religious Tests; but, tho' the People of Massachusetts have not in their new Constitution kept quite clear of them, yet, if we consider what that People were 100 Years ago, we must allow they have gone great Lengths in Liberality of Sentiment on religious Subjects; and we may hope for greater Degrees of Perfection, when their Constitution, some years hence, shall be revised. If Christian Preachers had continued to teach as Christ and his Apostles did, without Salaries, and as the Quakers now do, I imagine Tests would never have existed; for I think they were invented, not so much to secure Religion itself, as the Emoluments of it. When a Religion is good, I conceive that it will support itself; and, when it cannot support itself, and God does not take care to support, so that its Professors are oblig'd to call for the help of the Civil Power, it is a sign, I apprehend, of its being a bad one. But I shall be out of my Depth, if I wade any deeper in Theology, and I will not trouble you with Politicks, nor with News which are almost as uncertain; but conclude with a heartfelt Wish to embrace you once more, and enjoy your sweet Society in Peace, among our honest, worthy, ingenious Friends at the *London*.[1] Adieu,

B. FRANKLIN.

TO SAMUEL MATHER

Passy, May 12, 1784.

Rᴇᴠᵈ Sɪʀ,

I received your kind letter, with your excellent advice to the people of the United States, which I read with great pleasure, and hope it will be duly regarded. Such writings, though they may be lightly passed over by many readers, yet, if they make a deep impression on one active mind in a hundred, the effects may be considerable. Permit me to mention one little instance, which, though it relates to myself, will not be quite uninteresting to you. When I was a boy, I met with a book, entitled *"Essays to do Good,"* which I think was written by your father.[1] It had been so little regarded by a former possessor, that several leaves of it were torn out; but the remainder gave me such a turn of thinking, as to have an influence on my conduct through life; for I have always set a greater value on the character of a *doer of good,* than on any other kind of reputation; and if I have been, as you seem to think, a useful citizen, the public owes the advantage of it to that book.

You mention your being in your 78ᵗʰ year; I am in my 79ᵗʰ; we are grown old together. It is now more than 60 years since I left Boston, but I remember well both your father and grandfather, having heard them both in the pulpit, and seen them in their houses. The last time I saw your father was in the beginning of 1724, when I visited him after my first trip to Pennsylvania. He received me in his library, and on my taking leave showed me a shorter way out of the house through a narrow passage, which was crossed by a beam over head. We were still talking as I withdrew, he accompanying me behind, and I turning partly towards him, when he said hastily, *"Stoop, stoop!"* I did not understand him, till I felt my head hit against the beam. He was a man that never missed any occasion of giving instruction, and upon this he said to me, *"You are young, and have the world before you;* STOOP *as you go through it, and you will miss many hard thumps."* This advice, thus beat into my head, has frequently been of use to me; and I often think of it, when I see pride mortified, and misfortunes brought upon people by their carrying their heads too high.

I long much to see again my native place, and to lay my bones there. I left it in 1723; I visited it in 1733, 1743, 1753, and 1763. In 1773 I was in England; in 1775 I had a sight of it, but could not enter, it being in possession of the enemy. I did hope to have been there in 1783, but could not obtain my dismission from this employment here; and now I fear I shall never have that happiness. My best wishes however attend my dear country. *Esto perpetua.*[2] It is now blest with an excellent constitution; may it last for ever!

This powerful monarchy continues its friendship for the United States. It is a friendship of the utmost importance to our security, and should be carefully cultivated. Britain has not yet well digested the loss of its dominion over us, and has still at times some flattering hopes of recovering it. Accidents may increase those hopes, and encourage dangerous attempts. A breach between us and France would infallibly bring the English again upon our backs; and yet we have some wild heads among our countrymen, who are endeavouring to weaken that connexion! Let us preserve our reputation by performing our engagements; our credit by fulfilling our contracts; and friends by gratitude and kindness; for we know not how soon we may again have occasion for all of them. With great and sincere esteem, I have the honour to be, &c.   B. FRANKLIN.

TO EZRA STILES

*Philad*ᵃ, *March 9, 1790.*

Reverend and dear Sir,

I received your kind Letter of Jan'y 28, and am glad you have at length received the portrait of Gov'r Yale from his Family, and deposited it in the College Library. He was a great and good Man, and had the Merit of doing infinite Service to your Country by his Munificence to that Institution. The Honour you propose doing me by placing mine in the same Room with his, is much too great for my Deserts; but you always had a Partiality for me, and to that it must be ascribed. I am however too much obliged to Yale College, the first learned Society that took Notice of me and adorned me with its Honours, to refuse a Request that comes from it thro' so esteemed a Friend. But I do not think any one of the Portraits you mention, as in my Possession, worthy of the Place and Company you propose to place it in. You have an excellent Artist lately arrived. If he will undertake to make one for you, I shall cheerfully pay the Expence; but he must not delay setting about it, or I may slip thro' his fingers, for I am now in my eighty-fifth year, and very infirm.

I send with this a very learned Work, as it seems to me, on the antient Samaritan Coins, lately printed in Spain, and at least curious for the Beauty of the Impression. Please to accept it for your College Library. I have subscribed for the Encyclopædia now printing here, with the Intention of presenting it to the College. I shall probably depart before the Work is finished, but shall leave Directions for its Continuance to the End. With this you will receive some of the first numbers.

You desire to know something of my Religion. It is the first time I have been questioned upon it. But I cannot take your Curiosity amiss, and shall endeavour in a few Words to gratify it. Here is my Creed. I believe in one God, Creator of the Universe. That he governs it by his Providence. That he ought to be worshipped. That the most acceptable Service we render to him is doing good to his other Children. That the soul of Man is immortal, and will be treated with Justice in another Life respecting its Conduct in this. These I take to be the fundamental Principles of all sound Religion, and I regard them as you do in whatever Sect I meet with them.

As to Jesus of Nazareth, my Opinion of whom you particularly desire, I think the System of Morals and his Religion, as he left them to us, the best the World ever saw or is likely to see; but I apprehend it has received various corrupting Changes, and I have, with most of the present Dissenters in England, some Doubts as to his Divinity; tho' it is a question I do not dogmatize upon, having never studied it, and think it needless to busy myself with it now, when I expect soon an Opportunity of knowing the Truth with less Trouble. I see no harm, however, in its being believed, if that Belief has the good Consequence, as probably it has, of making his Doctrines more respected and better observed; especially as I do not perceive, that the Supreme takes it amiss, by distinguishing the Unbelievers in his Government of the World with any peculiar Marks of his Displeasure.

I shall only add, respecting myself, that, having experienced the Goodness of that Being in conducting me prosperously thro' a long life, I have no doubt of its Continuance in the next, though without the smallest Conceit of meriting such Goodness. My Sentiments on this Head you will see in the Copy of an old Letter enclosed, which I wrote in answer to one from a zealous Religionist, whom I had relieved in a paralytic case by electricity, and who, being afraid I should grow proud upon it, sent me his serious though rather impertinent Caution. I send you also the Copy of another Letter,[1] which will shew something of my Disposition relating to Religion. With great and sincere Esteem and Affection, I am, Your obliged old Friend and most obedient humble Servant   B. FRANKLIN.

P. S. Had not your College some Present of Books from the King of France? Please to let me know, if you had an Expectation given you of more, and the Nature of that Expectation? I have a Reason for the Enquiry.

I confide, that you will not expose me to Criticism and censure by publishing any part of this Communication to you. I have ever let others enjoy their religious Sentiments, without reflecting on them for those that appeared to me unsupportable and even absurd. All Sects here, and we have a great Variety, have experienced my good will in assisting them with Subscriptions for building their new Places of Worship; and, as I have never opposed any of their Doctrines, I hope to go out of the World in Peace with them all.

PART V

BAGATELLES AND DALLIANCES

A WITCH TRIAL AT MOUNT HOLLY

The Pennsylvania Gazette, *October 22, 1730.*

SATURDAY last, at Mount-Holly, about 8 Miles from this Place near 300 People were gathered together to see an Experiment or two tried on some Persons accused of Witchcraft. It seems the Accused had been charged with making their Neighbours' Sheep dance in an uncommon Manner, and with causing Hogs to speak and sing Psalms, etc., to the great Terror and Amazement of the king's good and peaceable Subjects in this Province; and the Accusers, being very positive that if the Accused were weighed in Scales against a Bible, the Bible would prove too heavy for them; or that, if they were bound and put into the River they would swim; the said Accused, desirous to make Innocence appear, voluntarily offered to undergo the said Trials if 2 of the most violent of their Accusers would be tried with them. Accordingly the Time and Place was agreed on and advertised about the Country; The Accusers were 1 Man and 1 Woman: and the Accused the same. The Parties being met and the People got together, a grand Consultation was held, before they proceeded to Trial; in which it was agreed to use the Scales first; and a Committee of Men were appointed to search the Men, and a Committee of Women to search the Women, to see if they had any Thing of Weight about them, particularly Pins. After the Scrutiny was over a huge great Bible belonging to the Justice of the Place was provided, and a Lane through the Populace was made from the Justice's House to the Scales, which were fixed on a Gallows erected for that Purpose opposite to the House, that the Justice's Wife and the rest of the Ladies might see the Trial without coming amongst the Mob, and after the Manner of Moorfields a large Ring was also made. Then came out of the House a grave, tall Man carrying the Holy Writ before the supposed Wizard etc, (as solemnly as the Sword-bearer of London before the Lord Mayor) the Wizard was first put in the Scale, and over him was read a Chapter out of the Books of Moses, and then the Bible was put in the other Scale, (which, being kept down before) was immediately let go; but, to the great Surprize of the Spectators, Flesh and Bones came down plump, and outweighed that great good Book by abundance. After the same Manner the others were served, and their Lumps of Mortality severally were too heavy for Moses and all the Prophets and Apostles. This being over, the Accusers and the rest of the Mob, not satisfied with this Experiment, would have the Trial by Water. Accordingly a most solemn Procession was made to the Mill-pond, where both Accused and Accusers being stripped (saving only to the Women their Shifts) were bound Hand and Foot and severally placed in the Water, lengthways, from the Side of a Barge or Flat, having for Security only a Rope about the Middle of each, which was held by some in the Flat. The accused man being thin and spare with some Difficulty began to sink at last; but the rest, every one of them, swam very light upon the Water. A Sailor in the Flat jump'd out upon the Back of the Man accused thinking to drive him down to the Bottom; but the Person bound, without any Help, came up some time before the other. The Woman Accuser being told that she did not sink, would be duck'd a second Time; when she swam again as light as before. Upon which she declared, That she believed the Accused had bewitched her to make her so light, and that she would be duck'd again a Hundred Times but she would duck the Devil out of her. The Accused Man, being surpriz'd at his own Swimming, was not so confident of his Innocence as before, but said, "If I am a Witch, it is more than I know." The more thinking Part of the Spectators were of Opinion that any Person so bound and placed in the Water (unless they were mere Skin and Bones) would swim, till their Breath was gone, and their Lungs fill'd with Water. But it being the general Belief of the Populace that the Women's shifts and the Garters with which they were bound help'd to support them, it is said they are to be tried again the next warm Weather, naked.

ADVICE TO A YOUNG MAN

Philadelphia, 25 June, 1745.

To My dear friend:

I know of no Medicine fit to diminish the violent natural Inclinations you mention; and if I did, I think I should not communicate it to you. Marriage is the proper remedy. It is the most natural state of Man, and therefore the State in which you are most likely to find solid Happiness. Your reasons against entering into it at present appear to me to be not well founded. The Circumstantial Advantages you have in View by postponing it, are not only uncertain, but they are small in comparison with that of the Thing itself, the being married and settled. It is the Man and Woman united that makes the complete human Being. Separate, she wants his force of Body and Strength of Reason; he her Softness, Sensibility and acute Discernment. Together they are more likely to succeed in the World. A single Man has not nearly the Value he would have in the State of Union. He is an incomplete Animal. He resembles the odd Half of a pair of Scissors.

If you get a prudent, healthy Wife, your Industry in your Profession, with her good Economy, will be a Fortune sufficient.

But if you will not take this Counsel, and persist in thinking a Commerce with the Sex inevitable, then I repeat my former Advice that in all your Amours you should prefer old Women to young ones. You call this a Paradox, and demand my reasons. They are these:

1. Because they have more Knowledge of the World, and their minds are better stored with Observations, their Conversation is more improving and more lastingly agreeable.

2. Because when Women cease to be handsome, they study to be good. To maintain their Influence over Men, they supply the Diminution of Beauty by an Augmentation of Utility. They learn to do a thousand Services, small and great; and are the most tender and useful of all Friends when you are sick. Thus they continue amiable. And hence there is hardly such a thing to be found as an old Woman who is not a good Woman.

3. Because there is no Hazard of Children, which irregularly produced may be attended with much Inconvenience.

4. Because through more Experience they are more prudent and discreet in conducting an Intrigue to prevent Suspicion. The Commerce with them is therefore safer with regard to your reputation. And with regard to theirs, if the Affair should happen to be known, considerate People might be rather inclined to excuse an old Woman, who would kindly take care of a young Man, form his manners by her good Counsels, and prevent his ruining his Health and Fortune among mercenary Prostitutes.

5. Because in every Animal that walks upright, the Deficiency of the Fluids that fill the Muscles appears first in the highest Part. The Face first grows lank and wrinkled, then the neck, then the Breast and Arms, the lower Parts continuing to the last as plump as ever; so that covering all above with a Basket, and regarding only what is below the Girdle, it is impossible of two Women to know an old one from a young one. And as in the Dark all Cats are grey, the Pleasure of Corporal Enjoyment with an old Woman is at least equal and frequently superior; every Knack being by Practice capable of Improvement.

6. Because the sin is less. The Debauching a Virgin may be her Ruin, and make her for Life unhappy.

7. Because the Compunction is less. The having made a young girl miserable may give you frequent bitter Reflections; none of which can attend making an old Woman happy.

8th, and lastly. They are so grateful!

Thus much for my Paradox. But still I advise you to marry immediately; being sincerely,

Your affectionate Friend,
BENJAMIN FRANKLIN.

THE SPEECH OF
POLLY BAKER

The Speech of Miss Polly Baker before a Court of Judicature, at Connecticut near Boston in New England; where she was prosecuted the fifth time, for having a Bastard Child: Which influenced the Court to dispense with her Punishment, and which induced one of her Judges to marry her the next Day—by whom she had fifteen Children.

"May it please the honourable bench to indulge me in a few words: I am a poor, unhappy woman, who have no money to fee lawyers to plead for me, being hard put to it to get a living. I shall not trouble your honours with long speeches; for I have not the presumption to expect that you may, by any means, be prevailed on to deviate in your Sentence from the law, in my favour. All I humbly hope is, that your honours would charitably move the governor's goodness on my behalf, that my fine may be remitted. This is the fifth time, gentlemen, that I have been dragg'd before your court on the same account; twice I have paid heavy fines, and twice have been brought to publick punishment, for want of money to pay those fines. This may have been agreeable to the laws, and I don't dispute it; but since laws are sometimes unreasonable in themselves, and therefore repealed; and others bear too hard on the subject in particular circumstances, and therefore there is left a power somewhere to dispense with the execution of them; I take the liberty to say, that I think this law, by which I am punished, both unreasonable in itself, and particularly severe with regard to me, who have always lived an inoffensive life in the neighbourhood where I was born, and defy my enemies (if I have any) to say I ever wrong'd any man, woman, or child. Abstracted from the law, I cannot conceive (may it please your honours) what the nature of my offense is. I have brought five fine children into the world, at the risque of my life; I have maintain'd them well by my own industry, without burthening the township, and would have done it better, if it had not been for the heavy charges and fines I have paid. Can it be a crime (in the nature of things, I mean) to add to the king's subjects, in a new country, that really wants people? I own it, I should think it rather a praiseworthy than a punishable action. I have debauched no other woman's husband, nor enticed any other youth; these things I never was charg'd with; nor has any one the least cause of complaint against me, unless, perhaps, the ministers of justice, because I have had children without being married, by which they have missed a wedding fee. But can this be a fault of mine? I appeal to your honours. You are pleased to allow I don't want sense; but I must be stupefied to the last degree, not to prefer the honourable state of wedlock to the condition I have lived in. I always was, and still am willing to enter into it; and doubt not my behaving well in it, having all the industry, frugality, fertility, and skill in economy appertaining to a good wife's character. I defy any one to say I ever refused an offer of that sort: on the contrary, I readily consented to the only proposal of marriage that ever was made me, which was when I was a virgin, but too easily confiding in the person's sincerity that made it, I unhappily lost my honour by trusting to his; for he got me with child, and then forsook me.

"That very person, you all know, he is now become a magistrate of this country; and I had hopes he would have appeared this day on the bench, and have endeavoured to moderate the Court in my favour; then I should have scorn'd to have mentioned it; but I must now complain of it, as unjust and unequal, that my betrayer and undoer, the first cause of all my faults and miscarriages (if they must be deemed such), should be advanced to honour and power in this government that punishes my misfortunes with stripes and infamy. I should be told, 'tis like, that were there no act of Assembly in the case, the precepts of religion are violated by my transgressions. If mine is a religious offense, leave it to religious punishments. You have already excluded me from the comforts of your church communion. Is not that sufficient? You believe I have offended heaven, and must suffer eternal fire: Will not that be sufficient? What need is there then of your additional fines and whipping? I own I do not think as you do, for, if I thought what you call a sin was really such, I could not presumptuously commit it. But, how can it be believed that heaven is angry at my having children, when to the little done by me towards it, God has been pleased to add his divine skill and admirable workmanship in the formation of their bodies, and crowned the whole by furnishing them with rational and immortal souls?

"Forgive me, gentlemen, if I talk a little extravagantly on these matters; I am no divine, but if you, gentlemen, must be making laws, do not turn natural and useful actions into crimes by your prohibitions. But take into your wise consideration the great and growing number of batchelors in the country, many of whom, from the mean fear of the expences of a family, have never sincerely and honourably courted a woman in their lives; and by their manner of living leave unproduced (which is little better than murder) hundreds of their posterity to the thousandth generation. Is not this a greater offense against the publick good than mine? Compel them, then, by law, either to marriage, or to pay double the fine of fornication every year. What must poor young women do, whom customs and nature forbid to solicit the men, and who cannot force themselves upon husbands, when the laws take no care to provide them any, and yet severely punish them if they do their duty without them; the duty of the first and great command of nature and nature's God, *encrease and multiply;* a duty, from the steady performance of which nothing has been able to deter me, but for its sake I have hazarded the loss of the publick esteem, and have frequently endured publick disgrace and punishment; and therefore ought, in my humble opinion, instead of a whipping, to have a statue erected to my memory."

TO THE EDITOR OF
A NEWSPAPER

Monday, May 20, [1765.]

Sir,

In your Paper of Wednesday last, an ingenious Correspondent that calls himself THE SPECTATOR, and dates from *Pimlico,* under the Guise of Good Will to the News-writers, whom he calls an "useful Body of Men in this great City," has, in my Opinion, artfully attempted to turn them & their Works into Ridicule, wherein if he could succeed, great Injury might be done to the Public as well as to those good People.

Supposing, Sir, that the *"We hears"* they give us of this & t'other intended Voyage or Tour of this & t'other great Personage, were mere Inventions, yet they at least offer us an innocent Amusement while we read, and useful Matter of Conversation when we are dispos'd to converse.

Englishmen, Sir, are too apt to be silent when they have nothing to say; too apt to be sullen when they are silent; and, when they are sullen, to hang themselves. But, by these *We hears,* we are supplied with abundant funds of Discourse, we discuss the Motives for such Voyages, the Probability of their being undertaken, and the Practicability of their Execution. Here we display our Judgment in Politics, our Knowledge of the Interests of Princes, and our Skill in Geography, and (if we have it) show our Dexterity moreover in Argumentation. In the mean time, the tedious Hour is kill'd, we go home pleas'd with the Applauses we have receiv'd from others, or at least with those we secretly give to ourselves: We sleep soundly, & live on, to the Comfort of our Families. But, Sir, I beg leave to say, that all the Articles of News that seem improbable are not mere Inventions. Some of them, I can assure you on the Faith of a Traveller, are serious Truths. And here, quitting Mr. Spectator of Pimlico, give me leave to instance the various numberless Accounts the Newswriters have given us, with so much honest Zeal for the welfare of *Poor Old England*, of the establishing Manufactures in the Colonies to the Prejudice of those of this Kingdom. It is objected by superficial Readers, who yet pretend to some Knowledge of those Countries, that such Establishments are not only improbable, but impossible, for that their Sheep have but little Wooll, not in the whole sufficient for a Pair of Stockings a Year to each Inhabitant; and that, from the Universal Dearness of Labour among them, the Working of Iron and other Materials, except in some few coarse Instances, is impracticable to any Advantage.

Dear Sir, do not let us suffer ourselves to be amus'd with such groundless Objections. The very Tails of the American Sheep are so laden with Wooll, that each has a little Car or Waggon on four little Wheels, to support & keep it from trailing on the Ground. Would they caulk their Ships, would they fill their Beds, would they even litter their Horses with Wooll, if it were not both plenty and cheap? And what signifies Dearness of Labour, when an English Shilling passes for five and Twenty? Their engaging 300 Silk Throwsters here in one Week, for New York, was treated as a Fable, because, forsooth, they have "no Silk there to throw." Those, who made this Objection, perhaps did not know, that at the same time the Agents from the King of Spain were at Quebec to contract for 1000 Pieces of Cannon to be made there for the Fortification of Mexico, and at N York engaging the annual Supply of woven Floor-Carpets for their West India Houses, other Agents from the Emperor of China were at Boston treating about an Exchange of raw Silk for Wooll, to be carried in Chinese Junks through the Straits of Magellan.

And yet all this is as certainly true, as the Account said to be from Quebec, in all the Papers of last Week, that the Inhabitants of Canada are making Preparations for a Cod and Whale Fishery this "Summer in the upper Lakes." Ignorant People may object that the upper Lakes are fresh, and that Cod and Whale are Salt Water Fish: But let them know, Sir, that Cod, like other Fish when attack'd by their Enemies, fly into any Water where they can be safest; that Whales, when they have a mind to eat Cod, pursue them wherever they fly; and that the grand Leap of the Whale in that Chase up the Fall of Niagara is esteemed, by all who have seen it, as one of the finest Spectacles in Nature. Really, Sir, the World is grown too incredulous. It is like the Pendulum ever swinging from one Extream to another. Formerly every thing printed was believed, because it was in print. Now Things seem to be disbelieved for just the very same Reason. Wise Men wonder at the present Growth of Infidelity. They should have consider'd, when they taught People to doubt the Authority of Newspapers and the Truth of Predictions in Almanacks, that the next Step might be a Disbelief in the well vouch'd Accts of Ghosts Witches, and Doubts even of the Truths of the Creed!

Thus much I thought it necessary to say in favour of an honest Set of Writers, whose comfortable Living depends on collecting & supplying the Printers with News at the small Price of Sixpence an Article, and who always show their Regard to Truth, by contradicting in a subsequent Article such as are wrong,—for another Sixpence,—to the great Satisfaction & Improvement of us Coffee-house Students in History & Politics, and the infinite Advantage of all future Livies, Rapins, Robertsons, Humes, and McAulays, who may be sincerely inclin'd to furnish the World with that *rara Avis*, a true History. I am, Sir, your humble Servant,

                                              A TRAVELLER.

THE TWELVE
COMMANDMENTS

TO MADAME BRILLON

Passy, March 10. [1777.]

I am charm'd with the goodness of my spiritual guide, and resign myself implicitly to her Conduct, as she promises to lead
me to heaven in so delicious a Road when I could be content to
travel thither even in the roughest of all ways with the pleasure
of her Company.

How kindly partial to her Penitent in finding him, on examining his conscience, guilty of only one capital sin and to call
that by the gentle name of Foible!

I lay fast hold of your promise to absolve me of all Sins past,
present, & future, on the easy & pleasing Condition of loving
God, America and my guide above all things. I am in Rapture
when I think of being absolv'd of the future.

People commonly speak of Ten Commandments.—I have
been taught that there are twelve. The first was increase & multiply & replenish the earth. The twelfth is, A new Commandment I give unto you, *that you love one another*. It seems to me
that they are a little misplaced, And that the last should have
been the first. However I never made any difficulty about that,
but was always willing to obey them both whenever I had an
opportunity. Pray tell me my dear Casuist, whether my keeping
religiously these two commandments tho' not in the Decalogue,
may not be accepted in Compensation for my breaking so often
one of the ten I mean that which forbids Coveting my neighbour's wife, and which I confess I break constantly God forgive

me, as often as I see or think of my lovely Confessor, and I am afraid I should never be able to repent of the Sin even if I had the full Possession of her.

And now I am Consulting you upon a Case of Conscience I will mention the Opinion of a certain Father of the church which I find myself willing to adopt though I am not sure it is orthodox. It is this, that the most effectual way to get rid of a certain Temptation is, as often as it returns, to comply with and satisfy it.

Pray instruct me how far I may venture to practice upon this Principle?

But why should I be so scrupulous when you have promised to absolve me of the future?

Adieu my charming Conductress and believe me ever with the sincerest Esteem & affection.

                                        Your most obed't hum. Serv.

THE EPHEMERA

An Emblem of Human Life

You may remember, my dear friend, that when we lately spent that happy day in the delightful garden and sweet society of the Moulin Joly, I stopt a little in one of our walks, and staid some time behind the company. We had been shown numberless skeletons of a kind of little fly, called an ephemera, whose successive generations, we were told, were bred and expired within the day. I happened to see a living company of them on a leaf, who appeared to be engaged in conversation. You know I understand all the inferior animal tongues: my too great application to the study of them is the best excuse I can give for the little progress I have made in your charming language. I listened through curiosity to the discourse of these little creatures; but as they, in their national vivacity, spoke three or four together, I could make but little of their conversation. I found, however, by some broken expressions that I heard now and then, they were disputing warmly on the merit of two foreign musicians, one a *cousin,* the other a *moscheto;* in which dispute they spent their time, seemingly as regardless of the shortness of life as if they had been sure of living a month. Happy people! thought I, you live certainly under a wise, just, and mild government, since you have no public grievances to complain of, nor any subject of contention but the perfections and imperfections of foreign music. I turned my head from them to an old grey-headed one, who was single on another leaf, and talking to himself. Being amused with his soliloquy, I put it down in writing, in hopes it will likewise amuse her to whom I am so much indebted for the most pleasing of all amusements, her delicious company and heavenly harmony.

"It was," said he, "the opinion of learned philosophers of our race, who lived and flourished long before my time, that this vast world, the Moulin Joly, could not itself subsist more than eighteen hours; and I think there was some foundation for that opinion, since, by the apparent motion of the great luminary that gives life to all nature, and which in my time has evidently declined considerably towards the ocean at the end of our earth, it must then finish its course, be extinguished in the waters that surround us, and leave the world in cold and darkness, necessarily producing universal death and destruction. I have lived seven of those hours, a great age, being no less than four hundred and twenty minutes of time. How very few of us continue so long! I have seen generations born, flourish, and expire. My present friends are the children and grandchildren of the friends of my youth, who are now, alas, no more! And I must soon follow them; for, by the course of nature, though still in health, I cannot expect to live above seven or eight minutes longer. What now avails all my toil and labor, in amassing honey-dew on this leaf, which I cannot live to enjoy! What the political struggles I have been engaged in, for the good of my compatriot inhabitants of this bush, or my philosophical studies for the benefit of our race in general! for, in politics, what can laws do without morals? Our present race of ephemeræ will in a course of minutes become corrupt, like those of other and older bushes, and consequently as wretched. And in philosophy how small our progress! Alas! art is long, and life is short! My friends would comfort me with the idea of a name, they say, I shall leave behind me; and they tell me I have lived long enough to nature and to glory. But what will fame be to an ephemera who no longer exists? And what will become of all history in the eighteenth hour, when the world itself, even the whole Moulin Joly, shall come to its end, and be buried in universal ruin?"

To me, after all my eager pursuits, no solid pleasures now remain, but the reflection of a long life spent in meaning well, the sensible conversation of a few good lady ephemeræ, and now and then a kind smile and a tune from the ever amiable *Brillante*.   B. FRANKLIN.

ELYSIAN FIELDS

M. Franklin to Madame Helvétius

Vexed by your barbaric resolution, announced so positively last evening, to remain single all your life in respect to your dear husband, I went home, fell on my bed, and, believing myself dead, found myself in the Elysian Fields.

I was asked if I desired to see anybody in particular. Lead me to the home of the philosophers.—There are two who live nearby in the garden: they are very good neighbors, and close friends of each other.—Who are they?—Socrates and Helvétius.—I esteem them both prodigiously; but let me see first Helvétius, because I understand a little French, but not one word of Greek. He received me with great courtesy, having known me for some time, he said, by the reputation I had there. He asked me a thousand things about the war, and about the present state of religion, liberty, and government in France.—You ask nothing then, I told him, of your dear friend Madame Helvétius; and nevertheless she still loves you excessively and I was at her place but an hour ago. Ah! said he, you make me remember my former felicity.—But it is necessary to forget it in order to be happy here. During several of the early years, I thought only of her. Finally I am consoled. I have taken another wife. The most like her that I could find. She is not, it is true, so completely beautiful, but she has as much good sense, a good deal of Spirit, and she loves me infinitely. Her continual study is to please me; and she has at present gone to hunt the best nectar and the best ambrosia in order to treat me this evening; remain with me and you will see her. I perceive, I said, that your old friend is more faithful than you: for several good offers have been made her, all of which she has refused. I confess to you that I myself have loved her to the point of distraction; but she was hard on me and absolutely rejected me for love of you. I pity you, he said, for your bad fortune; for truly she is a good and beautiful woman and very loveable. But the Abbé de la R****, and the Abbé M****, are they not still sometimes at her home? Yes, assuredly, for she has not lost a single one of your friends. If you had won over the Abbé M**** (with coffee and cream) to speak for you, perhaps you would have succeeded; for he is a subtle logician like Duns Scotus or St. Thomas; he arranges his arguments so well that they become nearly irresistible. Also, if the Abbé de la R**** had been bribed (by some beautiful edition of an old classic) to speak against you, that would have been better: for I have always observed, that when he advises her of something, she has a very strong penchant to do the reverse.—At these words the new Madame Helvétius entered with the nectar: at which instant I recognized her to be Madame Franklin, my old American friend. I called out to her, but she told me coldly, "I have been your good wife forty-nine years and four months, nearly a half century; be content with that. Here I have formed a new connection, which will endure to eternity."

Offended by this refusal of my Eurydice, I suddenly decided to leave these ungrateful spirits and return to the good earth, to see again the sunshine and you. Here I am! Let us take revenge!

THE WHISTLE

To Madame Brillon

Passy, November 10, 1779.

I RECEIVED my dear friend's two letters, one for Wednesday and one for Saturday. This is again Wednesday. I do not deserve one for to-day, because I have not answered the former. But, indolent as I am, and averse to writing, the fear of having no more of your pleasing epistles, if I do not contribute to the correspondence, obliges me to take up my pen; and as Mr. B. has kindly sent me word, that he sets out to-morrow to see you, instead of spending this Wednesday evening as I have done its namesakes, in your delightful company, I sit down to spend it in thinking of you, in writing to you, and in reading over and over again your letters.

I am charmed with your description of Paradise, and with your plan of living there; and I approve much of your conclusion, that, in the mean time, we should draw all the good we can from this world. In my opinion, we might all draw more good from it than we do, and suffer less evil, if we would take care not to give too much for *whistles*. For to me it seems, that most of the unhappy people we meet with, are become so by neglect of that caution.

You ask what I mean? You love stories, and will excuse my telling one of myself.

When I was a child of seven years old, my friends, on a holiday, filled my pocket with coppers. I went directly to a shop where they sold toys for children; and, being charmed with the sound of a *whistle*, that I met by the way in the hands of another boy, I voluntarily offered and gave all my money for one.

I then came home, and went whistling all over the house, much pleased with my *whistle,* but disturbing all the family. My brothers, and sisters, and cousins, understanding the bargain I had made, told me I had given four times as much for it as it was worth; put me in mind what good things I might have bought with the rest of the money; and laughed at me so much for my folly, that I cried with vexation; and the reflection gave me more chagrin than the *whistle* gave me pleasure.

This however was afterwards of use to me, the impression continuing on my mind; so that often, when I was tempted to buy some unnecessary thing, I said to myself, *Don't give too much for the whistle;* and I saved my money.

As I grew up, came into the world, and observed the actions of men, I thought I met with many, very many, who *gave too much for the whistle.*

When I saw one too ambitious of court favour, sacrificing his time in attendance on levees, his repose, his liberty, his virtue, and perhaps his friends, to attain it, I have said to myself, *This man gives too much for his whistle.*

When I saw another fond of popularity, constantly employing himself in political bustles, neglecting his own affairs, and ruining them by that neglect, *He pays, indeed,* said I, *too much for his whistle.*

If I knew a miser, who gave up every kind of comfortable living, all the pleasure of doing good to others, all the esteem of his fellow-citizens, and the joys of benevolent friendship, for the sake of accumulating wealth, *Poor man,* said I, *you pay too much for your whistle.*

When I met with a man of pleasure, sacrificing every laudable improvement of the mind, or of his fortune, to mere corporeal sensations, and ruining his health in their pursuit, *Mistaken man,* said I, *you are providing pain for yourself, instead of pleasure; you give too much for your whistle.*

If I see one fond of appearance, or fine clothes, fine houses, fine furniture, fine equipages, all above his fortune, for which he contracts debts, and ends his career in a prison, *Alas!* say I, *he has paid dear, very dear, for his whistle.*

When I see a beautiful, sweet-tempered girl married to an

ill-natured brute of a husband, *What a pity,* say I, *that she should pay so much for a whistle!*

In short, I conceive that great part of the miseries of mankind are brought upon them by the false estimates they have made of the value of things, and by their *giving too much for their whistles.*

Yet I ought to have charity for these unhappy people, when I consider, that, with all this wisdom of which I am boasting, there are certain things in the world so tempting, for example, the apples of King John, which happily are not to be bought; for if they were put to sale by auction, I might very easily be led to ruin myself in the purchase, and find that I had once more given too much for the *whistle.*

Adieu, my dear friend, and believe me ever yours very sincerely and with unalterable affection,

B. FRANKLIN.

MORALS OF CHESS

[PLAYING at chess is the most ancient and most universal game known among men; for its original is beyond the memory of history, and it has, for numberless ages, been the amusement of all the civilised nations of Asia, the Persians, the Indians, and the Chinese. Europe has had it above a thousand years; the Spaniards have spread it over their part of America; and it has lately begun to make its appearance in the United States. It is so interesting in itself, as not to need the view of gain to induce engaging in it; and thence it is seldom played for money. Those therefore who have leisure for such diversions, cannot find one that is more innocent: and the following piece, written with a view to correct (among a few young friends) some little improprieties in the practice of it, shows at the same time that it may, in its effects on the mind, be not merely innocent, but advantageous, to the vanquished as well as the victor.]

The Game of Chess is not merely an idle Amusement. Several very valuable qualities of the Mind, useful in the course of human Life, are to be acquir'd or strengthened by it, so as to become habits, ready on all occasions. For Life is a kind of Chess, in which we often have Points to gain, & Competitors or Adversaries to contend with; and in which there is a vast variety of good and ill Events, that are in some degree the Effects of Prudence or the want of it. By playing at Chess, then, we may learn,

I. *Foresight,* which looks a little into futurity, and considers the Consequences that may attend an action; for it is continually occurring to the Player, "If I move this piece, what will be the advantages or disadvantages of my new situation? What Use can my Adversary make of it to annoy me? What other moves can I make to support it, and to defend myself from his attacks?"

II. *Circumspection,* which surveys the whole Chessboard, or scene of action; the relations of the several pieces and situations, the Dangers they are respectively exposed to, the several possibilities of their aiding each other, the probabilities that the Adversary may make this or that move, and attack this or the other Piece, and what different Means can be used to avoid his stroke, or turn its consequences against him.

III. *Caution,* not to make our moves too hastily. This habit is best acquired, by observing strictly the laws of the Game; such as, *If you touch a Piece, you must move it somewhere; if you set it down, you must let it stand.* And it is therefore best that these rules should be observed, as the Game becomes thereby more the image of human Life, and particularly of War; in which, if you have incautiously put yourself into a bad and dangerous position, you cannot obtain your Enemy's Leave to withdraw your Troops, and place them more securely, but you must abide all the consequences of your rashness.

And *lastly,* we learn by Chess the habit of not being discouraged by present appearances in the state of our affairs, the habit of hoping for a favourable Change, and that of persevering in the search of resources. The Game is so full of Events, there is such a variety of turns in it, the Fortune of it is so subject to sudden Vicissitudes, and one so frequently, after long contemplation, discovers the means of extricating one's self from a supposed insurmountable Difficulty, that one is encouraged to continue the Contest to the last, in hopes of Victory from our own skill, or at least of getting a stale mate, from the Negligence of our Adversary. And whoever considers, what in Chess he often sees instances of, that particular pieces of success are apt to produce Presumption, & its consequent Inattention, by which more is afterwards lost than was gain'd by the preceding Advantage, while misfortunes produce more care and attention, by which the loss may be recovered, will learn not to be too much discouraged by any present success of his Adversary, nor to despair of final good fortune upon every little Check he receives in the pursuit of it.

That we may therefore be induced more frequently to chuse this beneficial amusement, in preference to others which are not attended with the same advantages, every Circumstance that may increase the pleasure of it should be regarded; and every action or word that is unfair, disrespectful, or that in any way may give uneasiness, should be avoided, as contrary to the immediate intention of both the Players, which is to pass the Time agreably.

Therefore, first, if it is agreed to play according to the strict rules, then those rules are to be exactly observed by both parties, and should not be insisted on for one side, while deviated from by the other—for this is not equitable.

Secondly, if it is agreed not to observe the rules exactly, but one party demands indulgencies, he should then be as willing to allow them to the other.

Thirdly, no false move should ever be made to extricate yourself out of difficulty, or to gain an advantage. There can be no pleasure in playing with a person once detected in such unfair practice.

Fourthly, if your adversary is long in playing, you ought not to hurry him, or express any uneasiness at his delay. You should not sing, nor whistle, nor look at your watch, nor take up a book to read, nor make a tapping with your feet on the floor, or with your fingers on the table, nor do any thing that may disturb his attention. For all these things displease; and they do not show your skill in playing, but your craftiness or your rudeness.

Fifthly, you ought not to endeavour to amuse and deceive your adversary, by pretending to have made bad moves, and saying that you have now lost the game, in order to make him secure and careless, and inattentive to your schemes: for this is fraud and deceit, not skill in the game.

Sixthly, you must not, when you have gained a victory, use any triumphing or insulting expression, nor show too much pleasure; but endeavour to console your adversary, and make him less dissatisfied with himself, by every kind of civil expression that may be used with truth, such as, "you understand the game better than I, but you are a little inattentive;" or, "you play too fast;" or, "you had the best of the game, but something happened to divert your thoughts, and that turned it in my favour."

Seventhly, if you are a spectator while others play, observe the most perfect silence. For, if you give advice, you offend both parties, him against whom you give it, because it may cause the loss of his game, him in whose favour you give it, because, though it be good, and he follows it, he loses the pleasure he might have had, if you had permitted him to think until it had occurred to himself. Even after a move or moves, you must not, by replacing the pieces, show how they might have been placed better; for that displeases, and may occasion disputes and doubts about their true situation. All talking to the players lessens or diverts their attention, and is therefore unpleasing. Nor should you give the least hint to either party, by any kind of noise or motion. If you do, you are unworthy to be a spectator. If you have a mind to exercise or show your judgment, do it in playing your own game, when you have an opportunity, not in criticizing, or meddling with, or counselling the play of others.

Lastly, if the game is not to be played rigorously, according to the rules above mentioned, then moderate your desire of victory over your adversary, and be pleased with one over yourself. Snatch not eagerly at every advantage offered by his unskilfulness or inattention; but point out to him kindly, that by such a move he places or leaves a piece in danger and unsupported; that by another he will put his king in a perilous situation, &c. By this generous civility (so opposite to the unfairness above forbidden) you may, indeed, happen to lose the game to your opponent; but you will win what is better, his esteem, his respect, and his affection, together with the silent approbation and good-will of impartial spectators.

TO MRS. ELIZABETH PARTRIDGE

Passy, Oct. 11. 1779.

MRS. PARTRIDGE

Your kind Letter, my dear Friend, was long in coming; but it gave me the Pleasure of knowing that you had been well in October and January last. The Difficulty, Delay & Interruption of Correspondence with those I love, is one of the great Inconveniencies I find in living so far from home: but we must bear these & more, with Patience, if we can; if not, we must bear them as I do with Impatience.

You mention the Kindness of the French Ladies to me. I must explain that matter. This is the civilest nation upon Earth. Your first Acquaintances endeavour to find out what you like, and they tell others. If 'tis understood that you like Mutton, dine where you will you find Mutton. Somebody, it seems, gave it out that I lov'd Ladies; and then every body presented me their Ladies (or the Ladies presented themselves) to be *embrac'd,* that is to have their Necks kiss'd. For as to kissing of Lips or Cheeks it is not the Mode here, the first, is reckon'd rude, & the other may rub off the Paint. The French Ladies have however 1000 other ways of rendering themselves agreable; by their various Attentions and Civilities, & their sensible Conversation. 'Tis a delightful People to live with.

I thank you for the Boston Newspapers, tho' I see nothing so clearly in them as that your Printers do indeed want new Letters. They perfectly blind me in endeavouring to read them. If you should ever have any Secrets that you wish to be well kept, get them printed in those Papers. You enquire if Printers Types may be had here? Of all Sorts, very good, cheaper than in England, and of harder Metal.—I will see any Orders executed in that way that any of your Friends may think fit to send. They will doubtless send Money with their Orders. Very good Printing Ink is likewise to be had here. I cannot by this opportunity send the miniature you desire, but I send you a little Head in China, more like, perhaps, than the Painting would be. It may be set in a Locket, if you like it, cover'd with Glass, and may serve for the present. When Peace comes we may afford to be more extravagant. I send with it a Couple of Fatherly Kisses for you & your amiable Daughter, the whole wrapt up together in Cotton to be kept warm.

Present my respectful Compliments to Mr Partridge.

Adieu, my dear Child, & believe me ever

Your affectionate Papah

DIALOGUE BETWEEN FRANKLIN AND THE GOUT

Midnight, October 22, 1780.

FRANKLIN. Eh! Oh! Eh! What have I done to merit these cruel sufferings?

GOUT. Many things; you have ate and drank too freely, and too much indulged those legs of yours in their indolence.

FRANKLIN. Who is it that accuses me?

GOUT. It is I, even I, the Gout.

FRANKLIN. What! my enemy in person?

GOUT. No, not your enemy.

FRANKLIN. I repeat it; my enemy; for you would not only torment my body to death, but ruin my good name; you reproach me as a glutton and a tippler; now all the world, that knows me, will allow that I am neither the one nor the other.

GOUT. The world may think as it pleases; it is always very complaisant to itself, and sometimes to its friends; but I very well know that the quantity of meat and drink proper for a man, who takes a reasonable degree of exercise, would be too much for another, who never takes any.

FRANKLIN. I take—Eh! Oh!—as much exercise—Eh!—as I can, Madam Gout. You know my sedentary state, and on that account, it would seem, Madam Gout, as if you might spare me a little, seeing it is not altogether my own fault.

GOUT. Not a jot; your rhetoric and your politeness are thrown away; your apology avails nothing. If your situation in life is a sedentary one, your amusements, your recreations, at least, should be active. You ought to walk or ride; or, if the weather prevents that, play at billiards. But let us examine your course of life. While the mornings are long, and you have leisure to go abroad, what do you do? Why, instead of gaining an appetite for breakfast, by salutary exercise, you amuse yourself, with books, pamphlets, or newspapers, which commonly are not worth the reading. Yet you eat an inordinate breakfast, four dishes of tea, with cream, and one or two buttered toasts, with slices of hung beef, which I fancy are not things the most easily digested. Immediately afterward you sit down to write at your desk, or converse with persons who apply to you on business. Thus the time passes till one, without any kind of bodily exercise. But all this I could pardon, in regard, as you say, to your sedentary condition. But what is your practice after dinner? Walking in the beautiful gardens of those friends, with whom you have dined, would be the choice of men of sense; yours is to be fixed down to chess, where you are found engaged for two or three hours! This is your perpetual recreation, which is the least eligible of any for a sedentary man, because, instead of accelerating the motion of the fluids, the rigid attention it requires helps to retard the circulation and obstruct internal secretions. Wrapt in the speculations of this wretched game, you destroy your constitution. What can be expected from such a course of living, but a body replete with stagnant humours, ready to fall a prey to all kinds of dangerous maladies, if I, the Gout, did not occasionally bring you relief by agitating those humours, and so purifying or dissipating them? If it was in some nook or alley in Paris, deprived of walks, that you played awhile at chess after dinner, this might be excusable; but the same taste prevails with you in Passy, Auteuil, Montmartre, or Sanoy, places where there are the finest gardens and walks, a pure air, beautiful women, and most agreeable and instructive conversation; all which you might enjoy by frequenting the walks. But these are rejected for this abominable game of chess. Fie, then Mr. Franklin! But amidst my instructions, I had almost forgot to administer my wholesome corrections; so take that twinge,—and that.

FRANKLIN. Oh! Eh! Oh! Ohhh! As much instruction as you please, Madam Gout, and as many reproaches; but pray, Madam, a truce with your corrections!

GOUT. No, Sir, no,—I will not abate a particle of what is so much for your good,—therefore—

FRANKLIN. Oh! Ehhh!—It is not fair to say I take no exercise, when I do very often, going out to dine and returning in my carriage.

GOUT. That, of all imaginable exercises, is the most slight and insignificant, if you allude to the motion of a carriage suspended on springs. By observing the degree of heat obtained by different kinds of motion, we may form an estimate of the quantity of exercise given by each. Thus, for example, if you turn out to walk in winter with cold feet, in an hour's time you will be in a glow all over; ride on horseback, the same effect will scarcely be perceived by four hours' round trotting; but if you loll in a carriage, such as you have mentioned, you may travel all day, and gladly enter the last inn to warm your feet by a fire. Flatter yourself then no longer, that half an hour's airing in your carriage deserves the name of exercise. Providence has appointed few to roll in carriages, while he has given to all a pair of legs, which are machines infinitely more commodious and serviceable. Be grateful, then, and make a proper use of yours. Would you know how they forward the circulation of your fluids, in the very action of transporting you from place to place; observe when you walk, that all your weight is alternately thrown from one leg to the other; this occasions a great pressure on the vessels of the foot, and repels their contents; when relieved, by the weight being thrown on the other foot, the vessels of the first are allowed to replenish, and, by a return of this weight, this repulsion again succeeds; thus accelerating the circulation of the blood. The heat produced in any given time, depends on the degree of this acceleration; the fluids are shaken, the humours attenuated, the secretions facilitated, and all goes well; the cheeks are ruddy, and health is established. Behold your fair friend at Auteuil; a lady who received from bounteous nature more really useful science, than half a dozen such pretenders to philosophy as you have been able to extract from all your books. When she honours you with a visit, it is on foot. She walks all hours of the day, and leaves indolence, and its concomitant maladies, to be endured by her horses. In this see at once the preservative of her health and personal charms. But when you go to Auteuil, you must have your carriage, though it is no further from Passy to Auteuil than from Auteuil to Passy.

FRANKLIN. Your reasonings grow very tiresome.

GOUT. I stand corrected. I will be silent and continue my office; take that, and that.

FRANKLIN. Oh! Ohh! Talk on, I pray you!

GOUT. No, no; I have a good number of twinges for you tonight, and you may be sure of some more tomorrow.

FRANKLIN. What, with such a fever! I shall go distracted. Oh! Eh! Can no one bear it for me?

GOUT. Ask that of your horses; they have served you faithfully.

FRANKLIN. How can you so cruelly sport with my torments?

GOUT. Sport! I am very serious. I have here a list of offences against your own health distinctly written, and can justify every stroke inflicted on you.

FRANKLIN. Read it then.

GOUT. It is too long a detail; but I will briefly mention some particulars.

FRANKLIN. Proceed. I am all attention.

GOUT. Do you remember how often you have promised yourself, the following morning, a walk in the grove of Boulogne, in the garden de la Muette, or in your own garden, and have violated your promise, alleging, at one time, it was too cold, at another too warm, too windy, too moist, or what else you pleased; when in truth it was too nothing, but your insuperable love of ease?

FRANKLIN. That I confess may have happened occasionally, probably ten times in a year.

GOUT. Your confession is very far short of the truth; the gross amount is one hundred and ninety-nine times.

FRANKLIN. Is it possible?

GOUT. So possible, that it is fact; you may rely on the accuracy of my statement. You know M. Brillon's gardens, and what fine walks they contain; you know the handsome flight of an hundred steps, which lead from the terrace above to the lawn below. You have been in the practice of visiting this amiable family twice a week, after dinner, and it is a maxim of your own, that "a man may take as much exercise in walking a mile, up and down stairs, as in ten on level ground." What an opportunity was here for you to have had exercise in both these ways! Did you embrace it, and how often?

FRANKLIN. I cannot immediately answer that question.

GOUT. I will do it for you; not once.

FRANKLIN. Not once?

GOUT. Even so. During the summer you went there at six o'clock. You found the charming lady, with her lovely children and friends, eager to walk with you, and entertain you with their agreeable conversation; and what has been your choice? Why to sit on the terrace, satisfying yourself with the fine prospect, and passing your eye over the beauties of the garden below, without taking one step to descend and walk about in them. On the contrary, you call for tea and the chess-board; and lo! you are occupied in your seat till nine o'clock, and that besides two hours' play after dinner; and then, instead of walking home, which would have bestirred you a little, you step into your carriage. How absurd to suppose that all this carelessness can be reconcilable with health, without my interposition!

FRANKLIN. I am convinced now of the justness of poor Richard's remark, that "Our debts and our sins are always greater than we think for."

GOUT. So it is. You philosophers are sages in your maxims, and fools in your conduct.

FRANKLIN. But do you charge among my crimes, that I return in a carriage from Mr. Brillon's?

GOUT. Certainly; for, having been seated all the while, you cannot object the fatigue of the day, and cannot want therefore the relief of a carriage.

FRANKLIN. What then would you have me do with my carriage?

GOUT. Burn it if you choose; you would at least get heat out of it once in this way; or, if you dislike that proposal, here's another for you; observe the poor peasants, who work in the vineyards and grounds about the villages of Passy, Auteuil, Chaillot, &c.; you may find every day, among these deserving creatures, four or five old men and women, bent and perhaps crippled by weight of years, and too long and too great labour. After a most fatiguing day, these people have to trudge a mile or two to their smoky huts. Order your coachman to set them down. This is an act that will be good for your soul; and, at the same time, after your visit to the Brillons, if you return on foot, that will be good for your body.

FRANKLIN. Ah! how tiresome you are!

GOUT. Well, then, to my office; it should not be forgotten that I am your physician. There.

FRANKLIN. Ohhh! what a devil of a physician!

GOUT. How ungrateful you are to say so! Is it not I who, in the character of your physician, have saved you from the palsy, dropsy, and apoplexy? one or other of which would have done for you long ago, but for me.

FRANKLIN. I submit, and thank you for the past, but entreat the discontinuance of your visits for the future; for, in my mind, one had better die than be cured so dolefully. Permit me just to hint, that I have also not been unfriendly to *you*. I never feed physician or quack of any kind, to enter the list against you; if then you do not leave me to my repose, it may be said you are ungrateful too.

GOUT. I can scarcely acknowledge that as any objection. As to quacks, I despise them; they may kill you indeed, but cannot injure me. And, as to regular physicians, they are at last convinced that the gout, in such a subject as you are, is no disease, but a remedy; and wherefore cure a remedy?—but to our business,—there.

FRANKLIN. Oh! oh!—for Heaven's sake leave me! and I promise faithfully never more to play at chess, but to take exercise daily, and live temperately.

GOUT. I know you too well. You promise fair; but, after a few months of good health, you will return to your old habits;

your fine promises will be forgotten like the forms of last year's clouds. Let us then finish the account, and I will go. But I leave you with an assurance of visiting you again at a proper time and place; for my object is your good, and you are sensible now that I am your *real friend*.

AN ECONOMICAL PROJECT

To the Authors of the Journal of Paris.

MESSIEURS,

You often entertain us with accounts of new discoveries. Permit me to communicate to the public, through your paper, one that has lately been made by myself, and which I conceive may be of great utility.

I was the other evening in a grand company, where the new lamp of Messrs. Quinquet and Lange was introduced, and much admired for its splendour; but a general inquiry was made, whether the oil it consumed was not in proportion to the light it afforded, in which case there would be no saving in the use of it. No one present could satisfy us in that point, which all agreed ought to be known, it being a very desirable thing to lessen, if possible, the expense of lighting our apartments, when every other article of family expense was so much augmented.

I was pleased to see this general concern for economy, for I love economy exceedingly.

I went home, and to bed, three or four hours after midnight, with my head full of the subject. An accidental sudden noise waked me about six in the morning, when I was surprised to find my room filled with light; and I imagined at first, that a number of those lamps had been brought into it; but, rubbing my eyes, I perceived the light came in at the windows. I got up and looked out to see what might be the occasion of it, when I saw the sun just rising above the horizon, from whence he poured his rays plentifully into my chamber, my domestic having negligently omitted, the preceding evening, to close the shutters.

I looked at my watch, which goes very well, and found that it was but six o'clock; and still thinking it something extraordinary that the sun should rise so early, I looked into the almanac, where I found it to be the hour given for his rising on that day. I looked forward, too, and found he was to rise still earlier every day till towards the end of June; and that at no time in the year he retarded his rising so long as till eight o'clock. Your readers, who with me have never seen any signs of sunshine before noon, and seldom regard the astronomical part of the almanac, will be as much astonished as I was, when they hear of his rising so early; and especially when I assure them, *that he gives light as soon as he rises*. I am convinced of this. I am certain of my fact. One cannot be more certain of any fact. I saw it with my own eyes. And, having repeated this observation the three following mornings, I found always precisely the same result.

Yet it so happens, that when I speak of this discovery to others, I can easily perceive by their countenances, though they forbear expressing it in words, that they do not quite believe me. One, indeed, who is a learned natural philosopher, has assured me that I must certainly be mistaken as to the circumstance of the light coming into my room; for it being well known, as he says, that there could be no light abroad at that hour, it follows that none could enter from without; and that of consequence, my windows being accidentally left open, instead of letting in the light, had only served to let out the darkness; and he used many ingenious arguments to show me how I might, by that means, have been deceived. I owned that he puzzled me a little, but he did not satisfy me; and the subsequent observations I made, as above mentioned, confirmed me in my first opinion.

This event has given rise in my mind to several serious and important reflections. I considered that, if I had not been awakened so early in the morning, I should have slept six hours longer by the light of the sun, and in exchange have lived six hours the following night by candle-light; and, the latter being a much more expensive light than the former, my love of economy induced me to muster up what little arithmetic I was master of, and to make some calculations, which I shall give you, after observing that utility is, in my opinion the test of value in matters of invention, and that a discovery which can be applied to no use, or is not good for something, is good for nothing.

I took for the basis of my calculation the supposition that there are one hundred thousand families in Paris, and that these families consume in the night half a pound of bougies, or candles, per hour. I think this is a moderate allowance, taking one family with another; for though I believe some consume less, I know that many consume a great deal more. Then estimating seven hours per day as the medium quantity between the time of the sun's rising and ours, he rising during the six following months from six to eight hours before noon, and there being seven hours of course per night in which we burn candles, the account will stand thus;—

In the six months between the 20th of March and the 20th of September, there are

Nights	183
Hours of each night in which we burn candles	7
Multiplication gives for the total number of hours	1,281
These 1,281 hours multiplied by 100,000, the number of inhabitants give	128,100,000
One hundred twenty-eight millions and one hundred thousand hours, spent at Paris by candle-light, which, at half a pound of wax and tallow per hour, gives the weight of	64,050,000
Sixty-four millions and fifty thousand of pounds, which, estimating the whole at the medium price of thirty sols the pound, makes the sum of ninety-six millions and seventy-five thousand livres tournois.	96,075,000

An immense sum! that the city of Paris might save every year, by the economy of using sunshine instead of candles.

If it should be said, that people are apt to be obstinately attached to old customs, and that it will be difficult to induce them to rise before noon, consequently my discovery can be of little use; I answer, *Nil desperandum*. I believe all who have common sense, as soon as they have learnt from this paper that it is daylight when the sun rises, will contrive to rise with him; and, to compel the rest, I would propose the following regulations;

First. Let a tax be laid of a louis per window, on every window that is provided with shutters to keep out the light of the sun.

Second. Let the same salutary operation of police be made use of, to prevent our burning candles, that inclined us last winter to be more economical in burning wood; that is, let guards be placed in the shops of the wax and tallow chandlers, and no family be permitted to be supplied with more than one pound of candles per week.

Third. Let guards also be posted to stop all the coaches, &c. that would pass the streets after sun-set, except those of physicians, surgeons, and midwives.

Fourth. Every morning, as soon as the sun rises, let all the bells in every church be set ringing; and if that is not sufficient, let cannon be fired in every street, to wake the sluggards effectually, and make them open their eyes to see their true interest.

All the difficulty will be in the first two or three days; after which the reformation will be as natural and easy as the present irregularity; for, *ce n'est que le premier pas qui coûte*. Oblige a man to rise at four in the morning, and it is more than probable he will go willingly to bed at eight in the evening; and, having had eight hours sleep, he will rise more willingly at four in the morning following. But this sum of ninety-six millions and seventy-five thousand livres is not the whole of what may be saved by my economical project. You may observe, that I have calculated upon only one half of the year, and much may be saved in the other, though the days are shorter. Besides, the immense stock of wax and tallow left unconsumed during the summer, will probably make candles much cheaper for the ensuing winter, and continue them cheaper as long as the proposed reformation shall be supported.

For the great benefit of this discovery, thus freely communicated and bestowed by me on the public, I demand neither place, pension, exclusive privilege, nor any other reward whatever. I expect only to have the honour of it. And yet I know there are little, envious minds, who will, as usual, deny me this, and say, that my invention was known to the ancients, and perhaps they may bring passages out of the old books in proof of it. I will not dispute with these people, that the ancients knew not the sun would rise at certain hours; they possibly had, as we have, almanacs that predicted it; but it does not follow thence, that they knew *he gave light as soon as he rose.* This is what I claim as my discovery. If the ancients knew it, it might have been long since forgotten; for it certainly was unknown to the moderns, at least to the Parisians, which to prove, I need use but one plain simple argument. They are as well instructed, judicious, and prudent a people as exist anywhere in the world, all professing, like myself, to be lovers of economy; and, from the many heavy taxes required from them by the necessities of the state, have surely an abundant reason to be economical. I say it is impossible that so sensible a people, under such circumstances, should have lived so long by the smoky, unwholesome, and enormously expensive light of candles, if they had really known, that they might have had as much pure light of the sun for nothing. I am, &c.

A SUBSCRIBER.

A PETITION OF
THE LEFT HAND

To Those Who Have the Superintendency
of Education

I ADDRESS myself to all the friends of youth, and conjure them to direct their compassionate regards to my unhappy fate, in order to remove the prejudices of which I am the victim. There are twin sisters of us; and the two eyes of man do not more resemble, nor are capable of being upon better terms with each other, than my sister and myself, were it not for the partiality of our parents, who make the most injurious distinctions between us. From my infancy, I have been led to consider my sister as a being of a more elevated rank. I was suffered to grow up without the least instruction, while nothing was spared in her education. She had masters to teach her writing, drawing, music, and other accomplishments; but if by chance I touched a pencil, a pen, or a needle, I was bitterly rebuked; and more than once I have been beaten for being awkward, and wanting a graceful manner. It is true, my sister associated me with her upon some occasions; but she always made a point of taking the lead, calling upon me only from necessity, or to figure by her side.

But conceive not, Sirs, that my complaints are instigated merely by vanity. No; my uneasiness is occasioned by an object much more serious. It is the practice in our family, that the whole business of providing for its subsistence falls upon my sister and myself. If any indisposition should attack my sister,— and I mention it in confidence upon this occasion, that she is subject to the gout, the rheumatism, and cramp, without making mention of other accidents,— what would be the fate of our poor family? Must not the regret of our parents be excessive, at having placed so great a difference between sisters who are so perfectly equal? Alas! we must perish from distress; for it would not be in my power even to scrawl a suppliant petition for relief, having been obliged to employ the hand of another in transcribing the request which I have now the honour to prefer to you.

Condescend, Sirs, to make my parents sensible of the injustice of an exclusive tenderness, and of the necessity of distributing their care and affection among all their children equally. I am, with a profound respect, Sirs, your obedient servant,

THE LEFT HAND.

PART VI

VIRTUOSO

TO PETER COLLINSON

Philad^a June 26. 1755

DEAR FRIEND

Mr. Bartram brings a Box to my House which has a little Vacancy in it, so I put in my Philosophical Pacquet, which I long since intended to send you, but one thing or other has prevented. I would not have any Part of it printed, unless you should think that printing the Papers relating to Whirlwinds and Water Spouts together with a Collection of all Accounts of Spouts and Whirlwinds that have been hitherto publish'd, might excite the Curiosity of Naturalists and the Attention of Shipmasters and other Travellers, so as to occasion more accurate Observations of the Phænomena and produce more particular Accounts, tending to a thorough Explanation. If you should be of that Opinion, I have no Objection to the Making that Use of the Papers on that Subject; but the rest are only for your private Amusement, and when perused I must request you to return them.

I also send you a few sheets of Paper made of the Asbestos. I am sorry it is so tender. I made some formerly that was much stronger. Please to present a Sheet of it to your noble President, if he will be so good as to accept such a Trifle.

I enclose you a second Bill for £25 Sterling on Account of the Library Company.

I must desire you to send us Johnson's Dictionary, and one for the Academy. The old Accounts of the first Settlem^t of the Colonies are very Curious, and very acceptable to the Library Company, who direct me to return you their hearty Thanks for your kindness in sparing them to the Library. The Box not being full, I have put in a few more of our Candles which I recommend for your particular Use when you have Occasion to read or write by Night; they give a whiter Flame than that of an other kind of Candle, and the Light is more like Daylight than any other Light I know; besides they need little or no Snuffing, and grease nothing. There is still a little Vacancy at the End of the Box, so I'll put in a few Cakes of American Soap made of Myrtle Wax, said to be the best Soap in the World for Shaving or Washing fine Linnens etc. Mrs. Franklin requests your Daughter would be so good as to accept 3 or 4 Cakes of it, to wash your Grandson's finest Things with.

In your Gentleman's Magazine for February 1755 I see a Letter from R. Brooke of Maryland mentioning an American Animal which he says he believes had not been seen or described in Europe. I imagine it to be the same that in New England is called a *Woodchuck* or Monack. When I was on my Journey in that Country last Winter one of them was killed in the Garden of an old Inn I put up at. Having never seen one of them before I immediately took some Notes towards a Description of it, to show our Friend Bartram, who tells me it is what we here call a *Ground hog*. I send you my Notes enclos'd.

I am endeavouring to Answer Dr. Parsons's Request relating to the Indian Names of the Cardinal Numbers. Please to give the enclos'd concerning an extraordinary Worm bred in a Woman's Liver to Dr. Clephane.

I hope you have got the Remainder of Douglas. I know I have sent it but forget by whom.

I have before me your Account dated May 2, 1754; in it I am charged with Dr. Blair's Chronology and Binding £2. 9. 0. As that Book was for the Academy, please to charge the Trustees of the Academy with it, and take it out of my Account, if there is, as I suppose there is, a Ballance of theirs in your Hands; if not, let it stand in my Acc^t and I will charge them.

I send you the Hospital Book, and our late Votes. In yours of Aug. 4 you express your Concern that such trifling Punctilios in our Publick Affairs should obstruct necessary Measures. You will see more of the same Trifling in these Votes on both sides.

I am heartily sick of our present Situation; I like neither the Governor's Conduct, nor the Assembly's; and having some Share in the Confidence of both, I have endeavour'd to reconcile 'em but in vain, and between 'em they make me very uneasy. I was chosen last Year in my Absence and was not at the Winter Sitting when the House sent home that Address to the King, which I am afraid was both ill-judg'd and ill-tim'd. If my being able now and then to influence a good Measure did not keep up my Spirits I should be ready to swear never to serve again as an Assembly Man, since both Sides expect more from me than they ought, and blame me sometimes for not doing what I am not able to do, as well as for not preventing what was not in my Power to prevent. The Assembly ride restive; and the Governor tho' he spurs with both heels, at the same time reins-in with both hands, so that the Publick Business can never move forward, and he remains like St. George on the Sign, Always a Horseback and never going on. Did you never hear this old Catch?

> Their was a mad Man—He had a mad Wife,
> And three mad Sons beside;
> And they all got upon a mad Horse
> And madly they did ride.

'Tis a Compendium of our Proceedings and may save you the Trouble of reading them.

There is one Mr. Hazard, who, happening to see last Fall a Paper of mine on the Means of settling a new Colony westward of Pensilvania (drawn up to divert the Connecticut Emigrants from their design of Invading this Province and so induce them to go where they would be less injurious and more useful) and picking out something farther from me in Conversation, has publish'd a Scheme for that purpose in my Absence, wherein he has added some Things and left out others, and now (like your Fire-hearth Man)[1] calls it his own Project. He aims at great Matters for himself, hoping to become a Proprietor like Mr. Penn etc, and has got, they say, a great Number of Settlers engag'd to go with him, if he can get a grant of the Land from the

Crown. It is certain that People enough may be had, to make a strong English Settlement or two in those Parts. I wish to see it done, and am almost indifferent how or by whom it is done; yet I think this Man not the fittest in the World to conduct such an Affair. I hear he intends soon for England.

Mr. Bird, I find, is of Opinion that it is impracticable to mend my broken Thermometer. The Tube was whole, and only the Ball broke. I got a thin Copper Ball nicely made, and fix'd to the Tube, with a Screw Plug entering the Ball at the Bottom, by means of which Screw going into the Cavity of the Ball, more or less, among the Mercury, I hoped to lessen or enlarge the Cavity at Pleasure, and by that Means find the true Quantity of Mercury it ought to contain, to rise and fall exactly with the others in the same Temperature of Air etc.

I only tell you this, that you and Mr. Bird may divert yourselves with laughing at me. I was much pleas'd with my Project, but I find Difficulties in the Execution which I did not foresee tho' they must occur to him immediately.

Our Academy goes on very well. Our Friend Smith will be very serviceable there. We have drawn our first Lottery, and are engag'd in a second, as you will see by our Papers. Mr. Smith will write fully about the Charity Schools, which I think cannot fail of Success, if suitable Funds are provided.

I purpose to write to the ingenious Mr. Canton on his very curious Experiment annext to my last Paper. I am oblig'd to him for the Kindness you mention. It is a great Pleasure to me that his Observations evince the various State of the Clouds (as to positive and negative Electricity) as well as mine. I was afraid of being thought out of my Senses.

I hope the Plan of Union which you express your Approbation of, or something like it, will take Place and be establish'd by the King and Parliament. 'Till it is done never expect to see an American War carried on as it ought to be, nor Indian Affairs properly managed.

I shall be glad to see Dr. Mitchel's Map and will endeavour to sell some for him if he sends them.

The Heirs of our Friend Logan have honourably settled the Library agreable to their Father's Intention. I am one of the

Trustees. The Books are now plac'd in the Library House he built and gave for that purpose. They deserve Praise for their Conduct; for some Children would have taken Advantage of the Settlement not being perfected by the Father, and refus'd to comply with it.

The Library Company will be glad to have Murray's Treatise of Ship-Building. We have the three first Vols of Shackford. The new Catalogue is now in the Press which I will send you as soon as finish'd. I do not remember that you have sent any of the Reviews, but will enquire.

I send you ten of my Fireplace Pieces, as you desire, which please to accept: and when Mr. Harris's Improvements come out please to communicate them to me.

I saw our Friend Elliot in my late New England Journey. He is very well, and still studying Improvements in Husbandry.

You are undoubtedly right in your Opinion that Niagara should be secur'd. Measures are now taking for that purpose of which no doubt you have already had Advices.

I will some Day muster up all the Papers and Letters I have relating to Swain's fruitless Expeditions and send them to you.

I like much your Proposal of setting some Person to write the History of this Colony; but a suitable Hand who has Leisure is hard to find.

Thus, my dear Friend, I have run thro' all your late Letters, answering every particular that requires an Answer. And now have only to request you would send my Wife Sattin sufficient for a Gown, somewhat darker than the enclos'd Pattern; which concludes this long Epistle from

Your affectionate Friend

B. FRANKLIN

Capt. Shirley I hear is going this Minute, so am prevented writing to my other London Friends, but hope to do it per Capt. Young who sails in a few Days.

TO DAVID HUME

Coventry, September 27, 1760.

DEAR SIR,

I have too long postponed answering your obliging letter, a fault I will not attempt to excuse, but rather rely on your goodness to forgive it, if I am more punctual for the future.

I am obliged to you for the favourable sentiments you express of the pieces sent to you; though the volume relating to our Pennsylvania affairs was not written by me, nor any part of it, except the remarks on the Proprietor's estimate of his estate, and some of the inserted messages and reports of the Assembly, which I wrote when at home, as a member of committees appointed by the House for that service. The rest was by another hand.

But though I am satisfied by what you say, that the Duke of Bedford was hearty in the scheme of the expedition, I am not so clear that others in the administration were equally in earnest in that matter. It is certain, that, after the Duke of Newcastle's first orders to raise troops in the colonies, and promise to send over commissions to the officers, with arms and clothing for the men, we never had another syllable from him for eighteen months; during all which time the army lay idle at Albany for want of orders and necessaries; and it began to be thought at last, that, if an expedition had ever been intended, the first design and the orders given must, through the multiplicity of business here at home, have been quite forgotten.

I am not a little pleased to hear of your change of sentiments in some particulars relating to America; because I think it of importance to our general welfare, that the people of this nation should have right notions of us, and I know no one, that has it more in his power to rectify their notions than Mr. Hume. I have lately read with great pleasure, as I do every thing of yours, the excellent Essay on the *Jealousy of Commerce*. I think it cannot but have a good effect in promoting a certain interest, too little thought of by selfish man, and scarcely ever mentioned, so that we hardly have a name for it; I mean the *interest of humanity*, or common good of mankind. But I hope, particularly from that Essay, an abatement of the jealousy, that reigns here, of the commerce of the colonies, at least so far as such abatement may be reasonable.

I thank you for your friendly admonition relating to some unusual words in the pamphlet. It will be of service to me. The *"pejorate,"* and the *"colonize,"* since they are not in common use here, I give up as bad; for certainly in writings intended for persuasion and for general information, one cannot be too clear; and every expression in the least obscure is a fault. The *"unshakeable"* too, though clear, I give up as rather low. The introducing new words, where we are already possessed of old ones sufficiently expressive, I confess must be generally wrong, as it tends to change the language; yet, at the same time, I cannot but wish the usage of our tongue permitted making new words, when we want them, by composition of old ones whose meanings are already well understood. The German allows of it, and it is a common practice with their writers. Many of our present English words were originally so made; and many of the Latin words. In point of clearness, such compound words would have the advantage of any we can borrow from the ancient or from foreign languages. For instance, the word *inaccessible,* though long in use among us, is not yet, I dare say, so universally understood by our people, as the word *uncomeatable* would immediately be, which we are not allowed to write. But I hope with you, that we shall always in America make the best English of this Island our standard, and I believe it will be so. I assure you it often gives me pleasure to reflect, how greatly the *audience* (if I may so term it) of a good English writer will, in another century or two, be increased by the increase of English people in our colonies.

My son presents his respects with mine to you and Dr. Monro. We received your printed circular letter to the members of the Society, and purpose some time next winter to send each of us a little philosophical essay. With the greatest esteem, I am, dear Sir, your most obedient and most humble servant,

B. FRANKLIN.

TO GIAMBATISTA
BECCARIA

London, July 13, 1762.

REVEREND SIR,

I once promised myself the pleasure of seeing you at *Turin;* but as that is not now likely to happen, being just about returning to my native country, *America,* I sit down to take leave of you (among others of my *European* friends that I cannot see) by writing.

I thank you for the honourable mention you have so frequently made of me in your letters to Mr. *Collinson* and others, for the generous defence you undertook and executed with so much success, of my electrical opinions; and for the valuable present you have made me of your new work, from which I have received great information and pleasure. I wish I could in return entertain you with any thing new of mine on that subject; but I have not lately pursued it. Nor do I know of any one here, that is at present much engaged in it.

Perhaps, however, it may be agreeable to you, as you live in a musical country, to have an account of the new instrument lately added here to the great number that charming science was before possessed of: As it is an instrument that seems peculiarly adapted to *Italian* music, especially that of the soft and plaintive kind, I will endeavour to give you such a description of it, and of the manner of constructing it, that you, or any of your friends may be enabled to imitate it, if you incline so to do, without being at the expence and trouble of the many experiments I have made in endeavouring to bring it to its present perfection.

You have doubtless heard the sweet tone that is drawn from a drinking-glass, by passing a wet finger round its brim. One Mr. *Puckeridge,* a gentleman from *Ireland,* was the first who thought of playing tunes, formed of these tones. He collected a number of glasses of different sizes, fixed them near each other on a table, and tuned them by putting into them water, more or less, as each note required. The tones were brought out by passing his fingers round their brims. He was unfortunately burnt here, with his instrument, in a fire which consumed the house he lived in. Mr. E. *Delaval,* a most ingenious member of our Royal Society, made one in imitation of it, with a better choice and form of glasses, which was the first I saw or heard. Being charmed by the sweetness of its tones, and the music he produced from it, I wished only to see the glasses disposed in a more convenient form, and brought together in a narrower compass, so as to admit of a greater number of tunes, and all within reach of hand to a person sitting before the instrument, which I accomplished, after various intermediate trials, and less commodious forms, both of glasses and construction, in the following manner.

The glasses are blown as near as possible in the form of hemispheres, having each an open neck or socket in the middle. (See Plate, Figure 1.) The thickness of the glass near the brim about a tenth of an inch, or hardly quite so much, but thicker as it comes nearer the neck, which in the largest glasses is about an inch deep, and an inch and half wide within, these dimensions lessening as the glasses themselves diminish in size, except that the neck of the smallest ought not to be shorter than half an inch. The largest glass is nine inches diameter, and the smallest three inches. Between these there are twenty-three different sizes, differing from each other a quarter of an inch in diameter. To make a single instrument there should be at least six glasses blown of each size; and out of this number one may probably pick 37 glasses, (which are sufficient for three octaves with all the semitones) that will be each either the note one wants or a little sharper than that note, and all fitting so well into each other as to taper pretty regularly from the largest to the smallest. It is true there are not 37 sizes, but it often happens that

ARMONICA.

Fig. 1.

Fig. 2.

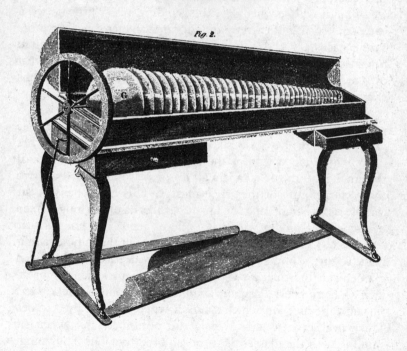

two of the same size differ a note or half note in tone, by reason of a difference in thickness, and these may be placed one in the other without sensibly hurting the regularity of the taper form.

The glasses being chosen and every one marked with a diamond the note you intend it for, they are to be tuned by diminishing the thickness of those that are too sharp. This is done by grinding them round from the neck towards the brim, the breadth of one or two inches, as may be required; often trying the glass by a well-tuned harpsichord, comparing the tone drawn from the glass by your finger, with the note you want, as sounded by that string of the harpsichord. When you come near the matter, be careful to wipe the glass clean and dry before each trial, because the tone is something flatter when the glass is wet, than it will be when dry; and grinding a very little between each trial, you will thereby tune to great exactness. The more care is necessary in this, because if you go below your required tone, there is no sharpening it again but by grinding somewhat off the brim, which will afterwards require polishing, and thus encrease the trouble.

The glasses being thus tuned, you are to be provided with a case for them, and a spindle on which they are to be fixed. (See Plate, Figure 2.) My case is about three feet long, eleven inches every way wide within at the biggest end, and five inches at the smallest end; for it tapers all the way, to adapt it better to the conical figure of the set of glasses. This case opens in the middle of its height, and the upper part turns up by hinges fixed behind. The spindle which is of hard iron, lies horizontally from end to end of the box within, exactly in the middle, and is made to turn on brass gudgeons at each end. It is round, an inch diameter at the thickest end, and tapering to a quarter of an inch at the smallest. A square shank comes from its thickest end through the box, on which shank a wheel is fixed by a screw. This wheel serves as a fly to make the motion equable, when the spindle, with the glasses, is turned by the foot like a spinning-wheel. My wheel is of mahogany, 18 inches diameter, and pretty thick, so as to conceal near its circumference about 25 lb of lead. An ivory pin is fixed in the face of this wheel, and about 4 inches from the axis. Over the neck of this pin is put the loop of the string that comes up from the moveable step to give it motion. The case stands on a neat frame with four legs.

To fix the glasses on the spindle, a cork is first to be fitted in each neck pretty tight, and projecting a little without the neck, that the neck of one may not touch the inside of another when put together, for that would make a jarring. These corks are to be perforated with holes of different diameters, so as to suit that part of the spindle on which they are to be fixed. When a glass is put on, by holding it stiffly between both hands, while another turns the spindle, it may be gradually brought to its place. But care must be taken that the hole be not too small, lest, in forcing it up the neck should split; nor too large, lest the glass, not being firmly fixed, should turn or move on the spindle, so as to touch and jar against its neighbouring glass. The glasses thus are placed one in another, the largest on the biggest end of the spindle which is to the left hand; the neck of this glass is towards the wheel, and the next goes into it in the same position, only about an inch of its brim appearing beyond the brim of the first; thus proceeding, every glass when fixed shows about an inch of its brim (or three quarters of an inch, or half an inch, as they grow smaller) beyond the brim of the glass that contains it; and it is from these exposed parts of each glass that the tone is drawn, by laying a finger upon one of them as the spindle and glasses turn round.

My largest glass is G, a little below the reach of a common voice, and my highest G, including three compleat octaves. To distinguish the glasses the more readily to the eye, I have painted the apparent parts of the glasses within side, every semitone white, and the other notes of the octave with the seven prismatic colours, *viz.* C, red; D, orange; E, yellow; F, green; G, blue; A, indigo; B, purple; and C, red again; so that glasses of the same colour (the white excepted) are always octaves to each other.

This instrument is played upon, by sitting before the middle of the set of glasses as before the keys of a harpsichord, turning them with the foot, and wetting them now and then with a spunge and clean water. The fingers should be first a little soaked in water, and quite free from all greasiness; a little fine chalk upon them is sometimes useful, to make them catch the glass and bring out the tone more readily. Both hands are used, by which means different parts are played together. Observe, that the tones are best drawn out when the glasses turn *from* the ends of the fingers, not when they turn *to* them.

The advantages of this instrument are, that its tones are incomparably sweet beyond those of any other; that they may be swelled and softened at pleasure by stronger or weaker pressures of the finger, and continued to any length; and that the instrument, being once well tuned, never again wants tuning.

In honour of your musical language, I have borrowed from it the name of this instrument, calling it the Armonica.[1]

With great esteem and respect, I am, &c.

B. FRANKLIN.

TO COURT DE GEBELIN

Passy, May 7, 1781.

DEAR SIR,

I am glad the little Book[1] prov'd acceptable. It does not appear to me intended for a Grammar to teach the Language. It is rather what we call in English a *Spelling Book,* in which the only Method observ'd is, to arrange the Words according to their Number of Syllables, placing those of one Syllable together, then those of two Syllables, and so on. And it is to be observ'd, that *Sa ki ma,* for Instance, is not three Words, but one Word of three Syllables; and the reason that *Hyphens* are not plac'd between the Syllables is, that the Printer had not enough of them.

As the Indians had no Letters, they had no Orthography. The Delaware Language being differently spelt from the Virginian may not always arise from a Difference in the Languages; for Strangers who learn the Language of an Indian Nation, finding no Orthography, are at Liberty in writing the Language to use such Compositions of Letters as they think will best produce the Sounds of the Words. I have observ'd, that our Europeans of different Nations, who learn the same Indian Language, form each his own Orthography according to the usual Sounds given to the Letters in his own Language. Thus the same Words of the Mohawk Language written by an English, a French, and a German Interpreter, often differ very much in the Spelling; and, without knowing the usual Powers of the Letters in the Language of the Interpreter, one cannot come at the Pronunciation of the Indian Words. The Spelling Book in question was, I think, written by a German.

You mention a Virginian Bible. Is it not the Bible of the Massachusetts Language, translated by Elliot, and printed in New England, about the middle of the last Century? I know this Bible, but have never heard of one in the Virginian Language. Your Observations of the Similitude between many of the Words, and those of the ancient World, are indeed very curious.

This Inscription, which you find to be Phenician, is, I think, near *Taunton* (not *Jannston*, as you write it). There is some Account of it in the old *Philosophical Transactions*. I have never been at the Place, but shall be glad to see your Remarks on it.

The Compass appears to have been long known in China, before it was known in Europe; unless we suppose it known to Homer, who makes the Prince, that lent Ships to Ulysses, boast that they had a *spirit* in them, by whose Directions they could find their way in a cloudy Day, or the darkest Night. If any Phenicians arriv'd in America, I should rather think it was not by the Accident of a Storm, but in the Course of their long and adventurous Voyages; and that they coasted from Denmark and Norway, over to Greenland, and down Southward by Newfoundland, Nova Scotia, &c., to New England; as the Danes themselves certainly did some ages before Columbus.

Our new American Society will be happy in the Correspondence you mention, and when it is possible for me, I shall be glad to attend the Meetings of your Society,[2] which I am sure must be very instructive. With great and sincere esteem, I have the honour to be, &c.

B. F[RANKLIN.]

TO NOAH WEBSTER

Philad^a, Decr 26, 1789.

DEAR SIR,

I received some Time since your *Dissertations on the English Language.* The Book was not accompanied by any Letter or Message, informing me to whom I am obliged for it, but I suppose it is to yourself. It is an excellent Work, and will be greatly useful in turning the Thoughts of our Countrymen to correct Writing. Please to accept my Thanks for it as well as for the great honour you have done me in its Dedication. I ought to have made this Acknowledgment sooner, but much Indisposition prevented me.

I cannot but applaud your Zeal for preserving the Purity of our Language, both in its Expressions and Pronunciation, and in correcting the popular Errors several of our States are continually falling into with respect to both. Give me leave to mention some of them, though possibly they may have already occurred to you. I wish, however, in some future Publication of yours, you would set a discountenancing Mark upon them. The first I remember is the word *improved.* When I left New England, in the year 23, this Word had never been used among us, as far as I know, but in the sense of *ameliorated* or *made better,* except once in a very old Book of Dr. Mather's, entitled *Remarkable Providences.* As that eminent Man wrote a very obscure Hand, I remember that when I read that Word in his Book, used instead of the Word *imployed,* I conjectured that it was an Error of the Printer, who had mistaken a too short *l* in the Writing for an *r,* and a *y* with too short a Tail for a *v;* whereby *imployed* was converted into *improved.*

But when I returned to Boston, in 1733, I found this Change had obtained Favour, and was then become common; for I met with it often in perusing the Newspapers, where it frequently made an Appearance rather ridiculous. Such, for Instance, as the Advertisement of a Country-House to be sold, which had been many years *improved* as a Tavern; and, in the Character of a deceased Country Gentleman, that he had been for more than 30 Years *improved* as a Justice-of-Peace. This Use of the Word *improved* is peculiar to New England, and not to be met with among any other Speakers of English, either on this or the other Side of the Water.

During my late Absence in France, I find that several other new Words have been introduced into our parliamentary Language; for Example, I find a Verb formed from the Substantive *Notice; I should not have* NOTICED *this, were it not that the Gentleman,* &c. Also another Verb from the Substantive *Advocate; The Gentleman who* ADVOCATES *or has* ADVOCATED *that Motion,* &c. Another from the Substantive *Progress,* the most awkward and abominable of the three; *The committee, having* PROGRESSED, *resolved to adjourn.* The Word *opposed,* tho' not a new Word, I find used in a new Manner, as, *The Gentlemen who are* OPPOSED *to this Measure; to which I have also myself always been* OPPOSED. If you should happen to be of my Opinion with respect to these Innovations, you will use your Authority in reprobating them.

The Latin Language, long the Vehicle used in distributing Knowledge among the different Nations of Europe, is daily more and more neglected; and one of the modern Tongues, viz. the French, seems in point of Universality to have supplied its place. It is spoken in all the Courts of Europe; and most of the Literati, those even who do not speak it, have acquired Knowledge enough of it to enable them easily to read the Books that are written in it. This gives a considerable Advantage to that Nation; it enables its Authors to inculcate and spread through other Nations such Sentiments and Opinions on important Points, as are most conducive to its Interests, or which may contribute to its Reputation by promoting the common Interests of Mankind. It is perhaps owing to its being written in French, that Voltaire's Treatise on *Toleration* has had so sudden and so great an Effect on the Bigotry of Europe, as almost entirely to disarm it. The general Use of the French Language has likewise a very advantageous Effect on the Profits of the Bookselling Branch of Commerce, it being well known, that the more Copies can be sold that are struck off from one Composition of Types, the Profits increase in a much greater Proportion than they do in making a great Number of Pieces in any other Kind of Manufacture. And at present there is no Capital Town in Europe without a French Bookseller's Shop corresponding with Paris.

Our English bids fair to obtain the second Place. The great Body of excellent printed Sermons in our Language, and the Freedom of our Writings on political Subjects, have induced a Number of Divines of different Sects and Nations, as well as Gentlemen concerned in public Affairs, to study it; so far at least as to read it. And if we were to endeavour the Facilitating its Progress, the Study of our Tongue might become much more general. Those, who have employed some Part of their Time in learning a new Language, must have frequently observed, that, while their Acquaintance with it was imperfect, Difficulties small in themselves operated as great ones in obstructing their Progress. A Book, for Example, ill printed, or a Pronunciation in speaking, not well articulated, would render a Sentence unintelligible; which, from a clear Print or a distinct Speaker, would have been immediately comprehended. If therefore we would have the Benefit of seeing our Language more generally known among Mankind, we should endeavour to remove all the Difficulties, however small, that discourage the learning it.

But I am sorry to observe, that, of late Years, those Difficulties, instead of being diminished, have been augmented. In examining the English Books, that were printed between the Restoration and the Accession of George the 2^d, we may observe, that all *Substantives* were begun with a capital, in which we imitated our Mother Tongue, the German. This was more particularly useful to those, who were not well acquainted with the English; there being such a prodigious Number of our Words, that are both *Verbs* and *Substantives,* and spelt in the same manner, tho' often accented differently in Pronunciation.

This Method has, by the Fancy of Printers, of late Years been laid aside, from an Idea, that suppressing the Capitals shows the Character to greater Advantage; those Letters prominent above the line disturbing its even regular Appearance. The Effect of this Change is so considerable, that a learned Man of France, who used to read our Books, tho' not perfectly acquainted with our Language, in Conversation with me on the Subject of our Authors, attributed the greater Obscurity he found in our modern Books, compared with those of the Period above mentioned, to a Change of Style for the worse in our Writers, of which Mistake I convinced him, by marking for him each *Substantive* with a Capital in a Paragraph, which he then easily understood, tho' before he could not comprehend it. This shows the Inconvenience of that pretended Improvement.

From the same Fondness for an even and uniform Appearance of Characters in the Line, the Printers have of late banished also the Italic Types, in which Words of Importance to be attended to in the Sense of the Sentence, and Words on which an Emphasis should be put in Reading, used to be printed. And lately another Fancy has induced some Printers to use the short round *s,* instead of the long one, which formerly served well to distinguish a word readily by its varied appearance. Certainly the omitting this prominent Letter makes the Line appear more even; but renders it less immediately legible; as the paring all Men's Noses might smooth and level their Faces, but would render their Physiognomies less distinguishable.

Add to all these Improvements *backwards,* another modern Fancy, that grey Printing is more beautiful than black; hence the English new Books are printed in so dim a Character, as to be read with difficulty by old Eyes, unless in a very strong Light and with good Glasses. Whoever compares a Volume of the *Gentleman's Magazine,* printed between the Years 1731 and 1740, with one of those printed in the last ten Years, will be convinced of the much greater Degree of Perspicuity given by black Ink than by grey. Lord Chesterfield pleasantly remarked this Difference to Faulkener, the Printer of the Dublin *Journal,* who was vainly making Encomiums on his own Paper, as the most complete of any in the World; "But, Mr. Faulkener," said my Lord, "don't you think it might be still farther improved by using Paper and Ink not quite so near of a Colour?" For all these Reasons I cannot but wish, that our American Printers would in their Editions avoid these fancied Improvements, and thereby render their Works more agreable to Foreigners in Europe, to the great advantage of our Bookselling Commerce.

Farther, to be more sensible of the Advantage of clear and distinct Printing, let us consider the Assistance it affords in Reading well aloud to an Auditory. In so doing the Eye generally slides forward three or four Words before the Voice. If the Sight clearly distinguishes what the coming Words are, it gives time to order the Modulation of the Voice to express them properly. But, if they are obscurely printed, or disguis'd by omitting the Capitals and long *s's* or otherwise, the Reader is apt to modulate wrong; and, finding he has done so, he is oblig'd to go back and begin the Sentence again, which lessens the Pleasure of the Hearers.

This leads me to mention an old Error in our Mode of Printing. We are sensible, that, when a Question is met with in Reading, there is a proper Variation to be used in the Management of the Voice. We have therefore a Point called an Interrogation, affix'd to the Question in order to distinguish it. But this is absurdly placed at its End; so that the Reader does not discover it, till he finds he has wrongly modulated his Voice, and is therefore obliged to begin again the Sentence. To prevent this, the Spanish Printers, more sensibly, place an Interrogation at the Beginning as well as at the End of a Question. We have another Error of the same kind in printing Plays, where something often occurs that is mark'd as spoken *aside.* But the Word *aside* is placed at the End of the Speech, when it ought to precede it, as a Direction to the Reader, that he may govern his Voice accordingly. The Practice of our Ladies in meeting five or six together to form a little busy Party, where each is employ'd in some useful Work while one reads to them, is so commendable in itself, that it deserves the Attention of

Authors and Printers to make it as pleasing as possible, both to the Reader and Hearers.

After these general Observations, permit me to make one that I imagine may regard your Interest. It is that *your Spelling Book* is miserably printed here, so as in many Places to be scarcely legible, and on wretched Paper. If this is not attended to, and the new one lately advertis'd as coming out should be preferable in these Respects, it may hurt the future Sale of yours.

I congratulate you on your Marriage, of which the Newspapers inform me. My best wishes attend you, being with sincere esteem, Sir, &c.

B. FRANKLIN.

Chronology

1706 Benjamin Franklin born in Boston January 17 (January 6, 1705, Old Style)

1710 *Population in colonies, 375,500*

1716 Schooling ends; works with father

1718 Begins apprenticeship in brother James's printing shop

1720 *Population, 474,400*

1723 Breaks indentures and goes to Philadelphia via New York; employed by printer Samuel Keimer

1724 Goes to London and is employed in print shops there after Governor Keith's promise to supply him with funds to establish his own shop in Philadelphia proves false

1726 Returns to Philadelphia; works in merchant Thomas Denham's shop

1727 At Denham's death returns to Keimer's print shop; during an illness composes *Epitaph*

1728 Founds own print shop in partnership with Hugh Meredith

1729 Son William born in this (or the following?) year—mother unknown; buys Keimer's magazine and changes its name to *Pennsylvania Gazette*

1730 *Population, 654,950*

Marries Deborah Read; William taken into household; appointed Public Printer by Pennsylvania Assembly; dissolves partnership with Meredith

1731 Founds Library Company of Philadelphia, first subscription library in America

1732 *George Washington born*

Son Francis Folger Franklin born

1735 *John Adams born*

1736 Chosen clerk of Pennsylvania Assembly; son Francis dies of smallpox

1740 *Population, 889,000*
Is first printer in America to publish a novel (Richardson's *Pamela*)

1741 *Jonathan Edwards, "Sinners in the Hands of An Angry God"*
Invents Pennsylvania fireplace (Franklin stove)

1743 *Thomas Jefferson born*

1744 Establishes American Philosophical Society; daughter Sarah born

1745 *King George's War (to 1748)*
Begins experimenting with electricity

1749 Founds the academy that later becomes the University of Pennsylvania

1750 *Population, 1,207,000*

1752 Kite experiment proves lightning is electrical

1753 Receives Copley Medal from Royal Society for electrical experiments; M.A. degrees awarded by Harvard and Yale; appointed deputy postmaster for North America

1754 *Jonathan Edwards,* FREEDOM OF WILL; *French and Indian War (to 1760); Albany Congress*
Commissioner to Albany Congress, proposes a plan of colonial union

1755 Helps to supply Braddock's forces; as colonel of militia oversees construction of forts on Pennsylvania frontier

1756 Elected fellow of Royal Society of London

1757 Arrives in England as agent of Pennsylvania Assembly to negotiate differences with the colony's proprietors

1758 Honorary degree of Doctor of Laws from St. Andrews University; title "Dr. Franklin" soon enters common usage; in Edinburgh begins personal acquaintanceships with Adam Smith, David Hume, Lord Kames, and other members of the Scottish Enlightenment

1760 *Population 1,610,000*

1761 Tours on European continent

1762 *Son William marries and is appointed Royal Governor of New Jersey*

Receives degree of Doctor of Civil Law from Oxford; perfects work on his musical armonica; returns to Philadelphia

1764 Departs Philadelphia to serve as Pennsylvania's agent in London to petition king for change from proprietary to royal government

1765 *Parliament passes Stamp Act*

1766 Examined in House of Commons about repeal of the Stamp Act

1767 Visits France where he meets French Physiocrats and is presented to Louis XV

1768 Appointed London agent for Georgia; writes preface to John Dickinson's *Letters from a Pennsylvania Farmer*

1769 Visits France; elected first president of American Philosophical Society; appointed London agent for New Jersey

1770 *Population 2,205,000*

Boston Massacre

Appointed London Agent for Massachusetts

1771 Begins *Autobiography;* tours Ireland and Scotland

1772 *First Committee of Correspondence*

1774 *First Continental Congress*

Sends Hutchinson-Oliver letters to Massachusetts, which leads in the next year to a scathing denunciation of him before the Privy Council and his dismissal as deputy postmaster; back in Philadelphia wife Deborah dies December 19

1775 Returns to America; chosen delegate to Second Continental Congress

1776 *Thomas Paine,* COMMON SENSE

Appointed to committee to frame Declaration of Independence; leaves Philadelphia for Paris to serve as one of the commissioners from Congress to the French court

1778 *Articles of Confederation*

1779 Minister plenipotentiary to French court

1780 *Population 2,781,000*

1781 Appointed one of the commissioners to negotiate peace treaty between England and the United States

1782 *Crèvecoeur, LETTERS FROM AN AMERICAN FARMER*
1783 *Webster, SPELLING BOOK*
  With John Jay and John Adams signs the Treaty of Paris
1784 Resumes work on *Autobiography* beyond 1731
1785 Resigns as Minister to French Court; returns to Philadelphia; President of Council of Pennsylvania
1786 *Shays Rebellion*
1787 *Jefferson, NOTES ON VIRGINIA*
  President of the Pennsylvania Society for the Abolition of Slavery; Pennsylvania delegate to Constitutional Convention
1788 *Constitution ratified*
  Resumes work on *Autobiography*
1789 *Washington administration; First United States Congress*
1790 *First national census: population 3,929,214*
  Benjamin Franklin dies in Philadelphia, April 17

Glossary of Correspondents

Sarah "Sally" [Franklin] Bache (1743–1808): Franklin's only daughter, proudly noted by him to have been a precocious child; later, a dutiful hostess and caretaker to him on his returns to Philadelphia in 1775 and 1785.

(Sir) Joseph Banks (1743–1820): British naturalist and explorer; highly influential president of the Royal Society, beginning 1778, and regular correspondent with Franklin concerning various scientific inquiries.

Giambatista Beccaria (1716–1781): Italian cleric and natural philosopher; an important advocate of Franklin's views on electricity and major theorist of such phenomena in his own right.

Madame Anne-Louise Boivin D'Hardancourt Brillon de Jouy (1744–1824): Franklin's neighbor in Passy; a skilled musician and witty, engaging friend he much admired.

Cadwallader Colden (1688–1776): New York naturalist, physician, ethnographer, and politician who frequently corresponded with Franklin regarding scientific matters.

Peter Collinson (1694–1768): London merchant and botanist; a close friend of Franklin's who supported his electrical investigations and furthered his connection to British scientific audiences.

La Sabliere (Charles Marie) de la Condamine (1701–1774): French geographer and scientist; commissioned to explore South America in 1735 by the Academy of Sciences.

(Sir) Alexander Dick (1703–1785): Scottish physician, medical scholar, and civic leader whose correspondence with Franklin predominantly concerned scientific questions.

Abiah [Folger] Franklin (1667–1752): Franklin's mother; married Josiah Franklin in 1689, Benjamin being the eighth of their ten children and youngest son.

Deborah [Read] Franklin (1705?–1774): Franklin's wife by common-law marriage, from 1730, with whom he had two children, Francis (who died at age four) and Sarah; faithful and sensible, she defended their Philadelphia home during the Stamp Act riots.

Josiah Franklin (1657–1745): Franklin's father, born and raised in Ecton, England, before emigrating to Boston in 1683; by trade first a dyer and then a candle-maker who had with his first wife, Anne Child, seven children, in addition to ten with Abiah Folger Franklin.

William Franklin (ca. 1730–1813): Franklin's son, recognized from birth though illegitimate, the eventual royal governor of New Jersey; at the time of the Revolution his Tory sympathies divided him from his father.

(Antoine) Court de Gebelin (1725–1784): French antiquarian and philologist; his reputation suffered as a result of his enthusiasm for Mesmer's theories of animal magnetism, which Franklin took a key role in refuting.

David Hartley (1732–1785): British statesman and scientist, son of the philosopher David Hartley; became friends with Franklin through shared interests and aided in the negotiations to end the Revolutionary War, having long been a vocal opponent of it.

Madame Anne-Catherine de Ligniville Helvétius (1719–1800): Neighbor of Franklin's at Auteuil near Passy; widow of the philosopher Claude-Adrien Helvétius, she developed a close friendship with Franklin, who playfully (yet earnestly?) proposed marriage in 1780.

Lord Richard Howe (1726–1799): Member of Parliament twice involved in negotiations with Franklin, secretly in 1774–75 and publicly in 1776, that aimed to avert war between the colonies and Britain.

Joseph Huey (?): Resident of Lancaster, Pennsylvania who wrote Franklin with concern about his religious views.

David Hume (1711–1776): Scottish moral philosopher and historian who Franklin befriended through William Strahan, twice visited in Edinburgh, in 1759 and 1771, and corresponded with regarding linguistic and scientific matters.

James Hutton (1715–1795): Franklin's longtime London friend, a bookseller and leader in the Moravian church.

Jared Ingersoll (1749–1822): American jurist who served in the Continental Congress and again during the Constitutional Convention; Ingersoll knew Franklin from early in life and was recommended by him to serve as an officer of the Stamp Act in Connecticut. Like other officers, Ingersoll was compelled to resign before the violent reactions to the act.

Samuel Mather (1706–1785): Son of Cotton Mather, a Boston minister with whom Franklin maintained a friendly correspondence late in life.

Oliver Neave (?): Member of a wealthy family of merchants who traded in London and Philadelphia.

Isaac Norris (1701–1766): Prominent Philadelphia merchant who as speaker of the Pennsylvania Assembly, beginning 1750, worked closely with Franklin.

Elizabeth [Hubbard] Partridge (?): Franklin's niece, the stepdaughter of his brother John.

Richard Price (1723–1791): English philosopher, demographer, and political radical; Franklin's fellow member of the Honest Whigs club who authored a popular pamphlet that endorsed the American Revolution in 1776.

Joseph Priestley (1733–1804): London minister and a distinguished chemist; with Franklin a member of the Royal Society and the London club Honest Whigs.

(Sir) John Pringle (1707–1782): Scottish physician, a close friend and continental traveling companion of Franklin's; made by King George III to resign his presidency of the Royal Society because of his defense of Franklin's views.

Catherine Shipley (1759–1840): Youngest daughter of Jonathan Shipley, Bishop of St. Asaph's, at whose residence Franklin commenced the *Autobiography* in 1771. She is the "Miss

Shipley" to whom "The Art of Procuring Pleasant Dreams" is addressed.

William Shirley (1694–1771): London lawyer and Massachusetts governor, 1741–1757, who discussed with Franklin how the colonies could be organized politically, as part of the British Empire.

Mary "Polly" Stevenson [Hewson] (1739–1795): Intelligent and charming daughter of Margaret Stevenson, from whom Franklin rented his rooms on Craven Street during stays in London, 1757–1762 and 1764–1775. A central portion of her correspondence with Franklin involved questions of natural philosophy and scientific experimentation.

Ezra Stiles (1727–1795): Congregationalist minister and President of Yale College from 1778 until his death.

William Strahan (1715–1785): London printer and member of Parliament whose close friendship with Franklin was resumed after the Revolution. He recommended David Hall to Franklin as a partner in his printing business.

Benjamin Vaughan (1751–1835): Secretary to the Earl of Shelburne and close friend of Franklin's who assisted in the negotiation of final peace treaties between America and England in 1782. He persistently encouraged the aged Franklin to finish his memoirs and to undertake and publish other works.

George Washington (1732–1799): Consulted with Franklin as commander in chief of the Revolutionary Army and later worked with him again when he presided over the Constitutional Convention.

Noah Webster (1758–1843): Federalist pedagogue and lexicographer who discussed linguistic matters with Franklin and went on to author specifically American spellers, readers, and eventually a dictionary that encouraged the unification of the new nation by language and culture.

"Charles de Weissenstein": Pseudonym adopted by the writer of a mysterious letter addressed to Franklin in 1778, which warned that France would betray America and proposed a reconciliation between the warring colonies and England. The letter intimated that Franklin and other prominent American leaders would be compensated for their cooperation with positions in a new colonial government; Franklin was indignant, and believing the letter to have been sent directly by King George III, he wrote but did not send the response included in this volume.

George Whatley (?): Franklin's friend, a London economist.

Editor's Notes

THE DOGOOD PAPERS

1. No. IV: *"An sum . . ."*—And furthermore whether I am to be taught to speak in Greek or Latin?
2. No. VII: *"Mæstus Composuit"*—Composed in sadness
3. No. VII: *"Mater me . . ."*—My mother gave birth to me, and soon the daughter will give birth to a mother.

EPITAPH

1. During March and April of 1728 Franklin was seriously ill, most likely with pleurisy, and at that time composed this darkly humorous epitaph. Although it seems particularly fitted for a journeyman printer, the same conceit was used in a seventeenth-century Puritan elegy with which Franklin was familiar.

PREFACE

1. *"New-stile"*—In 1752 England adopted the New Style (or Georgian) calendar in which the new year commenced on January 1st. Previously, the new year had begun on March 25th. The change necessitated the dropping of eleven days. Hence, for example, Franklin's birth date was January 6, 1705, Old Style, and is January 17, 1706, New Style.

PROMOTING USEFUL KNOWLEDGE

1. This paper and the American Philosophical Society that emerged from it are noted in the *Autobiography*.

EDUCATION OF YOUTH

1. The University of Pennsylvania is the modern descendant of the academy that was formed as a result of Franklin's proposal. It is

notable that unlike all previous American universities Franklin's is not founded on a religious denomination and that the ability to serve mankind and one's country is emphasized as the educational goal.

TO MARY STEVENSON (AMERICAN YOUNG BEGIN TO LISP)

1. The "young Painter now studying at Rome" is Benjamin West.
2. "Dr. Smith" is William Smith, an Episcopal minister who was made provost of the college that resulted from Franklin's proposal for the education of youth. A fierce conservative, he opposed the Quakers and political liberals such as Tom Paine and Franklin.

TO CADWALLADER COLDEN (INTENDS TO RETIRE)

1. The "Indian History" is Colden's *History of the Five Indian Nations* (1727).
2. "Mr. Bartram" is John Bartram, the internationally renowned botanist who resided in the vicinity of Philadelphia where he maintained his gardens.
3. "Swedish gentleman" is Peter Kalm, a disciple of Linnaeus's. He wrote a multivolume account of his 1748–51 visit to America.

TO DEBORAH FRANKLIN (CAMP LIFE)

1. "Capillaire" is a syrup flavored with orange flower water.

TO DEBORAH FRANKLIN (HOUSEHOLD ARRANGEMENTS)

1. The conclusion of this letter is lost.

TO WILLIAM FRANKLIN (RECONCILIATION?)

1. At the outbreak of the American Revolution William, then Royal Governor of New Jersey, remained loyal to the Crown and the rift between father and son that had been developing previously widened to a separation.
2. "Confide to your son" refers to William Temple Franklin, who like his father was born out of wedlock. He resided with his grandfather in Paris.

CODICIL TO LAST WILL AND TESTAMENT

1. In his last will and testament, signed and sealed in July 1788, Franklin disposed of lands and money to members of his family as well as making public benefactions. But apparently his zeal for civic improvement was not satisfied nor did he seem to be able to rest easy without exerting from beyond the grave some degree of the influence he had always exerted in civic matters; hence this codicil attached to the will eleven months later.

TO PETER COLLINSON (ON ELECTRICITY)

1. Franklin's notes to this letter are omitted.
2. *"positively . . . negatively"*—Franklin thus introduces these terms into the vocabulary of science; previously, experimenters had talked of "vitreous" and "resinous" electricity.

TO SIR JOSEPH BANKS (SOME SUPPOSE FLYING NOW TO BE INVENTED)

1. The second postscript, a note sent to Franklin in French, is here omitted.

INCREASE OF MANKIND

1. "pejorate"—See the 1760 letter to David Hume in Part VI of this book.
2. "Palatine boors"—The final two paragraphs with their slur on German immigrants and concern for a white America were omitted from all save the first edition of this essay.

THREE LETTERS TO GOVERNOR SHIRLEY

1. In his edition of Franklin's writings, Albert Henry Smyth supplied the following note: "Mr. John Adams said (in his *History of the Dispute with America,* first published in 1774); 'Dr. Franklin, who was known to be an active and very able man, and to have great influence in the province of Pennsylvania, was in Boston in the year 1754, and Mr. Shirley communicated to him the profound secret, the great design of taxing the colonies by act of Parliament. This sagacious gentleman and distinguished patriot, to his lasting honor, sent the governor an answer in writing.' "

TO WILLIAM STRAHAN (YOU ARE NOW MY ENEMY)

1. Franklin never sent this letter. After the war Strahan and he resumed their friendship.

A DISSERTATION ON LIBERTY AND NECESSITY, PLEASURE AND PAIN

1. In the *Autobiography* Franklin remarked that this piece was "not so clever a performance as I once thought it." But he left open the question of whether his regret arose from doubt about the truth of his assertions or a sense of it being impolitic to publish them. In a letter to Benjamin Vaughan, November 9, 1779, he said, "There was only an hundred copies printed, of which I gave a few to friends, and afterwards disliking the piece, as conceiving it might have an ill tendency, I burnt the rest, except one copy."

TO RICHARD PRICE (RELIGIOUS TESTS)

1. "the *London*"—a coffeehouse.

TO SAMUEL MATHER (MEMORY OF COTTON MATHER)

1. "your father"—Cotton Mather.
2. *"Esto perpetua"*—Let her be eternal.

TO EZRA STILES (SOMETHING OF MY RELIGION)

1. "the Copy of another Letter"—that to Joseph Huey, above.

TO PETER COLLINSON (CONTENTS OF A BUSY MIND)

1. "Like your Fire-hearth Man"—Franklin is referring to an English craftsman who copied his stove and then took out a patent on it, claiming the invention as his own. Franklin had earlier declined patenting the stove because, he said, it was not designed for his personal profit but for the benefit of the public. In his *Autobiography* he said, "as we enjoy great advantages from the inventions of others, we should be glad of an opportunity to serve others by any invention of ours; and this we should do freely and generously."

TO GIAMBATISTA BECCARIA (THE ARMONICA)

1. Franklin's instrument had a widespread but brief vogue. Mozart and Beethoven, among others, wrote pieces for it.

TO COURT DE GEBELIN (INDIAN LANGUAGES)

1. "the little Book"—a vocabulary of one of the North American tribes.
2. "your Society"—L'Academie des Inscriptions et Belles Lettres.

CLICK ON A CLASSIC
www.penguinclassics.com

The world's greatest literature at your fingertips

Constantly updated information on more than a thousand titles, from Icelandic sagas to ancient Indian epics, Russian drama to Italian romance, American greats to African masterpieces

•

The latest news on recent additions to the list, updated editions, and specially commissioned translations

•

Original essays by leading writers

•

A wealth of background material, including biographies of every classic author from Aristotle to Zamyatin, plot synopses, readers' and teachers' guides, useful web links

•

Online desk and examination copy assistance for academics

•

Trivia quizzes, competitions, giveaways, news on forthcoming screen adaptations

FOR THE BEST IN PAPERBACKS, LOOK FOR THE

In every corner of the world, on every subject under the sun, Penguin represents quality and variety—the very best in publishing today.

For complete information about books available from Penguin—including Penguin Classics, Penguin Compass, and Puffins—and how to order them, write to us at the appropriate address below. Please note that for copyright reasons the selection of books varies from country to country.

In the United States: Please write to *Penguin Group (USA), P.O. Box 12289 Dept. B, Newark, New Jersey 07101-5289* or call 1-800-788-6262.

In the United Kingdom: Please write to *Dept. EP, Penguin Books Ltd, Bath Road, Harmondsworth, West Drayton, Middlesex UB7 0DA.*

In Canada: Please write to *Penguin Books Canada Ltd, 90 Eglinton Avenue East, Suite 700, Toronto, Ontario M4P 2Y3.*

In Australia: Please write to *Penguin Books Australia Ltd, P.O. Box 257, Ringwood, Victoria 3134.*

In New Zealand: Please write to *Penguin Books (NZ) Ltd, Private Bag 102902, North Shore Mail Centre, Auckland 10.*

In India: Please write to *Penguin Books India Pvt Ltd, 11 Panchsheel Shopping Centre, Panchsheel Park, New Delhi 110 017.*

In the Netherlands: Please write to *Penguin Books Netherlands bv, Postbus 3507, NL-1001 AH Amsterdam.*

In Germany: Please write to *Penguin Books Deutschland GmbH, Metzlerstrasse 26, 60594 Frankfurt am Main.*

In Spain: Please write to *Penguin Books S. A., Bravo Murillo 19, 1° B, 28015 Madrid.*

In Italy: Please write to *Penguin Italia s.r.l., Via Benedetto Croce 2, 20094 Corsico, Milano.*

In France: Please write to *Penguin France, Le Carré Wilson, 62 rue Benjamin Baillaud, 31500 Toulouse.*

In Japan: Please write to *Penguin Books Japan Ltd, Kaneko Building, 2-3-25 Koraku, Bunkyo-Ku, Tokyo 112.*

In South Africa: Please write to *Penguin Books South Africa (Pty) Ltd, Private Bag X14, Parkview, 2122 Johannesburg.*